## DATE LOANED

# THE TRANSFORMATION OF
# AMERICAN FOREIGN RELATIONS
## 1865–1900

*The*

*New American Nation Series*

EDITED BY

HENRY STEELE COMMAGER

AND

RICHARD B. MORRIS

# THE TRANSFORMATION
# OF AMERICAN
# FOREIGN RELATIONS
# 1865 ★ 1900

## By *CHARLES S. CAMPBELL*

**ILLUSTRATED**

*1817*

## HARPER & ROW, PUBLISHERS
*New York, Hagerstown, San Francisco, London*

We are grateful to Prentice-Hall, Inc., for permission to use the following maps: The maps on pp. 125 and 300 are from *A History of United States Foreign Policy*, by Julius W. Pratt, 3rd edition, copyright © 1965, 1972, by Prentice-Hall, Inc. The map on p. 196 is from *A Diplomatic History of the American People*, by Thomas A. Bailey, copyright 1940, 1946, 1950 © 1955, 1958, 1969, 1974 by Prentice-Hall, Inc.

Library of Congress Cataloging in Publication Data

Campbell, Charles Soutter, date
    The transformation of American foreign relations,
1865–1900.
    (The New American Nation series)
    Includes bibliographical references and index.
    1. United States—Foreign relations—1865–1898.
I. Title.
E661.7.C36 1976        327.73        75–23877
ISBN 0–06–010618–2

76 77 78   10 9 8 7 6 5 4 3 2 1

FOR PATRICK AND FAMILY

# Contents

# *Illustrations*

# CARTOONS

# MAPS

# Editors' Introduction

THE years between the Civil War and the war with Spain witnessed a major turning point in American foreign policy. Those years found the central American traditions of missions and anticolonialism transformed beyond recognition. The first of these traditions had already been drastically altered, if not dissolved, in the acid bath of Manifest Destiny. Long before the Civil War many Americans had avowed the doctrine that the whole continent of North America, stretching across to the Pacific, belonged by right to the American people, a reality achieved by the annexation of Texas and the war with Mexico.

The second concept, a vigorous anticolonialism, had been exemplified both in the attitude of the Founding Fathers toward other people's empires as well as in that of Congress, which had consistently provided for the admission of newly acquired territory as states of the Union on a footing of equality with the original ones. In the years after 1865, however, an aggressive expansionism viewed the Caribbean and the Pacific as American lakes and, toward the end of the century, the acquisition by the United States of overseas possessions inhabited by people of alien cultures precipitated the issue of colonialism.

In this probing anlysis of America's diplomacy in the years 1865 to 1900, Dr. Campbell has convincingly demonstrated how deeply rooted was the anticolonial tradition, how opponents of expansionism came within an inch of blocking the purchase of Alaska, how all the attempts in the 1870s and 1880s to establish a naval base in the

Caribbean and build an Isthmian canal failed or lapsed when that arch antiexpansionist, Grover Cleveland, became President, and how even the annexations of Hawaii and part of the Samoan islands were blocked until the end of the century.

Just why America turned on its earlier traditions and assumed the mantle of imperialism by the end of the period reviewed in this book is a central question of concern to the author. While Dr. Campbell does not seek to give precise weight to each of the components which underlay a new sense of urgency in the acquisition of overseas possessions, he does show convincingly that the transformation of American society from an agricultural to an industrial nation was central to the change. If, as the author demonstrates, business interests were now exhibiting a growing concern about cultivating foreign markets in order to siphon off the products of America's excess industrial capacity, he also considers other ingredients in the imperialist brew. Included among them were Social Darwinism, racism, and the religious ardor of missionaries determined to convert the infidel. Not least of all were the geophysical views of Captain Alfred T. Mahan, with his stress upon the importance of seapower. To achieve dominance on the seas, the influential Mahan argued that a nation needed naval bases and, with the coming of the steam navy, coaling stations. The author sees a perceptive drift toward imperialism evident during Benjamin Harrison's administration, but the war with Spain created an American empire, entangling the United States in the Pacific permanently, with consequences so fateful to unborn generations.

Aside from the thrust of expansionism, the foreign relations of the United States in these years, as Dr. Campbell relates, were centrally involved with Great Britain. Catching Irish votes by twisting the lion's tail had long been a preoccupation of American politicians, but a perceptible change in America's attitude toward Great Britain followed the settlement of the *Alabama* claims. Relations come to a climax in this book, when the British take an unpredictably conciliatory line toward President Cleveland's jingoistic posture in the boundary dispute between Venezuela and Great Britain. British anger was now deflected toward Germany, which seemed the more imminent and tangible threat at that juncture. Indeed, as Dr. Campbell instructs us, the settlement of the Venezuela boundary dispute proved to be a turning point in America's foreign policy.

Henceforth, the American Secretaries of State were disposed to expound a broad interpretation of the Monroe Doctrine and the American government inclined to assume overseas responsibilities from which it had shied away in the most. This juncture also dates the beginning of a long and durable entente with Great Britain which has stood the test of two world wars.

Perhaps fortunately for the nation, and certainly for the interest of readers of books on this period like Dr. Campbell's, the era, though one of diminished presidential leadership, was enlivened by colorful and activist Secretaries of State, and through these pages march such notable personalities as William Henry Seward, Hamilton Fish, William Maxwell Evarts, and James G. Blaine, by any standards giants in the history of American diplomacy.

*The Transformation of American Foreign Relations, 1865–1900* is a volume in the New American Nation series, a comprehensive, cooperative survey of the area now embraced in the United States. Other aspects of the period covered by Professor Campbell are treated by the books of Messrs. Garraty and Faulkner, while a succeeding volume by Foster Rhea Dulles treats twentieth-century foreign relations.

Henry Steele Commager
Richard B. Morris

# *Preface*

U NITED STATES relations with other countries were very different at the end of the century from what they were in 1865, so different that it is no exaggeration to say that they had been transformed. During the six or seven years after the Civil War Americans viewed Great Britain with dislike, even hatred; but by 1898 an emotional friendship had replaced the earlier mood. A similar development took place with respect to the main goals of expansionists: bases in the Caribbean and Hawaii, and a Central American canal. Whereas for many years these proved to be utterly unobtainable, by 1900 the bases had been acquired and the groundwork for the Panama Canal had been well prepared. Relations with Great Britain and territorial expansion abroad were the principal themes of American foreign policy in the three and a half decades following the Civil War.

But interpretive titles of books should not be taken as complete and literal truth. Territorial expansion and the connection with Britain did not constitute the totality of American foreign relations. Not all the many aspects of these relations were transformed, although all of them did undergo profound changes. Moreover, even in the transformations strong continuities existed. Both expansion and the Anglo-American relationship had deep roots that steadily made themselves felt, even if the results did not become fully apparent until near the century's end. Despite these qualifications, however, the fact remains that in 1899 America's place in the world was utterly different from its place just after the Civil War.

I would like to thank Mrs. Catherine Tramz and Mrs. Toni Tosch for typing the manuscript diligently and expeditiously, and Mr. Parker Palmer for useful advice on various points. Mr. Stuart Anderson checked the manuscript for errors and made many helpful suggestions. I am grateful to Miss Corona Machemer of Harper & Row for faithfully shepherding the manuscript through the various stages of publication. I am also indebted to the editors of this series, Professor Richard B. Morris and Professor Henry Steele Commager, for their constructive criticism.

C.S.C.

# THE TRANSFORMATION OF
# AMERICAN FOREIGN RELATIONS
# 1865–1900

# CHAPTER 1

# Postwar Frustrations

I N April 1865 the Civil War ended. The United States had survived a fearful ordeal, and her republican, democratic institutions seemed beyond doubt to have vindicated themselves. National self-confidence and optimism soared; not until the mid-1890s were they seriously checked, and then not for long.

Americans had always regarded their country as morally superior to other countries. In an inarticulate way they thought of the New World as a place set apart by God until such time as people were ready to discard medieval ways and adopt a simpler, more natural form of society. The United States, in particular, was young, virtuous, progressive; and, as all Americans knew, she had a mission: the sacred mission of preserving her institutions as a beacon of hope for all mankind. For Americans still envisaged their Revolution as a turning point in the long, dismal history of man; before 1776 the road had been rough and dusty, apparently leading nowhere, but after that year it veered sharply toward a future that was bright.[1]

Outside the New World all seemed dark by comparison. Africa was hopelessly backward; Asia decadent. Even Europe, a place occupying a larger part of American attention than any other overseas area, was outmoded, although its culture still commanded respect. The Continental countries, and to a somewhat less extent Great

1. Edward McN. Burns, *The American Idea of Mission: Concepts of National Purpose and Destiny* (New Brunswick, 1957); Robert E. Spiller et al., *Literary History of the United States* (3 vols., New York, 1948), I, 192–215.

Britain, were the Old World—with emphasis on the derogatory connotations of the word "old."[2] Its feudal monarchies and effete aristocracies, its clogging traditions, its class-structured society, its rigid economy, offered no model for the United States. Americans would have agreed wholeheartedly with Mark Twain's characterization of Italy: "One vast museum of magnificence and misery . . . for every beggar in America, Italy can show a hundred—and rags and vermin to match";[3] and the rest of the Continent was about as bad. Bowed down under huge armies and navies, it nevertheless gloried in martial display and intricate alliances, and hopelessly abandoned itself to a never-ending round of war upon war.

Nothing so clearly demonstrated American superiority as the swarms of immigrants from Europe; and if any American doubted his country's preeminence, he had only to look around at these teeming newcomers. In 1873 almost 460,000 foreigners flooded into the United States; in 1882, almost 800,000. In 1890, out of a total population of about 63 million, 9,250,000 had been born abroad.[4] The great majority of them had come from the Old World (about one million were Europeans from Canada). "The phenomenon is . . . without a precedent in history . . . ," an Englishman reflected. "Now the idea of a new Europe on the other side of the Atlantic affects every speculation. . . . European governments can no longer have the notion that they are playing the first part on the stage of the world's political history."[5] Americans had no doubt that the United States would increasingly dwarf the Old World as the years passed.

The Civil War's triumphant outcome strengthened these beliefs immeasurably. The time was near, so Americans thought, for all vestiges of Europe to depart from the New World, and for at least North America and the nearby islands to become a happy fraternity of republics closely associated with the United States, perhaps politically united with her. In words presumably written by his expansionist-minded Secretary of State, William H. Seward, President Andrew Johnson urged "the acquisition and incorporation into our Federal Union of the several adjacent continental and insular com-

2. Cushing Strout, *The American Image of the Old World* (New York, 1963).
3. Mark Twain, *The Innocents Abroad* . . . (2 vols., New York, 1911), I, 266.
4. U.S. Bureau of the Census, *Historical Statistics of the United States, Colonial Times to 1957* (Washington, 1960), pp. 57, 66.
5. Chester W. Wright, *Economic History of the United States* (New York, 1941), p. 552. The remark was made in 1904, but similar notions were entertained years earlier.

munities as speedily as it can be done peacefully, lawfully, and without any violation of national justice, faith, or honor."[6] So sober, unromantic a man as Hamilton Fish, Secretary of State under President Ulysses S. Grant, wrote that Spanish Cuba "ought to belong to the great family of American republics. . . . The desire of independence on the part of Cubans is a natural and legitimate aspiration of theirs, because they are Americans. . . . their political separation is inevitable. It is one of those conclusions which have been aptly called the inexorable logic of events."[7]

In the early years of independence the United States had been compelled in self-defense to involve herself in European affairs, but now with her new-found strength and confidence she could go her own way, heedless of Europe. The old tradition of isolationism was still immensely strong, and it was to remain strong for several decades. Americans simply took it for granted that the United States had nothing to do with European quarrels; and indeed, apart from routine diplomacy, she did have very little official business with the Continental countries. Americans were not only following prudent policy, natural law, and virtue by steering clear of the Old World, but a vast, largely empty continent lay temptingly before them, its great plains and prairies crying out for cultivation. Moreover conditions were ripe for building transcontinental railroads and for developing industry, pursuits that would soon transform the economy and social structure. Meanwhile domestic problems clamored for attention. How to deal with the vanquished South? What to do with the millions of former slaves, now disoriented, unemployed, and roaming the countryside?

In addition to domestic issues, there were serious problems of foreign policy, and these are our main concern. One such problem arose from the presence of a French army in Mexico. France was the country of Lafayette, the country that had stood with America during the Revolution and had imitated the United States with her own revolution. But regard for France had fallen sharply when her Emperor, Napoleon III, had openly displayed his sympathy for the Confederacy and then, early in the Civil War, had sent French troops to Mexico, ostensibly to collect debts. In 1864 Archduke

6. Message of Dec. 9, 1868, James D. Richardson (ed.), *A Compilation of the Messages and Papers of the Presidents, 1789–1897* (10 vols., Washington, 1899), VI, 688.

7. Fish to Caleb Cushing (American minister to Spain), Feb. 6, 1874, *Papers Relating to the Foreign Relations of the United States, 1874* (Washington, 1874), p. 860.

Maximilian, brother of the Emperor of Austria, became Emperor of Mexico, supported by France. Although dismayed by the turn of events, the United States was fully occupied by her own struggle. Seward, a shrewd, cautious former Governor of New York, who was then Abraham Lincoln's Secretary of State, realized that careful treatment of France and Maximilian was necessary lest they be provoked to intervene on the side of the Confederacy.[8] But as northern fortunes improved, Americans began to view the French-backed monarchy south of the border with rising impatience. At a time when republicanism was vindicating itself, the appearance of yet another European monarchy in the free New World (Great Britain, Russia, and Spain were also there) was intolerable. When the war ended, General Ulysses S. Grant and other officers were eager to oust Maximilian; and Grant actually sent 50,000 soldiers to the border. Seward continued to proceed cautiously, fearing to force France into war by pushing too hard. But in early 1866 he asked Paris for "definitive information" about a withdrawal.[9] Already Napoleon had decided to pull out. Probably American diplomacy had nothing to do with his decision, although American military power may have had. The likelihood is, however, that other considerations weighed more heavily in Paris: guerrilla warfare by the Mexicans, the unexpectedly high cost of the intervention, its unpopularity in France, the menacing rise of Prussia.[10] A year later came Maximilian's tragic end. Gallantly but foolishly refusing to leave, he was captured and shot in 1867. Franco-American relations were definitely cool, and most Americans rejoiced when Napoleon was deposed in 1870 after France's defeat by Prussia.[11]

Much more important and lasting were the problems, some of

8. Egon C. Corti, *Maximilian and Charlotte of Mexico* (New York, 1928), describes the intervention. For American diplomacy see Dexter Perkins, *The Monroe Doctrine, 1826–1867* (Baltimore, 1933), chs. 6–9. For French attitudes during the Civil War see Lynn M. Case and Warren F. Spencer, *The United States and France: Civil War Diplomacy* (Philadelphia, 1970).

9. Seward to Marquis de Montholon, Feb. 12, 1866, *House Executive Documents*, 39 Cong., 1 Sess., No. 93 (Serial 1263), p. 34.

10. Henry Blumenthal, *A Reappraisal of Franco-American Relations, 1830–1871* (Chapel Hill, 1959), pp. 175–80; Perkins, *Monroe Doctrine, 1826–1867*, pp. 515–27; Clyde A. Duniway, "Reasons for the Withdrawal of the French from Mexico," *Annual Report*, American Historical Association, I (1902), 315–28.

11. Blumenthal, *Franco-American Relations*, ch. 7; John G. Gazley, *American Opinion of German Unification, 1848–1871* (New York, 1926).

them bequeathed by the Civil War, regarding Great Britain and regarding territorial expansion overseas. Anglo-American relations and expansion were the two main foreign-policy issues throughout the years dealt with in this book, and we must pay careful attention to the way the United States confronted these matters after hostilities ended in 1865.

Of all countries in the world, Great Britain was the one with which the United States had had the closest contacts. In fact Washington's attention was focused upon that one country more, probably, than on the rest of the world put together. The United States and Great Britain had already fought each other twice, during the Revolution and during the War of 1812. At many other times they had disputed angrily, and not infrequently more fighting had threatened to erupt. Britain was the world's strongest country, and wherever Americans took a step outside their own borders, there they seemed to run into British opposition. Britain blocked an American isthmian canal; she encouraged the Hawaiians to maintain their independence; her Caribbean bases warned off Americans from adventures in that sensitive area. Above all, along the Canadian border and off both Canadian coasts the United States kept encountering a firm British hand. Difficulties with Canada frequently strained America's relations with Britain.[12]

For other reasons, too, Americans disliked the British. They denounced Britain for her allegedly tyrannical rule over their colonial forefathers, and they resented the derisory attitude of her ruling classes toward republicanism and democracy, foolish and subversive doctrines in the predominant British view. Britain was the target of Irish-American venom and the citadel of the international gold standard excoriated in the 1890s by free-silverites and Populists. Furthermore, a significant element of apprehension, almost fear, characterized attitudes toward Great Britain. Her mighty power seemed to hover menacingly over the United States. In 1885 the first Canadian transcontinental railroad was completed, an iron band, as it seemed to Americans, hemming them in. Supplementing

12. Regarding these matters see Charles S. Campbell, *From Revolution to Rapprochement: The United States and Great Britain, 1783–1900* (New York, 1974), chs. 1–6. On the other hand, regarding influences that drew some sections of the British and American peoples close together see Frank Thistlethwaite, *The Anglo-American Connection in the Early Nineteenth Century* (Philadelphia, 1959).

it were Britain's many naval bases. "The British Empire . . . stands ready . . . to complete its chain of naval stations from Australia to British Columbia," General John M. Schofield warned in 1875.[13] "The Government of Canada is hostile to us"; "England [is] reaching out for every island in the Pacific"; her formidable West Indian bases "are a standing menace to our Atlantic seaboard."[14] So Senator Henry Cabot Lodge warned twenty years later. In full agreement was Senator John H. Mitchell of Oregon: "To-day the Pacific Ocean is dotted with British naval stations . . . as the stars dot the heavens. In the Atlantic . . . we find a line of British naval stations . . . connecting with the great transcontinental railway . . . while on the south the waters of the Gulf of Mexico are menaced at every strategic point by British naval establishments."[15]

During the Civil War, so northerners were firmly convinced, Britain had again displayed an abiding malevolence; she had scoffed at the conflict as a crusade against slavery; she had yearned for the destruction of democracy and of the sacred union itself, and had subtly striven to achieve these nefarious ends. The United States contended that Britain's neutrality proclamation, issued at the start of the war, was illegal and designed to aid the Confederacy. Moreover, Britain had sanctioned the construction of several Confederate cruisers in her ports: the *Alabama, Florida, Shenandoah,* and others. In part because of their depredations, the tonnage of the American merchant marine had fallen from 5,539,813 in 1861 to 1,602,528 in 1865, whereas that of British ships had risen from 5,895,369 to 7,322,604.[16] The United States insisted that Britain pay full compensation for the damage the cruisers had done. The

13. Schofield to Representative John K. Luttrell, Dec. 30, 1875, *Congressional Record,* 44 Cong., 1 Sess., p. 1489 (March 6, 1876).

14. Henry Cabot Lodge, "Our Blundering Foreign Policy," *Forum,* XIX (1895), 12, 9, 17.

15. *Congressional Record,* 53 Cong., 3 Sess., p. 708 (Jan. 7, 1895). For similar expressions see *ibid.,* 44 Cong., 1 Sess., pp. 1596, 1604 (March 9, 1876); 47 Cong., 2 Sess., p. 1559 (Jan. 24, 1883); 50 Cong., 2 Sess., p. 89 (Dec. 7, 1888); 52 Cong., 2 Sess., p. 1526 (Feb. 13, 1893); 53 Cong., 2 Sess., p. 1837 (Feb. 3, 1894); 53 Cong., 3 Sess., p. 353 (Dec. 17, 1894), p. 3083 (March 2, 1895); 54 Cong., 1 Sess., p. 112 (Dec. 10, 1895), p. 1789 (Feb. 17, 1896).

16. *Congressional Globe,* 41 Cong., 1 Sess., Appendix, p. 25 (April 13, 1869). For a general account of the cruisers see Adrian Cook, *The Alabama Claims, American Politics and Anglo-American Relations, 1865–1872)* (Ithaca, 1975); see also Maureen M. Robson, "The Alabama Claims and the Anglo-American Reconciliation, 1865–1871," *Canadian Historical Review,* XLII (1961), 1–22, and *Senate Executive Documents,* 41 Cong., 1 Sess., No. 11 (Serials 1394–1398).

American claims relating to all the ships built in Britain came to be known as the *Alabama* claims, and for nearly a decade they constituted an extremely dangerous, emotional issue between Britain and the United States. Americans believed that Britain had even permitted southerners to strike across the Canadian border at St. Albans, Vermont, and had little doubt that she would have intervened openly on the side of the South if northern power and European complications had not given her pause. As the war pursued its dreadful course, anger against Britain mounted; and it surged up with every fresh report of a northern ship sunk. At the end of the conflict a deep hatred of her and a resolve to wreak vengeance obsessed the country.

An easy way to retaliate lay close at hand. The Marcy-Elgin treaty of 1854 had provided for a measure of free trade between the United States and the British North American provinces, and had given Americans fishing rights in provincial waters. The fishing grounds were the oldest, and a perennial, source of British-American contention; and their peaceful regulation was no easy matter. Washington terminated the Marcy-Elgin treaty in 1866, the earliest date allowed by its terms.[17] Although this abrupt step reflected mainly a strong tide of protectionism, it demonstrated also how pervasive anti-British sentiment was. A dangerous state of affairs ensued. With the treaty terminated, the provincial governments naturally withdrew the fishing privileges they had bestowed; they did, however, offer to continue extending the privileges to those buying special licenses. Americans generally refused to buy them and fished anyhow. In 1870 Ottawa stopped issuing licenses and banned Americans from all inshore waters except the limited ones specified in a treaty of 1818. Canadian warships patrolled the fishing grounds; Americans armed themselves and continued to frequent the inshore waters.[18] United States relations with Great Britain, already strained by the *Alabama* claims, deteriorated further.

17. Lester B. Shippee, *Canadian-American Relations, 1849–1874* (New Haven, 1939), ch. 8.

18. *Ibid.*, ch. 11. According to *Senate Miscellaneous Documents,* 50 Cong., 1 Sess., No. 109 (Serial 2517), p. 11, Americans purchased 354 licenses in 1866, 281 in 1867, and 56 in 1868. For a petition from Gloucester, Massachusetts, protesting Canadian seizures, see *Congressional Globe,* 41 Cong., 3 Sess., p. 88 (Dec. 13, 1870). Sir Edward Thornton (British minister to the United States) forwarded the petition to Foreign Secretary Lord Granville, Dec. 19, 1870, Public Record Office (London), Foreign Office 5/1195.

Other controversies with Britain, not directly related to the Civil War, emerged. Ireland's centuries-old struggle with Great Britain was nearing a climax, and hundreds of thousands of Irish-Americans were more concerned with the plight of their ancestral home than with their new country. In June 1866, Irish Fenians invaded Canada from New York and Vermont. They were members of a secret organization, founded in the United States, which hoped to liberate Ireland by provoking an Anglo-American war.[19] The raids were fiascos, but they alarmed and angered Canadians, especially when Washington declined to suppress the Fenians. President Johnson was occupied by the quarrel with the Radical Republicans that led to his impeachment in 1868. Effective government was breaking down in Washington; in any case, few politicians dared alienate the Irish vote.

The American menace encouraged Canadians to form the Dominion of Canada in 1867.[20] The prospect of a unified British, monarchical country adjacent to themselves was repugnant to Americans. In the House of Representatives the famous Civil War general Nathaniel P. Banks, now a Representative from Massachusetts, declared that Canadian confederation was "in contravention of the rights and interests of this Government," and the House adopted a resolution opposing it. The Senate, too, indulged in hostile talk.[21]

The Anglo-American treaty of 1846 regarding Oregon had drawn the international boundary along the forty-ninth parallel from the Rocky Mountains to Georgia Strait, and had provided that between the mainland and Vancouver Island the line would follow the middle of the channel. Which channel? The United States contended that it went through Haro Strait near Vancouver Island; Great Britain that it went farther east, through Rosario Strait. Within the disputed area lay San Juan Island, which had strategic importance. In 1858 gold discoveries in British Columbia brought American settlers to San Juan. American soldiers followed them, and soon a

19. Arthur H. DeRosier, Jr., "Importance in Failure: The Fenian Raids of 1866–1871," *Southern Quarterly*, III (1965), 181–97; William D'Arcy, *The Fenian Movement in the United States: 1858–1886* (Washington, 1947); Brian Jenkins, *Fenians and Anglo-American Relations during Reconstruction* (Ithaca, 1969).

20. Donald G. Creighton, "The United States and Canadian Confederation," *Canadian Historical Review*, XXXIX (1958), 209–22.

21. *Congressional Globe*, 40 Cong., 1 Sess., p. 37 (March 8, 1867), p. 392 (March 27, 1867), p. 48 (March 11, 1867).

British force arrived. At the end of the Civil War the island was still under joint military occupation, with all the dangers of that situation.[22]

Much the most perilous of all these disputes were the *Alabama* claims, a settlement of which could not long be delayed if the specter of a third British-American war was to be removed. Lord John Russell, Britain's Foreign Secretary during the Civil War, had been primarily responsible for allowing the ships to be built and the neutrality proclamation to be issued. After the war Washington demanded damages or, failing that, arbitration. But the Foreign Secretary was quite unwilling to admit that he had been seriously at fault. In August 1865 he refused to permit either compensation or arbitration; he would consent only to the appointment of a commission to examine all Civil War claims "which the two powers shall agree to refer to the commissioners." Such cool treatment did not interest Americans, who longed for Britain to be humiliated.[23] In late 1865 Russell became Prime Minister; no progress could be made while he held power. But in June 1866 his ministry fell, and in July the Conservatives took office, first under Lord Derby, then in early 1868 under Benjamin Disraeli. Lord Stanley was the Foreign Secretary. The new leaders, who had not been responsible for Civil War policy, were more conciliatory.

Secretary Seward had the bad fortune to be in office at a time when the clash between Congress and the President made comprehensive policies impossible of execution. Despite the change of scene at Whitehall, he failed to settle any of the controversies with Great Britain. In response to his admonition that a resolution of the dispute over the *Alabama* claims and the neutrality proclamation was "urgently necessary," Stanley softened Russell's position by agreeing to "the principle of arbitration" as regards the claims, but not the proclamation. This was unacceptable to Seward.[24] Before leav-

22. James O. McCabe, *The San Juan Water Boundary Question* (Toronto, 1964).

23. Russell to Charles Francis Adams (American minister to Great Britain), Aug. 30 and Oct. 14, 1865, *Senate Executive Documents*, 41 Cong., 1 Sess., No. 11 (Serial 1396), pp. 562, 581; Adams to Foreign Secretary Lord Clarendon, Nov. 21, 1865, *ibid.*, p. 614.

24. Seward to Adams, Aug. 27, 1866, *Senate Executive Documents*, 41 Cong., 1 Sess., No. 11, p. 633; Stanley to Sir Frederick Bruce (British minister to the United States), Nov. 30, 1866, *ibid.*, pp. 652–53; Seward to Adams, Nov. 29, 1867, *ibid.*, p. 686. See also Glyndon G. Van Deusen, *William Henry Seward* (New York, 1967), ch. 34.

## " HOITY-TOITY ! ! ! "

(*Punch,* February 1, 1868)

MRS. BRITANNIA: "Hoity-toity! What's all this fuss about?"
JOHNNY BULL: "It's Cousin Columbia, Ma, and she says I broke her
ships, and I didn't—and I want to be friends—and she's a cross
thing—and wants to have it all her own way!"

ing office, however, he made one more attempt to resolve the dispute. A new United States minister, Reverdy Johnson, was sent to London; unlike his predecessor, Charles Francis Adams, he was not bound by rigid positions assumed during the war, but he alienated his fellow countrymen by what they considered to be his fawning attitude toward the British. Within a few months he had negotiated a treaty for the arbitration of the *Alabama* and other claims, and also a treaty for the arbitration by the President of Switzerland of the San Juan boundary; both were signed on January 14, 1869. The Johnson-Clarendon convention, as the claims treaty was called, provided that Great Britain and the United States would each appoint two commissioners to examine claims submitted by individuals, including those over the *Alabama,* and that if the four commissioners could not reach a decision an arbitrator would be selected, by lot if necessary.[25]

Congressional hatred of Andrew Johnson and all his works was intense at that time. Grant had been elected President in November 1868; he was known to have strong feelings about the *Alabama,* and Seward would have been well advised to leave the fate of both treaties to the incoming administration. Instead he allowed them to go to the Senate early in 1869. That body declined to consider the San Juan treaty and by a vote of 54 to 1 it defeated the Johnson-Clarendon convention on April 13, 1869 (a month after Grant entered the White House) following a devastating attack by Charles Sumner, chairman of the Foreign Relations Committee and a man of enormous authority in foreign policy. "The massive grievance under which our country suffered for years is left untouched . . . ," Sumner pronounced. "For all this there is not one word of regret or even of recognition." He stressed Britain's neutrality proclamation as the fount of all her misdemeanors. Because of it and the consequent negligence about the cruisers, Great Britain was responsible for direct damages, which he estimated at $125 million. But in addition, he contended, there were "national losses" resulting from British acts that had prolonged the war. "If, through British intervention, the war was doubled in duration, or in any way extended, as cannot be doubted, then is England justly responsible for the additional expenditure to which our country was doomed . . . ;"

25. *Senate Executive Documents,* 41 Cong., 1 Sess., No. 11, pp. 752–55.

and he estimated this extra expense at over $2 billion.[26]

Did the Senator really think that Britain should be assessed half the cost of the Civil War? Was he intimating, as some thought, that she should cede Canada in order to meet an enormous American claim? Sumner did want the Dominion, but only with its willing consent, which he thought would be forthcoming. He was convinced that if only the United States insisted on her grievance and refused to make a quick settlement, Britain would make the cession. Sumner had been an ardent Anglophile; he was still favorably disposed to the British, but his ill-advised speech persuaded many Americans that Britain was morally responsible for about half the total cost of the war. America's subsequent preoccupation with the national losses—or indirect claims, as they were usually called—complicated Anglo-American affairs enormously for the next three years.

What really interested Secretary of State Seward was territorial expansion, the second main theme of American foreign policy during more than three decades following the Civil War. To account for the national concern with expansion, especially overseas expansion, we must go back to 1848, the year the Mexican War ended. One consequence of that conflict was the acquisition of California, which, together with the Oregon Territory, gave the United States her Pacific coast. Gold discoveries in 1849 brought a stampede of fortune seekers to California. In 1850 it became a state, as did Oregon nine years later. All at once the United States had a considerable population on the west coast, and this was to affect foreign policy profoundly.

No transcontinental railway was completed until 1869. Before then, many travelers between the two coasts preferred the sea trip by way of Central America, broken only by a short land transit, to the difficult and dangerous journey across the United States. Acquaintance with Central America directed attention to the convenience of an isthmian canal, the eventual construction of which had been foreseen ever since the discovery of the narrow land barrier between the two oceans. Consequently, after 1848 American thought turned strongly to a canal. An isthmian waterway, though seldom an urgent matter, was one to which other important aspects

26. *Congressional Globe*, 41 Cong., 1 Sess., Appendix, pp. 21–26 (April 13, 1869); *Journal of the Executive Proceedings of the Senate . . .* (Washington, 1901), XVII, 163; Cook, *Alabama Claims*, ch. 4.

of foreign policy were related, and was a continuing and central American aspiration for more than fifty years until construction by the United States began early in the twentieth century. Even before the Civil War Washington had taken steps preliminary to construction. There were two promising routes: one across Nicaragua, the other across Panama, the latter a province of New Granada (as Colombia was called until 1861). In 1846 the United States made a treaty with New Granada giving transit (but not construction) rights; significantly, it was not approved until 1848, after the acquisition of California made the United States a major Pacific power. The next year an American diplomat signed a treaty with Nicaragua giving construction rights to the United States, but instead of ratifying it Washington decided to adopt a policy of cooperation with Great Britain. This took the form of the Clayton-Bulwer treaty of 1850, which provided that neither the United States nor Britain would colonize Central America, or exercise exclusive control over or fortify a Central American canal, and that both would guarantee the canal's neutrality.[27] Despite much British-American bickering over its meaning, the treaty lasted until 1901.

In an indirect way west coast settlement stimulated the traditional American interest in the Caribbean Sea, whose importance for the protection of a canal was recognized. As early as 1854 an American agent named William L. Cazneau drafted a treaty with Santo Domingo for the cession of Samaná Bay, potentially a first-rate naval base; the treaty failed when Santo Domingo made amendments unacceptable to the Senate. But it was particularly Cuba that occupied American attention. Unsuccessful filibustering expeditions sailed to that Spanish island in 1850 and 1851; and the Ostend Manifesto of 1854, written by three American diplomats in Europe, advised purchasing the island or, if Spain refused to sell, taking it by force. In 1858 Senator Stephen A. Douglas declared: "It is our destiny to have Cuba, and it is folly to debate the question."[28] Except for the sectional strife of the fifties, the United States might have invaded the island during the 1850s—and had her war with Spain some forty years early.

Settlement in the west of course sharpened interest in the Pacific

27. Hunter Miller (ed.), *Treaties and Other International Acts of the United States of America* (8 vols., Washington, 1931–43), V, 671–75.
28. Harold U. Faulkner, *American Political and Social History* (New York, 1941), p. 315.

Ocean, and especially in the Hawaiian Islands. Hawaii's significance for protecting a potential canal, and the west coast itself, was obvious. Hardly was California annexed when Secretary of State James Buchanan sent a commissioner to the islands to make a commercial treaty (concluded in 1849). When French forces seized Honolulu in 1849, the United States reacted strongly;[29] and the French soon withdrew. In 1854 Secretary of State William L. Marcy negotiated a treaty of annexation, but when Hawaii demanded an amendment that would make her a state, he decided not to submit the treaty to the Senate. For many years the United States had traded with China through Canton, the only open port. Taking advantage of two Anglo-French wars with China in the late 1850s, Washington demanded and received from the defeated Oriental empire privileges equal to those obtained by the Europeans. Japan, too, was an attractive market; by a mixture of threats and presents, Commodore Matthew Perry persuaded her to conclude a commercial treaty with the United States in 1854, and in 1857 and 1858 Japan granted additional concessions.

A powerful country like the United States, once settled along the Pacific Ocean, was certain to play a major role in a Central American canal, the Caribbean, and Hawaii. A canal, the Caribbean, Hawaii —inevitably these were basic objectives of foreign policy. Yet not for fifty years were the second and third of these objectives realized, and the first virtually assured. Then, after the Spanish-American War broke out in 1898, the long-pent-up forces were suddenly released, and in two momentous years the United States annexed Hawaii, occupied Cuba and took Puerto Rico, and moved decisively toward the construction of an isthmian canal. She also went much further, annexing Wake, Guam, part of Samoa, and all the thousands of Philippine islands.

What caused the half-century delay? Some of the reasons are obvious enough. During the thirteen years between the Mexican War and the Civil War the mounting sectional conflict precluded a sustained foreign policy; the rivalry between North and South did stimulate southern efforts to gain new lands for slavery and cotton in Central America and the Caribbean Sea, but a divided United States could not achieve these goals. And when the sectional quarrel

29. Samuel F. Bemis, *A Diplomatic History of the United States* (New York, 1955), p. 349.

erupted into war in 1861, expansion became altogether impossible. After the Civil War, however, the United States was strong enough to move again toward a Central American canal, the Caribbean, and Hawaii. Secretary of State Seward, clearly perceiving what may be called the continuing implications of 1848, wanted to do just this; and so did another fervent expansionist, President Grant. But their efforts largely failed; and after Grant left office in 1877, his successors during the next twenty years, for reasons that will become apparent, either opposed territorial expansion overseas or found the opposition to expansion insurmountable.

For many years Seward had had no doubt that the United States ought to expand and little doubt that she was destined to do so. One essential step, in his view, was to construct an isthmian canal. In June 1867 the United States minister to Central America and the Nicaraguan Foreign Minister signed the Dickinson-Ayón treaty, by which the United States got a nonexclusive right of transit over any route across Nicaragua, agreeing in return to protect the route and guarantee its innocent use.[30] The Senate approved the treaty the next year. Interested in the Panama route, too, Seward wanted to obtain construction rights there as well. In January 1869 the American minister, Peter J. Sullivan, signed a treaty with Colombia giving the United States, or a private company chosen by her, the sole right to build a canal through a strip of land twenty miles wide, to be under American control but not sovereignty. That these terms violated the Clayton-Bulwer treaty seems clear, but Great Britain never had to protest because the Colombian Senate rejected the treaty.[31]

Meanwhile, anticipating success in Colombia, Seward had twice in 1868 gone to New York City to persuade businessmen to organize a construction company. The Suez Canal was to be completed the next year, and a cogent argument could be made for an American waterway to balance the British one. Although dubious about raising enough money in the stringent postwar years, a group of capitalists formed the Isthmus Canal Company and got a charter

30. William M. Malloy (ed.), *Treaties, Conventions, International Acts, Protocols and Agreements between the United States of America and Other Parties, 1776–1909* (2 vols., Washington, 1910), II, 1279–87.

31. *Senate Documents*, 56 Cong., 1 Sess., No. 237 (Serial 3853), pp. 45–51; see also Gerstle Mack, *The Land Divided: A History of the Panama Canal and Other Isthmian Projects* (New York, 1944), p. 167.

from New York in September 1868.[32] The company came to nothing, but Seward's Nicaragua treaty remained in force for almost fifty years.

The Secretary of State also attempted to increase American strength in the Pacific Ocean. In August 1867 a naval officer, under instructions from the Navy Department, took the uninhabited Midway Islands.[33] Seward wanted to annex the Hawaiian Islands, and he had assurances from the American minister at Honolulu that the local inhabitants would like to be annexed. But he could not have been sanguine. Congress opposed overseas territorial expansion, especially when espoused by the hated Johnson administration. Furthermore, former abolitionists, notably Charles Sumner, were opposed in principle to depriving dark-skinned people of their independence. Nor did they want to aggravate America's already serious race problem, all the more because many of them, although genuinely condemning slavery on idealistic grounds, were quite certain that the black man was inherently inferior to the white man.[34] Other considerations also worked against overseas expansion; thus the Senate refused to approve even a reciprocity treaty of 1867 with Hawaii, partly because of pressure from American sugar interests fearful of competition.[35]

Seward was more hopeful about the Caribbean. The French intervention in Mexico and a recent short-lived Spanish occupation of Santo Domingo, as well as Civil War blockade problems, had shown the desirability of having naval bases in that sea. Bases would be

32. Sir Edward Thornton (British minister to the United States) to Foreign Secretary Lord Stanley, Oct. 26 and Nov. 2, 1868, Foreign Office 5/1132 and Foreign Office 5/1133; Van Deusen, *Seward,* pp. 517–18.

33. *Senate Reports,* 40 Cong., 3 Sess., No. 194 (Serial 1362), p. 6; see also *Senate Executive Documents,* 40 Cong., 2 Sess., No. 79 (Serial 1317).

34. Donald M. Dozer, "Anti-Expansionism during the Johnson Administration," *Pacific Historical Review,* XII (1943), 253–75. Regarding the belief in black inferiority see Robert F. Durden, "Ambiguities in the Antislavery Crusade of the Republican Party," in Martin B. Duberman (ed.), *The Antislavery Vanguard: New Essays on the Abolitionists* (Princeton, 1965), ch. 15; C. Vann Woodward, *The Burden of Southern History* (Baton Rouge, 1960), pp. 83–85.

35. *Senate Executive Documents,* 52 Cong., 2 Sess., No. 77 (Serial 3062), pp. 11, 133, 135–37, 139–40; James M. Callahan, *The Alaska Purchase and Americo-Canadian Relations* (Morgantown, W. Va., 1908), p. 27; John Patterson, "The United States and Hawaiian Reciprocity, 1867–1870," *Pacific Historical Review,* VII (1938), 14–26; Dozer, "Anti-Expansionism during the Johnson Administration," pp. 272–73. The Senate vote came on June 1, 1870, when Grant was President.

needed, too, for defending the potential canal. Early in 1865 he conferred with General Waldemar Raasloff, the minister of Denmark at Washington, about purchasing the Danish West Indies.[36] The negotiations at first made little headway. In January 1866 Seward sailed on a cruise "for his health" to the Danish West Indies, Santo Domingo, Haiti, and Cuba. Back in Washington, he offered $5 million for the three main Danish islands; but Denmark demanded $10 million for two islands and stipulated that the inhabitants must first vote for annexation. Agreement was finally reached on $7,500,000 for St. John and St. Thomas, which has the splendid harbor of Charlotte Amalie, conditional on a favorable plebiscite; and a treaty with these terms was signed in October 1867. But by then relations between President Johnson and the Congress had deteriorated sharply. Had the Danes acted promptly in 1865 or even 1866 the sale might have gone through, but the tense American political conditions made this unlikely in late 1867. Nature, too, was hostile. An earthquake, a tidal wave, and a hurricane devastated the islands. The U.S.S. *Monongahela* was washed ashore, then carried back and grounded on a coral reef. The House of Representatives was already confronted with a request to appropriate several million dollars for Alaska, and the thought of spending $7,500,000 more for the storm-wreaked little islands seemed intolerable. Pressure was strong to reduce the enormous Civil War debt. On November 25 the House resolved: "That in the present financial condition of the country any further purchases of territory are inexpedient and this House will hold itself under no obligations to vote money to pay for any such purchases unless there is greater necessity for the same than now exists."[37] The Senate did not even vote on the treaty.

Meanwhile Secretary Seward had another Caribbean harbor in mind—Samaná Bay in Santo Domingo.[38] Negotiations to purchase it petered out; however, after a revolt a new Dominican government was disposed to sell not only the bay but the entire country. Two Americans, William L. Cazneau (the man who had drafted the Dominican treaty of 1854) and Joseph W. Fabens, both of whom had

36. Charles C. Tansill, *The Purchase of the Danish West Indies* (Baltimore, 1932), chs. 1, 2; Halvdan Koht, "The Origin of Seward's Plan to Purchase the Danish West Indies," *American Historical Review*, L (1945), 762–67.

37. *Congressional Globe*, 40 Cong., 1 Sess., p. 792 (Nov. 25, 1867).

38. Charles C. Tansill, *The United States and Santo Domingo, 1798–1873: A Chapter in Caribbean Diplomacy* (Baltimore, 1938), pp. 234–35.

business ventures in Santo Domingo, tried to promote annexation. But before anything could be concluded, Johnson's impeachment trial was at hand; and it occupied all thoughts. Nevertheless the President in his annual message of 1868 urged the purchase not only of Santo Domingo but also of Haiti, which in Môle St. Nicolas has another fine harbor.[39] Following up this plea, Representative Nathaniel P. Banks, chairman of the House Foreign Affairs Committee, proposed a joint resolution extending American protection over Santo Domingo and Haiti whenever either country applied for protection or whenever the President was satisfied that either wanted to be protected. But although Banks insisted that he merely envisaged sending a warship, and perhaps advising revolutionists to behave properly, his proposal was soundly beaten.[40]

At various times Seward showed interest in other West Indian islands. He sounded out Spain on selling Culebra and Culebrita, considered buying St. Bartholomew Island from Sweden, and approached France about St. Pierre and Martinique. He gave some attention to Cuba and Puerto Rico, in the former of which a rebellion broke out in 1868 that was to cause much trouble for Washington.[41] None of these moves came to anything.

The eager Secretary was fully prepared to go beyond these basic objectives of a canal, the Caribbean, and Hawaii. Like many other Americans, he was convinced that someday the Dominion of Canada would gravitate peacefully to America's welcoming embrace. This was probably his main reason for toying with the idea of buying not only the Danish West Indies but also Danish Iceland and Greenland. These northern lands would outflank Canada on the northeast, just as Alaska, after 1867, outflanked her on the northwest; thus encircled, according to a hopeful State Department pamphlet, the Canadians would cheerfully join their great neighbor.[42] But Iceland and Greenland eluded Seward's grasp, just as did Tigre Island off

39. Annual Message, Dec. 9, 1868, Richardson, *Messages and Papers*, VI, 689.
40. *Congressional Globe*, 40 Cong., 3 Sess., p. 317 (Jan. 12, 1869); pp. 333–340 (Jan. 13, 1869). For a similar resolution see *ibid.*, p. 769 (Feb. 1, 1869).
41. Van Deusen, *Seward*, pp. 530–31.
42. Benjamin M. Pierce, *A Report on the Resources of Iceland and Greenland* (Washington, 1868). The pamphlet was issued in response to Seward's request for a report on the two islands. Minister Thornton sent a copy of it to London with the remark that Seward had his eye on Iceland and Greenland. Thornton to Stanley, Sept. 28, 1868, Foreign Office 5/1132.

the west coast of Central America, and two remote places on which, so rumor had it, he directed his wide-ranging attention: Borneo and Fiji.[43]

His one major success was the purchase of Russian-America (as Alaska was called). Why Russia decided to sell—this was the only instance in her history in which she peacefully ceded territory—is a matter about which we need say no more than that the Russian-American Company, which administered the huge area, was near bankruptcy; that Alaska would be difficult to defend against Great Britain, war with whom was a perennial possibility; and that St. Petersburg feared the day when swarms of American settlers invading Alaska would rebel and seek United States annexation, as the Texans had done.[44] Having decided to sell, Russia wanted Washington to make the first move. The Russian minister to the United States, Édouard de Stoeckl, succeeded in eliciting from Seward in early March 1867 a query as to whether the Czar would consider a sale. Over the next few days a treaty was drafted by which the United States offered to pay $7,200,000 (Russia was ready to accept $5 million). Stoeckl then used the new Atlantic cable, at American expense, to ask for permission to sign. Receiving a favorable reply, he went to Seward's home the evening of March 29 and proposed signing the next day. According to Seward's son the delighted Secretary replied, "Why wait till tomorrow, Mr. Stoeckl? Let us make the treaty tonight!"[45] Off the two men went to the State Department, where they assembled secretaries, put the last touches on the treaty, and signed it at four o'clock in the morning of March 30.

It is not difficult to understand why a man of Seward's expansive tastes jumped at the chance of getting Russian-America. Alaska dominated the north Pacific and reached out close to Asia. One may conjecture, moreover, that the Secretary, and the President too, hoped to revive their tottering prestige by the tremendous leap to

43. Van Deusen, *Seward*, p. 532.

44. Regarding Russia and Alaska see Hector Chevigny, *Russian America: The Great Alaskan Venture, 1741–1867* (New York, 1965). For general accounts of the purchase see Victor J. Farrar, *The Purchase of Alaska* (Washington, 1934); Thomas A. Bailey, "Why the United States Purchased Alaska," *Pacific Historical Review*, III (1934), 39–49; Frank A. Golder, "The Purchase of Alaska," *American Historical Review*, XXV (1920), 411–25; and Ernest N. Paolino, *The Foundations of the American Empire: William Henry Seward and U.S. Foreign Policy* (Ithaca, 1973), pp. 106–18.

45. Frederick W. Seward, *Reminiscences of a War-Time Statesman and Diplomat, 1830–1915* (New York, 1916), p. 362.

the north. Possibly considerations relating to Canada weighed more heavily still. Alaska could be expected to exert a heavy pressure propelling at least British Columbia toward its eager suitor. "The acquisition of Alaska was made with a view of extending national jurisdiction and republican principles in the American hemisphere," President Johnson reported to Congress; and Seward said candidly that Alaska would hasten Canada's destiny to join the United States.[46] Deeply concerned, the British minister at Washington, Sir Frederick Bruce, reported that the treaty symbolized a Russian-American rapprochement against Great Britain and foreshadowed America's eventual absorption of the whole continent.[47]

When the Senate convened in special session on April 1 to consider the treaty, approval seemed unlikely. The press was deriding Alaska as worthless, "Seward's Icebox," a "Polar Bear Garden." The very fact that Seward and Johnson wanted it argued against the purchase. Senatorial motives cannot easily be discerned because the debate was secret. But apparently most Senators became convinced that Alaska really was a valuable acquisition, and however much they begrudged the executive getting the credit, they dared not allow personal spite to outweigh national interest. Probably the decisive influence was a powerful speech by Charles Sumner. Opposed at first to the treaty, Sumner after intensive study changed his mind. Part of his three-hour address is worth quoting because it expressed prevailing views so well—the manifestly destined spread of republicanism, the inevitable doom of monarchy, Canada's destiny to join the United States, America's leadership in the New World: "The present treaty is a visible step in the occupation of the whole North American continent. . . . We dismiss one other monarch from the continent. One by one they have retired—first France, then Spain, then France again, and now Russia,—all giving way to the absorbing Unity declared in the national motto, *E pluribus unum.* . . . Sincerely believing that republican institutions under the primacy of the United States must embrace this whole continent, . . . I cannot disguise my anxiety that every stage in our predestined future shall be by natural processes, without war. . . ."[48] One more monarch

46. Annual message, Dec. 9, 1868, Richardson, *Messages and Papers,* VI, 688; Callahan, *Alaska Purchase,* p. 22.

47. Van Deusen, *Seward,* p. 544.

48. *The Works of Charles Sumner* (12 vols., Boston, 1873–77), XI, 223, 232–33.

remained, Queen Victoria; and, as Sumner surely implied, the treaty was "a visible step" toward her dismissal too. On April 9 the Senate approved the treaty overwhelmingly, 37 to 2.[49]

But the House of Representatives had still to appropriate the $7,200,000. After the Senate's approval, the House met for only short periods until December, when the second session began. By then relations between the executive and legislative branches were explosive. A House committee had offered a resolution for the President's impeachment, and the House had passed the resolution against purchases of territory. Although the Representative sponsoring the latter resolution had asserted that he was not referring "to the purchase of Walrussia," it was perfectly clear that both he and many of his colleagues had Alaska just as much in mind as the Danish West Indies. Johnson's impeachment trial lasted from March 25 to May 26, 1868. His narrow acquittal added to the bitter feelings; of the forty-three Representatives voting against the Alaska appropriation forty-one had supported impeachment.[50] Another matter militating against the appropriation related to an old monetary claim. During the Crimean War an American named Benjamin W. Perkins had made an agreement with Russia to supply equipment, but the war ended before it was delivered. Perkins unsuccessfully claimed damages for his expenses. Now in 1867 his widow and children, their appetites whetted by the $7,200,000, revived the matter; and a group of Representatives attempted to block payment for Alaska so as to force Russia to settle the claim.[51]

Nevertheless, sentiment for annexation won the day. Two points outweighed any other as the House debate proceeded in early July: first, Alaska was valuable economically and militarily; second, the United States should not offend Russia, the only country to befriend the North during the Civil War, by rejecting the territory which Washington itself had solicited.[52]

The affection felt for Russia at the time was truly remarkable. She and Great Britain were at opposite poles on the American scale of

49. *Journal of the Executive Proceedings of the Senate* . . . (Washington, 1886), XV, Pt. II, p. 662.
50. Van Deusen, *Seward*, p. 546.
51. *Congressional Globe*, 40 Cong., 2 Sess., Appendix, p. 403 (July 7, 1868); pp. 452–53 (July 14, 1868).
52. Bailey, "Why the United States Purchased Alaska," pp. 47–48.

affection.[53] The British had tried hard to cause the North to lose; the Russians, to help it to win; so Americans believed. For many years Russia had been popular, but friendship for her really soared when in the autumn of 1863, a critical time of the Civil War, two Russian fleets appeared, one at San Francisco, the other at New York.[54] Northerners concluded that the ships had come to serve warning on Britain and France not to intervene, and they gave the Russians a tremendous reception. For decades the myth lingered of how the Czar had stood with the beleaguered North in its hour of need; and even Russia's recall in 1871, under insistent American prompting, of her minister at Washington, Constantin de Catacazy (he was accused of meddlesome intrigue), ruffled the honeymoon only temporarily.[55] Not until 1915 was it revealed that the squadrons had taken their American posts so as not to be bottled up by Britain in the event of a European war that threatened to erupt over a revolt in Poland.[56] In 1867 and 1868, however, to challenge the myth would have been blasphemy, and gratitude to Russia may have been a large factor in the House's favorable vote. Sumner had expressed this consideration in the Senate, calling the treaty "a new expression of that *entente cordiale* between the two powers which is a phenomenon of history."[57] James G. Blaine, then a Representative, thought that the United States would have refused to buy Alaska from any other European country.[58]

Other considerations must have been present, even if little expressed. By July 1868 well over a year had elapsed since America's occupation of Alaska, and though the House resented being confronted with a fait accompli, it almost had to accept it. Alaska was in North America, so that its annexation did not conjure up dread visions of imperialism; nor was it thought to have, like the Caribbean, large numbers of dark-skinned natives (the Eskimos were

53. Albert A. Woldman, *Lincoln and the Russians* (Cleveland, 1952).

54. Frank A. Golder, "The Russian Fleet and the Civil War," *American Historical Review*, XX (1915), 807–9.

55. *Senate Executive Documents*, 42 Cong., 2 Sess., No. 5 (Serial 1478); Allan Nevins, *Hamilton Fish: The Inner History of the Grant Administration* (New York, 1936), pp. 503–11.

56. Golder, "Russian Fleet," pp. 801–12; Thomas A. Bailey, "The Russian Fleet Myth Re-Examined," *Mississippi Valley Historical Review*, XXXVIII (1951), 81–90.

57. *Works of Sumner*, XI, 228.

58. James G. Blaine, *Twenty Years of Congress: From Lincoln to Garfield* . . . (2 vols., Norwich, Conn., 1884–86), II, 333–34.

generally overlooked). Then, too, just as the desire to please Russia played a part, so did the wish to offend Great Britain and to speed Queen Victoria on her way from Canada. Less clear is the role of Minister de Stoeckl. Becoming deeply worried that the appropriation bill might fail in the House, he distributed large sums of money to lobbyists and the press. He may even have given funds to some Congressmen,[59] though this is not certain and in any case it seems unlikely that enough Representatives could have been bribed to clinch the final lopsided vote. This came on July 14: 113 voted for the appropriation, only 43 against it; 44 did not vote.[60] The bill became law on the twenty-seventh. Despite his many failures, Secretary Seward had brought an enormous and valuable territory to the United States. It was to be the last acquisition for many years to come.

Some recent writers have depicted Seward as a great prophet of empire with a carefully elaborated program of American expansion, a man whose far-reaching vision anticipated the course of United States foreign policy over the next thirty or forty years.[61] Seward was indeed an outstanding Secretary of State with a firm grasp of some basic requirements of expansion. Much of his energy was devoted to attempts at territorial expansion, but in addition he was deeply interested in commercial expansion. Imbued with the Hegelian concept that, as Seward expressed it, "empire has, for the last three thousand years . . . made its way constantly westward, and . . . must continue to move on westward until the tides of the renewed and of the decaying civilizations of the world meet on the shores of the Pacific Ocean."[62] He saw China as not only a crucial area of future political struggle among nations but as destined to

59. Golder, "Purchase of Alaska," pp. 411–25; Golder, who examined Russian archives, wrote: "It is clear that congressmen were bought . . . ," *ibid.,* p. 424. See also William A. Dunning, "Paying for Alaska: Some Unfamiliar Incidents in the Process," *Political Science Quarterly,* XXVII (1912), 385–98; Reinhard H. Luthin, "The Sale of Alaska," *Slavonic Review,* XVI (1937), 168–82; John Bigelow, *Retrospections of an Active Life* (5 vols., New York, 1909–13), IV, 216–17. The House investigated the purchase but uncovered no evidence of graft. *House Reports,* 40 Cong., 3 Sess., No. 35 (Serial 1388).

60. *Congressional Globe,* 40 Cong., 2 Sess., p. 4055 (July 14, 1868). *The Statutes at Large . . . of the United States of America . . .* (Boston, 1869), XV, 198.

61. See especially Walter LaFeber, *The New Empire: An Interpretation of American Expansion, 1860–1898* (Ithaca, 1963), pp. 24–32; and Paolino, *Foundations of Empire.*

62. LaFeber, *New Empire,* pp. 25–26.

provide an invaluable market for American exports. To promote American interests in China he worked closely with European nations, thereby anticipating the better-known policy of Secretary of State John Hay at the end of the century.

But Seward's cleverness and flashes of inspiration notwithstanding, one wonders whether he did in fact have the comprehensive vision sometimes attributed to him. Did he really foresee the full course of empire for the next generation and prepare the ground for the expansion at the turn of the century, or have historians, to some extent, read history backward and made an overly coherent pattern out of scattered remarks and actions of the Secretary? Seward's fame is secure enough not to require inflating his farsightedness. And whatever the truth about this matter, it is beyond dispute that, as Henry Adams said, the Secretary's policy "went somewhat too far and too fast for the public."[63] The most consummate diplomats are those who practice the art of the possible.

63. *Ibid.*, p. 31.

# CHAPTER 2

# The Quasi Settlement with Great Britain

WHEN Ulysses S. Grant became President in 1869 the dangerous controversy over the *Alabama* claims still clouded Anglo-
American relations. Nevertheless, conditions were more auspicious
for a British-American accord than during President Johnson's
years in office. Once Johnson had left the White House, the paralyz-
ing conflict between the President and the Radical Republicans
came to an end. Furthermore, Grant had an outstanding Secretary
of State. Hamilton Fish, a former Representative, United States
Senator, and Governor of New York, was a socially prominent man
of wealth and culture who had traveled widely in Europe. Strong-
willed and honest, he was a stalwart supporter of Grant and the only
Cabinet officer who, appointed in March 1869, still held his post
when the President's term expired in 1877. His faithful service was
a key factor in holding the administration together. Although somewhat unimaginative, occasionally inflexible, and not brilliant intel-
lectually, Fish possessed an unusual measure of that invaluable trait,
a sound judgment. He was completely lacking in experience in
diplomacy when he entered the State Department, but he proved to
be a remarkably successful secretary.

Both Grant and Fish wanted a settlement with Britain, and they
were fortunate in finding heads of government in London and Ottawa who were prepared to cooperate closely. William E. Gladstone
became Prime Minister of Great Britain in December 1868. During
the Civil War he had made remarks offensive to the North, but as

Prime Minister (1868–1874) he was a true friend of the United States, more than any other individual responsible for the coming accord of 1871–1872. His Foreign Secretary (beginning in 1870), Lord Granville, was another advocate of friendly British-American relations. Sir John A. Macdonald, the great Canadian Conservative leader, one of the founding fathers of the Dominion, had been Prime Minister since 1867. A strong Canadian nationalist, he was at the same time a realistic man who understood that the Dominion's weakness made concessions necessary—and for a British-American agreement, Canadian concessions were essential.

The new leaders quickly moved toward an accord. On July 8, 1869, informal talks opened in Washington between Secretary Fish and John Rose, Minister of Finance in Ottawa. Married to an American and a partner with Levi P. Morton (a future Vice-President of the United States) in a New York banking house, Rose had strong personal reasons to desire good Anglo-Canadian-American relations. He was a friend of the veteran American diplomat Caleb Cushing; and it was Cushing, together with Sir Edward Thornton, the British minister at Washington, who arranged the July meeting.[1] Rose's primary purpose was to obtain commercial reciprocity for Canada, but he and the Secretary perceived that Canadian-American accord could not be reached in an atmosphere of Anglo-American discord. They therefore turned to the *Alabama* claims, the root cause of the unhappy state of affairs. Fish warned that Britain must understand that Sumner's recent speech on the Johnson-Clarendon convention accurately expressed the American sense of grievance; he said that she must give "some kind expression of regret &c" for her Civil War conduct, must pay an indemnity, and in concert with the United States must establish laws of neutrality for the future. Rose thought an agreement along such lines might be worked out. The two men also discussed the advisability of a special British mission coming to Washington.[2] When Rose left on July 12, he and

1. Adrian Cook, *The Alabama Claims, American Politics and Anglo-American Relations, 1865–1872* (Ithaca, 1975), pp. 117–18; Charles Francis Adams, Jr., *Lee at Appomattox and Other Papers* (Boston and New York, 1902), pp. 122–23; Thornton to Foreign Secretary Lord Clarendon, July 12, 1869, A. H. U. Colquhoun, "The Reciprocity Negotiations with the United States in 1869," *Canadian Historical Review*, VIII (1927), 234.

2. Hamilton Fish Diary, Library of Congress (Washington), July 11, 1869; Adams, *Lee at Appomattox*, pp. 122–23.

Fish had reached a rough understanding that foreshadowed the eventual settlement.

Not only the new leaders but a series of developments now pushed both countries closer together. American businessmen were tired of the nagging trans-Atlantic dispute weighing down the economy. Secretary of the Treasury George S. Boutwell admitted that he wanted the tension relaxed in order to gain easier access to the London capital market, thereby facilitating the funding of America's enormous Civil War debt.[3] In May 1870 the Fenians raided Canada again. Although they failed ignominiously, the situation along the border was tense, and another raid was to take place in October 1871.[4] Ottawa, London, and Washington were thoroughly alarmed. And Canadians and Britons wondered why, if the United States failed to suppress Fenian raids, Great Britain should be held responsible for *Alabama* raids. The fishing grounds, too, were dangerous, with Canada determined to enforce a strict interpretation of the confining treaty of 1818, and Americans determined to fish. Responsible people saw the need to reach a settlement before the situation got out of control.

In June 1870 Charles Sumner, still chairman of the Senate Foreign Relations Committee, took the lead in defeating a treaty for the annexation of Santo Domingo; thereby he enraged Grant, who had set his heart on acquiring that country. The President retaliated by dismissing Sumner's friend John L. Motley, Reverdy Johnson's successor as minister at London. Motley had seen eye to eye with Sumner, to whom he owed his appointment, but his successor, Robert C. Schenck, who became minister in late 1870, cooperated closely with Secretary Fish.[5] This weakened Sumner's ability to delay a settlement with Great Britain.

Over the same months events on the Continent were alarming the British. As early as 1869 Gladstone's first Foreign Secretary, Lord Clarendon, told Queen Victoria that tension with America "to a

3. Rose to Foreign Secretary Lord Granville, Jan. 10, 1871, Public Record Office (London), Foreign Office 5/1298.
4. Arthur DeRosier, Jr., "Importance in Failure: The Fenian Raids of 1866–1871," *Southern Quarterly*, III (1965), 181–97; Brian Jenkins, *Fenians and Anglo-American Relations during Reconstruction* (Ithaca, 1969).
5. Allan Nevins, *Hamilton Fish: The Inner History of the Grant Administration* (New York, 1936), chs. 15, 16.

great extent paralyses our action in Europe."[6] Then in July 1870 the Franco-Prussian War jolted the Victorian peace. When in October Russia denounced clauses in the treaty of Paris of 1856 providing for the neutralization of the Black Sea, a serious war scare ensued. Britain was resolved to fight unless Russia backed down. On November 19 the First Lord of the Admiralty gave warning of the need for a settlement with the United States, and the Cabinet reviewed a grave memorandum written by Lord Tenterden, an able senior clerk in the Foreign Office (in 1871 he became Assistant Undersecretary of State for Foreign Affairs), calling an adjustment of the *Alabama* claims "a matter of national exigency."[7] A few days later Sir Edward Thornton told Fish that Britain wanted an accord; and Rose (now Sir John), who had left Canada and settled in England, wrote the Secretary intimating that London was ready to negotiate.[8]

Washington also was ready. On January 9, 1871, Rose arrived again in the capital; he took with him his New York partner, Levi P. Morton, so as to divert attention from his official mission. In about two weeks he and Fish reached substantial agreement. Fish at first proposed that Britain should cede Canada and pay a sum of money for the *Alabama*'s depredations, but he dropped both points because of Rose's inflexible opposition.[9] The two men agreed that an understanding about neutrality laws was needed, and that negotiations for a general settlement should be conducted by a special joint commission rather than through ordinary diplomatic procedures.[10]

But trouble threatened from Senator Sumner. The Senator was admonishing Sir John, "Haul down that flag [over Canada] and all will be right";[11] and on January 17 he sent Fish a challenging statement: "The greatest trouble . . . is from Fenianism, which is excited by the proximity of the British flag in Canada. Therefore the withdrawal of the British flag cannot be abandoned as a condition or preliminary of such a settlement as is now proposed. To make the

6. Clarendon to Victoria, May 1, 1869, Charles P. Stacey, "Britain's Withdrawal from North America, 1864–1871," *Canadian Historical Review*, XXXVI (1955), 192.

7. Spencer Childers, *The Life and Correspondence of the Right Hon. Hugh C. E. Childers, 1827–1896* (2 vols., London, 1901), I, 173–74; Lucien Wolf, *Life of the First Marquess of Ripon, K.G., P.C., G.C.S.I., D.C.L., Etc.* (2 vols., London, 1921), I, 238–39.

8. Fish Diary, Nov. 20, 1869; Rose to Fish, Nov. 24, 1870, *ibid.*

9. Rose to Granville, Jan. 10, 12, 31, 1871, Foreign Office 5/1298; Fish Diary, Jan. 9, 1871.

10. Rose to Granville, Jan. 12, 31, 1871, Foreign Office 5/1298.

11. Rose to Granville, Jan. 19, 1871, *ibid.*

settlement complete the withdrawal should be from this hemisphere, including provinces and islands."[12] If Sumner was to have his way, Britain would depart not only from Canada but from the entire hemisphere. His extreme stand irritated Fish. As for Grant, he was already so infuriated by the Senator's role in the treaty with Santo Domingo that he was said to shake his fist in incoherent rage whenever he passed Sumner's house. The administration now steeled itself to seek a settlement even at the cost of a break with the powerful chairman of the Foreign Relations Committee.[13]

Secretary Fish had also sounded out other members of the committee, almost all of whom favored an accord along the lines he and Sir John envisaged. The Cabinet supported negotiations on the condition that (as recorded by Fish in his diary) "Great Britain admit her liability for the losses sustained by the Acts of the Alabama, including the expenses of the Gov. incurred in her pursuit & capture, & that the question of liability for the losses sustained by the other vessels, together with the question of liability for any consequential damages should be referred to the decision of some tribunal to be eventually agreed upon."[14] The distinction between the *Alabama* and the other cruisers was not to hold, but throughout the subsequent negotiations the administration apparently felt somewhat bound by the Cabinet's insistence on a judicial decision about the "consequential," or indirect, damages.

It remained to get London's approval, and this was immediately forthcoming. Fish and Rose then exchanged public letters stating that a Joint High Commission would meet in Washington to consider the *Alabama* claims, the fisheries, and "any other questions" affecting Canadian-American relations.[15] With Motley dismissed, Sumner spurned, general lines of negotiation arranged, and a special commission about to convene, the Anglo-American scene had brightened immeasurably.

The Joint High Commission held its first meeting in Washington

12. Fish Diary, Jan. 17, 1871.
13. *Ibid.*, Jan. 17, 24, 1871.
14. *Ibid.*, Jan. 11, 13, 15, 17, 1871.
15. Rose to Granville, Feb. 2, 1871, Foreign Office 5/1298; Thornton to Fish, Jan. 26, 1871, Foreign Office 5/1304; Fish to Thornton, Jan. 30, 1871, *ibid.;* Thornton to Fish, Feb. 1, 1871, *ibid.;* Fish Diary, Jan. 9, Feb. 2, 1871. The letters were predated so as to give the impression that time had been allowed for their careful consideration.

on February 27, 1871. Fish headed the American delegation. Its other members were Schenck; E. Rockwood Hoar, Grant's former Attorney General; Supreme Court Justice Samuel Nelson; and Senator George H. Williams of Oregon, a state deeply interested in the San Juan boundary dispute. Earl de Grey (Marquess of Ripon in 1871), a close associate of Foreign Secretary Granville, headed the British delegation. The other commissioners were Sir Stafford Northcote (Earl of Iddesleigh in 1885), British Foreign Secretary in 1886; Sir John A. Macdonald; Sir Edward Thornton; and Mountague Bernard, an Oxford professor of international law who had written a book defending Britain's neutrality during the Civil War. The commission's two secretaries were Assistant Secretary of State John C. Bancroft Davis and Lord Tenterden, men who were to have outstanding roles in bringing about a settlement. Shortly after the commission met, Grant, by exerting great pressure, succeeded in getting Sumner ousted from his chairmanship of the Foreign Relations Committee. Probably this brightened prospects for an accord, although the feeling was widespread that the Senator had been treated unjustly.[16]

The treaty of Washington, which the commission drew up, was a major step toward an Anglo-American accord but not the definitive one usually portrayed. It actually exacerbated the dispute over the *Alabama* claims, and thereby almost produced an Anglo-American breach far more dangerous than the one supposedly healed at Washington. As for the fisheries, the treaty made what seemed to be a lasting settlement, but subsequent related developments so angered the United States that in 1885 she abrogated all the fishery articles. Thereupon the dispute flared up more dangerously than ever before. Furthermore, the treaty made no settlement at all of the Canadian claims for damages caused by the Fenian raids. Although the Fish-Thornton letters authorized consideration of the fisheries and "any other questions" affecting Canadian-American relations, Secretary Fish argued that these letters did not specifically mention the Fenian claims, and he made abundantly clear his resolve to terminate the negotiations rather than permit discussion of the politically explosive Fenians. In the end, despite the affront to Canada, Gladstone courageously agreed to waive the claims;[17] neither in

16. Thornton to Granville, March 13, 1871, Foreign Office 5/1215.
17. British commissioners to Granville, April 26, 30, 1871, Foreign Office 5/1308;

1871 nor ever did the United States pay compensation. Britain's abandonment of Canada's just claims was a major concession for which the Liberals were roundly denounced in Britain as well as in the Dominion. But without the Prime Minister's statesmanlike decision, which was one of several he made during the negotiations, no treaty would have been concluded.

The basic elements in the fishery negotiation were simple. The United States was determined to regain access to Canada's inshore fisheries and not to pay for this with another reciprocity agreement; Canada was just as determined not to yield her inshore waters without reciprocity, or at least substantial American tariff concessions; Great Britain wanted a settlement at almost any price short of totally alienating the Dominion. The Americans first offered $1 million for the inshore privileges; but London supported Macdonald in rejecting a proposition so far short of reciprocity.[18] After weeks of inconclusive talk the United States finally offered to buy the inshore rights for ten years with a sum of money to be determined by arbitration, and to import Canadian fish duty-free. But Macdonald insisted also on duty-free coal, salt, and lumber.[19] A deadlock resulted.

Even before the commission met, Gladstone, foreseeing that such a difficulty might arise, had suggested that Canada could be appeased "by some undertaking on account of the Fenian Raid."[20] De Grey now made use of the Prime Minister's imaginative suggestion. Calling on Sir John at his hotel, he in effect promised that, as a douceur for a Canadian retreat on the fisheries, Great Britain would pay Canada compensation for the raids.[21] Though doubtless tempted to accept, and probably realizing that in any event the game

and May 1, 1871, quoting a telegram received from Granville that date, Foreign Office 5/1304.

18. Donald G. Creighton, *John A. Macdonald: The Old Chieftain* (Toronto, 1955), p. 86; De Grey to Granville, March 7, 1871, quoted in Goldwin Smith, *The Treaty of Washington* (Ithaca, 1941), p. 54; Macdonald to Sir Charles Tupper, president of the Council in Ottawa, March 8, 1871, Creighton, *Macdonald,* pp. 86–87; Colonial Secretary Lord Kimberley to Lord Lisgar, March 11, 1871, *ibid.,* p. 87.

19. Macdonald to Ottawa, April 15, 1871 (two telegrams), quoted in British commissioners to Granville, April 16, 1871, Foreign Office 5/1302.

20. Paul Knaplund, *Gladstone and Britain's Imperial Policy* (New York, 1927), p. 122.

21. Creighton, *Macdonald,* p. 96; see also Gladstone's statement in Hansard, *Parliamentary Debates,* Third Series, CCX, 1934 (April 29, 1872). De Grey also hinted that Macdonald would be made a privy counsellor if the negotiations succeeded. Creighton, *Macdonald,* p. 94.

was up, Macdonald remained stubborn. De Grey appealed to London; it authorized him to accept the American proposal.[22] Sir John's first impulse was to resign, and his colleagues in Ottawa protested angrily against "a breach of faith, and an indignity never before offered to a great British possession."[23] But it was too late; London had spoken. In the end Sir John did not resign but signed the treaty. It stipulated that for ten years, and thereafter indefinitely subject to termination on two years' notice, Americans would have the inshore privileges on Canada's east coast, and Canadians would have corresponding privileges in American waters north of 39°; that Canada and the United States would admit each other's fish and fish oil duty-free; and that an arbitral commission would meet in Halifax, Nova Scotia, to determine what sum of money the United States would pay to offset the allegedly greater value of Canada's concessions as compared with America's. Similar provisions applied also to Newfoundland.

The Joint High Commission devoted several sessions to the San Juan water boundary question. Secretary Fish demanded at least San Juan Island, and hinted that Canada should cede Vancouver Island as well. After stubbornly rejecting arbitration, he finally accepted it, provided agreements were concluded on all the other disputes.[24] The treaty referred the controversy to the Emperor of Germany as arbiter. In 1872 he awarded San Juan Island to the United States.[25]

The treaty gave Americans free navigation forever of the St. Lawrence River, and Britons free navigation forever of the Yukon, Porcupine, and Stikine rivers (which flow from Canada through Alaska); it also gave Britons free navigation of Lake Michigan for at least ten years and provided that Canada and the United States could each transport goods in bond through the other country. A large number of routine Civil War claims were to be submitted to a British-Ameri-

22. De Grey to Granville, April 20, 1871, Foreign Office 5/1303; Gladstone to Granville, April 17, 1871, Creighton, *Macdonald*, p. 97; De Grey to Granville, April 21, 1871, *ibid.*

23. Macdonald to Tupper, April 27, 1871, Creighton, *Macdonald*, p. 98; Smith, *Treaty of Washington*, p. 80.

24. De Grey to Granville, March 17, 1871, Foreign Office 5/1308; British commissioners to Granville, April 15, 1871, Foreign Office 5/1302.

25. John Bassett Moore, *History and Digest of the International Arbitrations to Which the United States Has Been a Party* . . . (6 vols., Washington, 1898), I, 196–235.

can commission meeting in Washington; in 1873 it awarded British claimants $1,929,819, and dismissed the American claims.[26]

There remained the most dangerous issue of all, the *Alabama* claims; the negotiations over them, although unusually intricate, must be followed in some detail because a disposal of the claims was the key to better British-American relations. On March 8, 1871, Secretary Fish opened what turned out to be a crucial meeting by distinguishing two categories of losses, as Senator Sumner and the Cabinet had previously done: first, direct losses resulting from the destruction of vessels and cargoes by the *Alabama* and other cruisers, and from the cost of pursuing the cruisers; second, indirect losses resulting from the transfer of much of the American merchant marine to the British flag, from higher insurance costs, and from the war's prolongation. He declared that the direct losses amounted to about $14 million and (in words that should be carefully noted) "that, in the hope of an amicable settlement, no estimate was made of the indirect losses, without prejudice, however, to the right to indemnification on their account in the event of no such settlement being made." He asked Britain to express regret for the cruiser's depredations and suggested two procedures by which she could make restitution: she could admit liability, and the commission itself would then determine what sum of money she should pay; or the question of liability could be referred to an arbitral tribunal empowered to assess damages. He warned that the United States would not arbitrate without agreement on rules binding the tribunal, and he proposed several rules.[27]

The British commissioners refused to admit Britain's liability but agreed to arbitrate. They insisted, however, that the arbitrators should not be bound by rules that would, they feared with good reason, preclude an impartial consideration of the British case. Fish was adamant. He declared flatly that he would disband the commission rather than allow unrestricted arbitration.[28] An impasse ensued. Again it was necessary to have recourse to London; and again Prime Minister Gladstone saved the situation, and consequently the

26. *Ibid.*, I, ch. 15.
27. *Papers Relating to the Foreign Relations of the United States, 1872*, Pt. II, *Papers Relating to the Treaty of Washington* (Washington, 1872), I, 10; protocol of May 4, 1871, Articles I to XI, Foreign Office 5/1304; Andrew Lang, *Life, Letters, and Diaries of Sir Stafford Northcote, First Earl of Iddesleigh* (2 vols., Edinburgh, 1890), II, 10, 11n.
28. De Grey to Granville, March 17, 1871, Foreign Office 5/1308.

treaty. He agreed, "but reluctantly," to the American demand for binding rules, and after a "tremendous row" the Cabinet fell in line.[29] But the ministers successfully insisted that Fish's rules be softened. As incorporated in the treaty the rules of due diligence— so they came to be called—declared that a neutral must "use due diligence" to prevent the building or equipping of vessels to be used against a country with which it was at peace, and must not allow a belligerent to use the neutral's waters as a base of naval operations against another belligerent.

The treaty stipulated that all claims "growing out of the acts committed by the several vessels which have given rise to the claims generically known as the 'Alabama Claims' " (including the indirect claims?) be referred to a tribunal of five arbitrators, one each appointed by the United States, Great Britain, Italy, Switzerland, and Brazil, who would meet in Geneva and, in making their award, be guided by international law and the rules of due diligence. The treaty included an expression of Britain's regret "for the escape, under whatever circumstances, of the *Alabama* and other vessels from British ports, and for the depredations committed by those vessels." This was a remarkable apology by a great power; along with Britain's acceptance of the binding rules of due diligence and her yielding over the Fenians and fisheries, it showed the lengths to which the Gladstone ministry would go to accommodate the United States.

At long last all the controversies, except the Fenian claims, seemed to have been disposed of. Triumphant and pleased (all but Macdonald, sad over the fishery articles), the ten commissioners assembled in the State Department on May 8, 1871, to sign their treaty. So small was the Department that most of its employees were present, crowded into a room that Washington ladies had gaily decorated for the occasion. Catching the festive spirit, the commissioners shook hands and then ate strawberries and ice cream.

The United States Senate approved the treaty on May 24 by a vote of 50 to 12; Sumner sided with the majority. British ratification was a foregone conclusion, fulminations of Lord John Russell notwithstanding.[30] But for a long time it was uncertain whether Canada,

29. Granville to de Grey, and Forster to de Grey, both communications dated March 18, 1871, Wolf, *Ripon*, II, 246–47.

30. *Congressional Globe*, 42 Cong., 1 Sess., p. 891 (May 24, 1871); *Journal of the Executive Proceedings of the Senate* . . . (Washington, 1901), XVIII, 108–9; Cook, *Alabama*

where strong opposition to the treaty emerged, would follow suit. Not for a year did she act. During a bitter debate in the Canadian House of Commons, Macdonald, who had been under great pressure to cooperate, loyally defended the treaty; the House voted approval on May 16, 1872, and the Senate did likewise twelve days later.[31]

Meanwhile both countries had been preparing their cases for submission to the Geneva tribunal. In accordance with the treaty's terms, Lord Tenterden and Bancroft Davis met in Geneva in December 1871 to exchange the two cases. What was Britain's consternation to discover that the American case, in addition to advancing the direct claims, raised the question of British liability for the indirect claims as well. It argued: "Thus the Tribunal will see that, after the battle of Gettysburg, the offensive operations of the insurgents were conducted only at sea, through the cruisers; and observing that the war was prolonged for that purpose, will be able to determine whether Great Britain ought not, in equity, to reimburse to the United States the expenses [including interest at 7 percent calculated from July 1, 1863] thereby entailed upon them."[32] The total cost of the Civil War since the battle of Gettysburg, plus 7 percent interest—no wonder the British were staggered!

A furious outcry arose over what Britons universally believed was sharp Yankee practice. At the opening of Parliament in February 1872 Queen Victoria publicly denied that the indirect claims were properly within the American case, and Prime Minister Gladstone declared ringingly, "it amounts almost to an interpretation of insanity to suppose that any negotiators could intend to admit, in a peaceful arbitration, claims of such an unmeasured character. . . ."[33] In Washington, Thornton told Fish that Great Britain considered the indirect claims "beyond the province of the Geneva arbitra-

---

*Claims*, ch. 9. The text of the treaty is in William M. Malloy (ed.), *Treaties, Conventions, International Acts, Protocols and Agreements between the United States of America and Other Powers, 1776–1909* (2 vols., Washington, 1910), I, 700–16. For a resolution introduced by Russell opposing ratification see *Parliamentary Debates*, Third Series, CCVI, 1101–07 (May 22, 1871); 1823–1901 (June 12, 1871).

31. *Parliamentary Debates, Dominion of Canada, Fourth Session*, III, 647–48 (May 16, 1872); 868 (May 28, 1872).

32. *Senate Executive Documents*, 42 Cong., 2 Sess., No. 31 (Serial 1478), *The Case of the United States to Be Laid before the Tribunal of Arbitration . . .* (Washington, 1872), pp. 31, 185, 189; *Foreign Relations, 1872*, Pt. 2, I, 31, 185, 189.

33. *Parliamentary Debates*, Third Series, CCIX, 4, 85 (Feb. 6, 1872).

THE "MEN OF BUSINESS." *(Punch,* June 22, 1872)

COLUMBIA: "Ah, dear! If *your* man of business had only been less mealy-mouthed—"
BRITANNIA: "Yes, dear! And if *your* man of business had only been less—ahem!—'smart!' we should have settled the matter pleasantly enough!"

tion." But the Secretary retorted "very emphatically" that if London rejected them the United States would not arbitrate.[34]

How did so extraordinary a situation arise? How could two well-intentioned governments have produced a document permitting contradictory interpretations of so vital a matter? We must consider again the Joint High Commission's meeting of March 8. When Fish said "that, in the hope of an amicable settlement, no estimate was made of the indirect losses," did he mean that the indirect claims would be dropped if the treaty was successfully concluded? The British commissioners understood him to mean just that.[35] But Fish later argued that by "settlement" he had meant not the treaty but British acceptance of his first suggested procedure, namely, admission of liability before the Joint High Commission, followed by payment of money. He explained: "The Treaty is not, of itself, the settlement; it is an agreement between the Governments as to the mode of reaching a settlement. . . ." And he rejected as irrelevant the British rejoinder that the treaty, in its Preamble, was called "an amicable settlement."[36]

It is certainly true that nowhere does the treaty state that the indirect claims would not be arbitrated. Against this must be weighed a memorandum written by Gladstone in February 1872. Noting that Fish was now making an extremely limited definition of "settlement," namely, the payment of a sum of money, Gladstone asked, "If these limitations were in the mind of the American Commissioners, why were they never expressed or indicated?" Washington, he observed, had not mentioned the limited definition during the sessions of the Joint High Commission nor even when, later on, Britain made public her own contradictory construction of the treaty by official statements in Parliament. Not until months after the treaty's conclusion did the United States, when presenting her case, set forth her novel conception of "settlement."[37] The Prime

34. Granville to Thornton, and Thornton to Granville, Feb. 3, 1872, Foreign Office 5/1393; Fish Diary, Feb. 3, 1872.

35. British commissioners to Granville, March 8, 1871, Wolf, *Ripon*, I, 255; statement by Granville, *Parliamentary Debates*, Third Series, CCVI, 1852 (June 12, 1871).

36. Fish to Schenck, Feb. 27, 1872, *House Executive Documents*, 42 Cong., 2 Sess., No. 294 (Serial 1516), pp. 5–6; Granville to Schenck, March 20, 1872, *ibid.*, pp. 13–14; Cook, *Alabama Claims*, ch. 10.

37. Memorandum in Gladstone's handwriting, initialed "W.E.G." (William E. Gladstone), Feb. 28 (1872), Foreign Office 5/1394.

Minister was implying that Fish's argument was an afterthought. It is difficult to resist his contention that the indirect claims were not within the treaty.

But whatever the rights and wrongs, the plain fact was that a critical issue was squarely joined between Washington and London. No British government, after the Queen's address and the Prime Minister's forthright statement, could back down and admit the legitimacy of the indirect claims; nor could the government take the chance, however slight, that the tribunal would find her liable for about half the cost of the Civil War. Equally no American government, especially in a presidential election year, could withdraw the claims. "You can have no idea of the unanimity of the feeling here" in England, Rose wrote Macdonald. The American case, the British consul general in New York reported, "is a popular document, and the President & his Cabinet cannot now *afford* to modify it or withdraw it."[38] If the arbitration failed, so in all probability would the entire treaty of Washington. For if Great Britain refused to implement the provisions most important to Americans, the United States would be most unlikely to observe the articles favorable to Britain. The trans-Atlantic tension, temporarily abated, would rise up again, more strongly than before. "Affairs here are most critical and anxious," Benjamin Disraeli noted. "All is absorbed in the *Alabama* question." And William E. Forster, Vice-President of the Privy Council, said that he "never felt any matter so serious."[39]

It may be wondered why Secretary Fish, a moderate man, risked destroying the hard-won treaty of Washington by taking so extreme a stand. First of all, he felt bound by the public and Cabinet support of the indirect claims. But he had also come to perceive the desirability of securing a judical decision against the legal validity of such claims so that they would never be raised against the United States herself, a presumed neutral in future wars. He insisted on the claims, in short, in the hope that they would be rejected at Geneva.

Thornton's warning that Britain would not arbitrate the indirect

38. Rose to Macdonald, Sir John A. Macdonald Papers, Public Archives of Canada (Ottawa), CLXVII, 68765–66; Edward M. Archibald to Tenterden, Feb. 7, 1872, Foreign Office 5/1393.

39. Disraeli to Lord Cairns, Jan. 27, 1872, William F. Monypenny and George E. Buckle, *The Life of Benjamin Disraeli, Earl of Beaconsfield* (6 vols., New York, 1910–20), V, 177–78; Forster's diary, Jan. 30, 1872, T. Wemyss Reid, *Life of the Right Honourable William Edward Forster* (2 vols., London, 1888), II, 23.

claims launched a negotiation considerably longer and more difficult than that undertaken by the Joint High Commission. This resumed negotiation of 1872 should not be viewed as separate from the earlier one; there was in fact one single negotiation over the *Alabama* claims lasting from February 1871 when the commission met (omitting developments before then) to June 1872 when the arbitrators convened in Geneva—with a deceptive interlude between May 1871 and January or February 1872 when an agreement seemed to have been reached. From the British standpoint the United States, by advancing the indirect claims, had illegally resurrected an issue disposed of by the commissioners; in the American view Great Britain, by objecting to this routine step, was illegally seeking to evade an arbitration that she now, having perceived the strength of the American case, feared to lose.

Two further stages of negotiation took place: the first, conducted mainly through normal diplomatic channels, failed; the second, conducted at Geneva by subordinate officials, succeeded. After various suggestions of February and March 1872—for example, that Britain pay a large sum of money in lieu of arbitration, or that she cede Vancouver Island in exchange for cancelling the indirect claims—serious negotiations got under way over an American proposal for negotiating an additional treaty article stipulating that the United States would not request a monetary award for the indirect claims if Great Britain would allow the claims to go before the tribunal for a verdict on the abstract question of liability, and would also promise never to present such claims against a neutral America.[40] Such an accord would protect the United States against large claims in the future and would remove Britain's fear of being assessed an enormous sum at Geneva. Unfortunately, agreement on the wording of a new article proved impossible in the short time remaining before the tribunal was due to convene. Formal negotiations collapsed; the prospect for a successful arbitration seemed bleak indeed.

The tribunal met in Geneva on June 15. Count Frederico Sclopis (elected the tribunal's president) had been named by Italy; Viscount d'Itajubá, by Brazil; Jacques Staempfli, by Switzerland; Sir Alex-

40. Thornton to Granville, April 25, 1872, Foreign Office 5/1397; Fish Diary, April 25, 1872; Schenck to Fish, May 10, 1872, *Foreign Relations, 1872*, Pt. 2, II, 500; Cook, *Alabama Claims*, ch. 11.

(*Harper's Weekly*, July 6, 1872)

Our President Puts His Foot Down and the British Lion Will Have to Wriggle Out.

ander Cockburn, the Lord Chief Justice of England, by Great Britain; and Charles Francis Adams, the former American minister at London, by the United States. Lord Tenterden and John C. Bancroft Davis (the former secretaries at Washington) were the agents of their respective countries. Davis submitted the American summary of argument (that is, the final statement). The suspense was great when Tenterden arose; he declined to submit the British summary (without which a binding arbitration could not proceed) unless the indirect claims were excluded, and he requested an eight-month adjournment. Davis then asked for a two-day adjournment so that he could get instructions, and this was granted.

Four days of intense behind-the-scenes activity ensued. The surprising consequence was an accord over the indirect claims, Britain's decision to present her summary, and the commencement of the tribunal's regular sessions. To explain these developments we must go back to April 1872.

On the fifteenth of that month, as prescribed by the treaty of Washington, Davis and Tenterden had met in Geneva for the formal exchange of the countercases, that is, the replies to the cases exchanged in December. The Englishman said that no British government could arbitrate the indirect claims. Apparently he attached little hope to the proposed additional treaty article, negotiations about which were then beginning. He asked whether Davis had any suggestion. Davis did have one, which, he stressed, was personal and unofficial; but it furnished the key that broke the impasse. Let the counsel of the two countries, Davis proposed, confer together before June 15 and "agree together that the claims for indirect losses are not claims which the Tribunal can properly be called upon to give damages for as being contrary to the principles of American & English law."[41] Tenterden, at first dubious but then hopeful, proposed a modification that Davis accepted: instead of the *counsel*, let the five *arbitrators* meet for (as Davis expressed it) "the avowed purpose of relieving the two governments by consideration in advance of argument . . . of the question of the liability of Great

41. Tenterden to Granville, April 15, 1872, Lord Granville Papers, Public Record Office (London), Public Record Office 30/29/106. See also Tenterden memorandum, April 15/16, 1872, *ibid.*; Davis to Fish, April 15, 1872, John C. Bancroft Davis Papers, Alabama Claims, Letters from J. C. B. Davis, Library of Congress (Washington).

Britain for the indirect claims."[42] Their agreement was loose and informal, but the two agents hoped that a majority of the arbitrators would pronounce, extrajudicially, against the validity of the indirect claims under international law, and that thereafter the Grant administration could afford politically to drop its insistence that they be arbitrated. As shall appear, this is essentially what happened, although the arbitrators did not meet before June 15.

Yet there is no evidence that the Tenterden-Davis plan had any immediate impact on Washington or London. Davis wrote Fish about it, but the Secretary's reaction is unknown.[43] In England, Gladstone expressed himself as "much pleased"; Granville, too, viewed the plan favorably.[44] Neither government seems to have given further consideration to it before the tribunal met; presumably both were preoccupied with the additional article, the successful conclusion of which then seemed likely.

When Davis asked for a two-day adjournment on June 15, his real purpose was to communicate not with Washington but with Tenterden in order to obtain the extrajudicial decision the two men had discussed in April.[45] But first Davis had to dispose of a proposal, made by Adams on the fifteenth, to hold an immediate arbitration of the direct claims, leaving the question of the tribunal's jurisdiction over the indirect claims for later negotiation. When Davis told Tenterden of the suggestion, the Englishman retorted sharply that the request for an eight-month adjournment was the business before the tribunal and that the arbitration would not proceed unless the indirect claims were, once and for all, got rid of.[46] That was the end of the Adams plan. The first step toward drafting an extrajudi-

42. Davis to Fish, April 17, 1872, Davis Papers, Alabama Claims. Sir Edward Thornton suspected as early as February 1872 that Fish hoped "that the Tribunal, without claiming jurisdiction, should declare that we are not liable." Thornton to Granville, Feb. 27, 1872, Granville Papers, Public Record Office 30/29/67. Charles Francis Adams and Minister Schenck, perhaps having heard about the Tenterden-Davis plan, made a suggestion similar to it in May 1872. Granville to Thornton, May 7, 1872, Foreign Office 5/1398.
43. Davis to Fish, April 17, 1872, Davis Papers, Alabama Claims.
44. Gladstone to Granville, April 16, 1872, Granville Papers, Public Record Office 30/29/61; Granville to Sir Roundell Palmer, April 16, 1872, ibid. On the other hand, Palmer, writing to Granville on April 16, 1872, characterized Davis's proposal as "wholly chimerical." Ibid.
45. Davis to Fish, July 25, 1872, Davis Papers, Alabama Claims.
46. Tenterden to Granville, June 15, 1872, Granville Papers, Public Record Office 30/29/106; Frank W. Hackett, Reminiscences of the Geneva Tribunal of Arbitration, 1872, the Alabama Claims (Boston, 1911), pp. 240–60.

cial pronouncement, as envisaged by the two agents at their April meeting, was taken by Sir Roundell Palmer, a well-known legal expert and one of the British counsel, at Tenterden's request following his talk with Davis. Part of Palmer's draft read: "That the Arbitrators cannot give any judgment on the indirect Claims, as not being submitted to them by both parties, and that, therefore, any expression of opinion upon them, at the present time, would be simply extra-judicial."[47] Davis, Adams, and the American counsel (Caleb Cushing, Morrison R. Waite, and William M. Evarts) reviewed the draft, and the counsel then reshaped it. The American and British counsel, and also the arbitrators, made other changes. More time was needed, and Davis requested, and obtained, another two-day adjournment. By the nineteenth the thoroughly revised paper had been made acceptable to all.

When the tribunal reconvened on June 19, Britain's request for an eight-month adjournment was still pending. Count Sclopis opened the session by reading the prepared statement. It said that the arbitrators would not pass judgment on the point as to whether, under the treaty, they had jurisdiction over the indirect claims; they would merely declare "that these claims do not constitute, upon the principles of international law applicable to such cases, good foundation for an award of compensation or computation of damages between nations, and should, upon such principles, be wholly excluded from the consideration of the Tribunal in making its award. . . ."[48] This, of course, was an extrajudicial declaration because the tribunal had refused to decide whether it had jurisdiction over the indirect claims. The declaration's origin in the Tenterden-Davis plan of April is evident.

But would Washington and London now agree that the hearings could proceed? Convinced at last that the tribunal would not make a judicial decision about the indirect claims as he had demanded, and somewhat mollified at having obtained at least a firm declaration against them, Fish cabled his acceptance of Sclopis's statement. Granville did likewise;[49] he and the Liberals could take satisfaction in the tribunal's refusal to assume jurisdiction over the claims.

47. Tenterden to Granville, June 15, 1872, Granville Papers, Public Record Office 30/29/106.
48. *Foreign Relations, 1872*, Pt. 2, IV, 19–20.
49. Fish to Schenck, June 22, 1872, *ibid.*, II, 578–79; statement by Tenterden, June 27, 1872, *ibid.*, IV, 21–22.

Thereupon Tenterden withdrew the request for an adjournment and presented the British summary. Thus, at the last minute, was the arbitration rescued from the collapse that had seemed almost certain.

Formal sessions began in mid-July.[50] The arbitrators examined *seriatim* the case of each cruiser for which Great Britain was allegedly responsible. It exonerated her regarding all of them except the *Florida* (all the arbitrators except Cockburn found Britain failing in due diligence), the *Alabama* (all found Britain wanting in due diligence), and the *Shenandoah* after she had left Melbourne, Australia (three arbitrators declared Britain guilty). The hearings did not always proceed smoothly. Cockburn, a vivacious, excitable, highly intelligent man, frequently displayed his displeasure with his colleagues's opinions by outbursts of verbiage and angry pounding on the table. He antagonized the three neutral members, who could not have failed to contrast his overbearing manner with the calm, dignified, considerate demeanor of Charles Francis Adams; undoubtedly the contrast inclined Sclopis, Staempfli, and d'Itajubá to favor the United States. Although Sir Roundell Palmer was a greater legal scholar than any of the American counsel, he did not overawe them; the Americans were very well prepared and, confident of the strength of their case, soon had the upper hand in the debate. The veteran Caleb Cushing was particularly effective. After much contention about the correct amount, the tribunal assessed Great Britain $15,500,000 damages.

The formal judgment was publicly delivered on September 14, 1872, in a hall crowded with visitors.[51] Cockburn, believing the award unjust, declined to sign it. The spectators applauded enthusiastically when Count Sclopis pronounced the arbitration concluded, because they correctly believed they had witnessed a historic landmark in the peaceful settlement of international disputes. And indeed the arbitration was the prelude to several other major British-American arbitrations held during the remaining years of the century. The success at Geneva encouraged the recourse to the later tribunals; and by the century's end Britain and America would have an arbitral record that no other pair of countries could match.

50. *Ibid.*, I-IV; the protocols are in *ibid.*, IV, 15–48, and *British and Foreign State Papers, 1871–1872* (London, 1877), pp. 189–239.
51. *Foreign Relations, 1872*, Pt. 2, IV, 49–54.

To people of the nineteenth century international arbitration appeared to offer a real hope of ending the scourge of war, and to them the famous verdict of 1872 was not the tedious affair that it may seem today but thrilling evidence that mankind had at last turned the corner to better days.

But if the enthusiastic spectators at Geneva believed that all the controversies dealt with in the treaty of Washington had been settled, they were mistaken. True it was that the *Alabama* claims were never again to be a subject of dispute; but serious trouble over the fisheries was to occur as late as 1887. Moreover, not long after the Geneva tribunal disbanded, a protracted contention arose over establishing the Halifax fisheries commission. The treaty provided that Great Britain and the United States would each appoint a commissioner to serve at Halifax, and that if they could not agree on a third, neutral member by October 1873, the Austro-Hungarian ambassador at London would select him. Each country proposed various men as the third commissioner, but all were unsatisfactory to the other country. Among the British proposals was the Belgian minister at Washington, Maurice Delfosse; Secretary Fish rejected him outright as anti-American and as coming from a country controlled by Britain.[52] By then the deadline date of October 1873 had passed, but Fish, fearing a pro-British nomination, found excuses for refusing to turn to the Austro-Hungarian ambassador. Further time was lost when the two countries discussed the advisability of concluding a new reciprocity treaty as a substitute for arbitration. They actually drafted a treaty, but in early 1875 the Senate resolved that additional negotiations were not expedient.[53]

In July 1875 Great Britain appointed Sir Alexander T. Galt, an able Canadian and former Minister of Finance at Ottawa, as her commissioner. But Fish waited almost a year before naming the American commissioner, Ensign H. Kellogg, a minor Massachusetts

52. Thornton to Granville, Foreign Office 5/1558; Fish to Thornton, Aug. 21, 1873, *ibid.*, and *Senate Executive Documents*, 45 Cong., 2 Sess., No. 44 (Serial 1781), p. 5.

53. For the decision to negotiate see Lord Dufferin (Governor General of Canada) to Colonial Office, received Feb. 24, 1874, Foreign Office 5/1561; Foreign Office to Thornton, Feb. 27, 1874, *ibid.*; Thornton to Foreign Office, Feb. 28, 1874, *ibid.* The draft treaty is in *Congressional Record*, 50 Cong., 1 Sess., pp. 7530–32 (Aug. 14, 1888). Regarding the Senate's action see *Papers Relating to the Foreign Relations of the United States, 1875* (Washington, 1875), I, 653; Thornton to Foreign Secretary Lord Derby, Feb. 15, 1875, Foreign Office 5/1567.

politician,[54] and he continued to procrastinate about the third commissioner. Presumably he wanted to postpone the arbitration, which he feared the United States would lose, until after the presidential election of 1876; then, after the election, with the winner in doubt because of disputed returns, he may have thought an additional delay advisable. However, on February 1, 1877, less than five weeks before Grant's term was due to end, he told a surprised Thornton that he wanted the commission to be organized before he left office and that he would accept Maurice Delfosse.[55] How can this reversal be accounted for? The truth is that Fish, and Grant too, were immensely proud of their treaty of Washington. Eager to tidy up its unresolved points before their terms ended, they had to accept a man immediately agreeable to Britain. Great Britain and the United States quickly went through the formalities of requesting the Austro-Hungarian ambassador to name the third commissioner; and the ambassador selected Delfosse on March 2, 1877, just two days before Grant and Fish left office.[56] The two colleagues of eight eventful years could take deep satisfaction in the realization that, with the Halifax commission established, they had carried through to substantial fulfillment their treaty of Washington.[57]

It remains to describe briefly the Halifax commission and its unsettling aftermath. The commission convened on June 15, 1877, to decide upon the question: What, if anything, was the monetary value of the fishery privileges given Americans by the treaty of Washington for twelve years (the minimum period the privileges were to be operative), over and above the monetary value of the fishery privileges given British subjects? Five months later the three commissioners awarded the British $5,500,000 by a vote of two to one. Delfosse cast the deciding vote. Kellogg, the dissenter, went so far as to record the opinion that the fishery articles of the treaty actually favored not the United States but

54. Thornton to Derby, Aug. 3, 1875, Foreign Office 5/1567; Fish to Thornton, May 8, 1876, *Senate Executive Documents*, 45 Cong., 2 Sess., No. 44, pp. 19–21.

55. Thornton to Derby, Feb. 5, 1877, Foreign Office 5/1630.

56. Fish to Edwards Pierrepont (Schenck's successor as American minister to Great Britain), Feb. 13, 1877, *Senate Executive Documents*, 45 Cong., 2 Sess., No. 100 (Serial 1781), p. 9; Pierrepont to Fish, March 2, 1877, *ibid.*, p. 13.

57. By the treaty the United States and Great Britain were to invite other maritime countries to adhere to the rules of due diligence; they were unable to agree on the terms of the invitation.

Great Britain, and that in any event the commission's competence to make an award except by unanimous vote was "questionable."[58]

Both of Kellogg's charges gained widespread credence in the United States. Even a sober, somewhat pro-British journal like the *Nation* thought that the award "cannot be justified."[59] Yet almost everyone agreed that the country was, in honor, bound to pay; this it did in November 1878, but with an accompanying admonition that it did not consider the award "as furnishing any just measure" of the fishery privileges granted by the treaty.[60] The United States did well to pay, of course. Even though the award was unexpectedly heavy, Halifax, like Geneva, was the scene of an Anglo-American arbitration that did credit to the good sense of both countries. Nevertheless the award disenchanted Americans with the fishery articles; and unfortunately two further incidents, both related to the Halifax award, added to their disenchantment.

In 1878 Henry Youle Hind, a Canadian professor, happened to notice some false statistics in the British case; he wrote letters to many prominent men in which he accused Great Britain of intentional fraud.[61] Although for a while the American press scented a first-class scandal, and some sensational remarks were made in Congress,[62] Hind's activities attracted surprisingly little attention. Few Americans seem to have believed that Britain had been dishonest, and the government took no official action. The case soon dropped

58. *House Executive Documents*, 45 Cong., 2 Sess., No. 89 (Serials 1810, 1811, 1812), *Award of Fisheries Commission: Documents and Proceedings of Halifax Commission, 1877* . . . (3 vols., Washington, 1878), I, 76. For the commission's hearings see *ibid.*, all three volumes, and Moore, *International Arbitrations*, I, ch. 16.

59. *Nation*, XXVI (Feb. 28, 1878), 146.

60. John Welsh (American minister to Great Britain) to Foreign Secretary Lord Salisbury, Nov. 21, 1878, *Papers Relating to the Foreign Relations of the United States, 1878* (Washington, 1878), p. 334.

61. Some of the letters are in *Congressional Record*, 46 Cong., 3 Sess., pp. 421–42, 438 (Jan. 7, 1881); *Debates of the House of Commons . . . of Canada*, 4 Parl., 3 Sess., pp. 905–7 (Feb. 9, 1881); New York *World*, Feb. 8, 1881; Chester L. Barrows, *William M. Evarts, Lawyer, Diplomat, Statesman* (Chapel Hill, 1941), p. 398. Regarding the affair see Charles S. Campbell, *From Revolution to Rapprochement: The United States and Great Britain, 1783–1900* (New York, 1974), pp. 143–44; Oskar D. Skelton, *The Life and Times of Sir Alexander Tilloch Galt* (Toronto, 1920), 513n; New York *World*, Jan. 31, 1881.

62. New York *Herald*, Feb. 4, 1880; Washington *Capital*, Feb. 15, 1880; *Congressional Record*, 46 Cong., 2 Sess., p. 845 (Feb. 12, 1880), p. 442 (Jan. 7, 1881), p. 683 (Jan. 17, 1881).

from sight, but some uneasy doubts probably lingered in American minds.

The second incident also had its inception in 1878. On a Sunday in January of that year, in Fortune Bay, Newfoundland, several American boats were catching herring with seines when angry natives demanded that they stop because Sunday fishing was illegal; they even tore some of the nets. As a result the Americans sailed for home, suffering heavy financial losses. Secretary of State William M. Evarts protested to London. Lord Salisbury, Foreign Secretary under Benjamin Disraeli, refused to admit British fault. He insisted that the Americans had broken Newfoundland laws against Sunday fishing and against using seines for taking herring. Evarts retorted that fishing rights granted by the treaty of Washington took precedence over local Newfoundland legislation. He presented a bill for $105,305.02. But Salisbury contended that the treaty privileges were, by the terms of the treaty, "in common" with Newfoundlanders and that therefore Americans were obliged to observe local laws.[63] Americans were infuriated by what they considered to be his grudging attitude, which they contrasted with their own quick payment of the Halifax award.

A turn for the better came with the return to power in 1880 of William E. Gladstone and his Foreign Secretary, Lord Granville, the men who had been so helpful in the negotiations of 1871 and 1872. Becoming convinced that Salisbury's arguments were unsound, and worried over congressional moves looking to unilateral abrogation of the treaty of Washington's fishery articles, Granville declared that the conduct of the Newfoundlanders, in taking the law into their own hands, had been "quite indefensible," and that Britain would pay reparations. After some bargaining, she paid £15,000 on June 2, 1881.[64]

63. Evarts to Welsh, March 2, 1878, *House Executive Documents*, 46 Cong., 2 Sess., No. 84 (Serial 1925), p. 15; Salisbury to Welsh, Aug. 23, 1878, *ibid.*, p. 19; Evarts to Welsh, Sept. 28, 1878, *ibid.*, pp. 23–24; Evarts to Welsh, Aug. 1, 1879, *Papers Relating to the Foreign Relations of the United States, 1880* (Washington, 1880), pp. 530–39; Salisbury to William J. Hoppin (American chargé d'affaires at London), April 3, 1880, *ibid.*, pp. 571, 573. Regarding the affair see Campbell, *From Revolution to Rapprochement*, pp. 144–47; Raymond McFarland, *A History of the New England Fisheries* (New York, 1911), pp. 204–5.

64. Granville to Lowell, Oct. 27, 1880, *Foreign Relations, 1880*, pp. 589–90; Sir Edward Thornton (British minister to the United States) to Secretary of State James G. Blaine (who had just succeeded Evarts), June 2, 1881, *Papers Relating to the Foreign*

Thereby she staved off an illegal abrogation of the fishery articles. But Americans had been so angered by the $5,500,000 awarded at Halifax, and by Salisbury's stubbornness, that they were determined to get rid of all those articles at the earliest legal moment. In 1883 the United States gave Great Britain two years' notice (as required by the treaty of Washington);[65] and on July 1, 1885, she terminated all the fishery articles of 1871 and imposed duties upon fish. Serious clashes in the northeastern fishing grounds were not long in breaking out.

The failure of the treaty of Washington to settle the ancient fishery controversy was, of course, a serious matter. All the same, the treaty as supplemented by the Geneva arbitration, had made one enormous contribution: it had disposed of the *Alabama* claims that had been poisoning the atmosphere for almost ten years. Although Britain and America were still to experience much contention, and even a war scare, relations between them never again became so strained as in the dark post–Civil War years. For all its imperfections the treaty, with the arbitration, was an indispensable step toward the Anglo-American rapprochement that came at the end of the century.

---

*Relations of the United States, 1881* (Washington, 1882), p. 591. Regarding the unsoundness of Salisbury's arguments see, particularly, memoranda by Francis C. Ford (a Foreign Office official), June 4, 1880, Foreign Office 5/1826; and by Lord Northbrook (First Lord of the Admiralty), June 10, 1880, *ibid.* Regarding the congressional moves see *Congressional Record,* 46 Cong., 2 Sess., p. 2789 (April 27, 1880), pp. 2813, 2832 (April 28, 1880), p. 3527 (May 19, 1880), p. 4333 (June 9, 1880).

65. For the background of this step see *Congressional Record,* 47 Cong., 2 Sess., pp. 1041–42 (Jan. 10, 1883), pp. 3055–56 (Feb. 21, 1883), p. 3298 (Feb. 26, 1883), pp. 3673, 3717 (March 3, 1883).

CHAPTER 3

# A Caribbean Naval Base
# and an Isthmian Canal:
# the 1870s and 1880s

THE close attention the United States had paid to the Caribbean Sea prior to the Civil War continued, of course, after hostilities ended. In fact naval incidents pertaining to the blockade of the Confederacy had driven home the Caribbean's vital strategic importance, thus reinforcing the older and persisting influence of west coast settlement, and the consequent interest in an isthmian canal and its Caribbean approaches.

President Ulysses S. Grant, like Seward, strongly favored expansion, and Secretary of State Hamilton Fish was almost as zealous. But whereas Fish took the lead in setting policy toward Great Britain, Grant was mainly responsible for moves toward overseas expansion. Unlike Seward, the President could not have given a logical explanation of why he wanted to annex certain areas. He was what may be called an instinctive expansionist, a man with an elemental conviction that the acquisition of some places would increase United States power and that this was self-evidently desirable. He directed his efforts particularly toward the three basic objectives of American expansionists: toward Hawaii but also—and much more fervently—toward an isthmian canal and the Caribbean Sea.

On the northeastern shore of Santo Domingo was a magnificent harbor, Samaná Bay, that under the Stars and Stripes could have become a naval base guarding the eastern approaches to a future isthmian canal and enhancing American power in the Caribbean generally. Two close associates fed Grant's mind with these thoughts: Commodore Daniel Ammen and Cornelius Cole, a Senator from California, who wanted a shorter sea route between his state and the east coast.[1] The President was also swayed by men who, with investments in Santo Domingo, stood to benefit financially from annexation: Peter J. Sullivan (the former American minister to Colombia),[2] William L. Cazneau, and Joseph W. Fabens. The latter two (whose earlier interest in the island we have noted) were closely associated with Santo Domingo's dictator, Buenaventura Baez, who himself wanted annexation for the country he ruled only precariously. A leading New York financial house, Spofford, Tileston and Company, with which Fabens was connected and which in 1869 started a steamship line to Santo Domingo, also favored annexation and had influence in Washington.[3]

Grant became convinced that the Caribbean country was essential to the United States, and for several months he was obsessed with a burning desire to acquire it. Hardly installed in office, he ordered a warship to Santo Domingo; and in its wake he sent his White House aide, Brigadier General Orville E. Babcock. The young brigadier general sailed on a Spofford, Tileston steamer; among his fellow passengers were Cole, Sullivan, and Fabens, who, one can be sure, regaled him with the advantages of annexation.[4] Secretary Fish had instructed Babcock to gather information about the people's disposition toward the United States. After long conversations with President Baez, Babcock returned to Washington in September 1869. Going far beyond his official instructions, though presumably not beyond informal ones, he had signed a draft treaty of annexation.[5] After revising it, the two countries in November 1869 signed a final treaty providing for Santo Domingo's incorporation into the United States as a territory.[6]

Grant now summoned up all his formidable strength of will to

---

1. Allan Nevins, *Hamilton Fish: The Inner History of the Grant Administration* (New York, 1936), pp. 263–64.

2. Cornelius Cole, *Memoirs of Cornelius Cole, Ex-Senator of the United States from California* (New York, 1908), p. 324.

3. Nevins, *Fish*, pp. 252–56, 264–65.

4. *Ibid.*, p. 265.

5. Fish to Babcock, July 13, 1869, *Senate Executive Documents*, 41 Cong., 3 Sess., No. 17 (Serial 1440), p. 79; *Senate Reports*, 41 Cong., 2 Sess., No. 234 (Serial 1409), pp. 188–89.

6. *Senate Executive Documents*, 41 Cong., 3 Sess., No. 17, pp. 98–100; for an accompanying convention see *ibid.*, pp. 101–2.

persuade the Senate to approve it. He walked to Charles Sumner's house one evening to solicit the Senator's help, he lobbied personally in the Capitol, he authorized the negotiation of an additional article extending the ratification date, he demanded the Attorney General's resignation in order to curry favor with Senators whom that official had antagonized, and he welcomed several moves by Fish supporting the treaty. But all his efforts came to nothing. Sumner, still chairman of the Foreign Relations Committee, threw his great influence against the treaty, and on June 30, 1870, the Senate defeated it decisively.[7]

The truth is that the President was butting his head against a massive wall of opposition to southward expansion. Americans had no wish to admit additional thousands of nonwhites into the union. And of all conceivable places, the southeastern tropics were the least attractive to the Republicans, who recalled with distaste the prewar Democratic attempts to move into the Caribbean and Central America. Moreover, to the many supporters of the freedman there was something immoral about taking a region assigned by nature to darker-skinned people. "Already," said Charles Sumner, speaking of Santo Domingo, "by a higher statute is that island set apart to the colored race. It is theirs by right of possession; by their sweat and blood mingling with the soil; by tropical position; by its burning sun, and by unalterable laws of climate."[8] We have already noted that, paradoxically, a not always avowed conviction of black inferiority also swayed former abolitionists to oppose acquisitions in the Pacific and Caribbean. Later in the century sentiment toward tropical annexation would become more favorable; but in the early 1870s, as the British minister at Washington, Sir Edward Thornton, shrewdly observed, Americans thought it more advantageous to go northward, "where the fact of the territory's being dependents of a Monarchy, and that Monarchy the one from which the United States emancipated themselves, would give additional zest to any acquisition in that quarter."[9] In his obsession with Santo Domingo, the President was out of touch with the traditional and still fervent

7. New York *Tribune*, June 29, 30, July 1, 1870; *Journal of the Executive Proceedings of the Senate . . .* (Washington, 1901), XVII, 502–3; the vote was 28 for approval, 28 against.

8. *Congressional Globe*, 41 Cong., 3 Sess., pp. 226–27, 231 (Dec. 21, 1870).

9. Thornton to Foreign Secretary Lord Clarendon, Jan. 10, 1870, Public Record Office (London), Foreign Office 5/1191.

opposition of his countrymen to overseas expansion.

Grant's obsession with Santo Domingo, however strong, was a quickly passing matter of comparatively little national significance. Much more important was a Cuban rebellion against Spain that lasted from 1868 to 1878, almost coinciding with Grant's two terms in the White House. Not only did the rebellion last far longer than the Dominican affair, but it led to considerable Spanish-American friction that at times threatened to erupt in outright war and whose effects were still felt even in the 1890s.

Violent, destructive, embittered, the Cuban revolt seemed to portend the demise of Spain's once enormous New World empire, of which only Cuba and Puerto Rico remained. France had recently departed from Mexico, and Russia from Alaska; the pressure was on Great Britain to leave Canada. One by one, as Charles Sumner had happily noted,[10] the European monarchs were winding up their affairs in the republican New World. The rebellion seemed to portend, too, the early acquisition of a Caribbean naval base by the United States. Dominating shipping routes from the east coast to a potential Central American canal, the long island of Cuba occupied an area of immense strategic importance for the United States; and an American base there would be even more welcome than one in Samaná Bay.

In New York and other American cities lived many Cubans who, organized in Juntas, labored to assist their countrymen to cast off the Spanish yoke. They smuggled men and munitions to the nearby island, and they spread propaganda in the United States. They worked in a sympathetic milieu, for overwhelmingly Americans favored the rebels, New World republicans struggling to cast off the yoke of an Old World monarchy. Especially during the first year or two of hostilities the Juntas secretly organized illegal filibustering expeditions that sailed from American shores to Cuba. At the beginning Washington was remiss in enforcing the neutrality laws. Spain was naturally indignant, the more so because American aid did keep the rebellion alive. As a member of Congress admitted, without the filibusters the Cubans would lose "nearly the whole power of the revolution."[11]

The nearby turmoil caused many inconveniences in the United

10. See above, p. 20.
11. *Congressional Globe*, 41 Cong., 2 Sess., p. 4437 (June 14, 1870).

States—the Juntas' noisy agitation, the nuisance and cost of suppressing the filibusters, the destruction of American property in Cuba, the disruption of American trade. Yet there was little danger of a Spanish-American war in the 1870s. The American Civil War was too recent; domestic preoccupations—reconstruction, economic problems, the development of the West—were too absorbing. Opposition to Caribbean expansion (except possibly for a canal) was too strong, as we saw in the case of Santo Domingo. Moreover Secretary Fish was sternly opposed to war with Spain; and after some initial uncertainty about Grant's attitude he gained the President's backing.

Early in Grant's term a tragic episode revealed, like a flash of lightning, what the sanguinary chaos held in store for the United States. Two young Americans, wanting to go to Jamaica, had embarked on an American schooner; Cuban rebels seized the ship and sailed her to Cuba. There the Americans escaped and surrendered to the Spanish, who without proper trial shot them. One of the young men had written a pathetic farewell letter to his wife and child, and across the United States an outcry denounced the unspeakable Spaniard. An American consul on the island struck a note that was to be heard repeatedly, and even more resoundingly, after fighting again swept Cuba in 1895: "This has become a war of extermination. . . . The country is in complete anarchy. . . ." Spain's control seemed to be collapsing in a mire of bloodshed. Angrily Secretary Fish protested "against any longer carrying on this war in Cuba in this barbarous way."[12]

That the conflict was saturated with atrocities and that a foundering Spain had little authority in her colony were widespread beliefs among Americans. The feeling grew that the Cuban situation was out of control, decadent and rotten, a feeling that was stronger because slavery still flourished on the island. Americans who had recently fought to end slavery at home were not the people to countenance it for long just off their shores.

Although the most provocative single incident did not occur until late 1873, the greatest danger of war came during the first year or so of Grant's administration. It stemmed from a campaign to pro-

12. A. E. Phillips to Fish, June 19, 1869, *Senate Executive Documents*, 41 Cong., 2 Sess., No. 7 (Serial 1405), pp. 34–35; the farewell letter is in *ibid.*, p. 36; Fish to Daniel E. Sickles (American minister to Spain), Aug. 10, 1869, *ibid.*, pp. 40–41.

claim United States neutrality, in other words, to grant the rebels belligerent rights. Had the campaign succeeded, Spain would have been legally entitled to stop American ships on the high seas; and given all the other inflammatory factors—the strong American repugnance for the Spanish presence in the New World, the damage to the economy, incidents like the execution of the two Americans, the Junta propaganda—interference with American vessels might have touched off hostilities.

Among many Americans the belief ran deep that the United States had a moral duty to recognize the rebels. Ardently encouraged by his close friend Secretary of War John H. Rawlins, President Grant was inclined to share this view. Fish strongly dissented.[13] As a stickler for the law, he believed that recognition was not legally justified because the rebels had no settled government; as a diplomat, he perceived that recognition would undermine the case he was nurturing against Great Britain, a case based in part on her recognition of the Confederacy in 1861. But in July 1869 Grant signed a neutrality proclamation to be held ready against an emergency; and on August 14 he ordered Fish to issue it—unless the American minister to Spain, Daniel E. Sickles, had "received an entirely satisfactory reply" to a recent American mediation proposal.[14] The proposal envisaged Spanish recognition of Cuban independence in return for the payment by Cuba of a large sum of money guaranteed by the United States. By chance, on August 13, one day before Grant's neutrality order, Sickles had telegraphed Washington optimistically about Madrid's attitude toward mediation, and this gave Fish a pretext to ask Grant for a delay. With a diplomatic coup apparently in sight, the President could scarcely refuse.[15]

In fact, however, Sickles had misjudged the situation, and the American mediation failed. Yet Grant did not revert to his demand for a neutrality proclamation. He did not do so partly because Rawlins's death in early September removed a strong pro-rebel voice, but more importantly because at that very time the Presi-

13. Nevins, *Fish,* pp. 183–84, 921, 181–82.
14. *Ibid.,* pp. 236, 239.
15. Fish to Sickles, June 29, 1869, *House Executive Documents,* 41 Cong., 2 Sess., No. 160 (Serial 1418), p. 15; Sickles to Fish, Aug. 13, 1869, *ibid.,* p. 27; Nevins, *Fish,* pp. 239–40.

dent's attention was diverted to Santo Domingo by Babcock's return to Washington. If Santo Domingo was to be acquired, the help of Senator Charles Sumner would be indispensable. Yet Sumner was expressing "the greatest indignation" over the prospect of recognizing Cuban belligerency, which he (like Fish) realized would weaken the case against Great Britain.[16] Other Senators agreed with him. Grant must have perceived that he had to choose between rebel recognition and Dominican annexation; and after the twist of the scene in September, White House pressure for recognition diminished.

It did not yet disappear, however. In June 1870 the House Foreign Affairs Committee was about to issue a report favoring recognition. Perhaps calculating that only a special presidential message would prevent the report's adoption, Fish pressed hard for one. Grant resisted strongly; he yielded only when the Secretary threatened to resign.[17] The President's message, undoubtedly written by Fish, went to Congress on June 13, 1870; it ringingly defended the traditional American recognition policy. "The question of belligerency is one of fact, not to be decided by sympathies for or prejudices against either party"; and the Cuban facts did not justify recognition of belligerency.[18] The next day the committee report was issued, and the debate on it merged with the debate on the message.[19] In the end neither branch of Congress supported the committee's recommendation. Fish's policy had been sustained; never again was it to be seriously challenged. In retrospect one can see that the crucial month of June 1870 saw the end not only of any likelihood of Dominican annexation but also of the principal danger of war with Spain.

Nevertheless the rebellion lasted almost eight more years, and during them one relatively minor matter (significant, however, because it foreshadowed the prewar situation of 1895–1898) and one sharp crisis disturbed Spanish-American affairs. By October 1872

16. Thornton to Clarendon, Sept. 6, 1869, Foreign Office 5/1162.
17. Nevins, *Fish*, pp. 355–59.
18. James D. Richardson (ed.), *A Compilation of the Messages and Papers of the Presidents, 1789–1897* (10 vols., Washington, 1899), VII, 67.
19. For the debate see *Congressional Globe*, 41 Cong., 2 Sess., pp. 4436–41 (June 14, 1870); Appendix, pp. 454–65, 491–93, 504–10 (June 14, 1870); pp. 4478–87 (June 15, 1870); Appendix, pp. 499–501 (June 15, 1870); pp. 4506–7 (June 16, 1870); Appendix, pp. 495–96, 498 (June 16, 1870); p. 4537 (June 17, 1870); pp. 4753–54 (June 23, 1870); pp. 4806–8 (June 24, 1870); pp. 4832–33 (June 25, 1870); p. 4993 (June 29, 1870).

the fighting had been ravaging Cuba for four years. Secretary Fish decided that Madrid needed a stiff warning. He dispatched a note, soon familiar as No. 270, which charged bluntly that despite assurances of reform and despite a slave emancipation law, neither reform nor emancipation had occurred. Spanish Cubans simply refused to obey Madrid. "If Spain permits her authority to be virtually and practically defied in that island . . . is not this tantamount to an acknowledgement of inability to control?" This was an insistent American point, then and again during the 1895 rebellion: that Spanish authority had collapsed. Unless Spain reestablished her authority soon, Fish threatened, the United States would have to decide "whether duty to itself and to the commercial interests of its citizens" required a different—and presumably much sterner—policy.[20]

Unwisely Fish published No. 270 in early 1873. By doing so he stirred up such an outcry in Spain that the Prime Minister felt obliged to deny publicly that he had received the note (which was literally true, but misleading), and a Spanish-American "conflict of veracity" (as the Nation called it)[21] broke out. No. 270 served only to postpone reform and worsen relations with Madrid.

In November 1873 a report reached Washington that the Spanish had captured on the high seas a ship flying the American flag, the Virginius, and taken her to Santiago, Cuba; soon came news, later confirmed, that the authorities there had shot the captain, thirty-six of the crew, and sixteen passengers. The captain and some of the others were Americans. The dreadful story created a sensation in the United States. For days column upon column of the front pages of newspapers blazed forth with heady accounts of Spanish monsters and American military preparations. "From the President down there is the strongest feeling of horror and indignation," the New York Tribune reported, "and so enraged was public sentiment . . . when the news arrived that, if there had been the slightest excuse or encouragement, it would not have been difficult to obtain hundreds of volunteers for the purpose of driving the Spanish Cuban butchers from Christian countries."[22] Rumor spread wildly. Enormous public meetings were held in many cities, with the crowds

20. Fish to Sickles, Oct. 29, 1872, *Papers Relating to the Foreign Relations of the United States, 1872* (Washington, 1873), pp. 581–82.
21. *Nation,* XVI (Jan. 16, 1873), 33; *ibid.* (Jan. 23, 1873), p. 51.
22. New York *Tribune,* Nov. 13, 1873.

abandoning themselves to war hysteria.[23] Horrified like other Americans, Secretary Fish instructed Sickles on November 14 to demand the restoration of the ship and of crew and passengers still living, a salute in Santiago to the American flag, and the punishment of implicated officials; and if within twelve days Spain refused to make satisfactory reparation, to close the Legation and leave Madrid.[24] The demands were unjustifiably severe, because the Secretary knew that the *Virginius* might not really be American.[25]

No agreement had been reached by the twenty-sixth, when the twelve-day limit expired. Appealed to by the Spanish Foreign Minister, Sickles decided to delay his departure one day. Just in time a compromise was reached. On the twenty-seventh Spain offered terms that were formalized two days later and accepted by Washington: she would release the *Virginius* and the survivors forthwith, but would delay saluting the flag pending an investigation of the vessel's nationality; if she convinced the United States, by December 25, that the ship was not American the salute would be dispensed with, and the United States would punish any violators of American law; similarly, Spain would punish any violators of her laws and of treaty obligations, and would disclaim any intent to insult the United States. Accordingly Spain surrendered the *Virginius.* She established that the vessel was Cuban-owned, and so gave no salute. In 1875 she paid reparations of $80,000.[26]

There can be little doubt that Washington, if it had wished to, could have carried the country to war over the incident. But the crucial fact was that it did not so wish, and in default of a lead from the administration talk of war soon dwindled. The initial clamor notwithstanding, one does not get the impression of any deep-rooted public desire for a clash with Spain. The reasons for the moderation in the face of the strong provocation are fairly clear. Earlier in the year Spain had become (for a short time) a republic.

23. *Ibid.,* Nov. 15, 18, 19, 1873; the *Times* (London), Nov. 19, 1873; *Nation,* XVII (Nov. 20, 27, 1873), pp. 329, 345.

24. Fish to Sickles, Nov. 14, 1873, *Papers Relating to the Foreign Relations of the United States, 1874* (Washington, 1874), p. 936.

25. Fish to Sickles, Nov. 12, 1873, *ibid.,* p. 927.

26. Memorandum, Nov. 27, 1873, *ibid.,* pp. 986–87; protocol, Nov. 29, 1873, *ibid.,* pp. 987–88; Polo de Bernabé (Spanish minister to the United States) to Fish, Dec. 10, 1873, *ibid.,* pp. 991–1051; Fish to Polo, Dec. 22, 1873, *ibid.,* pp. 1051–52; Nevins, *Fish,* p. 689.

The United States promptly recognized the new government, and Congress passed a joint resolution of congratulation.[27] America's reaction contrasted with the withdrawal from Madrid of the representatives of the major European powers; and for a while a surge of trans-Atlantic emotionalism over republican virtues replaced the usual ill will. At the height of the *Virginius* crisis monarchists in Spain attacked the governmental forces, and a civil war in the motherland paralleled the one in Cuba. Americans may have felt indisposed to harass the besieged republic too severely, even though some of them would have welcomed a base in Cuba. Moreover, the severe panic of 1873 was then raging. But the main reason for the restraint —in this case as throughout the rebellion—was expressed at the height of the crisis by a former Confederate general: "Surely we have had war enough for one generation. . . ."[28] Few Americans who had experienced the Civil War wanted to fight again. In 1898, however, a new generation was on hand.

During the remainder of the rebellion Spanish-American relations were more amicable. In 1876 General Arsenio Martínez de Campos, one of Spain's ablest soldier-statesmen, became captain general of Cuba. By a judicious mixture of bribes and promises of amnesty and reform, he induced the insurgents to yield. In February 1878 the Pact of Zanjón brought temporary peace to the distracted island. But the promised reforms, made ineffectively or not at all, did not still the cry for independence. Seventeen years later the fires of rebellion lighted the Cuban skies again. In a real sense the new fighting was a continuation of the old; and Americans would have been much more tolerant of Spain's difficulties in the 1890s had they not remembered the 1870s. That nearby Cuba was so soon again in chaos proved too much for them to bear in 1898. War with Spain—and a wave of expansion that included a Cuban naval base and decisive steps toward a canal, and also the acquisition of Hawaii —ensued.

Of Grant's successors up to 1889 only the Chester A. Arthur administration took even faltering steps toward acquiring a Caribbean base (although Garfield and Secretary of State Blaine might well have moved vigorously had they been longer in office). Hayes

27. *Congressional Globe*, 42 Cong., 3 Sess., p. 1980 (March 1, 1873), p. 2070 (March 1, 1873).
28. New York *Tribune*, Nov. 19, 1873. The general was Roger A. Pryor.

was preoccupied with serious domestic problems, and Cleveland opposed expansion on principle. In 1883 President Arthur could easily have acquired an excellent naval base in Haiti, such a base as Grant had yearned for in Santo Domingo, and another in Venezuela.[29] The Haitian prospect was tempting enough to cause Cabinet discussion and the sending of a ship to investigate. But the government decided not to take a base in either country for a reason expressed by Secretary of State Frederick T. Frelinghuysen: "The policy of this Government," he said, "as declared on many occasions in the past, has tended toward avoidance of possessions disconnected from the main continent." Later he reiterated this view more specifically: "I wish to state distinctly, on the general question of annexation of outlying islands or territory—except in the North, and I make an exception there—that I trust we have seen the last of annexation, and in this remark I include the whole of the Mexican territory. . . ."[30] This was an authentic American view, and anticolonial sentiment persisted with remarkable vigor throughout the remainder of the century, and indeed still longer.

Even after 1889, when Benjamin Harrison became President, no Caribbean expansion occurred for nine years. The Harrison administration did make some minor moves in that area, but it accomplished nothing. The President admitted that he was "not much of an expansionist," although he did think the country had been "too conservative" about acquiring naval bases.[31] After Harrison, Cleveland was again in the White House. Despite the strong underlying pressures for territorial expansion, it would take the war with Spain to whip up emotions to a point where Americans would get their Caribbean base. Before then domestic preoccupations were too absorbing, the traditional opposition to overseas expansion too

29. Rayford W. Logan, *The Diplomatic Relations of the United States and Haiti, 1776–1891* (Chapel Hill, 1941), pp. 373–79; Ludwell L. Montague, *Haiti and the United States, 1714–1938* (Durham, N.C., 1940), p. 123; David M. Pletcher, *The Awkward Years: American Foreign Relations under Garfield and Arthur* (Columbia, Mo., 1962), pp. 131–36.

30. Frelinghuysen to John M. Langston (American minister to Haiti), June 20, 1883, John Bassett Moore, *A Digest of International Law* . . . (8 vols., Washington, 1906), I, 432; Moore incorrectly dates the instruction June 20, 1882. Frelinghuysen to Langston, Feb. 1, 1884, *Congressional Record*, 55 Cong., 2 Sess., p. 6340 (June 22, 1898).

31. Harrison to Secretary of State James G. Blaine, Oct. 1, 1891, Albert T. Volwiler, "Harrison, Blaine, and American Foreign Policy, 1889–1893," *Proceedings of the American Philosophical Society*, LXXIX (1938), 638–39.

great, for even a base in the strategic Caribbean Sea to be acquired. Was a canal also beyond reach? For many years Grant had advocated a Central American canal, and as President he hoped to get construction started.[32] A canal would increase the navy's mobility, an important consideration to a military-minded man, but more immediately persuasive was the opening of Ferdinand de Lesseps's Suez Canal in 1869, the very year Grant took office. Although in that same year the completion of America's first transcontinental railroad reduced her dependence on the isthmian transit, this did not offset the impact of de Lesseps's achievement. For by shortening the sea distance between Europe and the Far East, the new waterway gave European manufacturers an advantage in the Oriental markets over their rivals in the northeastern United States, who, consequently, now needed a Central American canal to restore their competitive position. "The great importance of the construction of a ship canal across the Isthmus of Darien has been constantly before the attention of the department," Grant's Secretary of the Navy, George M. Robeson, wrote in 1869. "Now that the Suez canal has been opened for navigation, we are doubly stimulated to such efforts as will lead to the success of our own great enterprise. . . . The time has come for action. . . ."[33]

Colombia's rejection of Seward's treaty of January 1869, giving the United States construction rights across Colombia's province of Panama, had so incensed Panama that it threatened to secede, and its legislature unanimously called for reconsideration. Thus when Grant entered the White House the situation was favorable for further negotiations. He appointed his old friend General Stephen A. Hurlbut as minister to Colombia, and in 1870 Hurlbut signed a new treaty. This time the Colombian Senate approved it, but only after making amendments unacceptable to the United States Senate.[34] Grant also hoped to obtain more favorable terms from Nicaragua than those in the Dickinson-Ayón treaty of 1867, which gave only transit rights, but Nicaragua refused to meet his wishes.[35] His

32. Lindley M. Keasbey, *The Nicaragua Canal and the Monroe Doctrine* . . . (New York, 1896), p. 313.

33. *Report of the Secretary of the Navy, 1869* (Washington, 1869), p. 24.

34. The text of the treaty is in *Senate Documents*, 56 Cong., 1 Sess., No. 237 (Serial 3853), pp. 51–61; see also Gerstle Mack, *The Land Divided: A History of the Panama Canal and Other Isthmian Canal Projects* (New York, 1944), p. 167.

35. *Ibid.*, p. 215; *House Reports*, 47 Cong., 1 Sess., No. 1698 (Serial 2070), Pt. 3, pp. 14–15.

two terms ended with the United States still having this treaty with Nicaragua, the equally unsuitable treaty of 1846 with Colombia (it, too, gave only transit rights), and the cramping Clayton-Bulwer treaty of 1850 with Great Britain.

But although his diplomacy failed, the President launched several governmental surveys of possible Central American canal sites, all the way from the Isthmus of Tehuantepec to the Isthmus of Darien.[36] In 1872 he appointed an Interoceanic Canal Commission. One of its three members was Daniel Ammen, a canal enthusiast who had helped stimulate Grant's interest in a canal as well as in Santo Domingo, and who in the 1880s became a key figure in a canal construction company in Nicaragua.[37] After examining the various survey reports, the commission unanimously recommended the Nicaragua route in 1876,[38] and this advice dominated American thinking throughout the rest of the century. Although Grant left office without a spadeful of soil having been turned, the negotiations and surveys he initiated had rekindled among Americans their pre–Civil War interest in a canal; and his successors in the White House during the next eight years strove hard to get sustained construction started.

After the Canal Commission reported in favor of the Nicaragua route, three construction companies became interested in different parts of Central America. The first of these was a French concern with a charter from the French government and a concession from Colombia for a canal across Panama; it was headed by no less a person than Ferdinand de Lesseps. The appearance of the French at Panama sent an apprehensive shudder through the American people, who had always assumed that when in the ripeness of time a canal was built they would be the builders. Hoping to reassure them, de Lesseps went to Washington in March 1880; there he visited President Rutherford B. Hayes and testified before a House Select Committee on Interoceanic Canals that had just been established in response to the ominous news about Panama.[39] Hayes reacted with a strong message to Congress on March 8: "The policy

36. *Senate Executive Documents*, 46 Cong., 1 Sess., No. 15 (Serial 1869); *Senate Documents*, 58 Cong., 2 Sess., No. 222 (Serial 4609), I, 38–40.
37. Keasbey, *Nicaragua Canal*, p. 318.
38. *Senate Executive Documents*, 46 Cong., 1 Sess., No. 15, pp. 1–2.
39. *House Miscellaneous Documents*, 46 Cong., 3 Sess., No. 16 (Serial 1981), pp. 50–55.

of this country is a canal under American control. . . . An interoceanic canal . . . would be the great ocean thoroughfare between our Atlantic and Pacific shores, and virtually a part of the coast line of the United States."[40] But de Lesseps was not easily dissuaded. To give an American color to his enterprise he set up an American Committee, headed for a short time by the Secretary of the Navy (Ulysses S. Grant having refused the post). The Committee had at its disposal some $1,500,000, and it would be instructive to know how it spent this large sum.[41] Energetic French excavation soon got under way at Panama, and it continued, with interruptions, for years to come.

The two other companies were American. The Interoceanic Ship-Railway Company envisaged not a waterway but a railway that would carry ships across the Isthmus of Tehuantepec in immense cradles. However bizarre, the project was the dream of one of America's greatest engineers, James B. Eads, and the House Select Committee, after hearing his testimony, reported that evidence for the ship-railway's practicability was "overwhelmingly in the affirmative." But although Eads got a concession from Mexico, nothing was to come of his venture.[42]

The third company, the Maritime Canal Company of Nicaragua, envisaged a canal across Nicaragua, and for a few years it looked as though the United States was going to have her canal in the near future. Closely associated with the Maritime Canal Company were such prominent men as Ulysses S. Grant, Daniel Ammen, Seth L. Phelps (who became the company's president), Representative Levi P. Morton, and General George B. McClellan.[43] Having obtained a 99-year concession from Nicaragua stipulating that it start construction and spend at least $2 million within three years and complete the canal within a further ten years, the company set about getting a charter from the United States government in the well-grounded belief that federal incorporation would help it raise funds.[44] Despite

40. Richardson, *Messages and Papers*, VII, 585–86.
41. E. Taylor Parks, *Colombia and the United States, 1765–1934* (Durham, N.C., 1935), pp. 363–64.
42. *House Reports*, 46 Cong., 3 Sess., No. 322 (Serial 1982), pp. 1–3; for the concession see *Senate Reports*, 47 Cong., 1 Sess., No. 213 (Serial 2004), pp. 9, 15.
43. Keasbey, *Nicaragua Canal*, p. 365; see Grant's article, "The Nicaragua Canal," *North American Review*, CXXXII (1881), 107–16.
44. *Senate Reports*, 47 Cong., 1 Sess., No. 368 (Serial 2006).

repeated efforts in Congress, however, a federal charter was not forthcoming. It seems extraordinary that Congress not only refused to incorporate the company but did little more than shelve favorable resolutions without serious debate. A large part of the explanation lies in the fact that each of the three rival enterprises—the French company, the Eads project, the Maritime Canal Company—tried to check the other two. Undoubtedly, too, the transcontinental railroads opposed a rival that would divert traffic from their lines. Particularly active was Collis P. Huntington, head of the Southern Pacific, who for years employed a former Treasury Department official as a lobbyist.[45] Unable to meet the deadline for construction by the third year, the Canal Company succeeded in getting the period of grace extended another year, to September 30, 1884. As this new date drew near and federal incorporation was still unobtainable, the company incorporated itself in Colorado and in desperation turned to Europe for capital.[46]

The move alarmed Washington, which feared that if a European country financed the canal if would soon get control of it, as Great Britain had of Suez. At this juncture the new President, Arthur, and Secretary of State Frelinghuysen seem to have made the momentous decision that the national interest could not be safeguarded unless the government itself built the Nicaragua canal.[47] Two major obstacles existed. The first was the Maritime Canal Company, which still had a concession. But the company proved unable to raise funds in Europe, and hopes for rescue by Grant's banking house, Grant and Ward, were dashed when the firm went bankrupt during the depression of 1884. Consequently the canal company went out of existence after its concession expired in September 1884.[48] A much more formidable obstacle was the Clayton-Bulwer treaty banning an American canal. The three preceding Secretaries of State—Fish, Evarts, and Blaine—had all approached Great Britain about abro-

45. See a newspaper clipping dated Aug. 13, 1900 in the John T. Morgan Papers, Library of Congress (Washington), X; and William L. Merry to Morgan, April 28, 1900, *ibid.*

46. Sarah G. Walton, "The Frelinghuysen-Zavala Treaty, 1884–1885" (M.A. thesis, University of Virginia, 1953), pp. 56, 53, 141; Cornelius A. Logan (American minister to Central America) to Frelinghuysen, March 21, 1882, *Papers Relating to the Foreign Relations of the United States, 1882* (Washington, 1883), pp. 34–35.

47. Walton, "Frelinghuysen-Zavala Treaty," p. 109; Pletcher, *Awkward Years,* p. 272.

48. Mack, *Land Divided,* p. 216.

gating or modifying that unpopular treaty, but without success.[49] Frelinghuysen tried his own hand at persuading London; but the British still refused to budge.[50] The Secretary now took the plunge and decided to ignore the old treaty. He initiated negotiations with Nicaragua and on December 1 signed a treaty with Joaquin Zavala, a former President of that country. The Frelinghuysen-Zavala treaty granted the United States permission to construct a canal through a strip of land two and a half miles wide; there would be a "perpetual alliance" between the two countries, and the United States would protect Nicaragua's territorial integrity.[51] The provisions for governmental construction and for a permanent entangling alliance with Nicaragua were unprecedented, but Arthur endeavored to inveigle the Senate into approving the treaty by holding out alluring trade prospects. The proposed canal, he told that body, would stimulate exports by speeding up communications between the east coast of the United States and the Pacific coast of South America, "a natural market," and also between the east coast and "the vast population of Asia."[52] Nevertheless, the Senators refused to approve the treaty during the short time that remained of Arthur's term, although they did agree to reconsider the vote.[53]

But reconsideration never took place. Grover Cleveland had just won the presidential election of 1884. A stubborn, courageous, but provincial person, Cleveland concerned himself little with foreign

49. *Ibid.*, p. 215; Mary W. Williams, *Anglo-American Isthmian Diplomacy, 1815–1915* (Washington, 1916), pp. 276–84; Blaine to James Russell Lowell (American minister to Great Britain), June 24, 1881, *Papers Relating to the Foreign Relations of the United States, 1881* (Washington, 1882), pp. 537–38; Blaine to Lowell, Nov. 19, 1881, *ibid.*, pp. 554–59; Granville to William J. Hoppin (American chargé d'affaires at London), Nov. 10, 1881, *ibid.*, p. 549; Blaine to Lowell, Nov. 29, 1881, *ibid.*, pp. 563–69; Granville to Sir Lionel S. Sackville West (British minister to the United States), Jan. 7, 14, 1882, *ibid.*, *1882*, pp. 304–14.

50. Frelinghuysen to Lowell, May 8, 1882, *Foreign Relations, 1882*, pp. 271–83; Granville to West, Dec. 30, 1882, *Papers Relating to the Foreign Relations of the United States, 1883* (Washington, 1884), pp. 484–90; Frelinghuysen to Lowell, May 5, Nov. 22, 1883, *ibid.*, pp. 418–21, 477–78; Granville to West, Aug. 17, 1883, *ibid.*, pp. 529–31.

51. *Senate Documents*, 58 Cong., 2 Sess., No. 222, I, 359–63. For the negotiations see Walton, "Frelinghuysen-Zavala Treaty," pp. 96–97, 124, 128–32.

52. Richardson, *Messages and Papers*, VIII, 258.

53. *Journal of the Executive Proceedings of the Senate* . . . (Washington, 1901), XXIV, 453; the vote, on Jan. 29, 1885, was 32 for approval, 23 against. The decision to reconsider came on Feb. 23, *ibid.*, pp. 456, 481.

policy, his views about which were shaped mainly by his moralistic abhorrence of imperialism and by his belief in a purer America as contrasted with an irredeemable Old World. In his inaugural address he denounced "ambitions upon other continents" and lauded "the policy of Monroe and of Washington and Jefferson—'Peace, commerce, and honest friendship with all nations; entangling alliances with none.' " "Maintaining, as I do," he explained later, "the tenets of a line of precedents from Washington's day, which proscribe entangling alliances with foreign states, I do not favor a policy of acquisition of new and distant territory or the incorporation of remote interests with our own."[54] Soon after taking office Cleveland withdrew the canal treaty from the Senate, chiefly on the ground that the proposed alliance with Nicaragua was unwise.[55] And so terminated the Frelinghuysen-Zavala treaty and—despite some halting steps by the Harrison and second Cleveland administrations in support of construction—all serious hopes of a canal for many years to come.

An isthmian canal and one or more Caribbean naval bases may have been basic objectives prescribed by underlying geographic, economic, and strategic forces, and keenly sought after by such powerful men as Seward and Grant, but as late as the 1880s, and even well into the 1890s, the acquisition of either a canal or a base was out of the question. The anti-colonial sentiment and domestic distractions were still too strong. Not until the end of the century could new expansionists in Washington, and a more outward-looking American people, acquire Caribbean bases and take essential steps toward a canal.

54. Richardson, *Messages and Papers*, VIII, 301, 327.
55. Annual message, Dec. 8, 1885, *ibid.*, VIII, 327–28. Cleveland called Eads's ship-railway project "entirely practicable."

CHAPTER 4

# Commitments in Hawaii and Samoa

A N isthmian canal and naval bases in the Caribbean Sea were two of the main objectives of American expansionists in the last three decades of the nineteenth century. The third objective was a naval base in the Hawaiian Islands, perhaps even the annexation of the entire archipelago; but throughout the 1870s and 1880s Hawaii was just as unobtainable as were a canal and Caribbean bases.

The final defeat in the Senate of Seward's 1867 reciprocity treaty with Hawaii did not occur until June 1, 1870, when Grant was President.[1] The expansionist Grant, and Secretary of State Fish too, would doubtless have been willing to go beyond reciprocity all the way to annexation. When the American minister at Honolulu asked Washington in 1870 and again in 1871 to consider taking the islands, Fish reacted favorably. He warned the Cabinet in late 1870 that American influence in Hawaii was declining, but no one else in the room said a word. Disgustedly he noted in his diary: "The indisposition to consider important questions of the future in the Cabinet is wonderful. A matter must be imminent to engage attention—indifference and reticence—alas!"[2] In the 1870s American public opinion was no more disposed to annexing Hawaii than Santo Domingo. But despite the apathy Grant and Fish succeeded

1. *Journal of the Executive Proceedings of the Senate* . . . (Washington, 1901), XVII, 466; the vote was 20 for approval, 19 against.
2. Minister Henry A. Peirce to Fish, Feb. 25, 1871, *Senate Reports*, 53 Cong., 2 Sess., No. 227 (Serial 3180), p. xxxix; Hamilton Fish Diary, Library of Congress (Washington), Dec. 20, 1870; see also *ibid.*, March 21, April 7, 1871.

in preparing the groundwork for acquiring Hawaii, just as they did regarding an isthmian canal—and just as they did, for that matter, regarding more amicable relations with Great Britain.

By the 1870s, as a result of the west coast's settlement and development, Hawaii's economy, particularly her sugar industry, was being molded into the much larger economy on the mainland, and it was imperative for the tiny kingdom to have the assurance of a reciprocity treaty with her powerful neighbor. But reciprocity meant little to the United States, as the defeat of Seward's treaty showed, and therefore Hawaii in 1873 offered to cede control of Pearl Harbor in return for tariff concessions.[3] Like Samaná Bay, Pearl Harbor could become a major naval base; not only would it guard a canal's western approaches but, as was more strongly emphasized before the 1890s, it would render America's Pacific coast practically invulnerable because no hostile fleet could launch a sustained attack on the coast without recoaling in Hawaii (or in Mexico or Canada).[4] For this reason, and also to prevent Hawaii's economy from deteriorating to the point where she would appeal for help to Great Britain or some other European power, the Cabinet heard the Pearl Harbor offer with much interest.

Hawaiian negotiators opened talks with Fish in November 1874; and seeking to stir up American support, the Hawaiian King, Kalakaua, came to the United States, the first reigning King ever to visit the country. After a triumphant tour he returned home with a reciprocity treaty, signed January 30, 1875.[5] It enumerated several Hawaiian agricultural products, including unrefined sugar, to be admitted duty-free into the United States for seven years (and thereafter indefinitely unless the treaty was denounced by either country), and a large number of American goods, including manufactures, for similar duty-free admittance into Hawaii. But because of growing opposition among Hawaiians to ceding control of any part of their country, it had no Pearl Harbor concession.[6]

3. Sylvester K. Stevens, *American Expansion in Hawaii, 1842–1898* (Harrisburg, Pa., 1945), pp. 116–17.
4. See a report of 1873 by Major General John M. Schofield and Lieutenant Colonel Burton S. Alexander, *American Historical Review*, XXX (1925), 561–65.
5. Stevens, *American Expansion*, pp. 119–23; Merze Tate, *The United States and the Hawaiian Kingdom: A Political History* (New Haven, 1965), p. 39.
6. William M. Malloy (ed.), *Treaties, Conventions, International Acts, Protocols and Agreements between the United States of America and Other Powers, 1776–1909* (2 vols., Washington, 1910), I, 915–17; Stevens, *American Expansion*, pp. 116–17.

Without some such concession American ratification of the treaty was unlikely. The Senate accordingly insisted on an amendment binding Hawaii not to give either the harbor or the commercial privileges to any other country. Even so, many opposed the treaty. East coast refiners and southern sugar-cane growers dreaded Hawaiian competition. California refiners, led by Claus Spreckels, the sugar magnate, also disliked the treaty, suspecting that Hawaiian sugar even if unrefined would undersell their refined product. Some Senators fought Hawaiian reciprocity as creating a precedent for renewed Canadian reciprocity;[7] Republican doctrine favored harassing Canada, not helping her, in order to drive her into the union. But strategic considerations relating to the west coast carried the day, and on March 18, 1875, the Senate gave its approval, 50 to 12.[8]

The treaty specified that Congress should enact enabling legislation, and this involved the House of Representatives. There, too, the advocates of sugar and security clashed. John K. Luttrell, Representative from California, emphasized security; Hawaii, he argued, was the only outpost for defending the Pacific coast. "Defeat this bill and in less than sixty days Great Britain will have secured a treaty with those islands, and will then control every naval station from Newfoundland in the east to Victoria in the North Pacific." Another Representative linked Hawaii with the isthmian canal, which in the "certain and, historically speaking, not distant future" would be built.[9] The vote on May 8, 1876, was surprisingly close: 115 favored the enabling legislation; 101 opposed it; 74 did not vote. Three months later the Senate accepted the enabling bill and, since Hawaii long since had ratified, the treaty went into effect.[10] Never again was the bulk of Hawaiian-American trade to be dutiable.

The removal of duties for at least seven years on Hawaii's exports to the United States revolutionized the islands' economy and whole society. Sugar production boomed. Between 1876 and 1880 its

7. *Ibid.*, pp. 131–33, 139; George S. Boutwell, *Reminiscences of Sixty Years in Public Affairs* (2 vols., New York, 1902), II, 277–78.

8. *Journal of the Executive Proceedings of the Senate* . . . (Washington, 1901), XX, 42; the *Journal* says that 51 approved, but lists 50 names.

9. *Congressional Record*, 44 Cong., 1 Sess., p. 1488 (March 6, 1876), p. 1596 (March 9, 1876), p. 1463 (March 4, 1876).

10. *Ibid.*, p. 3037 (May 8, 1876); for the Senate's action see *ibid.*, p. 5572 (Aug. 14, 1876).

annual value rose from $1,272,334 to $4,322,711, and exports to America nearly quadrupled. Sugar workers had to be imported, usually as contract laborers, coming mainly from China, Japan, and Portugal. As the American west coast population grew, more sugar was needed. By 1890, out of a total population of 89,990 on the islands, 15,301 were Chinese, 12,360 Japanese, and 8,602 Portuguese. Moreover, the native population was declining: from 58,000 in 1866 to 34,436 in 1890.[11] In short, the Hawaiian Islands, so vital to American security, were slipping into Oriental occupation.

The concentration on sugar brought prosperity to the islands, but at the cost of a dangerous dependence on the United States. More than ever Hawaii needed long-term access to the American market; consequently at the end of 1882, as the original seven-year period of guaranteed reciprocity neared its end, she opened negotiations for a new treaty. Chester A. Arthur was then President, and Secretary of State Frelinghuysen, a strong advocate of reciprocity with areas near the United States, favored renewing the Hawaiian treaty; then too, although the administration opposed annexing the islands, as it opposed overseas expansion in general, it wanted to ensure that no other country would annex them.[12]

Eastern refiners still opposed reciprocity; but Claus Spreckels, who had started to produce sugar in Hawaii (where he had great influence over King Kalakaua), had reversed his stand of 1876 and now supported a treaty that would benefit him as a producer. Southern sugar interests, of course, opposed renewal strongly, as did a new group, the sugar-beet growers of California and some other states. Partly because of their pressure, several anti-reciprocity resolutions had already been introduced in Congress; but in January 1883 the House Foreign Affairs Committee reported in favor of a new treaty, citing the familiar strategic considerations and also the newer reason of a growing commerce with Asia and Australia. These were the dominant arguments for a close relationship with Hawaii, but the opposition remained active and not until December

11. *House Executive Documents*, 53 Cong., 2 Sess., No. 47 (Serial 3224), pp. 73–74; Stevens, *American Expansion*, pp. 91, 141.
12. Draft dated Dec. 20, 1882, recopied for signature Jan. 9, 1883, and addressed to Charles G. Williams (chairman of the House Foreign Affairs Committee), Frederick T. Frelinghuysen Papers, Library of Congress (Washington).

6, 1884, did Frelinghuysen and the Hawaiian minister at Washington sign a treaty that extended reciprocity for seven years.[13] For two and a half years the Senate considered whether or not to approve it. Presumably the sugar interests remained busy behind the scenes. Eventually Arthur's successor, President Grover Cleveland, decided that the vacillation had gone on long enough; in his annual message of 1886 he explained why he—an opponent of reciprocity, and also of the entangling Frelinghuysen-Zavala treaty —supported this one rather entangling reciprocity treaty: "I express my unhesitating conviction that the intimacy of our relations with Hawaii should be emphasized. . . . those islands, on the highway of Oriental and Australasian traffic, are virtually an outpost of American commerce and a stepping-stone to the growing trade of the Pacific."[14] But just as the Senate had refused to approve the original treaty of 1875 without adding the restriction on Pearl Harbor, so it now insisted upon an amendment to the new treaty that gave the United States the exclusive right to a coaling and naval station in "the harbor of Pearl River."[15] The prospect of gaining so valuable a privilege, together with the administration's pressure, tipped the scales; and the Senate approved the treaty on January 20, 1887, with the far-reaching amendment.[16] Hawaii followed suit, although she had strong misgivings about Pearl River, and perhaps was aware of a prediction by the British consul general at Honolulu that "the acquisition of this Harbour by the United States would lead to the loss of Hawaiian independence." Her fears were only partially relieved by Bayard's assurance that American rights in the harbor would last no longer than the life of the treaty.[17]

13. Stevens, *American Expansion*, pp. 165–66; *Congressional Record*, 47 Cong., 1 Sess., Appendix, pp. 31, 33, 34 (March 10, 1882); *ibid.*, 47 Cong., 2 Sess., pp. 1003–5 (Jan. 9, 1883), pp. 3322–23 (Feb. 27, 1883); *ibid.*, 48 Cong., 1 Sess., p. 127 (Dec. 12, 1883), p. 166 (Dec. 19, 1883); *Senate Reports*, 47 Cong., 2 Sess., No. 1013 (Serial 2088), pp. 2, 5, 7; *ibid.*, 48 Cong., 1 Sess., No. 76 (Serial 2173). For the Committee on Foreign Affairs report see *House Reports*, 47 Cong., 2 Sess., No. 1860 (Serial 2159), pp. 1–2.
14. Message of Dec. 6, 1886, James D. Richardson (ed.), *A Compilation of the Messages and Papers of the Presidents, 1789–1897* (10 vols., Washington, 1899), VIII, 500–1.
15. *Senate Documents*, 56 Cong., 2 Sess., No. 231 (Serial 4054), Pt. 8, p. 244.
16. *Journal of the Executive Proceedings of the Senate . . .* (Washington, 1901), XXV, 708–10; Malloy, *Treaties*, I, 919–20. The treaty entered into force on Nov. 9, 1887.
17. Regarding Hawaii's misgivings and the ominous British prediction see James H. Wodehouse (the British consul general) to Captain Charles L. Oxley, H.M.S. *Conquest*, Oct. 19, 1887, Public Record Office (London), Foreign Office 58/241; for Bayard's assurances see Bayard to Henry A. P. Carter (Hawaiian minister to the

The Pearl River article represented the first small success of American expansionists toward achieving their trinity of basic objectives: an isthmian canal, a Caribbean base, and a Hawaiian base. But the article certainly did not satisfy even their Hawaiian aspirations. The limited privileges of 1887 might terminate in 1894, and, in any case, a coral reef blocked the river's mouth. Not for many years would the United States have an effective Pearl Harbor base.

In 1898 the United States annexed the Hawaiian Islands. We shall later analyze the various reasons for this, but a brief comment may be made here. We have seen that in 1875 and 1876 the main reasons advanced by advocates of a close tie with the islands were economic and strategic in nature. Which were more important: the economic or the strategic considerations? Different writers have offered varying interpretations.[18] But in the 1870s, the 1880s, and also the 1890s, the economic and strategic factors were inextricably interrelated. Without the Pearl Harbor restriction the United States would not have accepted commercial reciprocity in the seventies. Once the duty on Hawaiian sugar had been abolished, the islands became economically bound to the enormously larger mainland; however, equally significant was the fact that the economic tie gave rise to population changes in Hawaii that, because of strategic considerations, could not fail to alarm Washington profoundly. Thus for reasons of strategy and economics the reciprocity treaty, as renewed in 1887, made inevitable some kind of special relationship between Hawaii and the United States. Eventual annexation was a natural consequence.

By sponsoring reciprocity the Grant administration paved the way to Hawaii's acquisition. In a less compelling way the administration had a measure of responsibility for the future acquisition of another Pacific Ocean archipelago, the Samoan Islands. These islands are strategically situated in the south Pacific, as the Hawaiian Islands are in the north Pacific. Lying 2,260 miles from Hawaii (which is 2,100

---

United States), Sept. 23, 1887, *Papers Relating to the Foreign Relations of the United States, 1887* (Washington, 1888), p. 591. On both matters see Merze Tate, "British Opposition to the Cession of Pearl Harbor," *Pacific Historical Review,* XXIX (1960), 381–94.

18. Although not neglecting economic considerations, John A. S. Grenville and George B. Young give more attention to strategic considerations, *Politics, Strategy, and American Diplomacy: Studies in Foreign Policy, 1873–1917* (New Haven, 1966), pp. 102–15. For emphasis on economics see Walter LaFeber, *The New Empire: An Interpretation of American Expansion, 1860–1898* (Ithaca, 1963), pp. 408–10.

miles from San Francisco) and 2,355 miles from Sydney, Samoa is a perfectly placed stepping stone between California and the English-speaking lands in the Antipodes. Its significance for the protection of the potential isthmian canal was less apparent, though sometimes asserted. Should the United States acquire both Pearl Harbor and Pago Pago she would have two of the three best harbors in all the islands of the Pacific (outside Japan), the third being Manila Bay in the Philippines. Strategically, however, Samoa was much less important to the United States than Hawaii was. Its strategic importance related more to New Zealand, and somewhat as the United States was beginning to think of taking Hawaii, so New Zealand and Australia were asking London to annex Samoa.

In 1869, the year the first transcontinental railroad was completed, a New York promoter named William H. Webb started a steamship line that plied between San Francisco and Australia. Needing coaling facilities between Hawaii and Australia, he dispatched an associate, Edgar Wakeman, to investigate the Samoan Islands; and on receiving Wakeman's report he sent it to his friend President Grant. The report described Pago Pago, on Tutuila Island, as "the most perfectly land-locked harbor that exists in the Pacific Ocean."[19] With the age of steamships at hand, the great powers were seeking coaling stations around the world. Like Samaná Bay and Pearl Harbor, Pago Pago came into the navy's view as a possible American naval base.

It was a coincidence, however, that in 1872 Commander Richard W. Meade, acting without instructions, negotiated a treaty with the Tutuila chiefs giving the United States the exclusive right to establish a coaling station in Pago Pago and putting the natives under American protection.[20] Ever an expansionist, a delighted Grant asked the Senate to approve the treaty, recommending however some modification of the obligation to protect the natives.[21] But the Senate was far from ready for South Seas adventures, and true to the prevailing mood opposing tropical expansion that had wrecked

19. The report, dated Sept. 20, 1871, is in *House Executive Documents*, 44 Cong., 1 Sess., No. 161 (Serial 1691), pp. 7–11. See also Edgar Wakeman, *Report of Capt. E. Wakeman, to W. H. Webb, on the Islands of the Samoa Group . . .* (New York, 1872).

20. The Meade agreement, dated Feb. 17, 1872, is in *House Executive Documents*, 44 Cong., 1 Sess., No. 161, pp. 6–7. See also George H. Ryden, *The Foreign Policy of the United States in Relation to Samoa* (New Haven, 1933), ch. 3.

21. Special message, May 22, 1872, Richardson, *Messages and Papers*, VII, 168–69.

Grant's Santo Domingo dream and had contributed to the defeat of Seward's Hawaiian reciprocity treaty, it did not deign even to vote. Secretary of the Navy Robeson also supported the treaty; he called Pago Pago "absolutely the only land-protected harbor among the islands of the South Pacific."[22] Later Secretaries of the Navy expressed similar sentiments, and one suspects that they exerted a steady background pressure from which followed no little of America's increasing involvement.[23]

In 1873 the administration, acting on a suggestion from Webb, sent a special agent, Colonel Albert B. Steinberger, to Samoa to gather information about a possible naval station (as Babcock had gone to Santo Domingo). Steinberger arrived in the islands in August.[24] He found a loose government, incapable of suppressing the frequent fighting among the native chiefs. Although Steinberger may have been associated with an American company speculating in Samoan land, and was probably an opportunist of little principle, he endeared himself to the Samoans and strove sincerely to improve their lot. But rivalries among the great powers defeated his aspirations. Of all foreign countries Germany had much the largest economic stake in the islands. Since 1847 the Hamburg house of John Caesar Godeffroy and Son, with local headquarters in Apia, the capital (on Upolu Island), had traded with Samoa; its principal representative there, Theodor Weber, was also the German consul. Great Britain, because of her missionaries, pressure from New Zealand, and commercial connections, also interested herself in the distant archipelago.

In late 1873 Steinberger was back in the United States. He wrote Secretary Fish in glowing terms, predicting that ". . . Samoa, under guidance and protection, would develop and concentrate a great

22. Annual report, Nov. 26, 1872, *Report of the Secretary of the Navy, 1872* (Washington, 1872), pp. 13–14.

23. For later expressions of interest see *ibid., 1880* (Washington, 1880), p. 26; *ibid., 1883* (2 vols., Washington, 1883), I, 32; *ibid., 1884* (2 vols., Washington, 1884), I, 41; *ibid., 1889* (2 vols., Washington, 1889), I, 31–32; *ibid., 1899* (Washington, 1899), p. 27.

24. Steinberger to Grant, Aug. 17, 1872. *House Executive Documents*, 44 Cong., 1 Sess., No. 161, p. 3; Fish to Steinberger, March 29, 1873, *ibid.*, pp. 5–6. On Steinberger's mission see *Senate Executive Documents*, 43 Cong., 1 Sess., No. 45 (Serial 1581); *House Executive Documents*, 44 Cong., 1 Sess., No. 161; *ibid.*, 44 Cong., 2 Sess., No. 44 (Serial 1755); Ryden, *Foreign Policy of the United States*, chs. 4, 5; Joseph W. Ellison, "The Adventures of an American Premier in Samoa, 1874–1876," *Pacific Northwest Quarterly*, XXVII (1936), 311–46. Richard P. Gilson, *Samoa, 1830–1900: The Politics of a Multi-Cultural Community* (Melbourne, 1970), ch. 13.

trade."[25] Fish was sufficiently impressed to send the colonel back to Samoa. Steinberger first went to Germany and secretly agreed with Godeffroy and Son to back its Samoan interests; he arrived in the islands again in April 1875. So successful was he in ending their feuds that the natives made him a sort of prime minister. But his popularity with the Samoans was equaled by the dislike he aroused among the German, British, and American consuls. On February 8, 1876, they arrested the "prime minister" and deported him on a British warship.[26] Thus ended the Samoan career of Albert B. Steinberger.

But however inglorious its end, it had momentous consequences. Fearful of Germany, one faction of Samoan chiefs departed for Fiji, recently acquired by Great Britain as a shield for New Zealand, and solicited British annexation, while another sent a chief named Le Mamea to faraway Washington. At the end of 1877 Le Mamea met Assistant Secretary of State Frederick W. Seward, the expansionist son of the frustrated expansionist, former Secretary of State William H. Seward, and asked for annexation or at least a protectorate. Carefully warning his unusual visitor of the "strong opposition to the acquisition of any islands, near or remote, inhabited by any race but our own,"[27] Seward drafted a treaty that was signed on January 17, 1878. By it the United States gained the right to establish a naval and coaling station in Pago Pago, but instead of annexing the islands or establishing a protectorate she agreed merely to employ good offices if Samoa should have differences with a third country.[28] Although Grant had left office the year before, the treaty was the direct result of his sponsorship of Steinberger's mission.

Debating the treaty in executive session, the Senate approved it unanimously on January 30, 1878.[29] This behavior contrasted sharply with the cavalier disregard of the Meade treaty six years

25. Steinberger to Fish, undated but transmitted to Congress April 21, 1874, *Senate Executive Documents*, 43 Cong., 1 Sess., No. 45, pp. 41–42.

26. Steinberger to Fish, June 1, 1876, *House Executive Documents*, 44 Cong., 2 Sess., No. 44, pp. 79–84.

27. Frederick W. Seward, *Reminiscences of a War-Time Statesman and Diplomat, 1830–1915* (New York, 1916), p. 438.

28. Malloy, *Treaties*, II, 1574–76. Other articles gave commercial privileges, most-favored-nation treatment, and extraterritorial rights. The treaty was to remain in force for a minimum of ten years, and thereafter until twelve months after being denounced by either party. See also Ryden, *Foreign Policy of the United States*, ch. 7.

29. *Journal of the Executive Proceedings of the Senate . . .* (Washington, 1901), XXI, 220–21.

before, and the reason for the change is not altogether clear. The earlier treaty would have given the United States an exclusive naval base but (with Grant's proposed modification) no commitment; the 1878 treaty gave a nonexclusive base and a commitment to extend good offices. Perhaps the Senate's quick approval reflected an awareness of America's multiplying interests in the Pacific Ocean— as did its acceptance of reciprocity with Hawaii in 1875 after rejecting it in 1870. Commerce with Australia and New Zealand was already large enough so that in 1879 President Hayes commended Congress's attention to "the important and growing" trade with the former, and in 1879 and 1880 the United States participated in international exhibitions in Sydney and Melbourne.[30] The navy made a survey of Pago Pago in 1878 and deposited several hundred tons of coal there in 1880.[31]

This was Samoa's first treaty with a foreign country, and Washington occasionally cited the point as though it created a special American commitment to her. A commitment it did create, although looser than the one formed with Hawaii by the reciprocity treaty. All the same, the Samoan treaty of 1878, as we shall now see, proved to be the opening wedge for an American involvement that grew constantly deeper throughout the 1880s, with a much more binding commitment following in 1889 and outright annexation ten years later.

The treaty did not compel the American consul at Samoa to act as he did the very next year, but it is impossible to believe that he would have done so had the treaty not been in existence. In 1879 he, together with the British and German consuls, signed a convention providing that the town of Apia, the center of foreign activity, should in effect be neutralized and governed by a council composed of the three consuls.[32] Never submitted to the Senate, the convention had no legal force for the United States. Nevertheless, American consuls participated regularly on the council for many years, and in reality the three consuls governed not only Apia but, with some help from the natives, the entire archipelago. Washington,

30. Annual message, Dec. 1, 1879, Richardson, *Messages and Papers*, VII, 567; see also his annual message, Dec. 6, 1880, *ibid.*, p. 607.

31. Annual message, Dec. 2, 1878, *ibid.*, p. 497; *Report of the Secretary of the Navy, 1880*, p. 26.

32. *House Executive Documents*, 50 Cong., 1 Sess., No. 238 (Serial 2560).

however, sincerely wanted the islands to be self-governing.

For the United States this arrangement represented an unprecedented collaboration with European countries on a distant South Sea archipelago. It is not easy to account for it. In a way, the involvement just grew, step by step, as one thing led to another and no one step seemed significant enough to call for a halt. But it was also true that the United States was the strongest country facing the Pacific Ocean. Samoa had little actual but presumably much more potential value. Someday it might be an outpost for protecting the potential isthmian canal; someday it might be useful for commerce with Australia and New Zealand. Meanwhile European countries were seizing one Pacific Ocean island after another. It seemed wise to salvage for the future an archipelago that because of its stragetic position and splendid harbor might, in time, have great importance for the United States, and in each of his annual reports for 1883 and 1884 the Secretary of the Navy recommended putting the projected Pago Pago station "on a firm basis."[33]

The perils inherent in the consular rule soon manifested themselves. Disturbed by native actions that threatened Germany's economic position in Samoa, the German consul general intervened dramatically. Early in 1885 he ordered the seizure of Apia and of nearby Mulinuu peninsula, where the King, Malietoa Laupepa, resided; over Mulinuu he hoisted the German flag. There ensued four turbulent years that involved the United States in a growing altercation with Germany.[34]

The four years coincided with Grover Cleveland's first administration. Cleveland and his Secretary of State, Thomas F. Bayard, were unusual men. They were both prone to talk in moralistic terms; and although completely sincere, they often exasperated their auditors, who readily detected through the high moral tone a sharp eye to the national interest and, in Cleveland's case, to the requirements of domestic party politics. Bayard came from a distinguished family of government servants; he, his father, grandfather, and an uncle had all represented Delaware in the United States Senate. Some-

33. *Report of the Secretary of the Navy, 1883*, I, 32; *ibid., 1884*, I, 41.
34. About the dispute, see Clara E. Schieber, *The Transformation of American Sentiment toward Germany, 1870–1914* (Boston, 1923), ch. 2; Ryden, *United States in Relation to Samoa, pp. 293–429;* Alfred Vagts, *Deutschland und die Vereinigten Staaten in der Weltpolitik* (2 vols., New York, 1935), I, ch. 10; Otto zu Stolberg-Wernigerode, *Germany and the United States during the Era of Bismarck* (Reading, Pa., 1937), Pt. 2, ch. 3.

what aloof and patrician, he was a good-hearted, likable man of fine character. Not outstandingly intelligent and lacking any broad view of American foreign policy, he partially made up for these defects by courtesy, patience, even temper, and devotion to work. Instinctively pro-British, he was at the same time a resolute defender of American interests. As a negotiator he suffered from a certain vague elusiveness that sometimes created general confusion.

Both the President and Bayard reacted with dismay to the treatment of Malietoa. They detested anything that smacked of bullying defenseless natives, and Bayard could speak without hypocrisy of the "moral interests of the United States with respect to the islands of the Pacific." He reminded the American consul at Apia, Berthold Greenebaum, of the treaty obligation of 1878 to tender good offices. When the German minister at Washington, Friedrich von Alvensleben, told him that Berlin intended to assume political control of Samoa but would not tamper with American rights, the Secretary retorted sharply that such an arrangement was not acceptable.[35] Germany went ahead with her plans, however. She landed troops, and she very probably had a hand in a rebellion, led by a chief named Tamasese, that broke out against the King. Americans, already irritated by a German ban on imports of their pork, and disliking the domineering manner of Chancellor Otto von Bismarck, began to turn sharply against Germany.

In May 1886 Malietoa, desperate over the growing rebellion, invoked American good offices. Thereupon Greenebaum, quite without authorization, had the United States flag raised over Samoan public buildings and announced a temporary protectorate.[36] Evidently a German-American collision was in the making if consular recklessness continued much longer. An embarrassed Bayard hastened to disavow the protectorate; he proposed that all three consuls be replaced, and that he and the German and British ministers at Washington devise a new government for the distracted islands.[37] Germany and Great Britain accepted this sensible suggestion.

35. Bayard to Greenebaum, June 19, 1885, *House Executive Documents*, 50 Cong., 1 Sess., No. 238, pp. 10–11; Ryden, *United States in Relation to Samoa*, p. 299.

36. *House Executive Documents*, 50 Cong., 1 Sess., No. 238, p. 26.

37. Bayard to George H. Pendleton (American minister to Germany), June 1, 1886, *ibid.*, pp. 19–20.

Bayard and the two ministers met on June 25, 1887, for the first of several sessions. Their meetings ended in failure a month later when compromise proved impossible between an American plan envisaging an independent Samoan kingdom assisted by foreign advisers but with no one foreign power being predominant, and a German proposal that Britain and America give her a mandate to administer Samoa while maintaining a façade of native rule.[38]

Events now moved rapidly and ominously. Germany gave notice that she would study the American plan further and would respect American and British rights, but that she must have guarantees for her large Samoan interests.[39] On August 19, 1887, four German warships dropped anchor off Apia. On the twenty-third Germany presented sweeping demands; on the twenty-fourth she declared war on Malietoa personally; on the twenty-fifth she recognized Tamasese as King. More than seven hundred marines landed. Malietoa fled to the bush, but soon surrendered. Like Steinberger several years earlier, he was deported. The American consul general, Harold M. Sewall, described the scene: "All this morning he sat with his chiefs, and they were all in tears while the last talk was had. . . . As Malietoa walked to the wharf large crowds of people followed, crying and clinging to him as if they could not give him up."[40] In October Germany declared the municipal convention of 1879 provisionally in abeyance; she withdrew from it three months later.[41] Tamasese might be the King, but the real ruler was a German named Brandeis; according to Robert Louis Stevenson, who moved to Samoa in 1890, he gave the islands an excellent administration.[42]

Inevitably these startling events fanned America's smoldering

38. For the Washington conference see Ryden, *United States in Relation to Samoa*, ch. 10.

39. Bismarck to von Alvensleben, Aug. 7, 1887 (received at the State Department Aug. 29), *House Executive Documents*, 50 Cong., 1 Sess., No. 238, p. 60.

40. Harold M. Sewall to Assistant Secretary of State James D. Porter, Oct. 10, 1887, *ibid.*, pp. 79–80. Stolberg-Wernigerode, *Germany and the United States*, p. 251, says of Sewall: "Closely allied to commercial companies interested in Samoa, he followed an extreme policy on behalf of American interests."

41. Charles C. Tansill, *The Foreign Policy of Thomas F. Bayard, 1885–1897* (New York, 1940), p. 72; Dr. Becker (German consul at Samoa) to Sewall, Jan. 18, 1888, *Senate Executive Documents*, 50 Cong., 2 Sess., No. 31 (Serial 2610), p. 17.

42. Robert Louis Stevenson, *A Foot-Note to History: Eight Years of Trouble in Samoa* (New York, 1897), p. 439.

antipathy for Bismarck's Germany. Bayard bluntly told von Alvens-leben "that the first allegiance of this Government was to right and justice, and that they were not only to consider what were the rights of the German, English, and American Governments in Samoa, but . . . the rights of the natives in Samoa." His remark was underscored when the U.S.S. *Adams* sailed into Apia on October 20, 1887.[43] A situation already delicate became critical when a chief named Mataafa launched a rebellion against the Brandeis-Tamasese re-gime on September 4, 1888. Mataafa was a capable, popular leader whom Tamasese, without German aid, could not have resisted for long. The American public stirred restively as reports arrived of deep German implication. Had Berlin taken the fateful decision to go its own way in contemptuous disregard of the United States? So it began to seem. The imminent presidential election of 1888, and the consequent partisan attacks on Cleveland and the Democrats, added to the danger. Amid signs of increasing anger, some of it no doubt politically inspired, Secretary Bayard felt his way cautiously. War he was determined to avoid. "If peace can be had with honor and without war, what malediction should pursue the man that leads a people into strife?" he asked.[44] But a recent display of considera-tion for Canada had earned him a drubbing in the Republican press, and his refusal to sound the alarm over Samoa brought added censure. The influential New York *Tribune* characterized his policy as "surpassing in imbecility and pusillanimity anything that has ever been known in the annals of American diplomacy."[45]

Not far from Apia, at a place called Fangalili, a German force landed in December 1888. Mataafa attacked it. Twenty Germans were killed, thirty wounded, in a terrible disaster. The American vice-consul telegraphed excitedly: "Germans swear vengeance. Shelling and burning indiscriminately, regardless of American property. Protests unheeded. . . . Americans in boat flying American flag seized in Apia Harbor by armed German boat, but released. Admiral with squadron necessary immediately."[46] The horrifying news reached Washington on January 5, 1889, and for the next thirty days the situation was critical.

43. Bayard memorandum of conversation, Sept. 23, 1887, Tansill, *Bayard,* p. 74; for a similar utterance see *ibid.,* p. 80. Regarding the *Adams* see *ibid.,* p. 72.
44. Bayard to E. M. Shephard, Nov. 8, 1888, *ibid.,* p. 93.
45. *Public Opinion,* VI (Feb. 16, 1889), 388.
46. William Blacklock to Bayard, Jan. 5, 1889 (via Wellington, New Zealand), *Senate Executive Documents,* 50 Cong., 2 Sess., No. 68 (Serial 2611), p. 17.

For Germany, the defeat at Fangalili was most humiliating. America's sympathy for Malietoa, and now for Mataafa, was common knowledge in the Fatherland; and anger surged up against the interfering Yankees. President Cleveland's own anger was mounting likewise. Besides his moralistic hatred of imperialism he had a quick temper, and these traits spurred him to hasty action. Presumably with his approval, Rear Admiral Lewis A. Kimberley, commander of United States naval forces in the Pacific Ocean, hastened to Apia on his flagship, the *Trenton;* she would join the *Nipsic,* which had recently arrived to relieve the *Adams.* A few days later the *Vandalia,* too, sailed for Samoa.[47] Then, on January 15, Cleveland sent a special message to Congress. Germany, he observed tartly, still disavowed any wish to destroy the native government. "But thus far her propositions on this subject seem to lead to such a preponderance of German power in Samoa as was never contemplated by us and is inconsistent with every prior agreement or understanding. . . ." He said that he was now submitting the whole subject to Congress.[48]

This abandonment of the quiet procedures of diplomacy for the excitable arena of congressional declamation was most unfortunate. New anger broke out against Germany; the St. Louis *Republic* reported a "unanimity of American opinion," which it attributed to dislike of Bismarck.[49] A Senate committee recommended an appropriation of $500,000 for protecting United States interests in Samoa and another of $100,000 for making Pago Pago an effective base.[50] Soon Congress resounded to inflammatory remarks such as that of Senator John H. Reagan of Texas, who saw "the clear rights of the American people and Government . . . brutally overridden and trodden down by subalterns of Germany." Congress voted for the appropriations in February, and Cleveland signed them into law shortly before his term expired.[51]

It is clear that in January 1889 a flare-up of emotionalism joined

47. Bayard to Count von Arco-Valley (von Alvensleben's successor as German minister to the United States), Jan. 12, 1889, *ibid.,* pp. 20–21; the *Times* (London), Jan. 22, 1889.

48. Message of Jan. 15, 1889, Richardson, *Messages and Papers,* VIII, 804–5.

49. *Public Opinion,* VI (Feb. 2, 1889), 344.

50. *Congressional Record,* 50 Cong., 2 Sess., p. 1119 (Jan. 23, 1889).

51. *Ibid.,* p. 1816 (Feb. 13, 1889), p. 1984 (Feb. 16, 1889), p. 2418 (Feb. 27, 1889). Reagan's remark is in *ibid.,* p. 1337 (Jan. 30, 1889); for other extravagant statements by Senators see *ibid.,* pp. 1283–91 (Jan. 29, 1889), pp. 1325–37 (Jan. 30, 1889), pp. 1371–76 (Jan. 31, 1889).

the older naval and commercial considerations as a major influence upon United States policy. As with many flare-ups, this one subsided quickly. The last thing Bismarck wanted was hostilities with the United States. Much as Bayard had done earlier, he invited the United States and Great Britain on January 21 to a conference at Berlin. On February 5, 1889, Washington accepted.[52] With that, the worst of the crisis was over.

One month later Cleveland and Bayard left office. They were succeeded by Benjamin Harrison and Secretary of State Blaine. The Republican administration had no reason to make difficulty about the coming conference; and prospects for its success brightened, strangely enough, when a devastating hurricane struck Apia in March 1889. In addition to the three American warships at Apia, there were three German warships and one British. But after the hurricane only the British ship remained afloat. Nearly one hundred and fifty men were dead, forty-nine of them Americans.[53] The disaster's sobering effect was recounted by the New York *World:* "Surely the awful devastation wrought in the harbor of Apia makes our recent quarrel with Germany appear petty and unnatural. Can it not be confidently predicted that the bonds which now join us to Germany as together we mourn the fate of those who perished in their duty will make the coming diplomatic conference at Berlin a council of friends, not a quarrel of restless rivals?"[54]

As American commissioners to the Berlin conference, Blaine appointed John A. Kasson, a former Representative and a former minister to Austria-Hungary and to Germany; George H. Bates, who had recently made an official visit to Samoa; and William Walter Phelps, Blaine's close friend. The German commissioners were Count Herbert Bismarck (the Chancellor's son), Baron Friedrich von Holstein, and Dr. Richard Krauel; the British, Sir Edward Malet, Charles Stewart Scott, and Joseph Crowe. Blaine's instructions reflected America's deepening interest in the Pacific. They mentioned the need of a Pago Pago naval station; "our commerce with the East . . . developing largely and rapidly"; and "the certainty of an early

52. Bayard to Arco-Valley, Feb. 5, 1889, *Papers Relating to the Foreign Relations of the United States, 1889* (Washington, 1890), pp. 194–95.
53. J. A. C. Gray, "The Apia Hurricane of 1889," *United States Naval Institute Proceedings,* LXXXVI (1960), 35; Stevenson, *Foot-Note to History,* ch. 10.
54. *Public Opinion,* VI (April 6, 1889), 571–72.

opening of an Isthmian transit from the Atlantic to the Pacific (under American protection)."[55] Convening on April 29, 1889, the conference reached agreement with surprisingly little difficulty. By the General Act (as the Berlin treaty was called), signed June 14, 1889, Germany agreed to restore Malietoa Laupepa as King. Samoa would be independent, but her independence would be severely qualified. A chief justice, appointed by the three powers (or if they could not agree, by the King of Sweden and Norway), would have the final decision on disputes regarding the Samoan King or between one of the powers and Samoa. The former Apia municipal council would be restored; its president, to be nominated by a neutral country if the three powers could not agree, would advise the King.[56] The Senate approved the General Act on February 6, 1890, after a short debate;[57] Germany, Great Britain, and also Samoa ratified it.

For the first time in her history the United States found herself committed to help govern an overseas people. Not only that, but she was participating in an extremely entangling arrangement with two great European powers, and in a place where her existing interests were very limited. An American who just after the Civil War had tried to guess where overseas rule would first occur would have selected Cuba or Santo Domingo or Hawaii or several other places long before Samoa. But if the United States would neither abandon the islands nor consent to a mandatory or partition, she had no alternative except to govern them with Great Britain and Germany. According to the German minister at Washington, Blaine disliked this outcome, thought that Samoa was worth little to the United States, and said that if only public opinion would permit he would consider transferring to Germany the American claims.[58] But of course he did no such thing. The United States was in Samoa—and also in Hawaii—to stay.

55. Blaine to Kasson, Phelps, and Bates, April 11, 1889, *Foreign Relations*, p. 201.
56. Malloy, *Treaties*, II, 1576–89. Regarding Germany's opposition to Mataafa see William Walter Phelps to Blaine, Sept. 4, 1889, James G. Blaine Papers, Library of Congress (Washington).
57. *Journal of the Executive Proceedings of the Senate* . . . (Washington, 1901), XXVII, 422–24 (Feb. 4, 1890), 424–25 (Feb. 5, 1890), 434–35 (Feb. 6, 1890).
58. Stolberg-Wernigerode, *Germany and the United States*, pp. 266–67.

CHAPTER 5

# Commercial Expansion in the 1880s

FOR several decades the settlement of the west coast had been turning American attention toward territorial expansion overseas—especially in Central America, the site of a potential canal; in the Caribbean Sea; and in the Hawaiian Islands. Over the same years economic developments were creating pressure for commercial expansion. During the decades after the Civil War the American economy was growing at a tremendous rate. The gross national product quadrupled, rising from $9,110,000,000 for 1869–1873 to $37,100,000,000 for 1897–1901. The gross farm product almost tripled, increasing from a value of $1,484,000,000 in 1860 to one of $3,799,000,000 in 1900. In 1865, 35,085 miles of railway were under operation; in 1899, 250,143. As for manufacturing, the production index jumped from 17 in 1865 all the way to 100 in 1900.[1]

As one consequence of this extraordinary economic growth, exports mounted steadily. From 1865 to 1900 total exports increased in value from $281 million to $1,394 million. Exports to the United Kingdom rose in value from $103 million to $534 million; to Germany, from $20 million to $187 million; to France, from $11 million to $83 million; to Canada, from $29 million to $95 million; and to Cuba, from $19 million to $26 million.[2] Imports, too, were increasing, though less rapidly. As is to be expected in the case of a new

1. U.S. Bureau of the Census, *Historical Statistics of the United States, Colonial Times to 1957* (Washington, 1961), pp. 139, 284, 427, 429, 409.
2. *Ibid.,* pp. 550–51.

and underdeveloped country, imports had exceeded exports for many years; but the traditional pattern reversed itself in 1876, the centennial year, when merchandise exports first began to exceed imports consistently.

The historic change meant that the United States was producing a greater value of goods than she consumed. In the late 1870s and early 1880s informed people were becoming aware of this unfamiliar situation, a situation seeming to require the urgent cultivation of foreign markets. Thus as early as 1877 Abram S. Hewitt, a member of Congress from New York, thought that the country needed foreign markets "more than any other thing"; and in 1881 John A. Kasson (later on, the American delegate at the Samoan conference in Berlin) warned that if the United States did not find markets for her agricultural and industrial goods, "our surplus will soon roll back from the Atlantic coast upon the interior, and the wheels of prosperity will be clogged by the very richness of the burden which they carry, but cannot deliver."[3] Secretary of State Evarts found that all thinking people were worrying about "how to create a foreign demand for those manufactures which are left after supplying our home demand"; and in 1880 he inaugurated monthly consular reports giving up-to-date information about trade openings.[4] American participation in international exhibitions testified to the interest in foreign markets. Congress made appropriations for American displays at many exhibitions, at Vienna in 1873, Sydney in 1879, Berlin in 1880, Melbourne in 1880 and 1888, London in 1883, Barcelona and Brussels in 1888, and Paris in 1867, 1878, 1889, 1890, and 1900.[5]

Export promotion was chiefly the occupation not of the government but of thousands of individual producers who turned to foreign markets to absorb the goods they did not sell at home. But increasingly as the post–Civil War years passed, the government,

3. *Congressional Record,* 45 Cong., 1 Sess., p. 538 (Nov. 19, 1877); John A. Kasson, "The Monroe Doctrine in 1881," *North American Review,* CXXXIII (1881), 533.

4. Edward C. Kirkland, *Industry Comes of Age: Business, Labor, and Public Policy, 1860–1897* (New York, 1961), pp. 291–92; Brainerd Dyer, *The Public Career of William M. Evarts* (Berkeley, 1933), p. 238.

5. Merle Curti, "America at the World Fairs, 1851–1893," *American Historical Review,* LV (1950), 833–56; Joseph M. Rogers, "Lessons from International Expositions," *Forum,* XXXII (1901), 500–10; *House Reports,* 47 Cong., 1 Sess., No. 1413 (Serial 2069), pp. 1–2.

too, concerned itself in the matter; and because of the worry about the surplus (as it was beginning to be called), and also because of an economic depression in 1884, administrations in the late 1870s and especially in the 1880s made unprecedented efforts to expand exports. The worry about overproduction was considerably less than it was to become during the great depression of the 1890s, and consequently these early moves to foster exports occupied a relatively small part of official attention. Nonetheless, already in the 1880s commercial expansion in the New World, in Europe, and even in darkest Africa and little known areas in Asia was an important objective of United States foreign policy.

Some historians have strongly emphasized the agricultural and industrial surplus, with the consequent desire for commercial expansion abroad; they have depicted Washington, responsive to lobbying by special business interests, as preoccupied with commercial expansion—which frequently led also to territorial expansion; and they have argued that the foreign markets which were opened up to the burgeoning American exports constituted just as real an empire as if the Stars and Stripes had flown over these lands.[6] Although throughout the ages commercial expansion has sometimes been the precursor of territorial expansion, it is an oversimplification virtually to equate these two types of expansion. The question of their relationship is a complicated one, but in the present context it is sufficient to say that the political control associated with colonization assures a degree of continuity and certainty in trade and other arrangements that is unobtainable in an informal commercial "empire." Thus the United States, as we shall observe, became dissatisfied with the commercial control of Hawaii given by the reciprocity treaty and decided that outright political control was essential.

At any rate American administrations during the 1880s, which on the whole opposed colonization on principle, did not consider commercial expansion as a substitute for territorial expansion, although a few individuals did, including, probably, Secretary of State Frederick T. Frelinghuysen. For various reasons these administrations looked to Mexico, the west coast of South America, and the Caribbean islands, as New World markets that should be cultivated. Whereas it was mainly for reasons of security and naval strategy

6. See especially the writings of William A. Williams, and Walter LaFeber, *The New Empire: An Interpretation of American Expansion, 1860–1898* (Ithaca, 1963).

(although the influence of trade was already great too) that Washington directed its attention to the potential canal, the Caribbean, Hawaii, and Samoa, the strategic consideration was less significant in policy toward Mexico and South America. As regards Mexico, America's main purpose was simply to protect the Texan border from marauders, but the wish to gain a new market became increasingly strong. As regards South America, both ideology and strategy were important—the feeling, strongly encouraged by the Monroe Doctrine, that by the nature of things, as well as for her national security, the United States rather than Europe should shape Latin American destiny; but for a time in 1881 and 1882 American party politics strongly influenced foreign policy, and at all times export promotion was a major consideration.

To Rutherford B. Hayes's Secretary of State, William M. Evarts (whose role at the Geneva arbitration we have observed), fell the task of dealing with Mexico over a turbulent state of affairs on the Texan-Mexican boundary. Evarts was one of the most prominent living Americans, a leader of the American bar who had defended President Andrew Johnson in the impeachment trial of 1868. But despite his great abilities he was a mediocre Secretary of State. With little training for the position and little interest in it, he had no trouble finding plenty of time to absent himself from the State Department. Not much happened, as a matter of fact, that needed his presence, apart from the dispute with Mexico. In no previous administration had there been such a paucity of foreign-policy developments. Only three pages of Hayes's annual message in 1877 concerned foreign relations, only two in 1878, only four the next year; and in his 1880 message the President could truthfully say: "Our relations with all foreign countries have been those of undisturbed peace...."[7]

In the thinly populated desert along the Texan-Mexican border roamed bands of Indians, outlaws, and cattle thieves. Frequently raiding into the United States and then retreating to safety in Mexico, they spread disorder in southern Texas.[8] After Maximilian's

7. James D. Richardson (ed.), *A Compilation of the Messages and Papers of the Presidents, 1789–1897* (10 vols., Washington, 1899), VII, 606.

8. Robert D. Gregg, *The Influence of Border Troubles on Relations between the United States and Mexico, 1876–1910* (Baltimore, 1937); Daniel Cosío Villegas, *The United States versus Porfirio Díaz* (Lincoln, Neb., 1963), pp. 39–40. On a so-called Free Zone see *House Miscellaneous Documents*, 40 Cong., 3 Sess., No. 16 (Serial 1385); *Senate Reports*, 41 Cong., 2 Sess., No. 166 (Serial 1409); *ibid.*, 42 Cong., 3 Sess., No. 39 (Serial 1565), pp. 39–41.

assassination Mexico had been governed fairly well for a few years, but in 1876 a rebellion broke out under Porfirio Díaz; he was elected President in 1877, just before Hayes entered the White House, but at first his hold on power was shaky. Hayes's own position was weak. He may not, by a fair count, have won the election of 1876, and for months after election day uncertainty prevailed as to whether he or his Democratic opponent would be President. Even after Hayes's inauguration the situation continued to be uncertain; the British Legation in Washington believed that "at no time probably, except that which immediately preceded the Secession of the Southern States, have there been more elements of internal danger in the Union. . . ."[9] Weak governments do not make for strong foreign policies.

At first the United States refused to recognize the new Mexican regime. Evarts insisted that Díaz, before being recognized, take steps to suppress the border bandits.[10] Mexico refused to act without diplomatic relations. On June 1, 1877, the Secretary of War issued directives, for Brigadier General Edward O. C. Ord in command in Texas, "that in case the lawless incursions continue, he will be at liberty, in the use of his own discretion, when in pursuit of a band of the marauders, and when his troops are either in sight of them or upon a fresh trail, to follow them across the Rio Grande, and to overtake and punish them. . . ."[11] Mexico erupted with rage. She believed that highly placed Americans wanted war. Díaz had revoked some concessions given Americans by his precedessor, and these people hoped for his downfall.[12] The outcry forced Díaz to respond in kind to the hated Ord order. He instructed Mexican troops to attack American troops entering Mexico: "You will repel force by force should the invasion take place."[13] With Ord authorized to invade Mexico and Mexicans directed to repel him, a clash

9. F. R. Plunkett to Foreign Secretary Lord Derby, Nov. 17, 1877, Public Record Office (London), Foreign Office 5/1580.

10. Assistant Secretary of State Frederick W. Seward to Foster, May 16, 1877, *House Reports*, 45 Cong., 2 Sess., No. 701 (Serial 1824), p. 447.

11. Secretary of War George W. McCrary to General William T. Sherman, June 1, 1877, *House Executive Documents*, 45 Cong., 1 Sess., No. 13 (Serial 1773), pp. 99–100.

12. Foster to Evarts, June 22, 1877, *ibid.*, p. 20; J. Fred Rippy, *The United States and Mexico* (New York, 1931), pp. 296–97; Gregg, *Border Troubles*, p. 22.

13. Minister of War Pedro Ogazon to General Gerónimo Treviño, June 18, 1877, *House Executive Documents*, 45 Cong., 1 Sess., No. 13, pp. 102–3.

had become just as probable as Ord chose to make it. In June 1877, Mexican soldiers pursued some foes of Díaz into Texas. Evarts protested stiffly; Mexico apologized, but in the same breath demanded modification of the Ord order. Two months later bandits raided Texas, and then Mexico protested an invasion by the United States army.[14] In September and December American troops again moved south of the Rio Grande. The American minister to Mexico, John W. Foster, observed growing Mexican anger and a belief that hostilities could hardly be avoided.[15]

The United States, too, was concerned, and Congress reflected the anxiety. The concern arose from fears not of a possible war but of losing a potential market. In early 1878 the Senate appointed a committee to study ways of promoting commerce with Mexico, and the House considered resolutions calling upon Hayes to explain his refusal to recognize Díaz.[16] The congressional restiveness may have tipped the scales in favor of recognition. On March 23, 1878, Evarts issued instructions to recognize Díaz. The new regime, he stated rather lamely, seemed to think that recognition would promote a settlement, and so "it is better for this government to waive its own preferences as to the fittest manner and time of adjusting the difficulties. . . ."[17]

The Secretary tried to save face by telling Foster to make an agreement for reciprocal border-crossing privileges. But having obtained a major American retreat by sitting tight, Díaz was unlikely to change tactics. Everything now centered on the Ord order. Díaz demanded its withdrawal prior to negotiations—whereas Evarts declared that withdrawal would occur only when Mexico accepted arrangements making the order unnecessary. Once again, the famil-

14. Evarts to Foster, June 21, 1877, *ibid.*, p. 15; Foster to Evarts, July 9, 1877, *ibid.*, p. 34; Governor Richard B. Hubbard to Hayes, Aug. 13, 1877, *ibid.*, p. 43; Foreign Minister I. L. Vallarta to Chargé d'Affaires José T. De Cuellar, Aug. 18, 1877, *ibid.*, pp. 61–68.

15. De Cuellar to Evarts, Dec. 14, 1877, *Papers Relating to the Foreign Relations of the United States, 1878* (Washington, 1878), pp. 664–66; Foster to Evarts, Jan. 17, 1878, *ibid.*, pp. 540–41.

16. *Congressional Record*, 45 Cong., 2 Sess., p. 290 (Jan. 11, 1878), p. 1664 (March 11, 1878), p. 120 (Dec. 11, 1877); Gregg, *Border Troubles*, p. 79, 79n; *Historical Statistics*, pp. 550–51.

17. Evarts to Foster, March 23, 1878, *Foreign Relations, 1878*, pp. 543–44; James M. Callahan, *American Foreign Policy in Mexican Relations* (New York, 1932), p. 395; Gregg, *Border Troubles*, p. 80.

iar sequence of events repeated itself. In June 1878, American troops, pursuing raiders, invaded Mexico; the United States, Evarts threatened, would not tolerate the plundering of her soil, and revocation of the order "cannot now be entertained."[18] Anti-American feeling reached a climax on Mexico's national holiday, September 15, 1878, when an outburst of threatening cries in a theater in Mexico City that Foster was attending caused him to contemplate fleeing to the Legation.[19] At the end of the year, months after recognition, nothing was clearer than Díaz's refusal to settle anything without the termination of the Ord order.

Fortunately, border conditions were improving. During the last months of 1878 nearly complete quiet prevailed, and in October 1879 General Ord himself (perhaps inspired by an administration seeking a pretext to retreat) pronounced the order no longer necessary because Mexico was now suppressing the raids. On February 24, 1880, almost three years after its issuance, Washington withdrew the order.[20]

The improved conditions undoubtedly contributed to the government's action, but one suspects that the desire of American business interests to cultivate the nearby market was strongly influential in this matter, as well as in the decision to recognize Díaz. For some time Díaz had been making offers of lucrative trade and investment if only Hayes would mitigate his stand.[21] In a widely noticed speech in Chicago in the summer of 1878 the Mexican minister at Washington, Manuel Zamacona, had emphasized to the Manufacturers' Association of the Northwest "the astonishing fact" that whereas American exports found their way to distant Australia, the Indies, and South America, they largely bypassed adjacent Mexico.[22] But this lamentable state of affairs was not to endure. Follow-

18. Evarts to Foster, Aug. 13, 1878, *Foreign Relations, 1878,* pp. 573–74.

19. John W. Foster, *Diplomatic Memoirs* (2 vols., Boston and New York, 1909), I, 101–2; Rippy, *United States and Mexico,* p. 308.

20. Annual Report of the Secretary of War, Oct. 1, 1879, *House Executive Documents,* 46 Cong., 2 Sess., No. 1, Pt. 2 (Serial 1903), I, 93; Secretary of War Alexander Ramsey to General of the Army, Feb. 24, 1880, *Papers Relating to the Foreign Relations of the United States, 1880* (Washington, 1880), pp. 735–36.

21. Rippy, *United States and Mexico,* pp. 304, 310; Gregg, *Border Troubles,* pp. 119–20; David M. Pletcher, "Mexico Opens the Door to American Capital," *The Americas,* XVI (1959), 4.

22. Foster to Evarts, Oct. 9, 1878, *House Executive Documents,* 45 Cong., 3 Sess., No. 15 (Serial 1852), pp. 1–2; Pletcher, "Mexico Opens the Door," pp. 3–4.

ing the settlement of 1880 United States exports to Mexico increased dramatically. Whereas in the 1870s they had hovered around an annual value of $6 million (about a sixth of the exports to Canada), they rose to a value of $11 million in 1881, $15 million in 1882, and $17 million in 1883. Moreover, in September 1880 Mexico awarded two American companies concessions for railways, and at various later dates she gave Americans dozens of mining and other railway concessions.[23]

In March 1881 Hayes and Evarts were succeeded by James A. Garfield and James G. Blaine. At once one of the most revered and detested of American politicians, Blaine from around 1877 until his death in 1893 was (except during Garfield's brief tenure) the nation's outstanding Republican and the party's presidential nominee in 1884, when he lost by a hairbreadth to Grover Cleveland. Brilliant, resourceful, dynamic, with great magnetism and a vivid personality, Blaine might have become an outstanding Secretary of State. His "spirited policy," as it was called (a "pugilistic policy" in the view of his critics, who denounced him as "Jingo Jim"), envisaged an "American system" developing greater influence in Central America, where, he thought, a canal should soon be constructed, and also in the Caribbean and Hawaii. These basic objectives fitted America's needs of the time, and Blaine would doubtless have pursued them vigorously if he had been granted the eight consecutive years in the State Department that he had reason to expect. Overseas expansion and decisive steps toward building a canal—similar to the developments at the end of the century— might well have occurred a decade or more earlier, and their main author would have been James G. Blaine.

But Blaine's weaknesses perhaps surpassed his strengths. His distrust of Europe did not serve the national interest. He was excessively political, notably in his penchant for cultivating the Irish at Great Britain's expense. He was inclined to use his power to do favors for his friends; this failing led to widespread suspicion of corruption (which, however, has never been proved). Restless, impatient, and impulsive, he was deficient in the prudence and steady

23. *Historical Statistics*, pp. 550–51; Frank A. Knapp, Jr., "Precursors of American Investment in Mexican Railroads," *Pacific Historical Review*, XXI (1952), 62; Pletcher, "Mexico Opens the Door," pp. 5–6, 13; John W. Foster, *Diplomatic Memoirs* (2 vols., Boston, 1909), II, 111.

persistence essential to good diplomacy. Would his merits have outweighed his failings? No one can know because circumstances prevented him from having a fair test.

In the Republican convention of 1880 Blaine had been the leader in blocking Ulysses S. Grant's nomination for a third term, and in swinging the convention to Garfield. Chester A. Arthur, a Grant man, was nominated for the vice-presidency. But the split between the Blaine-Garfield "Halfbreeds" and the Grant "Stalwarts" was bitter. On July 2, 1881, after less than four months in office, Garfield was shot by a self-proclaimed Stalwart who hailed Arthur as President. For more than two months Garfield lingered, with no one knowing whether he would recover or not. He died on September 19, 1881. During the weeks of uncertainty Blaine's position was precarious; a coherent foreign policy was impossible. After Arthur succeeded to the presidency, he kept Blaine as Secretary of State for three months, a period during which Blaine's position was little easier than when Garfield was dying.

Apart from politics, Blaine during his tenure of the State Department was occupied mainly by a minor Mexican-Guatemalan boundary controversy, and by one more important affair, the War of the Pacific. The Secretary was apprehensive about European, especially British, influence in Latin America. He hoped to counter this by promoting an association of New World republics under the benevolent supervision of the United States, an association free of war because its members would pledge themselves to arbitrate their disputes. Although Blaine had genuine solicitude for Latin American welfare, he was by no means forgetful of the United States. Latin Americans imported most of their manufactured goods from Europe, and to the Secretary and his many business supporters this was most unfortunate. Blaine expected that Latin America, once the New World republics were associated together, would buy its industrial goods from its great neighbor to the north instead of from Europe. Thus the United States would acquire markets that were beginning to seem essential for her prosperity.

The improvement in Mexican-American relations following the accord of 1880 occurred in the face of an unwise intervention by the United States in the dispute between Mexico and Guatemala. Both Latin American countries claimed the border state of Chiapas, and in 1881 war seemed imminent. The Guatemalan dictator, Justo

Rufino Barrios, wanted to create a Central American political union. Welcoming the prospect of stability in a strategic area, Blaine sided with Guatemala, thereby incensing Mexico. But after he left office, Washington became more impartial; Guatemala had to yield, and in 1882 she recognized Mexico's title to Chiapas.[24]

The War of the Pacific between Peru and Bolivia on one side and Chile on the other began early in 1879, when Evarts was still Secretary of State. Bolivia's role was slight, and may be largely disregarded. Chile and Peru had close ties with Europe, far closer than with the United States. Peru had borrowed heavily from Europe, mainly from Great Britain; as security she offered the enormous holdings of guano and nitrates in her southern province of Tarapacá. She and Bolivia were no match for Chile, whose army, pushing northward, cut off Bolivia from the ocean and seized Tarapacá. In the summer of 1880 the Chileans took the provinces of Tacna and Arica, north of Tarapacá, and an end of the fighting seemed near. At this juncture Britain and France suggested joint mediation with the United States, but Evarts, true to the general American feeling that Europe should not interfere in the New World, declined the proposal. Instead, he offered mediation. Delegates from Chile, Peru, and Bolivia, together with the American ministers to those countries, met in October 1880 on the United States warship *Lackawanna* off the town of Arica. Chile demanded Tarapacá; Peru and Bolivia insisted on United States arbitration. The meeting broke up in failure.[25] Chile resumed her northward march, capturing Lima, Peru's capital, early in 1881. Organized fighting by Peru collapsed; however, a Peruvian named Francisco García Calderón established a provisional government near Lima.

This was the situation bequeathed to Secretary of State Blaine in

24. Blaine to Cornelius A. Logan (American minister to Central America), May 7, 1881, *Papers Relating to the Foreign Relations of the United States, 1881* (Washington, 1882), p. 102; Blaine to Philip H. Morgan (American minister to Mexico), June 21, Nov. 28, 1881, *ibid.*, pp. 768–69, 814–17; Secretary of State Frederick T. Frelinghuysen to Matías Romero (Mexican minister to the United States), March 24, 1882, *House Executive Documents*, 48 Cong., 1 Sess., No. 154 (Serial 2207), pp. 94, 188–90; David M. Pletcher, *The Awkward Years: American Foreign Relations under Garfield and Arthur* (Columbia, Mo., 1962), pp. 106–11.

25. Evarts to Thomas A. Osborn (American minister to Chile), July 29, 1880, *Senate Executive Documents*, 47 Cong., 1 Sess., No. 79 (Serial 1989), p. 116; Evarts to Isaac P. Christiancy (American minister to Peru), July 30, 1880, *ibid.*, p. 385; Christiancy to Evarts, Oct. 27, 1880, *ibid.*, p. 403.

March 1881. He viewed the conflict apprehensively. Interviewed by the press after he had left office, he declared that Britain had equipped the Chilean army and navy. "I think the result of this Peru-Chilian war destroys American influence on the South Pacific coast and literally wipes out American commercial interests in that vast region." He told a congressional committee: "It is a perfect mistake to speak of this as a Chilian war on Peru. It is an English war on Peru, with Chili as the instrument, and I take the responsibility of that assertion."[26] His basic purpose as Secretary was to bolster Peru as a counterweight to Chile and the latter's European mentor —if that could be done without resort to force, since he certainly did not want war. The United States would thereby enhance her security and gain a larger South American market for her booming industries. But the political circumstances of 1881 precluded effective action to realize these objectives.

Before Garfield's assassination about the only thing Blaine did to implement his anti-British, anti-Chilean, pro-Peruvian policy was to support Calderón. His political foes charged later that, in backing Peru, he had been moved by dishonest considerations: he had wanted Peru to keep her guano and nitrates because he had a hidden financial interest in them. In 1882 a House committee investigated the accusation but uncovered no convincing evidence against Blaine.[27]

If Blaine's own actions were restrained, the same cannot be said of his minister to Peru, Stephen A. Hurlbut (Grant's former minister to Colombia). Hurlbut gave the Chilean commander in Lima, Admiral Patricio Lynch, a memorandum warning Chile not to take territory unless Peru refused to pay an indemnity; and he issued a "Declaration to the Notables of Lima" announcing that Washington opposed any forced dismemberment of Peru. He tried to persuade Argentina to send a minister to Lima, a move alarming to Chile, since her own relations with Argentina were strained. He signed an agreement with Calderón giving the United States a naval base at a town named Chimbote. When Calderón's imminent arrest was

26. Washington *Post,* Jan. 30, 1882; testimony of April 26, 1882, *House Reports,* 47 Cong., 1 Sess., No. 1790 (Serial 2070), p. 217.
27. *House Reports,* 47 Cong., 1 Sess., No. 1790, *passim.* For indictments of Blaine see *Congressional Record,* 47 Cong., 1 Sess., pp. 5639–47 (July 5, 1882), and Perry Belmont, *Recollections of an American Democrat . . .* (New York, 1941), chs. 7, 8.

rumored, Hurlbut placed the Peruvian archives in the American Legation.[28] All this he did without any authorization from Washington. In the opinion of the amazed British minister at Lima, Hurlbut had taken Calderón and Peru under his protection and had encouraged in the Peruvians delusions of peace terms completely unacceptable to Chile.[29] Disturbed by Calderón's growing popularity, Chile arrested the provisional president on November 6, 1881, and spirited him away to Santiago. In Hurlbut's view, which Blaine heard with indignation, she intended the arrest "to be understood by the people at large as the reply of Chili to the known support of that [Calderón] government by the United States."[30]

Hurlbut later claimed to have received secret oral instructions from Garfield and Blaine that justified his behavior.[31] This is unlikely in view of the fact that the Secretary censured the bumptious minister severely. He delayed a long time, it is true, but in November 1881 he rebuked Hurlbut for almost everything he had done; as for Chimbote he called the project "desirable" but "not opportune."[32] No doubt Blaine was remiss in not curbing Hurlbut sooner, but this does not establish the charge of corruption. The simple explanation is, no doubt, the breakdown of government in Washington following Garfield's assassination.

In November, after his successor had already been named, Blaine decided to adopt a much stronger policy: one of active mediation and envisaging close association with the Latin American republics. The mediation move, which apparently had President Arthur's approval,[33] took the form of a special mission to Chile, Peru, and Bolivia. It was headed by William H. Trescot, an outstanding diplomat; he was assisted by Blaine's able son, Walker. Blaine's instruc-

28. Hurlbut to Lynch, Aug. 25, 1881, *Senate Executive Documents*, 47 Cong., 1 Sess., No. 79, pp. 516–17; Hurlbut to Blaine, Oct. 4, 5, 26, Dec. 22, 1881, *ibid.*, pp. 526–28, 530–31, 537–39, 591–93; Pletcher, *Awkward Years*, p. 49; Herbert Millington, *American Diplomacy and the War of the Pacific* (New York, 1948), p. 93.
29. Spenser St. John to Foreign Secretary Lord Granville, Sept. 28, Oct. 4, 1881, Foreign Office 61/334.
30. Hurlbut to Blaine, Nov. 9, 1881, *Senate Executive Documents*, 47 Cong., 1 Sess., No. 79, p. 561.
31. Hurlbut to his half-brother, William H. Hurlbert *(sic)*, Dec. 29, 1881, *House Reports*, 47 Cong., 1 Sess., No. 1790, p. 181.
32. Blaine to Hurlbut, Nov. 22, 1881, *Senate Executive Documents*, 47 Cong., 1 Sess., No. 79, pp. 565–66.
33. Washington *Post*, Jan. 30, 1882.

tions to Trescot cited Chile's supposed intent to affront the United States by arresting Calderón, and declared that diplomatic relations would be terminated if Santiago now avowed such a motive. Regarding Tarapacá, they called for payment of an indemnity by Peru rather than the province's cession to Chile, and warned that if Chile insisted on taking a large part of Peru, the United States would consider appealing to the other Latin American countries "to join it in an effort to avert consequences which cannot be confined to Chili and Peru."[34] These were menacing words, but it is noteworthy that the Secretary threatened to break diplomatic relations only if Chile *now* admitted a desire to insult the United States, and he threatened further action against Chile only if other countries agreed to support it—both unlikely contingencies.

At the same time Blaine made a surprising move: he invited all the New World republics to meet in Washington in a year "for the purpose of considering and discussing the methods of preventing war between the nations of America."[35] He had earlier agreed with Garfield to issue such an invitation, but in November 1881 he must have intended it to reinforce the warning to Chile. Surely, however, his main thought was to strengthen his own political position for the presidential election of 1884. He could hope to take the credit whether Arthur held fast to the strong line against Chile and forced her to yield or adopted a softer policy that failed; and he could similarly reap the benefit whether the new administration went ahead with his invitation or recalled it. Blaine later declared that he had viewed the conference as a means of promoting United States exports; and it is true that when he again became Secretary of State in 1889 he presided over an inter-American conference at which trade was prominently discussed.

On December 20, 1881, before the Trescot mission had had time to accomplish anything, Frelinghuysen succeeded Blaine as Secretary of State. Like his uncle, Theodore Frelinghuysen, and his great-uncle, Frederick Frelinghuysen, he was a lawyer and had represented New Jersey in the United States Senate; his uncle had been

34. Blaine to Trescot, Dec. 1, 1881, *Senate Executive Documents*, 47 Cong., 1 Sess., No. 79, pp. 176, 179.
35. For the text see Blaine to Osborn, Nov. 29, 1881, *Foreign Relations, 1881*, pp. 13–15; the same communication, *mutatus mutandi*, was sent to the other Latin American countries. See also Russell H. Bastert, "A New Approach to the Origins of Blaine's Pan American Policy," *Hispanic American Historical Review*, XXXIX (1959), 403–5.

the Whig candidate for Vice-President on the ticket with Henry Clay in 1844. Frederick Theodore Frelinghuysen, the new Secretary, had had considerable governmental experience but none in diplomacy. In temperament he was the antithesis of his predecessor. Whereas Blaine was flamboyant and mercurial, Frelinghuysen was stolid, unimaginative, and methodical. Rather than spirited, his policy was deliberate and cautious; and it was usually calculated in terms of America's existing interests rather than her potential interests, which always concerned Blaine. But to those who thought Blaine dangerously reckless, Frelinghuysen's sober policy came as a heartfelt relief.

The Senate had previously called for the diplomatic correspondence regarding the War of the Pacific, and Blaine had indicated which parts could properly be made public. But on January 26, 1882, Frelinghuysen released everything, even the instructions to Trescot.[36] Presumably this action, like Blaine's recent moves, was politically motivated. As the British minister at Washington, Sir Lionel S. Sackville West, observed, Blaine's ". . . South American action was dictated by personal and electioneering motives and . . . the policy of Mr. Frelinghuysen in reversing it is in great measure simply to throw discredit on his predecessor." Walking down a Washington street, Bancroft Davis (Frelinghuysen's Assistant Secretary) had the bad luck to meet Mr. and Mrs. Blaine. "An iceberg was warm in comparison," he wrote his former chief, Hamilton Fish.[37]

Partly for this political reason, partly because he thought the United States should have a quieter policy, Frelinghuysen twice telegraphed Trescot, on his way to South America, not to offend Chile, and then wrote to him: "What the President does seek to do, is to extend the kindly offices of the United States impartially to both Peru and Chili. . . ." He canceled the parts of the instructions that could be construed as threatening Chile.[38] Before receiving the revised instructions, Trescot arrived in Santiago and had several

36. *Congressional Record*, 47 Cong., 1 Sess., p. 79 (Dec. 13, 1881); the correspondence is in *Senate Executive Documents*, 47 Cong., 1 Sess., No. 79.
37. Sackville West to Granville, March 26, 1882, Foreign Office 5/1786; Davis to Fish, Feb. 4, 1882, John C. Bancroft Davis Papers, Library of Congress (Washington).
38. Frelinghuysen to Trescot, Jan. 3, 1882, *Papers Relating to the Foreign Relations of the United States, 1882* (Washington, 1883), p. 56; Frelinghuysen to American consul at Panama (for Trescot), Jan. 4, 1882, *ibid.*, p. 57; Frelinghuysen to Trescot, Jan. 9, 1882, *ibid.*, pp. 57–58.

talks with Foreign Minister José M. Balmaceda, who gave satisfactory assurances regarding Calderón's arrest and accepted American good offices in arranging a peace. Then came a bombshell. During a conversation on January 31, 1882, Balmaceda interjected: "It is useless. . . . Your instructions from Mr. Blaine have been published, and others are on their way to you modifying your original instructions in very important particulars." The American could not hide his astonishment. That a foreign government should be better informed about his mission than he himself was humiliating to a degree. He rebuked Frelinghuysen for having published the instructions.[39] His indignation was justified. The Chilean Legation in Washington had cabled Balmaceda the information, via Paris. It was disgraceful that Frelinghuysen had not bothered to cable his envoy; his disclosure of the secret correspondence was also indefensible.

But Trescot did his best to obtain the moderate peace terms desired by Washington. Chile would not back down; her military superiority over Peru was overwhelming, and she had nothing to fear from the United States, who had little naval strength and whose peaceful intentions had now been laid bare. She was not going to be balked of her guano and nitrates by Frelinghuysen's gentle exhortations.

There was no point in Trescot's remaining in Santiago. On March 28 he arrived in Lima. The day before, Hurlbut had suddenly died. Thousands of grieving Peruvians lined the streets and decked his bier with flowers as it moved to the railway station. "The deceased gentleman . . . was looked upon by the natives as the Champion of the country," a British Legation officer explained.[40] Hurlbut dead in Lima (and the American minister to Chile had died in Santiago a few months before), the secret correspondence published, previous policies reversed, Trescot humiliated—to such a ludicrous pass had America's makeshift diplomacy arrived in the spring of 1882. And in August of that year Arthur—acting again, no doubt, from political considerations—withdrew the invitations to the inter-American peace conference.[41]

With Trescot's departure from Santiago, America's role in the

39. Trescot to Frelinghuysen, Feb. 3, 1882, *Senate Executive Documents*, 47 Cong., 1 Sess., No. 181 (Serial 1991), pp. 12, 17, 19.
40. W. E. Graham to Granville, March 30, 1882, Froeign Office 61/399.
41. Frelinghuysen to Osborn, Aug. 9, 1882, *Foreign Relations, 1882*, p. 4; the same communication, *mutatus mutandi*, was sent to the other invited countries.

War of the Pacific pretty much ended; however, she continued intermittently her mediation efforts. Eventually Chile accepted somewhat milder terms, although Peru had to cede Tarapacá. Chile emerged from the conflict much stronger, of course; British influence there became even greater. And Blaine's hopes of stimulating United States exports to South America were dealt a devastating blow.

If Frelinghuysen displayed little interest in South America, he was unusually zealous in promoting exports to islands in the Caribbean Sea and to Hawaii, nearby areas with which he believed that the United States, for security as well as commercial reasons, should have close ties. For although he did want an American isthmian canal, he apparently considered close commercial relations as a substitute for the Hawaiian and Caribbean bases whose annexation he opposed. Export promotion as such was not a party matter; both Democrats and Republicans agreed it was essential. But whereas Democrats argued that exports could most effectively be stimulated by overall tariff reduction, Republicans sometimes advocated reciprocity treaties. Frelinghuysen drew up several such treaties with Caribbean countries and colonies, but Congress refused to accept any of them. His only success was the renewal of the Hawaiian reciprocity treaty. Despite the failures, however, the treaties reflected the increasing attention to America's exporting requirements and therefore need brief mention.

The treaty that came nearest to being ratified was with Mexico. In 1882 President Arthur appointed as commissioners to make a commercial treaty no less a person than Ulysses S. Grant and also William S. Trescot, back from his frustrating experiences in Santiago. These men and the Mexican minister at Washington, Matías Romero, negotiated a treaty, signed in January 1883, by which Mexico agreed to admit duty-free a number of American goods, mainly industrial, and the United States agreed to import duty-free several Mexican goods, including tobacco and sugar. The Senate approved the treaty in 1884 with an amendment requiring enabling legislation by the House.[42] This was to cause trouble.

Frelinghuysen also wanted reciprocity with several other nearby

42. William M. Malloy (ed.), *Treaties, Conventions, International Acts, Protocols and Agreements between the United States of America and Other Powers, 1776–1909* (2 vols., Washington, 1910), I, 1146–52; *House Reports*, 48 Cong., 1 Sess., No. 1848 (Serial 2258), p. 1; *Congressional Record*, 48 Cong., 1 Sess., p. 1775 (March 11, 1884).

areas, including the Spanish colonies of Cuba and Puerto Rico. He sent John W. Foster (the former minister to Mexico) to Madrid as minister, with instructions to conclude a treaty. This Foster successfully accomplished. His treaty, signed in November 1884, provided for duty-free import into the United States of many Cuban and Puerto Rican goods (including sugar and tobacco), and for duty-free import into those islands of many United States industrial and agricultural goods. An elated Foster predicted that the treaty would give the United States a near-monopoly of Cuba's trade, and that —and here he made a classic linkage of commercial and territorial expansion—"It will be annexing Cuba in the most desirable way."[43] A similar treaty was signed with Santo Domingo in December 1884; treaties with Great Britain (for the British West Indies), and with various other Latin American countries, were negotiated or considered but not signed.

Both the Dominican and the Spanish treaties went to the Senate at the end of 1884. The month before, Grover Cleveland, a strong advocate of general tariff reduction rather than reciprocity, had won the presidential election. Under his prompting the Senate disregarded the Dominican treaty, which sank into oblivion. The Spanish treaty was subjected to such a storm of invective by tobacco and sugar interests (no less intent on thwarting Caribbean reciprocity than Hawaiian) that the Senate refused to vote.[44] When Cleveland took office, he promptly withdrew the treaty.[45] It was never resurrected. As for the Grant-Romero treaty, the one reciprocity treaty that the Senate had approved, the House declined to act until Cleveland was in the White House; then, in 1886, the Democratic House shelved an enabling bill before it.[46] That was the end of the treaty.

Latin America was a natural market for the United States, but the Congo River basin was a strange place to which to attach hopes for commercial expansion. American interest in the Congo had been whetted by articles in the New York *Herald* describing vast trade opportunities there. In 1869 the *Herald* sent Henry M. Stanley (a

43. Foster to Secretary of the Treasury Walter Q. Gresham, Oct. 26, 1884, Pletcher, *Awkward Years*, p. 297; the text of the treaty is in *Congressional Record*, 48 Cong., 2 Sess., pp. 148–56 (Dec. 10, 1884).

44. Pletcher, *Awkward Years*, pp. 305–6; *Congressional Record*, 48 Cong., 2 Sess., p. 412 (Dec. 22, 1884), p. 422 (Dec. 23, 1884), p. 464 (Jan. 5, 1885), *Index*, p. 160.

45. Special message, March 13, 1885, Richardson, *Messages and Papers*, VIII, 303.

46. *Congressional Record*, 49 Cong., 1 Sess., p. 7341 (July 22, 1886).

British subject who mistakenly believed he had acquired American citizenship) to search for the Scottish missionary David Livingstone, who had disappeared in the Dark Continent. Stanley's sensational discovery of Livingstone directed worldwide attention to sub-Saharan Africa, and his subsequent explorations of the Congo continued to thrill a large public.

The Arthur administration decided that the Congo offered a promising field for exports. Its decision was in large measure the result of the lobbying of Colonel Henry S. Sanford, a flamboyant former American diplomat and a speculator in Florida real estate. Sanford was deeply interested in Africa; in 1879 he had advised the State Department that the Congo country could relieve the overproduction that was worrying some American industrialists.[47] Sanford (as well as Stanley) was an agent of King Leopold II of Belgium, who was scheming to develop the Congo. In November 1883 Sanford talked with the right people in Washington about an African International Association that Leopold was sponsoring. To his delight, President Arthur was "influenced by the idea of covering those unclad millions with our domestic cottons. He saw the point suggested to him, that but three yards per capita would make an enormous aggregate for our cotton mills. . . ."[48]

The discovery of a potential market in Africa struck a responsive chord during the hard times of 1884. Congress considered the trade opportunities supposedly lurking in the Congo, as did also the influential New York Chamber of Commerce, and Secretary Frelinghuysen sent an agent there, who reported enthusiastically.[49] In view of such interest it was not altogether surprising that the United States, departing from precedent, participated in an international conference on the Congo that met in Berlin from November 1884 to February 1885. The chief American delegate was John A. Kasson, recently named minister to Germany (and later one of the American

47. Pletcher, *Awkward Years*, p. 311.
48. Henry S. Sanford, "American Interests in Africa," *Forum*, IX (1890), 412.
49. *Congressional Record*, 48 Cong., 1 Sess., p. 520 (Jan. 21, 1884), p. 1339 (Feb. 25, 1884), p. 1378 (Feb. 26, 1884), p. 2275 (March 26, 1884); *Senate Miscellaneous Documents*, 48 Cong., 1 Sess., No. 59 (Serial 2171); *Senate Reports*, 48 Cong., 1 Sess., No. 393 (Serial 2175). Regarding the New York Chamber see William W. Halligan, Jr., "The Berlin West African Conference of 1884–1885 from the Viewpoint of American Participation" (M. A. thesis, University of Virginia, 1949), pp. 46–48. Willard P. Tisdel to Frelinghuysen, Nov. 23, 1884, *Papers Relating to the Foreign Relations of the United States, 1885* (Washington, 1886), p. 288; Pletcher, *Awkward Years*, p. 345.

delegates at the Berlin conference on Samoa); his two fellow delegates were none other than Leopold's associates, Sanford and Stanley. Frelinghuysen told them to work for "unrestricted freedom of trade in that vast and productive region" but not to depart from the policy of noninterference in European affairs,[50] two aims difficult to reconcile. After complicated negotiations Kasson thought he had succeeded. The General Act, as the final agreement was called, provided for free trade and neutrality for the Congo basin and recognized the African Association as the Congo Free State.[51]

But Cleveland was about to enter the White House, and along with Frelinghuysen's reciprocity treaties—and also, it will be recalled, his Nicaragua canal treaty—the General Act was doomed. Determined to assume no responsibilities in the remote Congo valley, Cleveland declined to submit the Act to the Senate;[52] that body never approved it. More significant than this anticlimax, however, was the fact that the United States, as early as 1884, had participated in a conference in the heart of Europe strongly smacking of colonialism. In darkest Africa, as in Mexico, South America, and the Caribbean, she had sanctioned unusual steps to search out foreign markets.

The Congo was, at best, a market for the future; American exports there were negligible. In quite another category were pork exports to Europe. In 1879 these were valued at $85,736,674, more than 12 percent of total merchandise exports.[53] Most of the pork went to Great Britain, Germany, and France. It was consequently no small matter that during the 1880s pork products were excluded in whole or in part from Germany and France (but never from Great Britain), and also from Denmark, Italy, Spain, Portugal, Austria-Hungary, Rumania, Greece, and Turkey. Most of these countries

50. Frelinghuysen to Kasson, Oct. 17, 1884, *House Executive Documents*, 48 Cong., 2 Sess., No. 247 (Serial 2304), pp. 20–21.

51. *Senate Executive Documents*, 49 Cong., 1 Sess., No. 196 (Serial 2341), pp. 284–93, 297–305. See also Henry M. Stanley, *The Congo and the Founding of Its Free State: A Study of Work and Exploration* (2 vols., New York, 1885), II, ch. 38; Sybil E. Crowe, *The Berlin West African Conference, 1884–1885* (London, 1942).

52. See Cleveland's explanation in his annual message, Dec. 8, 1885, Richardson, *Messages and Papers*, VIII, 329–30. See also Edward Younger, *John A. Kasson: Politics and Diplomacy from Lincoln to McKinley* (Iowa City, 1955), p. 337; John A. Kasson, "The Congo Conference and the President's Message," *North American Review*, CXLII (1886), 119–33.

53. *House Executive Documents*, 48 Cong., 1 Sess., No. 106 (Serial 2206), p. 16.

were such small markets that they can be disregarded; but further attention must be given to France and especially to Germany, with each of whom a protracted dispute developed.

During the decades after the Civil War, as America's plains and prairies were brought under cultivation and scientific methods of farming were developed, exports of agricultural goods increased by leaps and bounds. During the 1870s Europe had bad harvests and seemed in danger of being overwhelmed by the prodigious output of America's enormous expanses. This alarmed European landowners, who began to agitate for limiting the flood of agricultural goods from across the Atlantic. In the 1880s their attack centered on pork imports. A sensational letter in the London *Times* in February 1881 provided unexpected help. Written by an acting British consul in Philadelphia, it gave a frightful description of a Kansas farmer who had eaten diseased sausages: "Upon consulting a physician trichinae were found; worms in his flesh by the millions, being scraped and squeezed from the pores of the skin. They are felt creeping through his flesh and are literally eating up his substance."[54] The British government put a stamp of authenticity upon the letter by publishing it in a Blue Book.

The horrifying report gave France a weapon to defend a step she had just taken: the banning of American salted pork.[55] The American minister at Paris expressed his "profound regret"; Washington hinted at retaliatory action against French exports; the Cincinnati Chamber of Commerce and the Merchants' Exchange of St. Louis passed resolutions attesting to the purity of the American hog.[56] But not until late 1891 did France definitely rescind her ban.[57]

Germany had excluded American chopped pork and sausages as early as June 1880; but other pork products continued to flood her

54. Crump to Foreign Secretary Lord Granville, Dec. 21, 1880, the *Times* (London), Feb. 19, 1881.
55. John L. Gignilliat, "Pigs, Politics, and Protection: The European Boycott of American Pork, 1879–1891," *Agricultural History*, XXXV (1961), 6; *Foreign Relations, 1881,* p. 399.
56. Edward F. Noyes to the French Foreign Secretary, Barthélemy St. Hilaire, Feb. 20, 1881, *Foreign Relations, 1881,* p. 399; Blaine to Noyes, March 15, 1881, *ibid.,* p. 403; Blaine to Max Outrey (French minister to the United States), Nov. 25, 1881, *ibid.,* pp. 442–44. The Cincinnati resolution (March 5, 1881) and the St. Louis resolution (March 7, 1881) are in *ibid.,* p. 581.
57. Bingham Duncan, "Protectionism and Pork: Whitelaw Reid as Diplomat: 1889–1891," *Agricultural History,* XXXIII (1959), 190–95.

markets. Liking for Germany had increased in the United States almost in proportion as esteem for France had fallen in consequence of Napoleon III's sympathy for the South during the Civil War and his support of Maximilian's Mexican venture; in fact, Americans had hoped for a German victory in the Franco-Prussian War of 1870–1871.[58] Although Germany's growing strength under Chancellor Bismarck caused concern among Americans, who disliked her moves in Samoa, and suspected her of having designs on Latin America, they found much to admire in the rapidly progressing country in central Europe; in the 1880s more than two thousand Americans were studying in German universities, and American higher education was reshaping itself on German models.[59]

The apparent evidence that American pork was infested with trichinae stimulated Germany's landed interests, who numbered Bismarck among their ranks, to demand a total ban. No one could have been surprised when Berlin stopped all imports of American pork on March 6, 1883. American hog raisers, many of them German-Americans who disliked Bismarck, were infuriated, all the more so because Berlin had rejected an official invitation to investigate the American pork industry.[60] Their annoyance mounted higher when the President of France lifted the French ban in late 1883. Although the Chamber of Deputies soon reinstated it, Arthur had meantime publicly contrasted the considerate French repeal with the German declination of the "friendly invitation."[61]

The tension with Germany was aggravated by an incident involving a political foe of Bismarck, Eduard Lasker, who in 1883 and 1884 was lecturing in the United States. His speeches were critical

58. Henry Blumenthal, *A Reappraisal of Franco-American Relations, 1830–1871* (Chapel Hill, 1959), and *France and the United States: Their Diplomatic Relations, 1789–1914* (Chapel Hill, 1970); John G. Gazley, *American Opinion of German Unification, 1848–1871* (New York, 1926); Clara E. Schieber, *The Transformation of American Sentiment toward Germany, 1870–1914* (Boston, 1923).

59. Milton Plesur, *America's Outward Thrust: Approaches to Foreign Affairs, 1865–1890* (DeKalb, Ill., 1971), p. 112. See also Thomas N. Bonner, *American Doctors and German Universities: A Chapter in International Intellectual Relations, 1870–1914* (Lincoln, 1963); Jurgen F. H. Herbst, *The German Historical School in American Scholarship* (Ithaca, 1965); John A. Walz, *German Influence in American Education and Culture* (Philadelphia, 1936).

60. Frelinghuysen to Aaron A. Sargent (American minister to Germany), Feb. 15, 16, 1883, *Senate Reports*, 48 Cong., 1 Sess., No. 345 (Serial 2175), pp. 121–23; Louis L. Snyder, "The American-German Pork Dispute, 1879–1891," *Journal of Modern History*, XVII (1945), 20.

61. Annual message, Dec. 4, 1883, Richardson, *Messages and Papers*, VIII, 171.

of the Chancellor, who could not have been disconsolate when Lasker died in early 1884. But a month later Bismarck had an unpleasant surprise when the American minister, Aaron A. Sargent, handed him a House resolution avowing the belief that Lasker's liberal ideas had benefited Germany. Bismarck refused to transmit the resolution to the Reichstag, its intended destination. A flurry over an apparent affront now agitated the House; Representatives denounced the Chancellor, and the Foreign Affairs Committee pondered the incident.[62] But the committee recommended that the House's dignity was too great for it to be offended by the treatment of its resolution; and the House accepted this good advice. By then Bismarck had disavowed any intention of discourtesy and had invited Minister Sargent to a state dinner where, as was facetiously predicted in Congress, "they may give him American pork. . . ."[63] But whether or not pork was served, Germany stood firm on the ban; the trans-Atlantic hog was not for her.

In 1884 a Senate report pointed the way to the controversy's solution. It recommended inspecting pork for export and authorizing the President to exclude any product of a country discriminating against an American product.[64] But Congress failed to act during the remainder of Arthur's term, and Cleveland opposed exclusion on principle. Not until August 30, 1890, was a law enacted with provisions for inspection and retaliatory action.[65] This furnished Germany with both a face-saver and a threat. Reinforcing the threat was the McKinley tariff act of 1890, which put sugar (a valued German export) on the free list but empowered the President to reimpose the duty if Germany treated American commerce unfairly. Berlin now offered to lift the pork ban as soon as inspection became effective, on the understanding that German sugar would stay on the free list. The two countries reached agreement on this basis; Germany terminated her prohibition in September 1891.[66]

62. *Congressional Record,* 48 Cong., 1 Sess., p. 329 (Jan. 9, 1884), p. 1191 (Feb. 18, 1884), pp. 1463–65 (Feb. 28, 1884); *House Executive Documents,* 48 Cong., 1 Sess., No. 113 (Serial 2206), pp. 5–6.

63. *House Reports,* 48 Cong., 1 Sess., No. 988 (Serial 2256); *Congressional Record,* 48 Cong., 1 Sess., pp. 2073–83 (March 19, 1884).

64. *Senate Reports,* 48 Cong., 1 Sess., No. 345, p. 2.

65. *Statutes at Large of the United States of America . . .* (Washington, 1891), XXVI, 414–17. See also Alice F. Tyler, *The Foreign Policy of James G. Blaine* (Minneapolis, 1927), ch. 12.

66. A. Mumm Schwartzenstein (German chargé d'affaires at Washington) to Secre-

It is clear that America's increasing agricultural and industrial output had a marked effect upon her foreign policy in the 1880s. The influence of the so-called surplus, which was already noticeable during the border-crossing dispute with Mexico and, again, during the War of the Pacific, became especially apparent when Arthur was President. So prudent a Secretary of State as Frelinghuysen made vigorous attempts to find markets not only in familiar places like the Caribbean Sea, Hawaii, and Europe, but even in distant Africa. Although, thanks to Cleveland, all his Caribbean reciprocity treaties failed, as well as the Congo General Act, Frelinghuysen's wide-ranging efforts to relieve the surplus must have given rise to an uneasy suspicion throughout the country that the United States was confronting a difficult situation that might soon become critical. When the great panic of 1893 struck the country, the business community had no doubt that overproduction was the root cause. Business leaders and government officials redoubled their efforts to find foreign markets, and this time they were more successful.

---

tary of State John W. Foster, Aug. 22, 1891, *Senate Executive Documents*, 52 Cong., 1 Sess., No. 119 (Serial 2901), p. 110; the letters exchanged by these two officials consituted the so-called Saratoga Agreement. See also Alfred Vagts, *Deutschland und die Vereinigten Staaten in der Weltpolitik* (2 vols., New York, 1935), I, 41–62.

# CHAPTER 6

## *The Far East*

THE lure of Oriental trade had always fascinated Americans, who had followed closely behind Great Britain and France in opening China to Western commerce and had themselves taken the lead in Japan. During the 1870s and 1880s the desire to promote exports affected relations with China (but American relations with that country were characterized mainly by an immigration controversy); the same desire more strongly influenced relations with Japan; and it was extremely evident in relations with Korea. In this attention to commercial expansion American Far Eastern policy was similar to the policy we have noted regarding Mexico, South America, the Caribbean, the Congo, and Germany.

But Far Eastern policy had another feature; it resulted from the American proclivity to lump together all Chinese, Japanese, and Koreans as mysterious but inferior Orientals; and largely for this reason one can distinguish a general Far Eastern policy that was different from America's European and Latin American policies. If American policy toward Europe was influenced by isolationism, and policy toward Latin America by the Monroe Doctrine, policy toward the Far East was marked sometimes (especially when Seward was Secretary of State) by cooperation with racially-akin Europeans but more typically by a growing tendency to take the side of the Asiatics against the encroaching Europeans. But compared with Great Britain, Latin America, and Hawaii, the vast continent of Asia—with a limited exception in the case of China—was little heeded by the United States.

Americans thought more highly of Japan than of any other Asiatic country.[1] They greatly admired her "awakening" from the slumbers of past centuries, her energetic endeavors to modernize herself, and her flattering emulation of Western methods. In 1871 Japan sent a special mission to the United States, headed by Prince Tonomi Iwakura, which earned much esteem for her. At that time Japan was trying to free herself from various unequal treaties with the great powers, and the United States often supported her efforts. To the annoyance of the European capitals, Washington concluded a treaty with Japan in 1878 permitting her to set her own import duties; but in order to safeguard American exporters the treaty was not to become effective until other countries granted Japan the same privilege, which they did not do for many years.[2] In 1883 the United States again showed her sympathy when, no doubt mindful of the commercial opportunities that might ensue from cultivating Japanese good will, she returned to Japan $785,000.87, the American share of an indemnity the Japanese had been forced to pay for damage to foreign shipping in the early 1860s.[3] Japan still seemed the charming little fairyland depicted by Lafcadio Hearn, a country fit for condescending American praise and causing no apprehension —until her defeat of China in 1895 aroused sudden fears for the Hawaiian Islands. Elsewhere in Asia, India was a British preserve; and the Middle East, although the scene of much American missionary endeavor,[4] scarcely entered the consciousness of the American people.

Of the Far Eastern countries, only Korea, the Hermit Kingdom, remained closed to Western trade after the Civil War. Washington was anxious to establish diplomatic relations with Korea, partly to protect the increasing numbers of Americans sailing along her in-

1. Akira Iriye, *Across the Pacific: An Inner History of American-East Asian Relations* (New York, 1967), pp. 23–28.

2. Lawrence H. Battistini, *The Rise of American Influence in Asia and the Pacific* (East Lansing, 1960), p. 127; William M. Malloy (ed.), *Treaties, Conventions, International Acts, Protocols and Agreements between the United States of America and Other Powers, 1776–1909* (2 vols., Washington, 1910), I, 1021–24.

3. *Senate Reports*, 47 Cong., 1 Sess., No. 120 (Serial 2004); *House Reports*, 47 Cong., 1 Sess., No. 138 (Serial 2065); *Congressional Record*, 47 Cong., 1 Sess., No. 2722 (Feb. 15, 1883), p. 2769 (Feb. 16, 1883); Payson J. Treat, *Diplomatic Relations between the United States and Japan, 1853–1895* (2 vols., Stanford, 1932), I, ch. 10.

4. James A. Field, Jr., *America and the Mediterranean World, 1776–1882* (Princeton, 1969), pp. 345–59.

hospitable shores, partly to make a commercial treaty that would open a new market. In 1867 an American naval officer, Commander Robert W. Shufeldt, had sailed to Korea on a futile mission; four years later an American squadron had tried, with equal futility, to compel her to make a treaty.[5] Shufeldt wanted to go down in history as the man who opened the Hermit Kingdom, as Matthew C. Perry had opened Japan. Like a naval officer of future renown, Captain Alfred T. Mahan, he was strongly export-minded; in 1878 he wrote: "At least one-third of our mechanical and agricultural products are now in excess of our wants, and we must *export* these products or *deport* the people who are creating them."[6] Shufeldt, now a commodore, was a natural choice for command of the U.S.S. *Ticonderoga*, which in December 1878 left Hampton Roads on a two-year world cruise, one purpose of which was to investigate trade prospects. After visiting many other areas, he tried again with Korea, but with no more success than thirteen years before.

Korea now filled his thoughts, and he urged the government to send him back to the Far East. James G. Blaine, when briefly Secretary of State in 1881, was instrumental in getting the commodore assigned to the Peking Legation.[7] This time, Shufeldt was successful. He negotiated not with Korea but with Li Hung Chang, one of the most powerful officials in China, a country claiming suzerainty over Korea. Then in May 1882, on a signal from Li, he went to Korea and signed a treaty. It opened that country to American trade on a most-favored-nation basis, and provided for diplomatic and consular representation and extraterritorial rights. The Senate approved it the next year.[8]

In 1883 Washington appointed Lucius H. Foote the first American diplomatic representative at Seoul, and Korea sent a special mission to the United States. Headed by a high official named Min Yong Ik, the mission visited American cities and factories. In re-

5. M. Frederick Nelson, *Korea and the Old Orders in Eastern Asia* (Baton Rouge, 1945), pp. 119–26; J. F. terHorst, "Our First Korean War," *Marine Corps Gazette*, XXXVII (1953), 37–38.

6. Robert W. Shufeldt, *The Relations of the Navy to the Commerce of the United States* (Washington, 1878), p. 3.

7. Charles O. Paullin, "The Opening of Korea by Commodore Shufeldt," *Political Science Quarterly*, XXV (1910), 486–87.

8. Malloy, *Treaties*, I, 334–39; the resolution of approval, dated Jan. 9, 1883, is on p. 340.

sponse to Min's request for American advisers, the Arthur administration assigned a naval officer, Ensign George C. Foulk, who sailed with Min and his colleagues on the warship *Trenton* back to Korea.[9] Soon a violent struggle between pro-Chinese and pro-Japanese factions broke out. Min was severely wounded; he owed his life to an American medical missionary, Dr. Horace N. Allen. Dr. Allen remained in Korea for many years, creating much good will for Americans.[10] He served not only as a missionary but also as a diplomat, first for Korea and then for the United States. But his diplomatic role was ineffectual; the American Far Eastern expert, William W. Rockhill, described him superciliously as a "very good, honest fellow, with little or no judgment, in the conduct of official affairs I mean, with a fairly good education and good health. He has on one or two occasions rather mismanaged our affairs out there. . . ."[11] For the rest of the century American influence in Korea was slight in the face of a fierce contest for supremacy among China, Japan, and, later, Russia. Nor, despite Shufeldt's hopes, did exports increase appreciably. Korea furnished little relief for the American surplus.

Of all Asiatic countries it was the empire of China with which the United States was most actively involved. Immigration, although the most complicated aspect, was not necessarily the most significant aspect of the connection with China. The influence of American missionaries was tremendous.[12] China was the lodestone of the American missionary movement and, in consequence of her great population, the largest mission field. Year after year American missionaries, on leave from their stations in China, enthralled their friends, church organizations, and other groups all over the United States with accounts of their adventures in fabled Cathay. The missionaries created such a deep sympathy for China that Americans

9. David M. Pletcher, *The Awkward Years: American Foreign Relations under Garfield and Arthur* (Columbia, Mo., 1961), pp. 211–12; Tyler Dennett, *Americans in Eastern Asia: A Critical Study of United States' Policy in the Far East in the Nineteenth Century* (New York, 1922), p. 478.

10. Fred Harrington, *God, Mammon, and the Japanese: Dr. Horace N. Allen and Korean-American Relations, 1884–1905* (Madison, 1944).

11. Rockhill to James H. Wilson (an American engineer interested in Chinese railways), Oct. 27, 1896, James Harrison Wilson Papers, Library of Congress (Washington), Box 21.

12. Kenneth Scott Latourette, *A History of Christian Missions in China* (New York, 1929), chs. 13–20; Paul A. Varg, *Missionaries, Chinese, and Diplomats: The American Protestant Missionary Movement in China, 1890–1952* (Princeton, 1958).

came to entertain an almost paternalistic feeling for that country. This had far-reaching consequences for official policy. Much of the popular enthusiasm for the Open Door policy at the end of the century, for example, is attributable not to American trade but to the sentimental feeling toward the Chinese, a feeling inspired by the missionaries. And much of the hostility to Japan in the twentieth century can be traced to that same influence.

Somewhat as the 400 million Chinese attracted missionaries, so too did they cast a spell over American exporters. Yet exports to China were trifling as compared with those to Great Britain and other principal trading partners. Even exports to Mexico were greater. In 1865 exports to China were valued at only $3 million, and ten years later at $1 million; the figures climbed slowly to $4 million in 1878, and $8 million in 1886, but were down again to $3 million in 1890 and $4 million in 1895. They attained a peak for the century of $14 million in 1899.[13] Japan, with her much smaller population, was importing considerably more from the United States by the end of the century, in fact twice as much by value in 1898. American imports from China, though larger than exports to her, were much smaller than imports from several other countries and included no vital goods. By 1900 Americans had only $17,500,000 invested in China as compared with $185 million in Mexico.[14] Yet it was China that Americans saw as the greatest potential market, not Japan or contiguous Canada or Mexico. The lure of that market was at its height in the 1890s, but it existed long before then, and as early as the 1880s it influenced Washington fairly strongly. "It is the wise policy of the present Administration," James H. Wilson, an American with business interests in China, reflected in 1884, "to find markets for our surplus products and manufactures and while China is relatively a poor country it is certain, that with her vast population, if we could build for her a few thousand miles of railroad, we should not only supply the steel, the locomotives, and the cars but should greatly stimulate the demand for every other article manufactured by our countrymen."[15] At the end of the

13. *Historical Statistics of the United States, Colonial Times to 1957* (Washington, 1961), pp. 550–51. A convenient table of exports to and imports from China, Hong Kong, and Japan, 1865–1904, is in Dennett, *Americans in Eastern Asia,* p. 478.

14. For imports from China see *Historical Statistics,* pp. 552–53; for investments see Charles F. Remer, *Foreign Investments in China* (New York, 1933), p. 260.

15. Wilson to John W. Foster, Dec. 14, 1884, J. H. Wilson Papers.

century such sentiments were to contribute to moves by Washington to safeguard the supposedly enormous market across the Pacific Ocean.

Before then, however, American diplomatic encounters with the distant empire were pretty much of a routine nature—except as they related to Chinese immigrants. For most of the time the United States was content to leave the initiative in China to European powers, being careful, however, to insist upon most-favored-nation treatment by Peking, that is, to get as much from China as the Europeans got. Only occasionally was Washington more active. In the course of a trip around the world after leaving the White House, Ulysses S. Grant visited China and Japan in 1879. His attempt to persuade them to settle a current dispute had only fleeting success, but the publicity surrounding the famous ex-President directed American attention to the Far East.[16] Grant secured the appointment in 1882 of his former traveling companion, a journalist named John Russell Young, as minister to China. In the early 1880s China was at war with France. Acting through Young, she tried to persuade the United States to mediate, but Secretary of State Frelinghuysen made acceptance conditional upon French agreement. Paris, after at first showing interest, rejected the proposition; and consequently no mediation occurred.[17] During the Sino-Japanese War of 1894–1895 some further inconclusive American diplomatic activity took place. John W. Foster (the former minister to Mexico and Spain, and Secretary of State from 1892 to 1893), after helping defeated China raise a large loan in the United States, went to the Far East in an unofficial capacity to advise her in making peace.[18] Apparently he had very little influence in Peking.

Before the Civil War and for several years after it the United States welcomed Chinese immigrants, particularly in California and

16. John Russell Young, *Around the World with General Grant* . . . (2 vols., New York, 1879), II, chs. 38, 43, 44; Dennett, *Americans in Eastern Asia,* pp. 444–45.

17. Pletcher, *Awkward Years,* pp. 214–18.

18. Secretary of State Walter Q. Gresham wrote Thomas F. Bayard (ambassador to Great Britain), Dec. 24, 1894: "You can readily see that if Foster is not already a very rich man his prospects for becoming a millionaire are flattering" (because China was to pay him a large commission), Walter Q. Gresham Papers, Library of Congress; however, nothing unethical about Foster's services is known. See John W. Foster, *Diplomatic Memoirs* (2 vols., Boston, 1909), II, ch. 33. For a congressional resolution affirming Foster's unofficial capacity see *Congressional Record,* 53 Cong., 3 Sess., p. 709 (Jan. 7, 1895).

other western states, where labor was scarce. Chinese workers built the western section of the first transcontinental railroad, and without them the economic development of the West would have been much slower. Earlier than Japan or Korea, China sent a mission to the United States; it had the unusual distinction of being headed by an American, Anson Burlingame, who resigned as minister to China to take on this assignment. He and Secretary of State Seward concluded the so-called Burlingame treaty on July 28, 1868, which gave Chinese laborers the right to enter the United States freely.[19] Few Americans did not applaud it.

As the years passed, the applause diminished. More and more Chinese emigrated across the wide Pacific; almost all of them congregated in California, particularly in San Francisco. In 1860 there were about 35,000 of them in the United States, all in California; in 1870, 49,277 in California and 63,199 in the whole country; in 1880, 75,132 in California (about 9 percent of the state's population) and 105,465 in the whole country. Of this total, 102,102 lived in western states.[20] The concentration doomed the Chinese, for had they been scattered more evenly throughout the United States, the agitation against them might not have arisen. Keeping to themselves in "Chinatowns," they did not want to be assimilated; they showed little interest in their new country except for its money. Their appearance, clothes, speech, religion, and customs were strange. Exaggerated tales spread about their opium smoking and allegedly filthy habits. Chinese women were said to be mostly prostitutes; Chinese criminals supposedly abounded; down every dark alley there lurked a Fu Manchu. Worse yet, the Chinese accepted miserable wages and worked hard and long. At a time when labor unions were struggling for existence, the presence of these unorganized laborers on the Pacific coast was an abomination to American workers.

In California an anti-Chinese crusade gathered impetus.[21] Its

19. Malloy, *Treaties*, I, 234–36. The Burlingame treaty was, in form, an amendment of the treaty of Tientsin of 1858.
20. Mary R. Coolidge, *Chinese Immigration* (New York, 1909), p. 501. In the 1880s the figures started to decrease; in 1890 there were 72,472 Chinese in California (107,488 in the whole country); in 1900, 45,753 (as against 89,963). See also Gunther Barth, *Bitter Strength: A History of the Chinese in the United States, 1850–1870* (Cambridge, Mass., 1964).
21. Elmer C. Sandmeyer, *The Anti-Chinese Movement in California* (Urbana, Ill., 1939); Rodman W. Paul, "The Origin of the Chinese Issue in California," *Mississippi Valley Historical Review*, XXV (1938), 181–96. For a fairly moderate, but distinctly anti-

leader, an Irish-born rabble-rouser named Denis Kearney, exhorted his followers in San Francisco sandlots, "The Chinese must go!" Kearneyism led to frequent violence in the 1870s. In July 1877, San Francisco rioters looted and burned Chinese buildings; in the autumn of that year a Workingmen's party was organized in California and proclaimed itself the leader of anti-Chinese agitation.[22]

Over these years, as California's population grew, so did the state's importance in national politics. As early as 1874 President Grant recommended a ban on the importation of coolies under contract and of Chinese prostitutes, and such a law was passed the next year.[23] It was the first of a series of increasingly restrictive measures. In 1876, in response to a resolution of the California legislature for the modification of the Burlingame treaty, Congress sent a commission to San Francisco to investigate.[24] After hearing more than a hundred witnesses, it issued an enormous report in 1877. Written by a California Senator, Aaron A. Sargent (the minister to Germany during the pork dispute), it recommended amending the Burlingame treaty and enacting legislation to curtail immigration.[25]

The consequence was a bill submitted in the House in January 1878 and a year's study of it in committee. A short debate occurred in early 1879 on the committee's recommendation that any ship on any voyage be prohibited from carrying more than fifteen Chinese laborers to the United States. The measure was vigorously backed by easterners as well as by westerners. "We have this day to choose," James G. Blaine, then a Senator from Maine, declared

Chinese, contemporary account see G. B. Densmore, *The Chinese in California* (San Francisco, 1880); for a contemporary defense of the Chinese see George F. Seward (onetime American minister to China), *Chinese Immigration, in Its Social and Economical Aspects* (New York, 1881).

22. Coolidge, *Chinese Immigration,* p. 115.

23. Annual message, Dec. 7, 1874, James D. Richardson (ed.), *A Compilation of the Messages and Papers of the Presidents, 1789–1897* (10 vols., Washington, 1899), VII, 288; *Statutes of the United States of America* (Washington, 1897), XVIII, Pt. 3, pp. 477–78; the act was approved March 3, 1875.

24. *Congressional Record,* 44 Cong., 1 Sess., p. 901 (Feb. 7, 1876), p. 2639 (April 20, 1876), p. 4421 (July 6, 1876), p. 4678 (July 18, 1876).

25. *Senate Reports,* 44 Cong., 2 Sess., No. 689 (Serial 1734); for a dissenting report by Senator Oliver P. Morton, the commission's chairman, see *Senate Miscellaneous Documents,* 45 Cong., 2 Sess., No. 20 (Serial 1785). Sandmeyer, *Anti-Chinese Movement,* pp. 82–88.

melodramatically, "whether we will have for the Pacific coast the civilization of Christ or the civilization of Confucius"; and even such a moderate man as Thomas F. Bayard dismissed the Burlingame treaty by affirming that every nation had the right to decide when to "retire from a treaty stipulation."[26] After one day of debate the House passed the bill decisively, 155 to 72; the Senate passed it by a closer vote, 39 to 27.[27] President Hayes courageously vetoed it on March 1, 1879, arguing that Congress lacked the constitutional power to modify a treaty (as he contended the bill would do). He defended the traditional American attitude toward immigration: "Up to this time our uncovenanted hospitality to immigration, our fearless liberality of citizenship, our equal and comprehensive justice to all inhabitants, whether they adjured their foreign nationality or not, our civil freedom, and our religious toleration had made all comers welcome. . . ." But he recognized the "grave discontents" of the Pacific states and adverted to possible negotiations with China. Congress failed to override his veto.[28]

Nevertheless, the congressional action had revealed widespread and intense anti-Chinese sentiment. During the presidential election of 1880 the Republican candidate, James A. Garfield, was accused of favoring Chinese labor.[29] Although the "Morey" letter, in which he was supposed to have expressed this damaging partiality, was exposed as a forgery, the fact that the Democrats publicized it indicated the national importance the Chinese question had attained.

In May 1880 Hayes had appointed a special commission to negotiate in Peking a revision of the Burlingame treaty. It was headed by

26. *House Reports*, 45 Cong., 3 Sess., No. 62 (Serial 1866); *Congressional Record*, 45 Cong., 2 Sess., p. 318 (Jan. 14, 1878); *ibid.*, 45 Cong., 3 Sess., pp. 1303, 1310 (Feb. 14, 1879). Blaine was so proud of this speech and of another he delivered on Feb. 15 that he had them both published in his book *Political Discussions, Legislative, Diplomatic, and Popular, 1856–1886* (Norwich, Conn., 1887); see also his letter in the New York *Tribune*, Feb. 21, 1879.

27. *Congressional Record*, 45 Cong., 3 Sess., pp. 800–1 (Jan. 28, 1879), p. 1400 (Feb. 15, 1879); the House concurred in the Senate amendments, *ibid.*, pp. 1796–97 (Feb. 22, 1879).

28. Message of March 1, 1879, Richardson, *Messages and Papers*, VII, 514–20; *Congressional Record*, 45 Cong., 3 Sess., pp. 2275–77 (March 1, 1879). The House vote was 110 for the bill, 96 against it, well short of the required two-thirds; the Senate did not vote.

29. Robert G. Caldwell, *James A. Garfield, Party Chieftain* (New York, 1931), pp. 306–7.

James B. Angell, president of the University of Michigan and now named minister to China; William H. Trescot was another member. By a new treaty, signed in Peking on November 17, 1880, China agreed that the United States could "regulate, limit, or suspend," in a "reasonable" way, the immigration of Chinese laborers; the United States could not, however, "absolutely prohibit" immigration, and "Chinese laborers who are now in the United States shall be allowed to go and come of their own free will and accord. . . ."[30] Thus invited to "regulate, limit, or suspend," Congress passed a bill suspending entry for twenty years.[31]

Chester A. Arthur was then in the White House. Contending that so long a suspension was not "reasonable," he, too, showed courage by vetoing the bill on April 4, 1882. Significantly, he reminded Congress that "the trade of the East is the key to national wealth and influence," and that the key might slip into the hands of America's commercial rivals if the proud Chinese felt slighted. But he expressed his conviction that legislation was required and virtually asked Congress to prohibit immigration for a shorter period than twenty years.[32] Promptly Congress enacted a measure suspending immigration for ten years only; Arthur signed it on May 6, 1882.[33] The measure was a historic one—the first general exclusion of immigrants in American history.

The truth of the matter is that by the 1880s the enormous influx from Europe had aroused national opposition to immigrants not only from China but from many other countries as well. If the Chinese were Chinks, there were also Polacks, Hunkies, Dagoes, and Greasers. Pressure for banning the Chinese came from labor

30. Malloy, *Treaties*, I, 237–38; the Senate approved the treaty on May 5, 1881. For the negotiations see *Papers Relating to the Foreign Relations of the United States, 1881* (Washington, 1882), pp. 168ff.; *Senate Executive Documents*, 47 Cong., 1 Sess., No. 148 (Serial 1990). The commission's third member was John F. Swift, a Californian.

31. The Senate passed the bill, 29 to 15, on March 9, 1882; the House, 167 to 66, on March 23. *Congressional Record*, 47 Cong., 1 Sess., p. 1753 (March 9, 1882), p. 2227 (March 23, 1882).

32. Richardson, *Messages and Papers*, VIII, 112–18.

33. The Senate voted to override the veto, 29 in favor and 21 opposed, less than two-thirds, *Congressional Record*, 47 Cong., 1 Sess., p. 2617 (April 5, 1882). The House passed the new measure, 201 to 37, on April 17, 1882; the Senate, 32 to 15, on April 28; the House concurred in the Senate's amendments (no vote being recorded) on May 2, *ibid.*, pp. 2973–74 (April 17, 1882), p. 3412 (April 28, 1882), p. 3532 (May 2, 1882). The bill is in *Statutes at Large of the United States of America* . . . (Washington, 1883), XXII, 58–61.

unions, which ironically were themselves filled with immigrants. As regards the Chinese, it was the Workingmen's party of California that was the most eager in seeking a ban. On the other hand, the opposition to exclusion stemmed from the steamship companies that carried the Chinese, from the railroad owners who used their labor, and from other businessmen who welcomed the Chinese as hard workers and obstacles to unionism. Opposition to exclusion arose also from idealistic considerations. American missionaries defended the Chinese. So did a number of prominent public figures. Such a highly respected Senator as George Frisbie Hoar could declare during the debate on the 1882 bill: "For myself and for the State of Massachusetts . . . I refuse to consent to this legislation. . . . We go boasting of our democracy, and our superiority, and our strength. The flag bears the stars of hope to all nations. A hundred thousand Chinese land in California and everything is changed. . . . What argument can be urged against the Chinese which was not heard against the negro within living memory."[34] Charles Sumner of Massachusetts, Justin S. Morrill and George F. Edmunds of Vermont, William P. Frye of Maine, Henry L. Dawes of Massachusetts, and Joseph P. Hawley of Connecticut were other prominent Senators, all New Englanders, who steadfastly upheld the old tradition of welcome for all—even Chinese. But they stood apart from the mainstream. And even though the newcomers from Europe, especially those from southern and eastern Europe, were increasingly resented, they aroused nothing like the hostility that the hapless Orientals did.

Despite the ten-year ban, racial hostility continued to grow. Mention has been made of the California riots in the 1870s; others occurred there in the following decade.[35] In Colorado in 1880 one Chinese was killed, several injured, and much Chinese property stolen.[36] Worse was to follow. In 1885, in Rock Springs, Wyoming Territory, an enraged mob comprised of immigrants from Europe attacked some five hundred Chinese, killed twenty-eight, wounded many more, and drove most of the rest out of town.[37] China pro-

34. *Congressional Record*, 47 Cong., 1 Sess., pp. 1517, 1518 (March 1, 1882). See *ibid.*, 49 Cong., 1 Sess., pp. 3919–22 (April 28, 1886), and 53 Cong., 1 Sess., p. 2489 (Oct. 13, 1893), for memorials from missionaries.
35. Sandmeyer, *Anti-Chinese Movement*, pp. 97–98.
36. Battistini, *Rise of American Influence*, p. 105.
37. *House Executive Documents*, 49 Cong., 1 Sess., No. 102 (Serial 2398).

tested strongly and requested indemnification. Secretary of State Bayard, while denying that any indemnity was legally due, said that President Cleveland, "solely from a sentiment of generosity and pity," might ask Congress to appropriate funds.[38] The consequence was an act of February 25, 1887, providing for an indemnity of $147,748.74.[39] Other attacks on Chinese, destructive of property but not of lives, occurred in 1885 and 1886 in Tacoma and Seattle; and numerous incidents occurred in other places, including even Alaska.[40]

The outrages led Peking to conclude that, if it wanted to avoid the humiliation of a unilateral American ban on immigration, it had no recourse except to ask for a new treaty imposing a joint ban. Cleveland was willing to negotiate, and a treaty was signed on March 12, 1888; it "absolutely prohibited" the immigration of laborers for twenty years but, in accordance with the treaty of 1880 (which, it will be recalled, specified that "Chinese laborers who are now in the United States shall be allowed to go and come of their own free will and accord"), exempted Chinese returning to the United States from visits to their homeland.[41] The Senate approved it in May, but with far-reaching amendments that would have prevented the reentry of some twenty thousand Chinese who were in China with official assurance of being able to return to America.[42]

38. Cheng Tsao Ju (Chinese minister to the United States) to Bayard, Nov. 30, 1885, *Papers Relating to the Foreign Relations of the United States, 1886* (Washington, 1887), pp. 101–9; Bayard to Cheng Tsao Ju, Feb. 18, 1886, *ibid.,* pp. 158–68; Richardson, *Messages and Papers,* VIII, 383–86.

39. For the Senate votes see *Congressional Record,* 49 Cong., 1 Sess., p. 5235 (June 4, 1886), p. 1564 (Feb. 10, 1887); for the House vote, *ibid.,* p. 1511 (Feb. 8, 1887). There was some opposition to the measure along the line expressed by Senator Francis M. Cockrell (Democrat from Missouri): "As I understand, a parcel of Chinese came in and engaged in work there. Here was a parcel of Bohemians [*sic*] who came to the same place. They got into this controversy. The Bohemians wanted the Chinese to do in a certain way and the Chinese refused to do it, and they went to killing each other; and the American citizens, the taxpayers of this country, are to become responsible for their acts upon each other." *Ibid.,* p. 5111 (June 1, 1886).

40. Jules A. Karlin, "The Anti-Chinese Outbreak in Tacoma, 1885," *Pacific Historical Review,* XXIII (1954), 271–83, and "The Anti-Chinese Outbreaks in Seattle, 1885–1886," *Pacific Northwest Quarterly,* XXXIX (1948), 103–30. The Tacoma and Seattle affairs, like that at Rock Springs, seem to have been precipitated by foreign-born laborers. Coolidge, *Chinese Immigration,* p. 188. Chang Yen Hoon (Chinese minister to the United States) to Bayard, Feb. 25, 1887, *Papers Relating to the Foreign Relations of the United States, 1888* (Washington, 1889), Pt. 1, pp. 363–64.

41. The treaty is in *Foreign Relations, 1888,* Pt. 1, pp. 398–400.

42. Secretary of State Thomas F. Bayard to Chang Yen Hoon, May 8, 1888, *ibid.,* p. 398; Coolidge, *Chinese Immigration,* p. 195.

A presidential election was approaching. On September 1, 1888, the press reported a rumor that China had decided not to ratify the treaty as it stood; if true, there would be no ban on reentry. Two days later Cleveland's campaign manager, Representative William L. Scott, conferred hastily with the President and the Speaker of the House. A telegram had just arrived from the Democratic organization in California demanding speedy action against the Chinese so as not to jeopardize the western vote. Following the conference, Scott submitted a bill in the House providing that no Chinese laborer who had departed from the United States could reenter, no matter what family or property he might possess there. The bill passed the House the same day, and the Senate four days later.[43] One might think that Cleveland would have vetoed so infamous a measure, as Hayes and Arthur had vetoed bills that, by comparison, were models of equity. But the election month of November 1888 was near. Cleveland was soon to woo the eastern vote by dismissing the British minister. Pressure on him from the West was heavy.[44] He signed the Scott act on October 1, 1888.[45] As Senator Matthew C. Butler, Democrat of North Carolina, admitted, "this whole Chinese business has become a matter of political advantage, and we have not been governed by that deliberation which it would seem to me the gravity of the question requires. In other words, there is a very important Presidential election pending. One House of Congress passes an act driving these poor devils into the Pacific Ocean, and the other House comes up and says, 'Yes, we will drive them further into the Pacific Ocean, notwithstanding the treaties between the two governments.' "[46]

China did refuse to ratify the amended treaty of 1888, and she protested the Scott act. The United States Supreme Court declared

---

43. *Congressional Record,* 50 Cong., 1 Sess., pp. 8226–27 (Sept. 3, 1888); p. 8369 (Sept. 7, 1888).

44. John A. S. Grenville and George B. Young, *Politics, Strategy, and American Diplomacy: Studies in Foreign Policy, 1873–1917* (New Haven, 1966), pp. 55–57, 59–63.

45. *Statutes of the United States of America . . .* (Washington, 1888), XXV, 504. Cleveland recommended that the Chinese who had actually embarked and were on their way back to the United States be exempted from the act's provisions. Message of Oct. 1, 1888, Richardson, *Messages and Papers,* VIII, 634–35. But more than 600 Chinese on the high seas were refused entry. Tsui Kwo Yin (Chinese minister to the United States) to Secretary of State James G. Blaine, March 26, 1890, *Papers Relating to the Foreign Relations of the United States, 1890* (Washington, 1891), p. 212.

46. *Congressional Record,* 50 Cong., 1 Sess., p. 8218 (Sept. 3, 1888). See also *ibid.,* 53 Cong., 1 Sess., pp. 2492–93 (Oct. 13, 1893); Sandmeyer, *Anti-Chinese Movement,* p. 101.

the act in contravention of the treaty of 1880 but not unconstitutional.[47] It continued, therefore, to be law of the land.

The treaty of 1888 having failed, Chinese immigration was regulated only by the ten-year ban of 1882. It would expire in 1892, the date of another presidential election. The coincidence of dates helps explain why Representative Thomas J. Geary of California introduced a bill in January 1892 excluding Chinese laborers not for a term of years but permanently. So sweeping a prohibition aroused concern. The Chinese minister at Washington contended that the Geary bill "violates every single one of the articles" of the 1880 treaty, and—since it denied bail, required white witnesses, and permitted arrests without warrants—was even worse than the Scott act.[48] Collis P. Huntington, the California railway magnate, warned that the "wicked bill" might exclude not only Chinese laborers from the United States but also American exports from China, with her "400,000,000 people"; and a Senator called China "the most promising country in the whole world" for cotton textile exports.[49] But no possibility existed of the Geary bill's failing in the election year of 1892, although its opponents did succeed in reducing the ban from perpetuity to ten years. President Benjamin Harrison signed the bill on May 5, 1892.[50] Thus, by two successive acts, each for ten years, Congress had achieved the twenty-year exclusion that Arthur's veto had thwarted in 1882.

47. *Supreme Court Reporter* 623–32; John Bassett Moore, *A Digest of International Law* . . . (8 vols., Washington, 1906), IV, 198. For the protest see Chang Yen Hoon to James G. Blaine, July 8, 1889, *Papers Relating to the Foreign Relations of the United States, 1889* (Washington, 1890), pp. 132–39. The diplomatic correspondence regarding the Scott act is in *Senate Executive Documents*, 51 Cong., 1 Sess., No. 41 (Serial 2682), and *ibid.*, 52 Cong., 2 Sess., No. 54 (Serial 3056).

48. Tsui Kwo Yin to Blaine, April 12 and May 5, 1892, *Papers Relating to the Foreign Relations of the United States, 1892* (Washington, 1893), pp. 147, 149, 150. See also *Senate Executive Documents*, 52 Cong., 2 Sess., No. 54. Senator Cushman K. Davis (Republican from Minnesota) called the bill "a rank, radical, unblushing, unmitigated repudiation of every treaty obligation which remains between us and China. . . ." *Congressional Record*, 52 Cong., 1 Sess., p. 3531 (April 22, 1892).

49. Collis P. Huntington to Senator William P. Frye (Republican from Maine), April 15, 1892, *Congressional Record*, 52 Cong., 1 Sess., pp. 3481–82 (April 21, 1892); speech of Frye, *ibid.*, p. 3532 (April 22, 1892).

50. *Statutes of the United States of America* . . . (Washington, 1892), XXVII, 25–26. For the one-sided congressional votes see *Congressional Record*, 52 Cong., 1 Sess., p. 2916 (April 4, 1892), p. 3629 (April 25, 1892), p. 3879 (May 3, 1892), p. 3925 (May 4, 1892). The Supreme Court declared the bill constitutional on May 15, 1893, 13 *Supreme Court Reporter* 1016–41.

As she had in 1888, China again petitioned for a new treaty, evidently because she still preferred to have her subjects excluded by a joint treaty rather than by a unilateral American law. She signed a treaty with the United States on March 17, 1894; the Senate approved it in August. Unlike the abortive amended treaty of 1888, it "absolutely prohibited" the immigration of laborers for ten years (instead of twenty) and permitted a Chinese resident to return from a visit to his homeland provided he had a family or a minimum of property in the United States.[51] This last provision, together with a decision of the Attorney General, repealed the Scott act. Consequently after 1894 Chinese residents no longer had to choose between cutting all ties either with their homeland or with the United States.[52]

Thereafter the immigration controversy subsided. In 1904 China terminated the treaty of 1894, in accordance with its provisions, but the United States continued to prohibit immigration. Not until 1943, when the exigencies of World War II made it desirable to treat China more equitably, did the United States permit a token annual admission of Chinese.

To a degree difficult to appraise, the anti-Chinese laws and treaties were the result of labor-union pressure. They reflected, too, the deep-rooted American feeling of superiority toward Orientals. Nonetheless these unhappy contentions over immigration constituted an exceptional phase of United States foreign policy, far removed from the main lines of policy at the time. Quite different was the commercial aspect of Sino-American relations. Although trade between the United States and China remained at a low level throughout the rest of the century, the idea of a great potential Chinese market took ever firmer hold of the American mind; and Secretary of State John Hay's Open Door at the century's close was to become, in the twentieth century, one of the principal objectives of the United States.

51. Malloy, *Treaties*, I, 241–43.
52. Coolidge, *Chinese Immigration*, p. 237; Moore, *Digest*, IV, 198.

# CHAPTER 7

# Anglo-American-Canadian Controversies in the Northeastern Fisheries and the Bering Sea

I N 1883, as will be recalled, the United States, responding to the indignation over the Halifax award, gave Great Britain notice that the fishery articles of the treaty of Washington would terminate on July 1, 1885. Grover Cleveland became President in March 1885, and his administration had to deal with the altercation which, after the termination of the articles, broke out with Great Britain and Canada over the northeastern fisheries. But whereas Cleveland inherited this controversy from the Republicans, he himself was responsible for a similar controversy over a herd of fur seals far to the northwest in the Bering Sea. The fisheries constituted one of the world's greatest natural resources and had for decades been keenly contested between Britain and America; the Bering Sea fur seals, the largest herd in the world, were less valuable but another prize well worth struggling for. Silver, gold, diamonds, and other precious materials have aroused international strife throughout the ages; so, in the 1880s and later, did the fish and the fur seals envenom Anglo-American affairs.

Cleveland was the first Democratic President since before the Civil War. Republicans viewed the rise to power of the party of rebellion as not only a Republican but a national disaster; consequently during his four years in office American foreign policy was subjected to the baneful influence of party politics even more than usual, almost as much, in fact, as during Blaine's brief tenure as Secretary of State in 1881. This unfortunate circumstance complicated the two maritime disputes, particularly the fisheries dispute.

If Canada was no longer to enjoy the duty-free treatment of her fish granted by the treaty of Washington ("free fish," the privilege was often called), she certainly would not tolerate the quid pro quo of fishing by Americans within her three-mile limit ("free fishing"). After the fishery articles expired in 1885, Great Britain, who controlled her Dominion's foreign policy, waited a year in the hope of making a broad agreement with Washington; but when none was forthcoming she permitted the Canadians to ban free fishing. Accordingly, in 1886 and 1887 Canadian police boats seized American vessels fishing in Canadian waters.[1] Fishery interests in the United States reacted angrily over the interference with what they regarded as virtually an inalienable right; they believed that most of the Canadian actions were illegal and suspected that Ottawa's real purpose was to force Washington to make the sort of reciprocity agreement that Sir John A. Macdonald (again Prime Minister since 1878) had striven for at the Joint High Commission in 1871.[2] Congress, too, was indignant. It passed a measure giving the President discretionary authority to bar Canadian ships, fish, or "any other product" from American ports; Cleveland, his anger apparently aroused over what looked like bullying of poor fishermen, signed it on March 3, 1887.[3] If he used these powers, and if the Canadians made further seizures in 1888, America's relations with Great Britain and Canada would plummet. Already they were being harmed by the parallel controversy over the fur seals.

The Pribilof Islands, in the Bering Sea, comprised part of Seward's Alaska purchase of 1867. On these four small islands there congregated every year, during the breeding season from early May to mid-November, the great fur seal herd. In 1870 Congress had given an American sealing company, the Alaska Commercial Company, a twenty-year lease of the islands. The company agreed to pay rental, plus royalties for the seal skins it took; and, in order to

1. *Senate Executive Documents,* 49 Cong., 2 Sess., No. 55 (Serial 2448).

2. Charles S. Campbell, "American Tariff Interests and the Northeastern Fisheries, 1883–1888," *Canadian Historical Review,* XLV (1964), 216.

3. *Congressional Record,* 49 Cong., 2 Sess., pp. 2127–28, 2150 (Feb. 23, 1887); *The Statutes at Large of the United States of America* (Washington, 1887), XXIV, 475–76.

ensure the herd's survival, to slaughter only on land and not more than 100,000 male seals a year (and no females). Secure in its monopoly, the company prospered; between 1870 and 1880 the price per skin more than quadrupled.[4] With killings limited, even the herd flourished.

But over the years the picture changed. As the population increased on the west coast, more people became aware of the nearby wealth. Sailing into the Bering Sea, they killed seals far from land. The Canadian fleet, based on Victoria, British Columbia, consisted of only fourteen schooners in 1882, but fifty in 1891.[5] The new type of sealing—pelagic sealing, it was called—was wasteful; many seals, including females, were slaughtered but lost in the water. Conservationists feared that the herd would become extinct, as several other herds already were. With seals being taken both on land and at sea, the supply of skins increased so greatly that by 1885 the price per skin had dropped by half.

Proof is lacking, but the speculation is irresistible that behind the scenes the Alaska Commercial Company sought Washington's assistance in suppressing this disastrous competition. The government would have listened sympathetically. It did not want to lose revenue from the Pribilof Islands, and it was beginning to regard the seals as United States property because they so regularly frequented the four islands (much as American fishermen had come to regard Canada's inshore waters as their own). Moreover, the indiscriminate slaughter outraged President Cleveland. In his righteous anger he was less heedful of international law than of the urgent need (as he believed) to stop pelagic sealing in order to save the seals. In 1886 and 1887 Treasury Department revenue cutters arrested Canadian pelagic sealers far outside territorial waters, the same years when thousands of miles away Canadian police boats were apprehending American fishermen in inshore waters. Just as the United States protested when Americans were arrested, so did Great Britain protest the

4. *Fur Seal Arbitration, Proceedings of the Tribunal of Arbitration . . .* III, *Appendix to the Case of the United States* (15 vols., Washington, 1895), II, 561–62; the company's lease is in *ibid.,* II, *Appendix to the Case of the United States* (Washington, 1892), I, 104–6.

5. Robert C. Brown, *Canada's National Policy, 1883–1900: A Study in Canadian-American Relations* (Princeton, 1964), pp. 44–45; Henry F. Angus (ed.), et al., *British Columbia and the United States: The North Pacific Slope from Fur Trade to Aviation* (Toronto, 1942), p. 320.

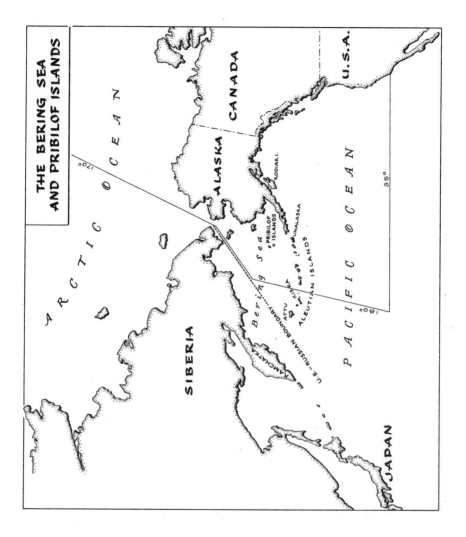

THE BERING SEA
AND PRIBILOF ISLANDS

ARCTIC OCEAN

SIBERIA

JAPAN

KAMCHATKA

Bering Sea

U.S.-RUSSIAN BOUNDARY

ATTU
AGATTU
ALEUTIAN ISLANDS
UNALASKA

PRIBILOF
ISLANDS

KODIAK I.

ALASKA

CANADA

U.S.A.

PACIFIC OCEAN

170°

180°

35°

Bering Sea developments;[6] and each controversy, by a reciprocal reaction, intensified the other.

From the beginning Secretary of State Bayard had been dubious about the propriety of seizing ships on the high seas. To check pelagic sealing he advocated international regulation, not unilateral policing. He therefore authorized negotiations in London in early 1888 looking to an agreement for safeguarding the species. Ottawa denied that the herd was endangered; it refused to accept international restraints on Canadian sealers while the Alaska Commercial Company was unrestrained (except by the United States alone), and it claimed damages for the illegal American arrests.[7] The Canadian stand brought the negotiations to an abrupt end. With no accord in sight, it was fortunate that Bayard finally persuaded the President that the seizures must stop. Largely because of the Secretary, American cutters did not arrest a single pelagic sealer in 1888.[8] But the peace in the northwestern waters was not to last.

Bayard had also been trying to negotiate a fishery agreement. "I feel we stand at 'the parting of the ways,'" he told a Canadian official in 1887. "In one direction I can see a well-assured, steady, healthful relationship . . . on the other, a career of embittered rivalries, staining our long frontier. . . ."[9] Preliminary talks proceeded smoothly, and on November 22, 1887, another British-American commission met in Washington.

The American members were Bayard; William L. Putnam, a lawyer from the fishing state of Maine; and James B. Angell, the former minister to China. Their British counterparts were Joseph Chamberlain, the Colonial Secretary; Sir Charles Tupper, the Canadian Minister of Finance; and Sir Lionel S. Sackville West, the British

6. See, for example, Sir Lionel S. Sackville West (British minister to the United States) to Bayard, Jan. 9, 1887, Great Britain, Foreign Office, *Blue Book, United States, No. 2 (1890): Correspondence Respecting the Behring Sea Seal Fisheries, 1886–1890* (London, 1890), pp. 37–38.

7. Lord Stanley (Governor General of Canada) to Colonial Secretary Lord Knutsford, Aug. 3, 1888, enclosing a report by George E. Foster (Acting Minister of Marine and Fisheries), July 7, 1888, *ibid.,* pp. 212–15; Charles S. Campbell, "Edward J. Phelps and Anglo-American Relations," in Harry C. Allen and Roger F. Thompson (eds.), *Contrast and Connection: Bicentennial Essays in Anglo-American History* (London, 1976), pp. 214–18.

8. Salisbury to Sackville West, April 3, 1888, *ibid.,* p. 189; Bayard to Sackville West, April 10, 1888, *ibid.,* p. 198.

9. Bayard to Sir Charles Tupper (Canadian Minister of Finance), May 31, 1887, *Senate Documents,* 61 Cong., 3 Sess., No. 870 (Serial 5931), III, 942–44. See also Campbell, "Edward J. Phelps," pp. 211–14.

minister to the United States. Once again the arguments heard by the Joint High Commission of 1871 were heard. The Canadians wanted free fish and, if possible, comprehensive reciprocity. Cleveland, having put an end to Frelinghuysen's reciprocity treaties, was pushing hard, just then, for a general reduction of the American tariff; and at this critical moment it became clear that the Republican Senate, determined to save the protective system, would not sanction the lowering of any duty, let alone the politically sensitive fish duties. After weeks of futile talk, accordingly, the British abandoned the demand for free fish, and this cleared the road to an agreement.[10]

The Bayard-Chamberlain treaty, signed February 15, 1888, defined which Canadian bays and waters would be open to American fishermen, and what rights and duties the fishermen would have in the inshore waters. Article XV held out a sort of bribe: if the United States ever granted free fish, Canada would let American fishermen buy supplies, transship catches, and take on crews in the inshore waters. Accompanying the treaty was a *modus vivendi* offered by Britain. Suspecting that the treaty would not be ratified, and fearing a showdown with the United States if the Dominion's antifishing measures were enforced much longer, Chamberlain had secured London's approval for a *modus* as a possible alternative accord.[11] The *modus* provided that for two years, pending the treaty's ratification, Americans purchasing annual licenses could enter Canadian waters for the three purposes listed in Article XV.[12]

A sustained chorus of disapproval greeted the treaty in the United States. The fishery interests, which had wanted enforcement of the retaliation law of March 3, 1887, instead of an agreement, called it a "shameful surrender."[13] Not a chance existed that the Republican

10. Chamberlain to his daughter Beatrice, Jan. 26, Feb. 10, 1888, James L. Garvin, *The Life of Joseph Chamberlain* (3 vols., London, 1932–34), II, 332; Tupper to Sir John A. Macdonald, Feb. 8, 1888, John A. Macdonald Papers, Public Archives of Canada (Ottawa), CLXXVII. Regarding the British desire for reciprocity see *Senate Executive Documents*, 50 Cong., 1 Sess., No. 127 (Serial 2513), pp. 2–3.
    11. Chamberlain to Prime Minister Salisbury, Dec. 22, 1887, Lord Salisbury Papers, Christ Church Library (Oxford).
    12. The text of the treaty is in *Senate Miscellaneous Documents*, 50 Cong., 1 Sess., No. 109 (Serial 2517), pp. 155–61; the text of the *modus* is in *ibid.*, p. 164. Both the treaty and the *modus* applied also to Newfoundland.
    13. Letter dated May 4, 1888, to the New York Sun, in *Congressional Record*, 50 Cong., 1 Sess., p. 8317 (Sept. 5, 1888); see also Charles C. Tansill, *The Foreign Policy of Thomas F. Bayard, 1885–1897* (New York, 1940), p. 300n.

Senate, in a presidential election year, would allow a Democratic President to settle the ancient controversy. Voting on August 21, 1888, a few weeks before the election, 27 Senators approved the treaty, 30 opposed it—far short of the required two-thirds.[14]

Was peace, then, not to come to the fisheries as it had, for a deceptive moment, to the Bering Sea? Thanks to Chamberlain's foresight, the *modus vivendi* now entered into force; American fishermen showed themselves ready to buy the proffered licenses; and consequently the northeastern waters, no less than the northwestern, were untroubled in 1888. Not only that, but at the end of the two years when the *modus* was due to expire, Great Britain renewed it, and she kept on doing so until in 1912 she and the United States reached a definitive settlement. The supposedly temporary *modus vivendi* turned out to be surprisingly permanent, and in 1888 the old fishery dispute ended forever.[15]

The Cleveland administration handled these maritime altercations with mixed ability. It deserves much credit for its patient negotiation of the fishery dispute; even the petty Republican Senate could not prevent the virtual settlement of America's oldest diplomatic controversy. On the other hand, in the Bering Sea affair the President's penchant for giving sweeping moralistic considerations an overly dominant role was only too apparent. It was all very well to be solicitous for the fur seals, but the solicitude led to no effective protection for them; on the other hand, the administration put the country in the wrong under international law and, as shall appear, it laid the ground for a sharp dispute with Great Britian.

Furthermore, the administration deserves censure for its conduct during a completely unexpected development that followed from the rejection of the Bayard-Chamberlain treaty. Republicans had catered to the Irish vote by proscribing the treaty as pro-British. Although Irish-Americans did not present so great a threat to relations between the United States and Great Britain as they had during the years just after the Civil War when Fenians were raiding into Canada, American politicians still felt it advisable to defer to them. As American minister at London from 1880 to 1885, James Russell Lowell, the famous poet (and one of several literary figures who

14. *Congressional Record*, 50 Cong., 1 Sess., p. 7768 (Aug. 21, 1888).
15. "The result bore out a well-known diplomatic axiom, 'Nothing is so permanent as the provisional.' " Garvin, *Chamberlain*, II, 330.

served as American minister or ambassador at the Court of St. James's during the Gilded Age), had had to deal with a number of difficult cases concerning men of Irish extraction, imprisoned by Britain, who claimed to be naturalized Americans. His tactful handling of these cases, although pleasing the British and creating much good will for the United States, had infuriated Irish-Americans.[16] Altogether the Irish question was fairly acute in the United States in the 1880s, and the Republican characterization of the fisheries treaty as pro-British presented a serious problem for President Cleveland in an election year. As Sackville West observed, Cleveland had to prevent the Republicans from "dominating his action, and he resolved at once to dominate their action by proposing to go even farther than they did, in adopting retaliatory measures."[17] In a message to Congress on August 23, 1888, two days after the Senate rejected the treaty, the President pronounced the 1887 retaliation act much too mild and asked for authorization to suspend the passage through the United States of Canadian goods in bond. The 1887 act was designed to limit fish imports into Republican New England; Cleveland's retaliation was aimed at New England railways (which carried the bonded Canadian goods). Thus the President was both soliciting the Irish vote and turning the tables against a Republican area.[18]

Perceiving the implications of Cleveland's clever move, the Democratic House of Representatives passed a bill giving the President the requested authorization.[19] Thereupon the Republican Senate found itself in a quandary: if the Republicans rejected the measure, they would alienate the Irish, with the election less than two months away; if they supported it, they would offend their wealthy New

16. Richard C. Beatty, *James Russell Lowell* (Nashville, 1942), ch. 21; Martin Duberman, *James Russell Lowell* (Boston, 1966); Beckles Willson, *America's Ambassadors to England (1785–1929)* (New York, 1929), pp. 374–88.

17. Sackville West to Salisbury, Sept. 4, 1888, Campbell, "American Tariff Interests," p. 225.

18. See Cecil Spring Rice (an officer in the British Legation in Washington and a future ambassador to the United States) to Jervoise (a Foreign Office official), Sept. 6, 1888, Public Record Office (London), Foreign Office 5/2049. According to information reaching Prime Minister Macdonald, Cleveland sent the message without Bayard's knowledge. Charles Tupper Papers, Public Archives of Canada (Ottawa), IX.

19. *Senate Executive Documents,* 50 Cong., 1 Sess., No. 251 (Serial 2514), p. 4; *Congressional Record,* 50 Cong., 1 Sess., p. 7901 (Aug. 23, 1888), pp. 8439–40 (Sept. 8, 1888).

## THE CUT DIRECT.   *(Punch,* September 8, 1888)

PRESIDENT CLEVELAND: "Don't know ya! *(Aside.)* At any rate, for the present!!"

England business supporters. But they found a way out by directing a committee to make a special study and report after the election.[20] Cleveland was generally considered too pro-British to suit Irish-Americans, and his support of the Bayard-Chamberlain treaty appeared to confirm this embarrassing reputation. But would not his advocacy of commercial war against Canada clear his name? The possibility worried the Republican managers. Eagerly they seized upon an unexpected opportunity to reestablish the President's pro-British credentials. In early September, Minister Sackville West received a letter signed "Charles F. Murchison." Murchison (whose real name was George Osgoodby) wrote as a naturalized Englishman who had intended to vote for Cleveland until he read the retaliation message, but was now puzzled as to which candidate was more friendly to Great Britain: Cleveland or his Republican antagonist, Benjamin Harrison. Most unwisely Sackville West, in a letter marked "Private," implicitly recommended Cleveland.[21] Osgoodby gave the letter to Republican officials. The press published it on October 21, in the midst of the closely contested election. The apparent proof that Her Majesty's minister favored Cleveland was a calamitous blow; Irish-Americans were reported to be rushing to Harrison in droves. "I . . . almost feel," a worried Cleveland wrote Bayard, "that if this stupid thing does not greatly endanger or wreck our prospects, it will only be because this wretched marplot is recalled. . . . I am afraid it is too much just what the enemy wants to have him remain here."[22] Sackville West would have to be sacrificed; that was clear to the President; four days later Bayard gave him his passports. Angered by an action that, with good reason, she considered much too hasty, Great Britain refused to replace him until after Cleveland left the White House in March 1889, defeated

20. Campbell, "American Tariff Interests," p. 227; *Congressional Record,* 50 Cong., 1 Sess., p. 8644 (Sept. 17, 1888), pp. 8979–80 (Sept. 27, 1888).

21. Regarding this incident see Tansill, *Bayard,* ch. 11; Charles S. Campbell, "The Dismissal of Lord Sackville," *Mississippi Valley Historical Review,* XLIV (1958), 635–48. Murchison had written, Sept. 5, 1888, essentially the same letter to Sir Charles Tupper, then in England. Sir Charles had the good sense to reply, Oct. 5, 1888: "My official position as the representative of Canada in Great Britain makes it quite impossible . . . for me to offer any opinion on the question you raise, as I am sure on reflection you will immediately comprehend." Macdonald Papers, CCCXXVII.

22. Cleveland to Bayard, Oct. 26, 1888, Thomas F. Bayard Papers, Library of Congress (Washington), CXXXI. See also Campbell, "Edward J. Phelps," pp. 218–22.

by Harrison, in some part because of the Murchison letter.

No one could have foreseen in August 1888 that the rejection of the Bayard-Chamberlain treaty would set in motion a train of events eventuating in the British minister's dismissal. But unexpected things happen in presidential election years, and it was lucky that the political exigencies of 1888 caused only temporary harm to British-Canadian-American affairs.

If Cleveland felt guilty over abandoning the defenseless fur seals, as he in effect did by permitting pelagic sealing to proceed unchallenged in 1888, he perhaps salved his conscience by signing on March 2, 1889, two days before leaving office, an unwise measure directing the President to warn annually that any pelagic sealer entering "all the dominion of the United States in the waters of Behring Sea" would be subject to arrest.[23] As required, President Harrison gave the warning on March 22, 1889. During that year Treasury Department revenue cutters arrested five Canadian sealers far outside the three-mile limit. All of them—surely by American intent—escaped.

The sudden resumption of arrests, following the suspension of 1888, naturally alarmed the Canadians, and London protested.[24] A long, fruitless debate ensued between London and Washington on legal and historical matters. Secretary of State James G. Blaine contended that the United States had exclusive jurisdiction in the Bering Sea, and that in effect she owned the fur seals. His arguments were weak; Prime Minister Lord Salisbury (who was also the Foreign Secretary) had no difficulty demolishing them. But Salisbury realized that safeguards were necessary to save the herd, and he admitted privately that "the Americans have a moral basis for their contention which it is impossible to ignore."[25]

In 1890 the twenty-year lease of sealing rights that had been awarded the Alaska Commercial Company came up for renewal.

23. *Statutes of the United States of America* . . . (Washington, 1889), XXV, 1009–10.
24. Salisbury to H. G. Edwardes (British chargé d'affaires at Washington), Aug. 22, 1889, Great Britain, Foreign Office, *Blue Book, United States, No. 2 (1890)*, p. 300. Regarding the Bering Sea controversy see Charles S. Campbell, *From Revolution to Rapprochement: The United States and Great Britain, 1783–1900* (New York, 1974), ch. 12.
25. Salisbury to Sir Julian Pauncefote (Sackville West's successor as British minister to the United States), March 28, 1890, Salisbury Papers. For a summary of the debate see John Bassett Moore, *History and Digest of the International Arbitrations to Which the United States Has Been a Party* . . . (6 vols., Washington, 1898), I, 785–87, 793–98.

The new award went to a different concern, the North American Commercial Company, partly, one may surmise, because two of the company's five or six stockholders were close associates of Blaine.[26] Unwisely, the Secretary took steps that the British minister at Washington, Sir Julian Pauncefote (Sackville West's successor), suspected, probably correctly, were designed to benefit his friends in the new concern. Blaine first proposed a time during which pelagic sealing would be banned every year. The Canadians refused to restrict their activities;[27] they saw no reason why Americans should be permitted to kill thousands of seals on the Pribilof Islands, whereas they would be prohibited from killing on the open sea. Exasperated, the Secretary asked Sir Julian to suggest some way to protect the seals. After consulting with Canada, the minister proposed a joint investigatory commission to report within two years, during which time sealing on land as well as at sea would be severely restricted.[28]

More than three weeks passed, with no reply from Blaine, when Pauncefote read in a newspaper that the administration intended to reject his proposal and to arrest pelagic sealers. Harrison had just issued his second annual warning to sealers not to enter the Bering Sea. Sir Julian hastened to the State Department, where he and Blaine exchanged angry remarks; Blaine, doubtless mindful of the North American Commercial Company, refused to consider a significant limitation on land killing. Overhastily, Pauncefote telegraphed Whitehall to expect more seizures.[29] His report provoked a strong reaction. With Queen Victoria's approval, the Cabinet decided to protest formally and to detach four warships for possible use in the Bering Sea. Pauncefote delivered the protest on June 14: ". . . Her Britannic Majesty's Government must hold the Government of the United States responsible for the consequences which may ensue from acts which are contrary to the principles of interna-

26. Charles S. Campbell, "The Anglo-American Crisis in the Bering Sea, 1890–1891," *Mississippi Valley Historical Review*, XLVIII (1961), 393–414.

27. Charles H. Tupper (Canadian Minister of Marine and Fisheries) to Macdonald, March 3, April 10, 1891, Macdonald Papers, XXX, XXXI, respectively; Pauncefote to Salisbury, Feb. 22, 1890, *Blue Book, United States, No. 2 (1890)*, p. 412. Regarding an approach by Blaine to Russia see Baron Rosen, *Forty Years of Diplomacy* (2 vols., London, 1922), I, 78–80.

28. Pauncefote to Salisbury, March 21, 1890, *Blue Book, United States, No. 2 (1890)*, pp. 419–20; Pauncefote to Blaine, April 29, 1890, *ibid.*, pp. 455–59.

29. Pauncefote to Salisbury, May 22, 23, 1890, *ibid.*, pp. 465–66, 469–71.

tional law." He also told the Secretary about the four warships. An incensed Blaine called them "a menace" that would not cause the United States to delay the seizures "for a single day."[30]

The controversy was at its height. "If both sides push their pretensions to an extreme," Salisbury had warned, "a collision is inevitable."[31] Pelagic sealers and at least one revenue cutter sailed into the Bering Sea. The British warships were stationed nearby. There can be no doubt that Britain would have used the ships, if necessary to protect Canadian sealers. While it is difficult to believe that war could have broken out, Salisbury's "collision," if it had occurred, would not have been easily resolved. Most fortunately, therefore, the American cutters did not interfere with the sealing vessels. The chances are that the British threats were not responsible for this outcome, and that Washington had never intended to authorize arrests in 1890 but, rather, had hoped to bluff the British into an agreement favorable to the North American Commercial Company. At any rate, as events were to show, the seizures of 1889 were the last ever to occur; and once the crisis of 1890 had been surmounted, Bering Sea waters began to become more tranquil.

During the season of 1890 Salisbury had sensibly proposed that the controversy be arbitrated.[32] Lengthy negotiations followed. They were complicated by the approaching season of 1891. Would the revenue cutters, this time, resume arrests? A *modus vivendi* signed June 15, 1891, staved off the danger. It banned pelagic sealing altogether and permitted the North American Commercial Company to take a mere 7,500 seals; these restrictions were to be effective until May 1892. Although Blaine had not been responsible for the final stages of the talks leading to this arrangement, which had taken place while he was ill, he had suggested its essential provisions.[33]

30. *Ibid.*, pp. 507–8; Pauncefote to Salisbury, June 16, 1890, Foreign Office 5/2108. For the Cabinet's decision see Salisbury to Pauncefote, May 31, 1890, Foreign Office 5/2107; Evan MacGregor (an Admiralty official) to Undersecretary of State, Foreign Office, Sept. 11, 1890, Foreign Office 5/2111.

31. Salisbury to Pauncefote, March 28, 1890, Campbell, "Anglo-American Crisis," p. 398.

32. Salisbury to Pauncefote, Aug. 2, 1890, *Blue Book, United States, No. 2 (1890)*, p. 520.

33. Blaine to Pauncefote, May 4, 1891, *Papers Relating to the Foreign Relations of the United States, 1891* (Washington, 1892), p. 555. Regarding the background of the *modus* see Campbell, "Anglo-American Crisis," pp. 402–14; its terms are in William

The *modus* of 1891 facilitated the conclusion of an arbitration treaty, signed on February 29, 1892. It provided for seven arbitrators—two each from the United States and Great Britain (or Canada), and one each from France, Italy, and Sweden and Norway—who would meet in Paris to decide upon the conflicting British and American contentions; they would also determine questions of fact regarding damages claimed by Canada for the seizures and would impose sealing regulations if the need arose.[34]

Before the arbitrators could convene, however, the fourth sealing season of Harrison's administration drew near, with the *modus* of 1891 due to expire on May 1, 1892. Canadians had strongly resented the 1891 ban on pelagic sealing; and London feared they would not accept another one. President Harrison insisted that an arbitration could scarcely be held if in the meantime Canadians were destroying the seals that were to be the subject of its deliberations. Blaine was ill again; he was also worried about Harrison's diplomacy. Though "too sick" to sign it, he wrote the President a warning on March 6 not to "get up a war cry and send naval vessels in Behring Sea."[35] Matters remained at loggerheads during the rest of the month, so much so that on the twenty-second the President's excitable private secretary feared that war was coming.[36]

Blaine resumed work at the end of March. He and Sir Julian put the final touches on a new *modus vivendi,* which they signed on April 18, 1892. It resembled the previous *modus* except for an article regarding damages that London and Ottawa insisted upon: if the outcome of the arbitration favored Great Britain, the United States would compensate Canadian sealers for their losses caused by refraining from sealing under the new *modus;* but if the outcome favored the United States, then Great Britain would compensate the

M. Malloy (ed.), *Treaties, Conventions, International Acts, Protocols and Agreements between the United States of America and Other Powers, 1776–1909* (2 vols., Washington, 1910), I, 743–44.

34. *Ibid.,* I, 746–50. The Senate approved the treaty unanimously on March 29.

35. Sidney Y. Smith (Blaine's private secretary) to Elijah W. Halford (Harrison's private secretary), March 6, 1892, Charles S. Campbell, "The Bering Sea Settlements of 1892," *Pacific Historical Review,* XXXII (1963), 360.

36. Diary of Everard F. Tibbott, March 22, 1892, Albert T. Volwiler, "Harrison, Blaine, and American Foreign Policy, 1889–1893," *Proceedings of the American Philosophical Society,* LXXIX (1938), 647–48.

American government and the North American Commercial Company for their losses.[37]

The arbitrators met in Paris for regular sessions on April 4, 1893. Supreme Court Justice John M. Harlan and Senator John T. Morgan, a Democrat from Alabama and chairman of the Foreign Relations Committee, were the American arbitrators; Lord Hannen, member of the High Court of Appeals, and Sir John S. D. Thompson, Attorney General of Canada, were the British members. The other arbitrators were Baron Alphonse de Courcel, a French Senator and the tribunal's president; Marquis Emilio Visconti Venosta, a former Italian Foreign Minister; and Gregers Gram, Minister of State of Sweden and Norway. Their award of August 15 went against the United States on all counts; however, they imposed regulations for pelagic sealing that went part way toward meeting American wishes for adequate safeguards. Pelagic sealing was banned in a zone extending outward sixty miles from the Pribilof Islands; it was also banned from May 1 through July 31 on the high seas north of the 35th parallel and east of the 180th longitude.[38] Thereafter the Bering Sea, like the northeastern fisheries after the *modus vivendi* of 1888, held no perils for British-American peace. But Anglo-Canadian-American squabbling about the seals did continue in a minor way until a definitive settlement was reached in 1911.[39]

Harrison and Blaine had inherited a complex dispute from Cleveland. Blaine in particular—but Salisbury too must be given much credit—had steered it to a successful resolution, although his diplomacy was marred by an absence of calm perseverance and by unwise efforts to help the North American Commercial Company. Both Americans had shown courage in agreeing to arbitrate. Harrison was denounced by critics when the United States lost the award, much as Prime Minister Gladstone (who, curiously enough, was again Prime Minister at the time of the Bering Sea award) had been over the Geneva award. Nonetheless the Paris arbitration and the *modi vivendi* of 1891 and 1892 were remarkable instances of the

37. Malloy, *Treaties*, I, 760–62. For the negotiations see Campbell, "Bering Sea Settlements," pp. 360–65.

38. For the arbitration see *Fur Seal Arbitration;* the award is in *ibid.*, I, *Award of the Tribunal . . .* , pp. 75–84. For a useful summary see Moore, *International Arbitrations*, I, ch. 17.

39. Thomas A. Bailey, "The North Pacific Sealing Convention of 1911," *Pacific Historical Review*, IV (1935), 1–14.

## THE POOR VICTIM!

(*Punch*, August 26, 1893)

JOHN: "Hm! Good; might be better!"
JONATHAN: "Hm! Bad; might be worse!"
THE SEAL: "Three months' close-time! Hm! Might ha' made it twelve!!"

growing British and American propensity to settle their quarrels reasonably and peacefully.

The bad taste left in America by the Paris decision contributed to a five-year delay in settling Bering Sea claims advanced by Canada. The tribunal had unanimously found that the United States had interfered with British sealers outside the three-mile limit; and in 1894 Washington and London agreed upon an American payment of $425,000. But Congress refused to appropriate the money. Thereupon the two countries appointed a joint commission to determine the proper sum; in December 1897 it assessed the United States $473,151.26.[40] Although Americans angrily denounced the award as excessive, Congress made the appropriation in June 1898.[41] "There could scarcely be a better proof of the changed feeling . . . towards England," the London *Times* was pleased to record. "It is only an act of justice which has been performed, but it has been performed ungrudgingly and with ardent cordiality."[42] Tactfully the *Times* refrained from mentioning that the United States was at war with Spain and constrained not to alienate one of her few sympathizers.

Despite these bickerings over the Canadian claims, relations between the United States and Great Britain were more amicable after the arbitration of 1893 than at any other time since the Civil War. The improvement was, of course, ascribable in part to the settlement of the *Alabama* claims reached at Washington and Geneva. The Irish question remained troublesome, as the Sackville West affair had demonstrated; but Washington would never again tolerate Fenian military activity along the northern border. And with the practical termination of the fishery and fur seals controversies there simply were not many remaining matters of serious contention. The Clayton-Bulwer treaty was a perennial source of irritation; and dangers still lurked in the Caribbean Sea, where rising American military power confronted the still powerful, but declining, British establishment. But for the time being these issues were not pressing. There were, moreover, strong underlying forces, notably a flourish-

40. *House Executive Documents*, 53 Cong., 3 Sess., No. 132 (Serial 3319), pp. 10–11; Malloy, *Treaties*, I, 766–70.
41. *Congressional Record*, 55 Cong., 2 Sess., pp. 5849–51 (June 13, 1898), p. 5853 (June 14, 1898); *Statutes at Large of the United States of America* . . . (Washington, 1899), XXX, 470.
42. The *Times* (London), June 15, 1898.

ing British-American commerce and a common heritage in language and literature, that were having a moderating effect on Anglo-American relations. Anyone looking below the surface would have perceived that the old rancors were becoming less intense.

# CHAPTER 8

# *Currents of the 1890s and Territorial Expansion*

B Y the 1890s the enormous growth in the American economy, which already in the 1880s had aroused considerable interest in commercial expansion, had convinced not only Washington but most business leaders and many publicists that it was essential to cultivate foreign markets. Arthur and Frelinghuysen had favored commercial expansion but had opposed territorial expansion; in the 1890s many Americans came to wonder whether exports could be significantly increased without the acquisition of colonies, which not only would themselves provide markets but, more important, would serve as points of strength for ensuring access to larger markets nearby. The new attention to territorial expansion resulted from the continuing economic growth at home, from changing policies abroad, and from new ideas and outlooks. We must examine these various matters.

The Arthur administration's attempts to boost exports had come to grief, for the most part, when Cleveland shipwrecked Freling-huysen's reciprocity treaties and the Congo General Act. Under Benjamin Harrison the Republicans again experimented with reci-procity. By authority of the McKinley tariff act of 1890 they con-cluded reciprocity treaties with Austria-Hungary, Brazil, Santo Domingo, Spain (for Cuba and Puerto Rico), Salvador, Great Brit-ain (for British West Indian islands and British Guiana), Nicaragua, Honduras, and Guatemala. But the familiar story repeated itself:

1. Secretary of State William H. Seward.

2. Senator Charles Sumner.

(*Harper's Weekly*, March 24, 1866)

3. President Ulysses S. Grant.
(Library of Congress)

4. Secretary of State Hamilton
(Library of Congress)

5. Prime Minister William E. Gladstone.
(Reproduced by permission of The Huntington Library, San Marino, California)

Sir John A. Macdonald, Prime Minister f Canada.
Library of Congress)

'oreign Secretary Lord Granville.
roduced by permission of The Hunt-n Library, San Marino, California)

8. The Geneva Conference—the American arbitrator and counsel. William M. Evarts, in the upper right-hand corner, later became Secretary of State.

*(Harper's Weekly,* February 3, 1872)

Sir Alexander Cockburn, Lord Chief
e and British arbitrator at Geneva.

10. President and Mrs. Rutherford B.
Hayes.

roduced by permission of The Hunt-
n Library, San Marino, California)

(Reproduced by permission of The Huntington Library, San Marino, California)

11. The projected Nicaragua canal.     (*Harper's Weekly,* January 19, 1889)

12.   The United States coaling station, Pago Pago, with King Tamasese (left) and King Malietoa.

(*Harper's Weekly*, February 2, 1889)

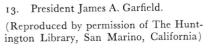

13. President James A. Garfield.
(Reproduced by permission of The Huntington Library, San Marino, California)

Secretary of State James G. Blaine.
produced by permission of The Hunt-
on Library, San Marino, California)

15. President Chester A. Arthur.

(Reproduced by permission of The H[unt]ington Library, San Marino, Califor[nia])

16. President Grover Cleveland.

(Library of Congress)

17. Secretary of State
Frederick T. Frelinghuysen.

*(Harper's Weekly,* May 30, 1885)

8. John W. Foster, Minister to Mexico
nd Spain and, later, Secretary of State.
Reproduced by permission of The Hunt-
ngton Library, San Marino, California)

19. Secretary of State Thomas F. Bayard.
(Reproduced by permission of The Huntington Library, San Marino, California)

). Porfirio Díaz, President of Mexico.
Harper's Weekly, January 17, 1885)

21. Commodore Robert W. Shufeldt.
(Library of Congress)

22. Prime Minister and Foreign
Secretary Lord Salisbury.
(Library of Congress)

23. Senator George Frisbie Hoar.
(Reproduced by permission of The Hun
ington Library, San Marino, Californi

4. Captain Alfred T. Mahan.

5. Secretary of the Navy Benjamin F. Tracy.

6. President Benjamin Harrison.

27. Sir Julian Pauncefote, British Minister and, then, Ambassador to the United States.

(*Harper's Weekly*, November 2, 1889)

28. Secretary of State Richard Olney.

(Reproduced by permission of The Huntington Library, San Marino, California)

29. John Sherman, Senator and, then, Secretary of State.

(Reproduced by permission of The Huntington Library, San Marino, California)

30. Senator John T. Morgan.

(Reproduced by permission of The Huntington Library, San Marino, California)

31. Thomas B. Reed, Speaker of the House of Representatives.

(Reproduced by permission of The Huntington Library, San Marino, California)

32. Theodore Roosevelt in his new uniform.

(Reproduced by permission of The Huntington Library, San Marino, California)

33. Senator Henry Cabot Lodge.

(Reproduced by permission of The Huntington Library, San Marino, California)

34. President William McKinley.

(Reproduced by permission of The Huntington Library, San Marino, California)

35. Secretary of State John Hay.

(Reproduced by permission of The Huntington Library, San Marino, California)

36. Senator Redfield Proctor.

(Reproduced by permission of The Huntington Library, San Marino, California)

37.   The Battle of Manila Bay.      *(Harper's Weekly,* May 14, 1898)

38.   Jules Cambon, French Minister to the United States, signs the armistice with Spain on August 12, 1898, as Secretary of State William R. Day, seated at Cambon's right, and President McKinley, standing at the end of the table, and others, look on.

(Reproduced by permission of The Huntington Library, San Marino, California)

39. William W. Rockhill, John Hay's adviser on Far Eastern policy.

(Reproduced by permission of The Huntington Library, San Marino, California)

40. Rear Admiral George Dewey in Manila.

(Reproduced by permission of The Huntington Library, San Marino, California)

Cleveland, again President in 1893 and still opposed to preferential tariff arrangements, terminated them all in 1894.[1]

If export promotion was so important, why did not American business interests induce Washington to act more resolutely? The fact is that most businessmen were apathetic about exporting until the mid-1890s. The home market was, generally speaking, quite adequate for their needs—although we have observed the considerable interest in Mexican and South American markets, in pork exports to Europe, and in such remote places as Korea and the Congo. Moreover, most exports consisted of agricultural goods, notably wheat and cotton; in 1875 exports of these two items alone had a value of $251 million, as compared with $499 million for total exports; in 1881, $416 million against $884 million.[2] For many years after 1874 crops were poor in Europe, where the great bulk of American agricultural produce went; in the "black year" of 1879 they were catastrophic. A British royal commission of 1879 and another of 1893 foresaw no end to the avalanche pouring in from the American plains and prairies. In these circumstances there was little reason for anxiety about foreign markets.[3] No wonder that American consuls in the 1870s and 1880s were described as being "almost pathetic" in begging business interests back home to wake up to the trade opportunities theirs for the asking.[4] Worry about exporting simply did not exist on a large scale until the 1890s.

During that decade a major change occurred in the trade balance of manufactured goods; and it not only transformed ideas about

1. Edgar J. Gibson, "Reciprocity and Foreign Trade," *Forum*, XXXII (1901), 466–80; *Senate Executive Documents*, 52 Cong., 1 Sess., No. 119 (Serial 2901); *House Reports*, 54 Cong., 1 Sess., No. 2263 (Serial 3466), pp. 7–13, 21–26. The Dingley tariff of 1897 authorized extremely limited reciprocity agreements; through 1900 four were concluded (with France, Germany, Italy, and Portugal), but they had very minor importance.

2. U.S. Bureau of the Census, *Historical Statistics of the United States, Colonial Times to 1957* (Washington, 1960), pp. 545–47.

3. William Trimble, "Historical Aspects of the Surplus Food Production of the United States, 1862–1902," *Annual Report of the American Historical Association, 1918* (2 vols., Washington, 1921), I, 229–30. See also Morton Rothstein, "America in the International Rivalry for the British Wheat Market, 1870–1914," *Mississippi Valley Historical Review*, XLVII (1960), 401–18. Regarding American agricultural interests and foreign policy see William A. Williams, *The Roots of the Modern American Empire: A Study of the Growth and Shaping of Social Consciousness in a Marketplace Society* (New York, 1969).

4. Ferdinand W. Peck, "The United States at the Paris Exposition in 1900," *North American Review*, CLXVIII (1899), 27.

exporting, but it directly affected industrialists, a group that had much more influence in Washington than agriculturalists had. We have seen that a favorable balance of trade for all kinds of merchandise, agricultural as well as industrial, was first achieved on a continuing basis in 1876; but the balance of manufactures remained on the debit side. Trends of commerce, however, indicated an early reversal; and in 1894 exports of manufactures passed imports; they continued to be greater during the years to come.[5] The reversal came mainly from the staggering increase in American industrial output; this gave rise, in turn, to an equally staggering increase in exports of manufactures: from $89 million in 1865 to $805 million in 1900. Contrasting with this more than ninefold rise was an increase in imports of manufactures from $174 million in 1865 to $470 million in 1900, less than a threefold rise.[6]

It was highly gratifying, of course, to have such a booming economy;[7] but at the same time it was worrying. For where could ever-expanding markets be found for the ever-increasing industrial output? The domestic market, businessmen believed, was not large enough. Nor were the traditional markets in industrialized Europe, which absorbed the American agricultural output, expected to take this quite different, industrial output. The lesson of the rising tide of manufactures seemed clear: somehow, and at all costs, the United States must increase her exports; otherwise the home market would become saturated with a mounting surplus.

Much of the alarm about the surplus is attributable to the panic of 1893 and the great depression that followed. These events rocked the country to its foundations. Not only was the economic distress severe, but social disorders and the rise of the Populist party appeared to portend dire calamity. For conservatives, everything was going alarmingly wrong. Catastrophic business conditions,

5. *Historical Statistics,* pp. 544–45; manufactured foodstuffs and semimanufactures are taken into the calculation as well as finished manufactures. See also Worthington C. Ford, "The Turning of the Tide," *North American Review,* CLXI (1895), 187–95.

6. *Historical Statistics,* pp. 544–45; these figures include semimanufactures and manufactured foodstuffs as well as finished manufactures.

7. Paul S. Holbo, "Economics, Emotion, and Expansion: An Emerging Foreign Policy," in H. Wayne Morgan (ed.), *The Gilded Age* (2d ed., Syracuse, 1970), p. 202, does well to emphasize that "the productive capacity was not seen primarily as an economic problem, but evidence of strength and prosperity." See also *ibid.,* pp. 204–11.

widespread radicalism, violent strikes—such dreadful happenings seemed to presage the disintegration of the social structure itself. After a century of brilliant success, were American institutions and ideals about to founder in chaos?

What caused the depression? Farmers typically attributed it to a scarcity of money and prescribed the free coinage of silver. Most business leaders, on the other hand, put the blame on overproduction, particularly of manufactured goods, and prescribed not financial tinkering but exporting the surplus.[8] The worst of the distress came during Grover Cleveland's second administration (1893–1897). A strong gold-standard, low-tariff man, the President attempted to restore the plummeting economy by acting on two fronts: one relating to the currency; the other, the tariff. Both had direct implications for exporting. To strengthen the currency he fought hard and successfully for the repeal in 1893 of part of the Sherman Silver Purchase Act, which required the government to buy large quantities of silver every month, and he also replenished the Treasury's gold holdings by selling bonds. Businessmen in general strongly applauded these steps, partly because they accepted the overproduction thesis with its corollary that the surplus must be exported. They and the administration were in full accord that the gold standard, which Cleveland's measures were supporting, provided the stable exchange rates necessary for thriving international commerce— and consequently for export expansion. This was the accepted, orthodox doctrine. It contrasted sharply with the beliefs of free-silverites, who generally put less emphasis on foreign markets because they thought that if more money was created, Americans could themselves purchase enough goods to prevent a surplus from arising. Some silverites, but fewer in number, agreed with the gold-standard advocates on the importance of foreign markets. In many cases highly respectable businessmen, they advocated bimetallism not through free silver but by international agreement; and every President from Hayes through McKinley sent missions to Europe or participated in bimetallic conferences in the vain hope of arranging European and American bimetal-

8. Charles S. Campbell, *Special Business Interests and the Open Door Policy* (New Haven, 1951), ch. 1; Walter LaFeber, *The New Empire: An Interpretation of American Expansion, 1860–1898* (Ithaca, 1963), ch. 4.

lism—or at least of quieting the clamor for free silver.[9]

Cleveland's second device for dealing with the depression—the Wilson-Gorman tariff of 1894—also brought up considerations of overproduction and overseas markets. The chief purpose of the McKinley tariff of 1890 had been to protect the home market, but it had also provided for the small measure of reciprocity we have noted. Republicans extolled reciprocity as an ingenious device to gain foreign markets while retaining protection against cheap foreign labor. Democrats scoffed at this view.[10] They agreed, to be sure (at least before 1896), that foreign markets were essential in order to prop up the collapsing economy. But their prescription for exporting the surplus was not reciprocity but duty-free raw materials; and the contention that export promotion depended on cheaper raw materials furnished perhaps the main argument for the tariff of 1894. Thus Representative William L. Wilson, who had charge of the bill in the House, reported for the Ways and Means Committee that every duty on raw materials raised the price of the finished product and thereby narrowed export possibilities; and the Senate's leading supporter of the bill, Roger Q. Mills, argued: "It is the tax on the materials of manufacture alone that keeps us out of foreign markets. . . ."[11]

The tariff measure as passed by the House on February 1, 1894, contained a long duty-free list that included many components of industrial exports. But the Senate, as a result of pressure from special interests, deleted everything on the list except wool, copper, and lumber, an altogether inadequate basis for export promotion.

9. *House Miscellaneous Documents,* 49 Cong., 1 Sess., No. 396 (Serial 2430), Pt. 2; *Senate Executive Documents,* 45 Cong., 3 Sess., No. 58 (Serial 1832); *ibid.,* 50 Cong., 1 Sess., No. 34 (Serial 2504); *ibid.,* 52 Cong., 2 Sess., No. 82 (Serial 3062); *Proceedings of the International Monetary Conference* . . . (Washington, 1887); Henry B. Russell, *International Monetary Conferences* . . . (New York, 1898); Jeannette P. Nichols, "Silver Diplomacy," *Political Science Quarterly,* XLVIII (1933), 565–88, and "A Painful Lesson in Silver Diplomacy," *South Atlantic Quarterly,* XXXV (1936), 251–72.

10. See, for example, George G. Vest, "The Real Issue," *North American Review,* CLV (1892), 401–6; William L. Wilson, "The Republican Policy of Reciprocity," *Forum,* XIV (1892), 255–64.

11. Roger Q. Mills, "The Wilson Bill," *North American Review,* CLVIII (1894), 242; *Congressional Record,* 53 Cong., 2 Sess., pp. 1796–97 (Feb. 1, 1894). See also Cleveland's annual message, Dec. 4, 1893, James D. Richardson (ed.), *A Compilation of the Messages and Papers of the Presidents, 1789–1897* (10 vols., Washington, 1899), IX, 459.

The Senate passed the emasculated bill on July 3, 1894; Cleveland reluctantly signed it the next month.[12]

Cleveland Democrats backed both the gold standard and low tariffs; Republicans, although generally supporting the gold standard, advocated high tariffs and, in some cases, reciprocity. But Cleveland Democrats and Republicans alike typically attributed the depression to surplus production and emphasized the necessity of cultivating foreign markets—although for Republicans, maintaining high tariff rates had first priority.[13] Commercial expansion became a much more important objective of policy than it had been in the 1880s.

Where were foreign markets to be found? For many years Americans had looked to Latin America and, even more, to the great potential market of China with its 400 million supposedly eager customers.[14] And now the depression of the 1890s clarified and intensified these older views. So did other developments. The fact was that Latin America and China were desirable not only on their own merits; they were desirable also because most other large markets seemed in danger of being closed to American exports. In the middle years of the century colonies had been unfashionable in Western countries—a "mill-stone round our necks," Benjamin Disraeli, soon to be a leading British imperialist, had called them as late as 1852.[15] But in the 1880s the great powers of Europe, now including Germany, embarked again upon a race for colonies, and in the 1890s Japan joined them. Two new and powerful navies, the German and Japanese, made their appearance; and Japan's intentions in Hawaii came to seem to Americans as sinister as Germany's in Samoa.

By the late 1890s the slicing up of Africa among the great powers, with the consequent erection of discriminatory tariffs, had been practically completed. There were signs that even America's Euro-

12. *Congressional Record,* 53 Cong., 2 Sess., p. 7136 (July 3, 1894). See also Festus P. Summers, *William L. Wilson and Tariff Reform* (New Brunswick, N.J., 1953), chs. 10–12; John R. Lambert, *Arthur Pue Gorman* (Baton Rouge, 1953), ch. 10.

13. Holbo, "Economics, Emotion, and Expansion," pp. 203–11.

14. Campbell, *Special Business Interests,* ch. 2.

15. William F. Monypenny and George E. Buckle, *The Life of Benjamin Disraeli, Earl of Beaconsfield* (6 vols., New York, 1910–20), III, 385; Carl A. Bodelsen, *Studies in Mid-Victorian Imperialism* (Copenhagen, 1924).

pean markets might soon be walled in. In a much-noticed speech regarding the perils for Europe posed by the colossal American economic machine, Count Agenor Goluchowski, Foreign Minister of Austria-Hungary, warned: "The destructive competition with transoceanic countries . . . requires prompt and thorough counteracting measures. . . . The European nations must close their ranks in order successfully to defend their existence." This and other such remarks worried Americans.[16] About that same time the most dynamic public figure in Great Britain, Colonial Secretary Joseph Chamberlain, was campaigning for imperial preference by which the British empire, hitherto open to world commerce, would erect a tariff wall against outside countries. Should the vast British world abandon free trade, American exporters would be hard hit. China, too, seemed in danger of being partitioned, but Americans could hope to influence events there more than in Africa, Europe, and the British empire.

For United States foreign policy, the lesson of these domestic and international economic trends of the 1890s was clear. Everyone agreed that, to be more competitive with her European rivals, the United States needed a shorter sea route between her industrial center in the northeast and her potential markets in China and on the west coast of South America. This an isthmian canal would provide. In short, the economic trends of the 1890s, now reinforcing the older strategic and geographic considerations attendant upon west coast settlement, pointed urgently to a canal and to the Caribbean and Hawaiian bases needed for its protection. As yet, however, there was nothing like a consensus for even these basic objectives, and the old-fashioned repugnance for anything smacking of territorial expansion overseas remained remarkably strong.[17] Notwithstanding the historic shift to an export surplus of manufactured goods, and notwithstanding the depression of the 1890s and the ominous signs of closing markets around the world, both the government and the business community continued to have faith in commercial expansion, unaccompanied by territorial expansion, as adequate to relieve the surplus.[18] The faith was somewhat old-

16. Campbell, *Special Business Interests,* pp. 6–8.
17. Regarding the anti-imperialist tradition see Ernest R. May, *American Imperialism: A Speculative Essay* (New York, 1967), ch. 5.
18. Julius W. Pratt, *Expansionists of 1898: The Acquisition of Hawaii and the Spanish Islands* (Baltimore, 1936), ch. 7.

fashioned in a world of high and proliferating tariff walls (outside the British empire); it had in fact been greatly weakened, and a canal and bases in the Caribbean and Hawaii had come much more into national favor. But not until the Spanish-American War did sentiment turn irresistibly to territorial expansion.

If economic developments of the 1890s reinforced the pressures making for territorial expansion, so did currents of thought.[19] During the last decades of the nineteenth century, the fashionable philosophy in the United States was that expounded by an Englishman, Herbert Spencer. Although himself an original thinker, Spencer derived his most influential ideas from the theory of evolution advanced by Charles Darwin, whose *Origin of Species* had been published in 1859. Spencer believed that evolution operated not only in biological species but in human society. Social Darwinism, as his extension of Darwin's theory came to be called, made a tremendous impact on the United States, where it was thought to hold a lesson for foreign policy.[20] The lesson, as often interpreted, was this: Just as an ever-exerting force of natural selection drives a biological species either to progress or else to decay, so it does too with a nation. Consequently a nation such as the United States, if it is not to perish in the brutal struggle for survival of the fittest, must compete fiercely with other nations. It must fight unceasingly for its place in the sun, and to that end it must ruthlessly swallow up weaker lands.

Spencer's ideas, and distortions of them, filled American publications during the 1880s and 1890s. They contributed to a more aggressive climate of opinion, and therefore to a more aggressive foreign policy. Sometimes they were applied to particular situations. Thus John Barrett, former American minister to Siam, appealing in 1898 for the annexation of the Philippine Islands, argued that "now is the critical time when the United States should strain every nerve and bend all energies to keep well to the front in the mighty struggle that has begun for the supremacy of the Pacific

19. Henry S. Commager, *The American Mind: An Interpretation of American Thought and Character since the 1880's* (New Haven, 1950), ch. 4; LaFeber, *New Empire*, ch. 2; Frederick Merk, *Manifest Destiny and Mission in American History: A Reinterpretation* (New York, 1963), ch. 11.

20. Richard Hofstadter, *Social Darwinism in American Thought* (New York, 1959). See also Albert K. Weinberg, *Manifest Destiny: A Study of Nationalistic Expansionism in American History* (Baltimore, 1935), p. 212; Bert J. Loewenberg, "Darwinism Comes to America, 1859–1900," *Mississippi Valley Historical Review*, XXVIII (1941), 339–68.

Seas. . . . The rule of the survival of the fittest applies to nations as well as to the animal kingdom." And a contemporary of his wrote: "By repeated annexations we advanced to the Pacific. . . . To advance still further is in accordance with the uninterrupted tendency of the country. . . . The survival of the fittest seems to be the law of nations as well as a law of nature."[21]

Often associated with Social Darwinism was a belief in inherent racial inequality. The belief had been given an apparently scientific foundation by Count Arthur Gobineau, whose *Moral and Intellectual Diversity of Races* was published in the United States in 1856. Gobineau's thesis was popularly supposed to explain the accomplishments of the Anglo-Saxons. For unless Anglo-Saxons were inherently superior, how could one account for the astounding expansion of Great Britain, two tiny isles on whose far-flung empire the sun never set? And how account for the success of the United States, who in a century had conquered a continent and achieved world economic supremacy? For Darwin, too, Anglo-Saxon superiority was manifest, but he attributed it to the struggle for survival. "There is apparently much truth," he wrote, "in the belief that the wonderful progress of the United States, as well as the character of the people, are the results of natural selection . . ."; and he quoted approvingly a remark in a recent book: "All other series of events —as that which resulted in the empire of Rome—only appear to have purpose and value when viewed in connection with, or rather as subsidiary to . . . the great stream of Anglo-Saxon emigration to the west."[22] In the 1890s Anglo-Saxonism was pervasive and deeprooted in American thinking; its consequences for foreign policy were enormous.

Anglo-Saxonism of course affected relations with Great Britain, but it also influenced territorial expansion. One could argue, and many did, that if the Anglo-Saxons were superior, they had a positive duty to spread the blessings of their rule to less-favored people. By this teaching, moralistic aversion to imperialism disappeared; it

21. John Barrett, "The Problem of the Philippines," *North American Review*, CLXVII (1898), 267; Charles K. Adams, "Colonies and Other Dependencies," *Forum*, XXVII (1899), 46. Regarding Barrett see Salvatore Prisco III, *John Barrett, Progressive Era Diplomat: A Study of a Commercial Expansionist, 1887–1920* (University, Alabama, 1973).

22. Charles Darwin, *The Descent of Man and Selection in Relation to Sex* (New York, 1896), p. 142. Darwin's quotation is from Foster B. Zincke, *Last Winter in the United States* . . . (London, 1868), p. 29.

was expansionists who donned the mantle of virtue. However, the influence of racism was ambivalent. It cut two ways: it led to a belief in the righteousness of annexing supposedly inferior people, but it led also to a disinclination to annex them, out of fear that the superior stock would be depreciated. We have seen that in the 1870s abolitionists had opposed annexing tropical areas, in part because of the strong belief held by many of them that the black man, however deserving of freedom, was inferior to the white man. This consideration had contributed to the Senate's defeat of Grant's treaty for the annexation of Santo Domingo; and because of its pervasiveness in the United States a writer has asked, "Is it not likely that racism, prior to the war with Spain, was a deterrent to imperialism rather than a stimulant of it?"[23] One cannot be sure of the answer to this searching question, but a reasonable guess is that whereas racism was a deterrent in the 1870s, it was not in the 1890s. In this later decade arguments abounded that the United States had a moral duty to extend her civilization and rule to supposedly inferior natives; and there is every reason to suppose that Americans found the arguments convincing. On balance, the belief in Anglo-Saxon supremacy encouraged territorial expansion at the end of the century.

The most effective American popularizer of Social Darwinism and Anglo-Saxonism was John Fiske. With something approaching religious zeal he delivered his famous lecture on "Manifest Destiny" hundreds of times all over the country. "It is enough," Fiske would declaim, "to point to the general conclusion that the work which the English race began when it colonized North America is destined to go on until every land on the earth's surface that is not already the seat of an old civilization shall become English in its language, in its religion, in its political habits and traditions, and to a predominant extent in the blood of its people."[24] This message, so often repeated, made an impact.

During the 1870s, 1880s, and 1890s an important shift occurred

23. Merk, *Manifest Destiny*, p. 247; see also pp. 24–28.
24. John Fiske, "Manifest Destiny," *Harper's New Monthly Magazine*, LXX (1885), 588. Milton Berman, *John Fiske: The Evolution of a Popularizer* (Cambridge, Mass., 1961). Merk, *Manifest Destiny*, pp. 238–39, shows that historians have exaggerated Fiske's racism.

in the ideas of British and Continental writers about colonialism.[25] It paralleled the change in national policies: away from the disinclination to acquire colonies that characterized the middle years of the century to the territorial expansion practiced by every major European power in the 1880s and 1890s. Such influential writers as Paul Leroy-Beaulieu, Friedrich Fabri, James Anthony Froude, Benjamin Kidd, and Charles H. Pearson challenged the older opinion that colonies were worthless to the colonial powers; Froude, Charles W. Dilke, and John R. Seeley also stressed the benefits bestowed upon the colonial natives. Imperialism again became fashionable among intellectuals in Europe. Did the new vogue spread to America? It is reasonable to suppose that, at a time when most educated American readers still looked to Europe for fresh ideas, the new views about imperialism had a profound effect in the United States. Similarly the renewed European practice of imperialism was persuasive, because activity so general must be based on some good reason; at any rate, it was natural for Americans to suspect this.[26] Altogether the European ideas and practices contributed to an atmosphere in the United States much more conducive to territorial expansion overseas.

An American who popularized the ideas of the 1890s, while also, unlike John Fiske, contributing an original idea of his own, was Captain Alfred T. Mahan, president of the Naval War College at Newport, Rhode Island, from 1886 to 1889 and from 1892 to 1893. His famous book, *The Influence of Sea Power on History, 1660–1783,* appeared in 1890. It presented the thesis that throughout history sea power furnished the key to national supremacy. Argued with great cogency and literary ability, the thesis took its place as another germinal idea in the 1890s.[27] But Mahan, a career naval officer, was not interested merely in formulating a theory; "the practical object

25. May, *American Imperialism,* ch. 6.
26. *Ibid.,* ch. 7.
27. William D. Puleston, *Mahan: The Life and Works of Captain Alfred Thayer Mahan, U.S.N.* (New Haven, 1939); William E. Livezey, *Mahan on Sea Power* (Norman, Okla., 1947); Robert Seager II, "Ten Years before Mahan: The Unofficial Case for the New Navy, 1880–1890," *Mississippi Valley Historical Review,* XL (1953), 491–512, shows that considerable American awareness of the significance of sea power existed before 1890. See also John A. S. Grenville and George B. Young, *Politics, Strategy, and American Diplomacy: Studies in Foreign Policy, 1873–1917* (New Haven, 1966), ch. 1; Kenneth J. Hagan, *American Gunboat Diplomacy and the Old Navy, 1877–1889* (Westport, Conn., 1973).

of this inquiry," he wrote, "is to draw from the lessons of history inferences applicable to one's own country. . . ."[28] In a series of articles during the 1890s he drew the inferences, military and economic, for American foreign policy.

Mahan's conception of the country's military requirements was simple. The United States needed enough capital ships to command a wide zone off both coasts.[29] The relationship between sea power and economic requirements was more complex. Mahan was deeply worried about the mounting industrial surplus.[30] Ever since the Civil War, he wrote in 1890, the United States had concentrated on preserving the home market. This goal was now out of date. "Whether they will or no, Americans must now begin to look outward. The growing production of the country demands it." The "growing production" demanded also extensive shipping. Shipping, in turn, depended upon a navy.[31] But the reverse was also true: "Durable naval power . . . depends ultimately upon extensive commercial relations . . . ," because the large number of people gaining their livelihood from shipping would constitute an indispensable pressure group for a navy.[32]

In addition to a large commerce, extensive shipping, and a powerful navy, the scholarly captain argued for colonial acquisitions. He did not envisage an empire on the British model; America's colonies, rather than themselves providing markets for the surplus, would serve as bases that would enable the navy to hold open the doors to the really important markets in independent countries.[33]

Throughout Mahan's writings ran a strong vein of Social Darwinism and Anglo-Saxonism. "In the rivalries of nations, in the accentuation of difficulties, in the conflict of ambitions, lies the pres-

28. Alfred T. Mahan, *The Influence of Sea Power upon History, 1660–1783* (Boston, 1898), p. 83.
29. Harold and Margaret Sprout, *The Rise of American Naval Power, 1776–1918* (Princeton, 1939), pp. 204–5.
30. Mahan, *Influence of Sea Power*, ch. 1; Walter LaFeber, "A Note on the 'Mercantilistic Imperialism' of Alfred Thayer Mahan," *Mississippi Valley Historical Review*, XLVIII (1962), 674–85.
31. Alfred T. Mahan, "The United States Looking Outward," *Atlantic Monthly*, LXVI (1890), 816; *Influence of Sea Power*, p. 26.
32. Alfred T. Mahan, "Preparedness for Naval War," *Harper's New Monthly Magazine*, XCIV (1897), 588; *Influence of Sea Power*, p. 88.
33. *Ibid.*, p. 28.

ervation of the martial spirit, which alone is capable of coping firmly with the destructive forces that from outside and from within threaten to submerge all that the centuries have gained." Europe and America he portrayed as an "oasis set in the midst of a desert of barbarism"; and to safeguard the oasis he advocated close cooperation with the British, for whom he had enormous respect as wielders of sea power and fellow Anglo-Saxons.[34]

Both military and economic considerations pointed to one prime need: an isthmian canal. (But Mahan cautioned that the United States should not build one until she had a navy large enough to guard it.)[35] A canal would increase the navy's mobility, and it would foster exports. As potential markets Mahan emphasized Latin America and, still more, China; he wrote that "the consequences of an artificial waterway that shall enable the Atlantic coast to compete with Europe, on equal terms as to distance, for the markets of eastern Asia, and shall shorten by two-thirds the sea route from New York to San Francisco, and by one-half that to Valparaiso, is too evident for insistence."[36] So vital a waterway would have to be protected. This could be done by acquiring bases in the Caribbean Sea and by annexing the Hawaiian Islands. (Mahan told his country-men that a Hawaiian rebellion of 1893 held out "a warning that the time has come when we must make up our minds.") Besides guard-ing the canal, these bases would be "resting-places" for American warships, which in wartime, without bases, "will be like land birds, unable to fly far from their own shores."[37]

A canal, bases in the Caribbean and Hawaii, a strong navy with capital ships—these, he hammered home in his many persuasive articles, should be the principal objectives of United States foreign policy. They were the same objectives, although with more explicit reference to a navy, as those prescribed by the geographic and economic forces that we have observed—and hence the power of Mahan's writings.

What was his influence? Among a small group of men strategically

34. Alfred T. Mahan, *The Interest of America in Sea Power, Present and Future* (Boston, 1898), p. 122; "Possibilities of an Anglo-American Reunion," *North American Review*, CLIX (1894), 556.

35. Mahan, "United States Looking Outward," p. 819.

36. Alfred T. Mahan, "The Isthmus and Sea Power," *Atlantic Monthly*, LXXII (1893), 471.

37. *Ibid.*, pp. 470–72; Mahan, *Influence of Sea Power*, pp. 33–35, 83.

placed, it was enormous; among the general public, less but still very significant. Mahan was in close touch with a number of men in high places: Benjamin F. Tracy, Secretary of the Navy from 1889 to 1893; Hilary A. Herbert, Tracy's immediate successor; John Hay, who moved from the London Embassy to become Secretary of State in 1898; Whitelaw Reid, owner of the New York *Tribune,* the country's leading Republican newspaper; Henry Adams, son of Charles Francis Adams and grandson of John Quincy Adams, and himself a distinguished writer on historical and other subjects; Albert J. Beveridge, who became a Senator in 1899; and Albert Shaw, editor of the *Review of Reviews.* Particularly noteworthy was the captain's influence on Henry Cabot Lodge and Theodore Roosevelt. Although neither of these men had as yet the power they would later acquire, both occupied positions of some importance. Lodge, a Senator from Massachusetts, was appointed to the Foreign Relations Committee in 1895; Roosevelt became Assistant Secretary of the Navy in 1897. They were fervent apostles of what Lodge called the "large policy";[38] it envisaged, essentially, constructing an isthmian canal and acquiring Caribbean and Hawaiian bases—exactly what their naval mentor was advocating in his articles and in many letters to his two friends.

With similar ideas and backgrounds, some of these men constituted a closely knit little coterie. They frequented Henry Adams's mansion on H Street, across Lafayette Square from the White House; and, around the corner on Sixteenth Street, John Hay's residence.[39] They accepted Mahan's main ideas; they advocated overseas commercial and territorial expansion. Intelligent and determined, they served as a channel between Mahan, with his synthesis of the seminal ideas of the day and his emphasis on sea power, and men in the highest seats of power. If only because of his influence upon this well-placed group, Alfred T. Mahan did much to mold American policy toward territorial expansion.

38. Lodge to Roosevelt, May 24, 1898, *Selections from the Correspondence of Theodore Roosevelt and Henry Cabot Lodge, 1884–1918* (2 vols., New York, 1925), I, 300; see also Julius W. Pratt, "The 'Large Policy' of 1898," *Mississippi Valley Historical Review,* XIX (1932), 219–42.

39. Matthew Josephson, *The President Makers: The Culture of Politics and Leadership in an Age of Enlightenment, 1896–1919* (New York, 1940), ch. 1; Harold D. Cater, *Henry Adams and His Friends: A Collection of His Unpublished Letters* (Boston, 1947), preface; Arthur F. Beringause, *Brooks Adams: A Biography* (New York, 1955), chs. 5, 6.

Two other Americans, both original thinkers, should be mentioned. One of the frequenters of Henry Adams's house was his brother Brooks. In his book *The Law of Civilization and Decay: An Essay in History,* first published in 1895, Brooks Adams formulated the hypothesis that society, under compulsion of his Law, oscillated between barbarism and civilization; and he suggested that Western civilization, now dominated by an arid commercialism, was doomed to revert to barbarism before long. His other pre-1900 writing (three magazine articles) reflected the current determinism, Social Darwinism, alarm over the surplus, and fixation on an isthmian canal and on China as a potential market: "Such great movements . . . are not determined by argument, but are determined by forces which override the volition of man"; "Nothing under the sun is stationary: not to advance is to recede"; ". . . America has been irresistibly impelled to produce a large industrial surplus"; "The expansion of any country must depend on the markets for its surplus product; and China is the only region which now provides almost boundless possibilities of absorption"; "a canal to the Pacific must be built."[40]

*The Law of Civilization and Decay* made a deep impression on Theodore Roosevelt, who wrote a long review of it in 1897.[41] No doubt some of the other visitors at Henry Adams's house read the book, and also the articles; and one may hazard the guess that through conversations with these men Brooks Adams helped prepare the ground for the coming territorial expansion. But his book and articles had very limited circulation. His impact on American foreign policy, before 1900, was not comparable to Mahan's.[42]

In 1893 a young professor, Frederick Jackson Turner, published an essay on "The Significance of the Frontier in American History."

40. Brooks Adams, "The Spanish War and the Equilibrium of the World," *Forum,* XXV (1898), 651; "England's Decadence in the West Indies," *Ibid.,* XXVII (1899), 477; "The Commercial Future: I. The New Struggle for Life among Nations (From an American Standpoint)," *Fortnightly Review,* LXV (1899), 276; "Spanish War and the Equilibrium of the World," p. 649; "England's Decadence in the West Indies," p. 477. His book *America's Economic Supremacy* was published in New York in 1900.

41. Theodore Roosevelt, "The Law of Civilization and Decay," *Forum,* XXII (1897), 575–89.

42. Thornton Anderson, *Brooks Adams, Constructive Conservative* (Ithaca, 1951), p. 193; Beringause, *Brooks Adams,* pp. 205–6. For a somewhat contrary view see William A. Williams, "Brooks Adams and American Expansion," *New England Quarterly,* XXV (1952), 217–32. See also Charles Vevier, "Brooks Adams and the Ambivalence of American Foreign Policy," *World Affairs Quarterly,* XXX (1959), 3–18; LaFeber, *New Empire,* pp. 80–85.

Throughout their history Americans had cherished the comforting belief that if ever things became too difficult at home, they could begin life anew on the beckoning frontier in the golden west. But now, Turner pronounced, "never again will such gifts of free land offer themselves"; never again will the frontier provide "a gate of escape from the bondage of the past." "And now," he concluded sadly, "four centuries from the discovery of America, at the end of a hundred years of life under the Constitution, the frontier has gone, and with its going has closed the first period of American history."[43] What did the future hold? To those who pondered the melancholy pronouncements of the young historian, that future looked bleak. And coupling, as some did, the end of the frontier with the coming of the surplus compounded the dilemma.[44]

The frontier thesis, if true, presented a far more profound interpretation of the collapse of the 1890s than did either the overproduction or the free-silver theory. Both these theories offered facile cures. But could there be a cure for so deep-rooted a malady as the end of the frontier? Perhaps Turner had one in mind when he wrote in the same essay: "He would be a rash prophet who should assert that the expansive character of American life has now entirely ceased. Movement has been its dominant fact, and, unless this training has no effect upon a people, the American energy will continually demand a wider field for its exercise."[45] Certainly the reference to the "expansive character" and the "wider field" did not have to be construed as advocacy of overseas territorial expansion. But it was easy so to construe it. For if American genius and prosperity had derived from expansion along a continental frontier (which no longer existed), was it not now incumbent upon the United States to develop a new frontier overseas?[46]

The essay appeared at a time when various unsystematized notions about a closing frontier were already under discussion.[47] Turner brought them into sharper focus. His thesis, however, was

43. Frederick J. Turner, *The Frontier in American History* (New York, 1921), pp. 37, 38.

44. A. Lawrence Lowell, "The Colonial Expansion of the United States," *Atlantic Monthly*, LXXXIII (1899), 145–54.

45. Turner, *Frontier*, p. 37.

46. Lawrence S. Kaplan, "Frederick Jackson Turner and Imperialism," *Social Sciences*, XXVII (1952), 12–16; William A. Williams, "The Frontier Thesis and American Foreign Policy," *Pacific Historical Review*, XXIV (1955), 379–95.

47. Herman C. Nixon, "The Precursors of Turner in the Interpretation of the American Frontier," *South Atlantic Quarterly*, XXVIII (1929), 83–89.

familiar only to a small number of intellectuals and politicians, some of them of considerable influence. Theodore Roosevelt read the essay not later than 1894, when he congratulated the professor on his "first class ideas."[48] Although Turner's impact was not widely felt until the next century, he undoubtedly contributed somewhat to the gathering mood of the 1890s for territorial expansion.[49]

More influential in promoting territorial expansion in the 1890s was a new United States navy. After the Civil War the navy had seriously deteriorated.[50] Garfield's Secretary of the Navy, William H. Hunt, took the first steps toward rebuilding it, but he could accomplish little before the President's assassination. Hunt's successor, William E. Chandler, was responsible for four steel vessels—the so-called White Squadron, completed between 1885 and 1887—which marked the beginning of a modern navy. Cleveland's first Secretary of the Navy, William C. Whitney, won authorization for thirty vessels, including the ill-fated *Maine* and the *Olympia*, Commodore George Dewey's flagship at Manila Bay in 1898. Nevertheless, the traditional conception of a defensive navy continued to prevail through the 1880s.

48. Elting E. Morison (ed.), et al., *The Letters of Theodore Roosevelt* (7 vols., Cambridge, Mass., 1951), I, 363.

49. For other ideas current in the 1890s see Pratt, *Expansionists of 1898*, ch. 1; May, *American Imperialism*, ch. 6. Two frequently cited writers are Josiah Strong and John W. Burgess. Strong wrote in 1885: "The time is coming when the pressure of population on the means of subsistence will be felt here as it is now felt in Europe and Asia. Then will the world enter upon a new stage of its history—*the final competition of races, for which the Anglo-Saxon is being schooled.* . . . If I read not amiss, this powerful race will move down upon Mexico, down upon Central and South America, out upon the islands of the sea, over upon Africa and beyond. And can anyone doubt that the result of this competition of races will be the 'survival of the fittest'?" *Our Country: Its Possible Future and Its Present Crisis* (New York, 1885), p. 175. These expansionist sentiments have been much quoted in the twentieth century, but apparently were little noticed in the nineteenth. Strong's book had big sales, but its influence on foreign policy was minimal. See Merk, *Manifest Destiny*, pp. 245–47. See also Dorothea R. Muller, "Josiah Strong and American Nationalism: A Reevaluation," *Journal of American History*, LIII (1966), 487–503. Burgess, *Political Science and Comparative Constitutional Law* (2 vols., Boston, 1890), expressed mildly racist views and had some influence. But he was a strong anti-imperialist. See Pratt, *Expansionists of 1898*, pp. 9–10; Merk, *Manifest Destiny*, pp. 240, 245.

50. For general naval histories see John R. Spears, *The History of Our Navy from Its Origin to the End of the War with Spain, 1775–1898* (5 vols., New York, 1902); Sprout, *Rise of American Naval Power;* Allan Westcott (ed.), *American Sea Power since 1775* (Chicago, 1947); Walter R. Herrick, Jr., *The American Naval Revolution* (Baton Rouge, 1966).

The Sad State of the U.S. Navy

By 1890 circumstances were favorable for building capital ships that could act aggressively far from home. Benjamin Harrison, a big-navy advocate, had entered the White House the year before; his Secretary of the Navy, Benjamin F. Tracy, a man of considerable ability, also favored naval expansion. Then, too, the concern over the surplus drew attention to a strong navy that could be a spearhead of worldwide commerce. Tracy was influenced by Mahan's ideas; his first annual report, of 1889, had language that the captain might have written: "To carry on even a defensive war with any hope of success we must have armored battle-ships. . . . We must have the force to raise blockades. . . . we must be able to divert an enemy's force from our coast by threatening his own, for a war, though defensive in principle, may be conducted most effectively by being offensive in its operations."[51] Responsive to these views, Congress in 1890 authorized the construction of "three sea-going coast-line battleships designed to carry the heaviest armor and most powerful ordnance."[52] The momentous step proved to be no transient aberration. Tracy's successor, Hilary A. Herbert, a Democrat, championed capital ships just as warmly;[53] and notwithstanding the depression, Congress authorized several more battleships during Cleveland's second administration.

What effect did the new naval ideas and the great battleships of the 1890s have on United States foreign policy? The old navy had depended on sails; even after steam power came into use, naval vessels carried both sails and coal for many years. When steam power won out, the navy, deprived of its sails, became more dependent on coaling stations around the world; Secretaries Chandler, Tracy, and Herbert all agitated for bases in the Caribbean Sea, the Pacific Ocean, and the Far East.[54] The change to coal undoubtedly stimulated some of the interest in Pago Pago and Pearl Harbor, as well as in the bases taken later from Spain. Furthermore, although the new navy did not dictate territorial expansion, it made this more

51. *Report of the Secretary of the Navy, 1889* (2 vols., Washington, 1889), I, 4.
52. *Congressional Record,* 51 Cong., 1 Sess., pp. 3395–97 (April 15, 1890), p. 5298 (May 26, 1890).
53. *Report of the Secretary of the Navy, 1893* (Washington, 1893), p. 38.
54. *Ibid., 1883* (2 vols., Washington, 1883), I, 32; *ibid., 1884* (2 vols., Washington, 1884), I, 40–41; *ibid., 1889,* I, 31–32; *ibid., 1893,* pp. 101–3; *ibid., 1894* (Washington, 1894), pp. 80–82; Seward W. Livermore, "American Naval-Base Policy in the Far East, 1850–1914," *Pacific Historical Review,* XIII (1944), 113–35.

feasible; and when circumstances became favorable, expansion followed.

The greater emphasis on naval bases and coaling stations is clear enough. Less certain is the validity of such an assertion as that of the New York *Journal of Commerce and Commercial Bulletin,* that "unquestionably naval officers are impatient to use their new fighting machines, and the people have . . . begun to catch the infection from the naval officers."[55] That some jingoism existed in the 1890s is certain, and it is easy to find additional evidence. "I for one have been disturbed and made anxious," Senator Eugene Hale said in 1896, "by the growth of what I may call the aggressive spirit. . . ."[56] "It would be unsafe to deny that there does exist among a body of voters . . . an undefined but not less real feeling that would readily join in a hurrah for war, with whatever nation and for whatever cause," Edward J. Phelps, a former minister to Great Britain, reflected gloomily that same year.[57] And John Bassett Moore, a distinguished international lawyer and Third Assistant Secretary of State during Cleveland's first administration, wrote his old chief, Thomas F. Bayard, in November 1895: "Since the panic two years ago, there has grown up quite a war party, which, while professing no actual grievance, thinks that a war would be a good thing for the country." (But Moore added that "the quiet, honest people . . . form the unclamorous and uncounted majority . . ."; and it is as important to remember this fact, which it surely was, as the existence of a jingoistic minority.)[58]

How is the jingoism to be accounted for? The *Journal of Commerce*'s attribution of it to the new navy, though not without a germ of truth, is too simple. A contemporary of the times observed that America "suffered from that intangible element . . . styled a general 'lack of confidence.' "[59] A more recent writer drew attention to what he

55. Walter Millis, *The Martial Spirit: A Study of Our War with Spain* (Boston, 1931), p. 35; the remark was probably made in 1896.

56. *Congressional Record,* 54 Cong., 1 Sess., p. 2594 (March 9, 1896).

57. Edward J. Phelps, "Arbitration and Our Relations with England," *Atlantic Monthly,* LXXVIII (1896), 27.

58. Charles C. Tansill, *The Foreign Policy of Thomas F. Bayard, 1885–1897* (New York, 1940), pp. 714–15n. For other indications of jingoism see the *Nation,* LXI (Nov. 7, 1895), 322; (Nov. 14, 1895), 340; (Nov. 28, 1895), 377; (Dec. 26, 1895), 460.

59. Harry T. Peck, *Twenty Years of the Republic, 1885–1905* (New York, 1907), p. 627.

called the "psychic crisis of the 1890's."[60] He contended that be-cause of such events as the great depression, the end of the frontier, the rise of gigantic trusts, the domestic social strife—and to this list could be added the disappearance of the old agricultural society under a proliferation of cities and factories, the frightening surplus, the apparent closing of foreign markets, and the encircling Euro-pean bases—because of all these disturbing developments, large numbers of Americans were feeling intensely frustrated. Was the number large enough to be significant? It is difficult to know. And is it true, as the psychic crisis argument goes on to say, that "we tend to respond to frustration with acts of aggression, and to allay anxie-ties by threatening acts against others"?[61] Perhaps so, although psychological theories about frustration and aggression are too con-troversial to be used with confidence.[62] It may be that in some way, still not understood and perhaps not subject to much understand-ing, the deep worries of the 1890s created an irrational desire to lash out. Perhaps frustration did induce a savage impulse to strike Spain and to grab territory; and perhaps these emotions were felt by enough Americans to influence policy. If they were, frustration and a jingoistic spirit help explain the territorial expansion of the late 1890s.

At any rate, the profound influence of America's extraordinary economic growth, of the great depression of the 1890s, of closing markets abroad, of the new navy, and of the current ideas is beyond question. They were not the only forces pointing to territorial ex-pansion overseas, particularly to an isthmian canal and to Caribbean and Hawaiian bases. But except for them the American people would not so readily have accepted territorial expansion during the closing years of the century. The war with Spain, and the conse-quent flare-up of imperialist sentiment, might still have occurred; but overseas expansion would probably have been more moderate and the acquisition of the Philippine Islands and the promulgation of the Open Door policy might not have happened at all.

60. Richard Hofstadter, "Manifest Destiny and the Philippines," in Daniel Aaron (ed.), *America in Crisis* (New York, 1952), p. 173.
61. *Ibid.*, p. 198.
62. See John Dollard, et al., *Frustration and Aggression* (New Haven, 1939); John F. Hall, *Psychology of Motivation* (Chicago, 1961), pp. 236–52.

# CHAPTER 9

## *Unjingo Jim*

"JINGO Jim," as Secretary of State James G. Blaine was called by his enemies, sometimes spoke in a blustering manner, but his words were harsher than his deeds. When he was head of the State Department under President Benjamin Harrison, political conditions were less troubled than when he had been Secretary under Garfield and Arthur, and he was granted a longer incumbency. But no longer did he have the energy and ambition of the man of 1881. His health was failing; from early May to late October 1891, a critical period for foreign policy, he was on sick leave at his home in Bar Harbor, Maine. Tragedy clouded his last years. In January 1890 his son Walker, who had accompanied William H. Trescot to Chile in 1882 and had helped Blaine in the State Department, died; hardly a fortnight later his eldest daughter died too. In February 1892 his youngest son was divorced; and four months afterward came the death of another son. Crushed by these blows, seriously ill, and at odds with the President (who suspected him of intriguing for the nomination in 1892), Blaine resigned on June 4, 1892. He died the following January 27.

Nevertheless Blaine's second term was a remarkable one, not least because, far from being a jingo, he strove hard and successfully to keep the peace. He had become, it is true, more of an expansionist, but he was a moderate one. Early in 1891 he tried to lease Môle St. Nicolas in Haiti as a naval base; however, when that country resisted, he dropped the matter. He also made a half-hearted, and unsuccessful, attempt to obtain a base in Samaná Bay, which had formerly interested President Grant so greatly. But Blaine advised Harrison that only three noncontinental places had sufficient value to be "taken": Hawaii, Cuba, and Puerto Rico, and that no decision was needed for a generation except possibly in the case of Hawaii.[1] The exception was significant, for Blaine had an indirect part in the Hawaiian revolution of 1893.

Blaine deserves mixed credit in the two controversies he inherited from the Cleveland administration. As regards Samoa, he did little more than permit the Berlin conference, arranged by Cleveland and Bayard, to proceed to a successful conclusion; as for the Bering Sea, however, he succeeded in settling that dangerous clash with the British, although not without a good deal of foolish rhetoric and unwise procedure.

Equally pacific was his policy toward Latin America, still the part of the world of preeminent interest to him. His influence for peace was marked in an International American Conference of 1889; in a dangerous confrontation with Chile in 1891 and 1892, reminiscent of the problems during the War of the Pacific; and in a minor skirmish with Italy in 1891, the significance of which lay chiefly in its bearing upon the Chilean episode.

The 1889 conference evolved from the inter-American peace conference for which Blaine had issued invitations when Secretary of State in 1881. After Arthur called off that earlier meeting, Blaine wrote a defense of the "Foreign Policy of the Garfield Administration" that was published in September 1882; that policy's two main objectives, he declared, were to prevent wars in the New World and to promote United States exports to Latin America.[2] The statement attracted national attention. Blaine always had a strong appeal, and many people believed that Arthur had missed an excellent opportu-

1. Blaine to Harrison, Aug. 10, 1891, Albert T. Volwiler (ed.), *The Correspondence between Benjamin Harrison and James G. Blaine, 1882–1893* (Philadelphia, 1940), p. 174. Regarding Môle St. Nicolas see Rayford W. Logan, *The Diplomatic Relations of the United States with Haiti, 1776–1891* (Chapel Hill, 1941), chs. 14, 15; Frederick Douglass (American minister to Haiti), "Haiti and the United States: Inside History of the Negotiations for the Môle St. Nicolas," *North American Review*, CLIII (1891), 337–45, 450–59. Regarding Samaná Bay see Sumner Welles, *Naboth's Vineyard: The Dominican Republic, 1844–1924* (2 vols., New York, 1928), I, 476–93.

2. James G. Blaine, *Political Discussions, Legislative, Diplomatic, and Popular, 1856–1886* (Norwich, Conn., 1887), pp. 411, 415, 419; Alice F. Tyler, *The Foreign Policy of James G. Blaine* (Minneapolis, 1927), pp. 170–73.

nity to promote both peace and exports. In 1882, 1883, and 1884 congressional resolutions called for a conference. Arthur felt compelled to send a special mission to Central and South America; its voluminous report advised that every country except Chile favored a conference with "warmth."[3]

By 1888 a vague Pan-Americanism, no doubt fostered by the growing attention to foreign markets, had become so popular in the United States that Congress enacted legislation (without the signature of President Cleveland, still the advocate of general tariff reduction) authorizing the President to invite the Latin American countries to meet in Washington; in July 1888, seven years after Blaine's invitations, the new invitations went out. All but Santo Domingo (still aggrieved over the failure of Frelinghuysen's reciprocity treaty) accepted.[4]

Sessions began in Washington on November 18, 1889. Secretary Blaine was elected president of the conference; it disbanded on April 19, 1890.[5] The main topics discussed were a customs union, a so-called Three-Americas Railway (from North to South America), arbitration, and customs regulations. Blaine still wished to redress the unfavorable trade balance with Latin America. But Latin American countries were fearful of economic subservience to their great neighbor; in addition, an Argentine delegate expressed another powerful consideration: "Affection and love for America are not wanting in me. I do not lack confidence in or gratitude towards Europe. I do not forget that Spain, our mother, is there . . . that Italy,

3. Commissioners to Arthur, Dec. 31, 1884, *House Executive Documents*, 48 Cong., 2 Sess., No. 226 (Serial 2304), p. 32. Regarding Congress see *International American Conference: Reports of Committees and Discussions Thereon.* Vol. IV: *Historical Appendix* . . . (Washington, 1890), pp. 294–99. See also A. Curtis Wilgus, "James G. Blaine and the Pan-American Movement," *Hispanic American Historical Review*, V (1922), 677–78, 679n, 685–87; John A. Caruso, "The Pan American Railway," *ibid.*, XXXI (1951), 608–39.

4. *International American Conference*, I, 9–11, 12–29; regarding an invitation to Hawaii see *ibid.*, pp. 29–37. For the congressional bill see *Congressional Record*, 50 Cong., 1 Sess., pp. 3928, 3932 (May 10, 1888); *Statutes of the United States of America* . . . (Washington, 1888), XXV, 155–56.

5. The official records are in *International American Conference*. Regarding a trip in the United States taken by the delegates see *ibid.*, III. A useful survey is Wilgus, "Blaine and the Pan-American Movement," pp. 692–707; see also Thomas F. McGann, *Argentina and the United States, and the Inter-American System, 1880–1914* (Cambridge, Mass., 1957), pp. 130–64, and J. Lloyd Mecham, *The United States and Inter-American Security, 1889–1960* (Austin, 1961), pp. 52–58.

our friend, is there, and France, our sister."[6] He and other delegates feared that a rupture of commercial ties with Europe would end precious cultural bonds as well. Consequently the conference merely recommended that countries interested in reciprocity should negotiate agreements between themselves. It also advocated surveys for an inter-American railway, the obligatory arbitration of all controversies except those a disputant considered as imperiling its independence, and the establishment of a Commercial Bureau to collect information about the economies of American countries.[7]

Some reciprocity agreements were concluded, and had a railway been built and compulsory arbitration adopted, the conference would have gone down in history as remarkably successful. But the railway still has not been completed; and most countries, including the United States, declined to ratify the arbitration plan. The Commercial Bureau, however, was established; in 1910 it was renamed the Pan American Union and housed in Washington in a handsome building donated by Andrew Carnegie, a well-chosen delegate of 1889. To judge the conference merely by its concrete results would be short-sighted. Bringing together in a friendly meeting all but one of the independent countries in the western hemisphere was a remarkable achievement. Blaine's conciliatory disposition impressed the Latin Americans; as Matías Romero, the former Mexican minister to the United States, said, most of the delegates had gone to Washington suspicious of the United States, but they left believing that she "had only sentiments of respect and consideration" for her sister republics.[8] Moreover, by its physical presence in Washington the Pan American Union helped consolidate the Pan American movement. Blaine was no simple, idealistic prophet of Pan Americanism, but he must be given credit for a significant part of whatever success the movement has had.

While the International American Conference was in session, the House of Representatives was debating the McKinley tariff bill. It appeared that duties would be taken off coffee and unrefined sugar and would be imposed on hides, which had long been duty-free. Since these were leading Latin American exports to the United

6. *International American Conference*, I, 130–31.
7. *Ibid.*, pp. 96, 98–99, 101–2, 264, 404–8; II, 1078–83.
8. Matías Romero, "The Pan-American Conference," *North American Review*, CLI (Sept. and Oct., 1890), 356, 421.

States, Blaine was dismayed. To tax hides, he thought, would be "a slap in the face" of the countries meeting in Washington; to put sugar on the free list would cause every principal import from Latin America, except wool, to be duty-free (more than 87 percent of products imported from Latin America were free already), so that the United States would have little bargaining power for negotiating the reciprocity treaties the conference recommended. The Secretary went before the Ways and Means Committee to urge his views. Nevertheless the House passed a bill he disliked, though it did restore hides to the free list.[9]

After the bill went to the Senate, Blaine had more success. In a widely noticed open letter to President Harrison he suggested that the McKinley bill could be adapted to obtain "profitable markets for the products of which we have so large a surplus." Specifically, he proposed that the President be empowered to admit duty-free the products of any American nation that imposed no export duties on those products and admitted duty-free a list of specified United States goods. This, he contended, would promote exports, provided Congress did not repeal the sugar duty.[10] He pursued his campaign vigorously with other open letters and in talks with Senators. The consequence was a compromise that put sugar, molasses, coffee, tea, and hides on the free list, and directed the President to impose duties on any of these items whenever, after January 1, 1892, he decided that a country producing them was treating United States exports unreasonably.[11] This proviso gave the United States something of the negotiating power Blaine wanted.

The large number of reciprocity treaties concluded under the McKinley tariff all lapsed in consequence of the Wilson-Gorman tariff of 1894, and sugar again became dutiable. Evidently Blaine's reciprocity was of no great consequence. All the same, except for his interposition there would have been no reciprocity at all; with duties levied on hides, the Latin American companies would indeed have felt slapped in the face and the limited success of the International American Conference would have been jeopardized.

9. Blaine to Representative William McKinley, April 10, 1890, Tyler, *Blaine*, p. 184; New York *Tribune*, July 26, 1890; *Congressional Record*, 51 Cong., 1 Sess., pp. 5112–13 (May 21, 1890).
10. Blaine to Harrison, June 4, 1890, *Congressional Record*, 51 Cong., 1 Sess., pp. 6257–59 (June 19, 1890).
11. *Statutes at Large of the United States of America . . .* (Washington, 1891), XXVI, 612.

Blaine's role was less prominent in the altercation with Italy, the only nineteenth-century dispute of any consequence with that country. In New Orleans lived many Italian-Americans, some of them members of the Mafia. In the autumn of 1890 the superintendent of police was murdered. Several Italians were arrested; they were acquitted by jurors who were generally thought to have been intimidated.[12] Convinced that further legal action would be futile, some New Orleans citizens organized a Committee of Fifty. On March 14, 1891, it led a mob into a prison and lynched eleven prisoners of Italian origin, including three Italian subjects.

Violent anger erupted in Italy. The Italian minister at Washington, Baron Francesco Fava, was ordered to protest and to demand reparations. Blaine at once told the Louisiana governor that the guilty should be brought to justice.[13] But the days passed without action against the Committee of Fifty. On March 24 Rome telegraphed Fava that if satisfaction was not immediately forthcoming, he would be recalled "from a country where he is unable to obtain justice."[14] Although the threat was premature, coming a scant ten days after the lynching, Washington was in an awkward position. However sincerely it deplored the mob action, the federal government had no jurisdiction over a state crime. Secretary Blaine endeavored to explain the complexities of federation; the Italians were in no mood for a lecture. At the end of March, Fava gave notice that, no suitable assurances having been received, he was leaving Washington.[15]

A brief press sensation followed, with some irresponsible talk of war. As the London *Times* observed, however, 5,324 Italian immigrants landed in New York in March, and in such circumstances the

12. Regarding the affair see John E. Coxe, "The New Orleans Mafia Incident," *Louisiana Historical Quarterly*, XX (1937), 1067–1110; J. Alexander Karlin, "The Italo-American Incident of 1891 and the Road to Reunion," *Journal of Southern History*, VIII (1942), 242–46, and "The Indemnification of Aliens Injured by Mob Violence," *Southwestern Social Science Quarterly*, XXV (1945), 235–46.

13. Fava to Blaine, March 15, 1891, *Papers Relating to the Foreign Relations of the United States, 1891* (Washington, 1892), p. 666; Blaine to Francis T. Nicholls, March 15, 1891, *ibid.*, pp. 666–67.

14. Premier Antonio di Rudini to Fava, March 24, 1891, *ibid.*, p. 673. The remark frequently attributed to Blaine—"I do not recognize the right of any government to tell the United States what it should do"—seems to have been made verbally; so it may have been misquoted. Regarding the remark see Coxe, "Mafia Incident," pp. 1094–95.

15. Fava to Blaine, March 31, 1891, *Foreign Relations, 1891*, p. 676.

## A FAIR EXCHANGE. *(Punch,* April 11, 1891)

UNCLE SAM: "See here, Umberto! Give us back your *'Minister,'* and take away that darn'd *'Mafia,'* and we'll call it a square deal!!"

quarrel "tends to become ridiculous."[16] Some weeks later the American minister departed from Rome on leave of absence; although a chargé d'affaires remained in each Legation, Italo-American negotiations were suspended for the rest of 1891. A Louisiana grand jury investigating the crime reported in May; it made no indictments; no one was ever brought to trial.[17]

And thus matters stood for months. No doubt the inactivity was mainly due to Blaine's long illness. When he returned to the capital in late October 1891, things started to move again. In passages in his annual message, presumably written by the Secretary, Harrison called the lynchings "most deplorable" and, with reference to Italy's claims, said that Washington had already agreed to investigate whether there was "an obligation upon the United States."[18] Long before then the excitement in Italy had died down.

In reopened talks of 1892 Rome at first insisted that, before Fava resumed his duties, Washington must recognize that in principle an indemnity was due; the United States contended that Harrison had already done this in his annual message. After further discussion, the United States agreed in March to send the American minister back to Rome, and the next month she offered an indemnity of $24,330.90. Italy accepted; Minister Fava returned to Washington; Italian-American relations resumed their usual friendly course.[19]

This disturbance with Italy was to exert a small influence upon a much more serious clash with Chile. Early in 1891 civil war broke out in that country. With the support of the navy, the Congressionalists, as the rebels were called, established their headquarters at Iquique in the north, near the Tarapacá nitrate fields that had so worried Secretary Blaine ten years earlier. Backed by the army, President José M. Balmaceda (with whom Trescot had had his embarrassing conversation in 1882) stood supreme elsewhere. As during the War of the Pacific, British-American rivalry for

16. The *Times* (London), April 2, 1891.
17. John Bassett Moore, *A Digest of International Law* . . . (8 vols., Washington, 1906), VI, 839.
18. Annual message, Dec. 9, 1891, James D. Richardson (ed.), *A Compilation of the Messages and Papers of the Presidents, 1789–1897* (10 vols., Washington, 1899), IX, 182–83.
19. Acting Secretary of State William F. Wharton to H. Remsen Whitehouse (American chargé d'affaires at Rome), March 16, 1892, Moore, *Digest,* VI, 841; Blaine to Marquis Imperiali (Italian chargé d'affaires at Washington), April 12, 1892, *Foreign Relations, 1891*, pp. 727–28; Imperiali to Blaine, April 12, 1892, *ibid.*, p. 728.

commercial supremacy in Chile was an important factor behind the scenes. Blaine's suspicions of 1881 and 1882 about Great Britain still lingered, as did his determination to promote hemispheric solidarity and trade. The large British colony in Chile sympathized strongly with the Congressionalists, who, after their eventual victory, could not do enough to express their gratitude to British naval men for what John G. Kennedy, Her Majesty's minister at Santiago, called "their steady sympathy and service towards the Chilean Fleet since the beginning of the revolution. We Britishers [he continued] are now in tremendous favour with all classes. There is no doubt our Naval Officers and the British community of Valparaiso and all along the Coast rendered material assistance to the opposition and committed many breaches of neutrality."[20]

On the other hand, Americans favored the Balmacedists, and several events earned them the intense dislike of the Congressionalists. One such event concerned a Chilean ship, the *Itata*, which, after being seized by the rebels, sailed into San Diego in May 1891.[21] Rightly suspecting that she was there to get weapons, Balmaceda's minister at Washington made representations to have her apprehended. A federal marshal boarded the ship, but on May 5 she steamed out of the harbor, put the marshal ashore, transferred a cargo of arms and munitions from another vessel she met at sea, and headed for Iquique. The Harrison administration (Blaine's illness began May 7) ordered the warship *Charleston* to pursue her. The American ship reached Iquique first, without having sighted the *Itata*. When the *Itata* did arrive, the rebels agreed to surrender her; and eventually they agreed to give up the cargo, too, though they argued that it was legally theirs, having been transshipped on the high seas. The delighted Balmacedists praised Harrison for his "great services."[22] On July 4 the *Itata* arrived back at San Diego. Three months later—by then the Congressionalists had won the civil war—she was released under bond; and an American court later declared she had been wrongly detained by the United States.

20. Kennedy to "My dear Sanderson" (Sir Thomas Sanderson, Permanent Undersecretary of State, Foreign Office), Sept. 15, 1891, Public Record Office (London), Foreign Office 16/266.

21. See Osgood Hardy, "The Itata Incident," *Hispanic American Historical Review*, V (1922), 195–226; *House Executive Documents*, 52 Cong., 1 Sess., No. 1, Pt. 1 (Serial 2931), *Report of the Secretary of the Navy, 1891*, pp. 25–26.

22. Kennedy to Salisbury, May 21, June 23, 1891, Foreign Office 16/265.

In late August the United States recognized the Congressionalist provisional government established in Santiago. Balmaceda committed suicide. "We may now dismiss our fears for the safety of Tarapaca and in regard to the United States influence in Chili," Minister Kennedy rejoiced. "The triumph of President Balmaceda would have involved the triumph of the ideas of Mr. Blaine, with a great diminution of the influence and commercial prosperity of Great Britain, France, and Germany."[23] But if British standing was high, American was abysmally low. The American minister at Santiago, Patrick Egan, reported a "bitter feeling against the United States." As early as September 1891 Washington felt it necessary to make contingency plans for war. Captain Alfred T. Mahan was summoned to the capital, where he, Secretary of the Navy Benjamin F. Tracy, and others met secretly to plan operations in Chilean waters.[24]

Part of the trouble arose from friction between Egan and the provisional government. A leading opponent of British rule in Ireland, Egan had fled from that country in 1882; in the United States he became a faithful backer of Blaine, who sent him to Chile in 1889. The British there were most suspicious of his intentions, and their attitude influenced the new government. Kennedy was pleased to report that Egan was "in very bad odour."[25] A particularly acute point of friction concerned the asylum extended by Egan to Balmacedist refugees. At first the American Legation housed eighty refugees; and in October 1891 fifteen still remained. Chile demanded that they be surrendered; Egan refused. Chile then surrounded the Legation with secret police. President Harrison, taking the position that since Santiago allowed other countries to grant asylum it must let the United States do the same, was extremely indignant.[26]

On October 16 America's already strained relations with Chile

23. Kennedy to Sanderson, Sept. 4, 1891, Foreign Office 16/266; Kennedy to Salisbury, Oct. 6, 1891, *ibid.*

24. Egan to Blaine, Sept. 17, 1891, *House Executive Documents*, 52 Cong., 1 Sess., No. 91 (Serial 2954), p. 74. Walter R. Herrick, Jr., *The American Naval Revolution* (Baton Rouge, 1966), p. 126.

25. Kennedy to Sanderson, Sept. 4, 1891, Foreign Office 16/266.

26. Regarding the refugees see *House Executive Documents*, 52 Cong., 1 Sess., No. 91, pp. 76–105, and *passim;* regarding the legal aspects see John Bassett Moore, "Asylum in Legations and Consulates and in Vessels," *Political Science Quarterly*, VII (1892), 1–37, 197–231, 397–418. See also Egan to Blaine, Oct. 8, 1891, *Foreign Relations, 1891*, p. 184.

were enormously exacerbated by a far more explosive incident than any that had yet occurred. Rather unwisely, in view of the unfriendly Chilean mood, Captain Winfield S. Schley, U.S.S. *Baltimore,* granted 117 sailors shore leave in Valparaiso. A mob riot broke out, reminiscent of the one in New Orleans seven months earlier; one sailor was killed; another died later of injuries; seventeen were wounded, five seriously. After investigating hastily, Schley reported to Secretary of the Navy Tracy that the sailors had not provoked the attack and that it was "designed."[27]

Blaine was still sick in Maine. Suspecting an affront to the national honor, Harrison told Tracy to prepare a telegram to Egan; the Secretary of the Navy was just as nationalistic as his chief, and throughout the ensuing crisis he exerted a strong influence for a hard policy.[28] Although the United States had only recently failed to satisfy Italy about the New Orleans riot, the President seized upon the fact that the sailors had been in uniform to insist that the Valparaiso affair was altogether different: it was an attack upon the country. Tracy's note asserted that the attackers, some of them "public police," had been "animated in their bloody work by hostility to these [American] men as sailors of the United States," and that if Schley's facts were correct Washington would expect "prompt and full reparation." His words were read in Santiago by a resolute man, Manuel A. Matta, the new Foreign Minister, a leading Radical politician who had long distrusted the United States. Matta retorted that a court investigation was under way and that he could promise nothing before it was finished.[29]

27. *House Executive Documents,* 52 Cong., 1 Sess., No. 91, pp. 105ff., and *passim;* for a later incident see *ibid.,* pp. 611–64. Schley to Tracy, Oct. 23, 1891, *ibid.,* pp. 293–95.

28. Surely exaggerated are the reports of Sir Michael Herbert (an officer in the British Legation in Washington and a future ambassador to the United States) that Tracy desired war in order to arouse popular enthusiasm for the navy and to persuade the House to appropriate money for more ships, and that Harrison wanted war in order to secure his renomination. Herbert to Barrington (a British Foreign Office official), Jan. 22, 1892, Lord Salisbury Papers, Christ Church Library (Oxford). Cecil Spring Rice (like Herbert, an officer in the British Legation in Washington and a future ambassador to the United States) wrote, Jan. 19, 1892, that "the President and the navy are bent on it [war]," Albert T. Volwiler, "Harrison, Blaine, and American Foreign Policy, 1889–1893," *Proceedings of the American Philosophical Society,* LXXIX (1938), 645.

29. Wharton (who signed the note) to Egan, Oct. 23, 1891, *House Executive Documents,* 52 Cong., 1 Sess., No. 91, pp. 107–8; Matta to Egan, Oct. 27, 1891, *ibid.,* pp. 120–21. See also Frederick B. Pike, *Chile and the United States, 1880–1962: The Emergence of Chile's Social Crisis and the Challenge to United States Diplomacy* (South Bend, Ind., 1963), pp. 72–73.

Although not fully restored to health, Blaine resumed his official duties at this critical moment, October 26 (it was then, too, that he picked up the threads of the New Orleans affair). He disapproved of Tracy's telegram and urged patience, perhaps reminding the President that Italy had been asked to await the results of an American inquiry; he spoke so reassuringly to the Chilean minister at Washington, Pedro Montt, that even Matta acknowledged his "conciliatory language."[30] Undoubtedly because of his pacific counsel the administration reconciled itself to a delay of several weeks while the Valparaiso investigation proceeded slowly and secretly. The American public, too, refused to get excited.

The suspense was abruptly shattered by the fiery Matta. His ire aroused by passages dealing with the *Baltimore* affair in Harrison's annual message to Congress and in Tracy's annual report (Harrison put the onus squarely on Chile and accused Matta of using "an offensive tone"; Tracy said that several of the sailors had bayonet wounds, "clearly showing the participation of the Chilean police"),[31] the Foreign Minister dashed off a most injudicious telegram to Montt; it asserted baldly that there was "no exactness nor sincerity in what is said at Washington," that Harrison's account of the episode was "deliberately incorrect," and that Chile would prevail despite "the threats which come from so high." Although Montt had the good sense not to deliver the telegram to the State Department, Matta foolishly read it to the Chilean Senate on December 11 and newspapers then published it.[32] Harrison was enraged by the unflattering description of himself; and Egan broke off personal relations with the provisional government.

Just at this worst of times Santiago saw fit to tighten its surveillance of the American Legation "in an offensive manner," and Egan heard apparently well-founded (but false) rumors that it was planning to evict the refugees by burning the building. The Argentine minister, as dean of the diplomatic corps, protested. Egan's dignified bearing in the emergency aroused the admiration of even the British minister—no mean feat.[33] But Egan believed that hostilities were certain unless Matta was dismissed; and Harrison's private

30. Kennedy to Salisbury, Nov. 8, 1891, Foreign Office 16/266.
31. Message of Dec. 9, 1891, Richardson, *Messages and Papers*, IX, 185–86; *Report of the Secretary of the Navy, 1891*, p. 22.
32. Egan to Blaine, Dec. 12, 14, 1891, *House Executive Documents*, 52 Cong., 1 Sess., No. 91, pp. 178–80, 182.
33. Kennedy to Salisbury, Dec. 31, 1891, Foreign Office 16/266.

secretary noted that the President, too, feared that war was coming.[34]

The situation was eased partly by Secretary Blaine; presumably to allow time for emotions to cool, he insisted that no demands be made upon Santiago for the time being. The formation of a new Chilean ministry on January 1, 1892, with the conciliatory Luis Pereira replacing Matta as Foreign Minister, helped too. Pereira exchanged friendly visits with Egan, who resumed his relations with the government and predicted a settlement of all the disputes—over the *Baltimore* affair, the Legation, the refugees.[35] He was right about the Legation and the refugees. Chile removed the agents around the building and intimated that the refugees could go to Valparaiso quietly without fear of arrest. On January 12 the indomitable Minister Egan escorted them there to the safety of the U.S.S. *Yorktown*.[36]

Egan was wrong about the *Baltimore*, however. One obstacle to a settlement, it is true, was removed when the Chilean court finally concluded its inquiry (it took only slightly longer than the New Orleans grand jury had needed to investigate the lynchings). On January 8, 1892, Montt gave Blaine a summary of its findings: the court defended the police but brought charges against three Chileans and one American; and the government expressed "very sincere regret."[37] But by that date Washington's attention had reverted to Matta's accusatory telegram, for Harrison could no longer contain his wrath. Hard pressed by the President, one may be sure, Blaine instructed Egan to ascertain whether everything in the telegram offensive to the President would be withdrawn.[38] "We are on the verge of a war," an officer in the British Legation in Washington predicted, although he added that Blaine "has prevented war with Chile so far, and may do so still."[39] The new ministers hesitated to

34. Egan to Blaine, Dec. 14, 22, 1891, *House Executive Documents*, 52 Cong., 1 Sess., No. 91, pp. 183, 184; Kennedy to Salisbury, Dec. 31, 1891, Foreign Office 16/266; Volwiler, "Harrison, Blaine, and American Foreign Policy," p. 643.

35. Kennedy to Salisbury, Jan. 15, 1892, Foreign Office 16/276; Egan to Blaine, Jan. 1, 1892, *House Executive Documents*, 52 Cong., 1 Sess., No. 91, pp. 187–88.

36. Egan to Blaine, Jan. 12, 1892, *House Executive Documents*, 52 Cong., 1 Sess., No. 91, p. 188; Kennedy to Salisbury, Jan. 15 and 27, 1892, Foreign Office 16/276. Moore, *Digest*, II, 798, incorrectly dates the trip to the *Yorktown* as Jan. 9.

37. Montt to Blaine, Jan. 8, 1892, *House Executive Documents*, 52 Cong., 1 Sess., No. 91, pp. 227–28.

38. Blaine to Egan, Jan. 8, 1892, *ibid.*, p. 188.

39. Cecil Spring Rice wrote this, Jan. 19, 1892, Volwiler, "Harrison, Blaine, and American Foreign Policy," p. 645.

withdraw any part of the telegram, since it would be dangerous to humiliate the politically powerful Matta. Nevertheless they agreed, somewhat equivocally, to withdraw "all that may be considered disagreeable to" America.[40] An amicable accord was probably close —when Chile made a gross blunder. On January 20, 1892, she suddenly asked for the recall of Patrick Egan as *persona non grata*.

In Washington the request landed with the impact of a high-explosive shell. Harrison reacted in cold anger. According to information reaching the British Legation, he had been on the verge of sending a warlike message to Congress but had postponed it when Blaine on January 19, after making an emotional appeal for peace, broke up a Cabinet meeting by feigning dizziness.[41] Harrison now rejected a State Department draft to Minister Egan as too mild, and with Blaine's apparent agreement a strong note that was basically the President's went off to Santiago on January 21. It amounted to an ultimatum. Harrison refused to accept the court's findings regarding the *Baltimore* affair; that incident, he insisted, still bore the aspect of an "attack upon the uniform of the U.S. Navy," and he asked for "a suitable apology and for some adequate reparation for the injury done to this Government." As for the Matta telegram, he warned that if the offensive parts were "not at once withdrawn, and a suitable apology offered, with the same publicity that was given to the offensive expressions," the United States would terminate diplomatic relations with Chile. Finally, he said contemptuously that he did "not deem it necessary to make any present response" to the request for Egan's recall.[42]

Egan presented these demands on Saturday, the twenty-third. Two days later Chile replied. She gave way completely. She could hardly have done otherwise, since warnings had come from London, Berlin, and Paris that Harrison was in dead earnest and that no European nation would help her in the event of war.[43] Expressing willingness to pay reparations, Chile proposed that either the

40. Kennedy to Salisbury, Jan. 15, 1892, Foreign Office 16/276; Egan to Blaine, Jan. 16, 1892, *House Executive Documents*, 52 Cong., 1 Sess., No. 91, p. 190.

41. Herbert to Eric Barrington (Salisbury's private secretary), Jan. 22, 1892, Salisbury Papers.

42. Blaine to Egan, Jan. 21, 1892, *Foreign Relations, 1891*, pp. 307–8. See also Volwiler, "Harrison, Blaine, and American Foreign Policy," pp. 645–46.

43. Egan to Blaine, Jan. 22, 1892, *Foreign Relations, 1891*, p. 309; Pike, *Chile and the United States*, p. 78; Herrick, *Naval Revolution*, p. 128.

United States Supreme Court or an arbitration tribunal name the sum; she deplored those expressions in the Matta telegram "which are offensive in the judgment of your Government"; she declared that she "absolutely withdraws" them and would give this step "such publicity as your Government may deem suitable"; and she agreed to make no move regarding Egan without American consent.[44] With this capitulation the crisis really ended: Washington's demands had been fully met, the refugees were safe, the Legation was no longer spied upon, and reparations for the *Baltimore* affair were assured.

But strangely enough a fleeting war scare was to sweep over the United States. While the Chileans were preparing their reply on Sunday, January 24, President Harrison, harboring what dark thoughts no one can know, was drawing up a special message to Congress. It went to that body on the twenty-fifth. After reviewing the various disputes and reiterating the charge that the attack on the sailors was "upon the uniform—the nationality—and not upon the men," the message concluded, "I have as yet received no reply to our note of the 21st instant [it had been delivered only two days previously, on a weekend], but in my opinion I ought not to delay longer to bring these matters to the attention of Congress for such action as may be deemed appropriate."[45] Who can say that this lamentable decision to abandon diplomacy and turn matters over to Congress would not have precipitated war, had not the news of Chile's precipitous retreat become known the very next day? Thereupon the President could only send off another message, informing Congress that all was well. Blaine happily closed Harrison's crisis by notifying Chile of the "great pleasure" her concessions had given Washington and the American people.[46]

The sequel is quickly told. In February 1892 a Chilean court sentenced the three Chileans implicated in the riot to imprisonment. In July Santiago offered $75,000 in reparations; Washington accepted the sum as adequate. Egan stayed on as minister, but when, during a short-lived rebellion of 1893, he again offered asy-

44. Pereira to Egan, dated and received Jan. 25, 1892, *Foreign Relations, 1891*, pp. 309–12.
45. Richardson, *Messages and Papers*, IX, 222, 226. Regarding the war scare see *Public Opinion*, XII (Jan. 30, 1892), 419–22.
46. Message of Jan. 28, 1892, Richardson, *Messages and Papers*, IX, 227; Blaine to Egan, Jan. 30, 1892, *Foreign Relations, 1891*, pp. 312–13.

lum, another American President, Grover Cleveland, ordered him to surrender his new refugees.[47]

Evidently James G. Blaine was not an ideal Secretary of State during his service under Benjamin Harrison—any more than he had been under James A. Garfield. Especially during the Bering Sea controversy he was much too impulsive, and overly reliant on the quick mind that had frequently enabled him to retrieve positions unwisely taken in public speech but that could not save him from errors in a formal diplomatic document. Yet Blaine was a far better secretary under Harrison than usually represented. Above all, he was not a jingo. However ill-advised many of his contentions about the fur seals, he arranged an arbitration; showing himself tactful and considerate, he earned the respect of the Latin American delegates at the International American Conference; he worked for a face-saving compromise in the rather absurd disturbance with Italy; and he may well have staved off outright war with Chile. Furthermore, Blaine was not simply a talented improviser. We have already noted his large view of relations with Latin America, and we shall see that he had a global conception of the objectives of United States foreign policy that can compare favorably, in its soundness, with the ideas of William H. Seward, and that antedated the opinions of such a brilliant prophet of expansion as Captain Alfred T. Mahan.

47. Henry C. Evans, Jr., *Chile and Its Relations with the United States* (Durham, N.C., 1927), pp. 152–53; Moore, *Digest*, II, 798–800.

CHAPTER 10

# The Hawaiian Revolution of 1893
## and Its Aftermath

I N a remarkable instruction of 1881 to the American minister at
Honolulu, an instruction foreshadowing the ideas advanced by
Captain Alfred T. Mahan a decade later, Blaine had given his views
about the Hawaiian Islands. After referring (as President Hayes had
done) to the "proposed Panama Canal as a purely American waterway to be treated as part of our own coast line," and to the vital
importance of extending "commercial empire" on the Pacific, he
went on to say: "The situation of the Hawaiian Islands, giving them
the strategic control of the North Pacific, brings their possession
within the range of questions of purely American policy, as much
so as that of the Isthmus itself." Hawaii, he reasoned, "holds in the
western sea much the same position as Cuba in the Atlantic. It is the
key to the maritime dominion of the Pacific States, as Cuba is the
key to the Gulf trade. . . . under no circumstances can the United
States permit any change in the territorial control of either which
would cut it adrift from the American system, whereto they both
indispensably belong."[1] Now in 1889, back in the State Department,
Blaine still believed in the vital importance of a canal, Hawaii, and
Cuba, but his thinking had advanced somewhat. Whereas in 1881

1. Blaine to James H. Comly (American minister to Hawaii), Dec. 1, 1881 (the first
of two instructions of that date), *Senate Executive Documents*, 53 Cong., 2 Sess., No. 13
(Serial 3160), pp. 8, 9.

he had not favored annexing the Pacific archipelago, he advised the President in 1891 that "Hawaii may come up for decision at any unexpected hour, and I hope we shall be prepared to decide it in the affirmative."[2]

As minister to Hawaii, the Secretary named a longstanding friend, John L. Stevens. One may assume that Stevens shared Blaine's ideas and that he owed his appointment to the strategic post somewhat to that fact. One may also assume that he studied Blaine's Hawaiian instruction of 1881; the Secretary specifically told him to read the previous Legation correspondence.[3] Not long after entering upon his new duties Stevens wrote Blaine in terms that showed he had learned his lesson well: "Left to themselves," he said, "the prevailing logical force of things would ultimately drive out the best American elements and swamp these islands with adverse influences. . . . The vital question, one that can not be possibly ignored or held in abeyance, is: Shall Asiatic or American civilization ultimately prevail here?" This reflected the Secretary's own thinking exactly. "The Hawaiian Islands," he had written in 1881, "can not be joined to the Asiatic system." He had said that America's nonannexation policy depended on "the perpetuity of the rule of the native race as an independent government," and had noted an "alarming diminution" of that race.[4] Since 1881 the influx of Chinese into Hawaii had continued, and it had been supplemented by a swelling tide of immigrants from Japan. Unquestionably this worried Blaine and encouraged his belief that the time for annexation was close.

In the Legation archives Stevens found another interesting instruction, this one written by Secretary of State Bayard to Minister George W. Merrill in 1887. A petty revolution in that year—it began and ended on July 1—had caused King Kalakaua to proclaim a new constitution giving greater powers to the wealthy white residents. It also caused Bayard to instruct Merrill that, in the event of another revolution, American commerce, lives, and property should be pro-

2. For Blaine's 1881 opinion see *ibid.,* p. 9; for his 1891 opinion see Blaine to Harrison, Aug. 10, 1891, Albert T. Volwiler (ed.), *The Correspondence between Benjamin Harrison and James G. Blaine, 1882–1893* (Philadelphia, 1940), p. 174.

3. Blaine to Stevens, June 26, 1889, National Archives (Washington), Record Group 59, State Department Records, Hawaii, Instructions.

4. Stevens to Blaine, March 20, 1890, *House Executive Documents,* 53 Cong., 2 Sess., No. 48 (Serial 3224), pp. 50–51; Blaine to Comly, Dec. 1, 1881 (the first of two instructions of that date), *Senate Executive Documents,* 53 Cong., 2 Sess., No. 13, p. 10.

tected; and that "the assistance of the officers of our Government vessels, if found necessary, will therefore be promptly afforded to promote the reign of law and respect for orderly government in Hawaii."[5] Two years later, in July 1889, the native royalists attempted to regain their lost ground, but this *émeute*, even pettier than the one of 1887, failed utterly. During the excitement of 1889 Merrill, doubtless recalling Bayard's instruction to promote law and order, arranged that marines be landed from the U.S.S. *Adams*, a step the State Department subsequently approved.[6] These trivial commotions of 1887 and 1889 had a large significance for Hawaii's future. Having gained power in 1887, white Hawaiians were determined to keep it; and Bayard's instruction, combined with the landing of forces, pointed the way to another landing in 1893 that would overturn the monarchy for all time.

In early 1891 King Kalakaua, whose reign had witnessed the enormous tightening of Hawaiian-American commercial links, died. He was succeeded by his sister, Liliuokalani, who disliked the pro-white constitution of 1887—the "Bayonet Constitution," she called it—and was reputed to be somewhat anti-American. Stevens informed Washington that she was surrounding herself with the worst elements in the country.[7] These events deeply disturbed the American faction in Hawaii. So did a depression following the McKinley tariff act of 1890. That act not only put sugar on the free list, thereby terminating the advantage enjoyed by Hawaiian sugar in the United States, but it gave American sugar producers a bounty of two cents a pound. Hawaiian sugar slumped badly, and property values were estimated to have fallen by at least $12 million.[8] Revolutionary sentiment began to loom large.

5. Bayard to Merrill, July 12, 1887, *Papers Relating to the Foreign Relations of the United States, 1887* (Washington, 1888), p. 581. For the revolution of 1887 see Sylvester K. Stevens, *American Expansion in Hawaii, 1842–1898* (Harrisburg, Pa., 1945), pp. 151–53.

6. Merrill to Blaine, Aug. 1, 1889, *Papers Relating to the Foreign Relations of the United States, 1894* (Washington, 1895), Appendix II, pp. 282–84; Third Assistant Secretary of State John Bassett Moore to Merrill, Aug. 12, 1889, *House Executive Documents*, 53 Cong., 2 Sess., No. 48, p. 22; Acting Secretary of State William F. Wharton to Merrill, Aug. 23, 1889, *Foreign Relations, 1894*, Appendix II, p. 289.

7. Stevens to Blaine, Feb. 22, 1891, *House Executive Documents*, 53 Cong., 2 Sess., No. 48, p. 77.

8. Julius W. Pratt, *Expansionists of 1898: The Acquisition of Hawaii and the Spanish Islands* (Baltimore, 1936), pp. 42–45; Stevens to John W. Foster (Blaine's successor as Secretary of State), Nov. 20, 1892, *Foreign Relations, 1894*, Appendix II, p. 382.

From then on, Minister Stevens's dispatches were often alarmist. Some are extremely significant in the light of the coming revolution: "The present political situation is feverish and I see no prospect of its being permanently otherwise until these islands become a part of the American Union or a possession of Great Britain. . . . a 'new departure' by the United States as to Hawaii is rapidly becoming a necessity . . . a 'protectorate' is impracticable, and . . . annexation must be the future remedy. . . ."[9] "If the Government here should be surprised and overturned . . . should the United States minister and naval commander confine themselves exclusively to the preservation of American property, the protection of American citizens, and the prevention of anarchy? . . . I desire to know how far the present minister and naval commander may deviate from established international rules and precedents. . . . I have information which I deem reliable that there is an organized revolutionary party on the islands. . . ."[10] "I want you [Secretary Blaine] to write me in as few or many words as you please—are you for Annexation?"[11] "Hawaii has reached the parting of the ways. She must now take the road which leads to Asia, or the other, which outlets her in America, gives her an American civilization and binds her to the care of American destiny. . . . I cannot refrain from expressing the opinion with emphasis that the golden hour is near at hand."[12]

Now the most significant point about these dispatches is that they were not answered, except by way of formal acknowledgment or infrequent perfunctory comment. Neither Blaine nor Acting Secretary William F. Wharton (during Blaine's illnesses), nor John W. Foster, Blaine's successor, replied to the specific queries or reprimanded Stevens for his annexationist sentiments. What steps should the minister and the naval commander take in the event of

---

Regarding sugar and the revolution of 1893 see Richard D. Weigle, "Sugar and the Hawaiian Revolution," *Pacific Historical Review*, XVI (1947), 41–58. See also Merze Tate, *Hawaii: Reciprocity or Annexation* (East Lansing, 1968), ch. 8.

9. Stevens to Blaine, Feb. 8, 1892, *House Executive Documents*, 53 Cong., 2 Sess., No. 48, pp. 87–88.

10. Stevens to Blaine, March 8, 1892, *Foreign Relations, 1894*, Appendix II, p. 182.

11. Stevens to "Bro. Blaine," March 25, 1892, Pratt, *Expansionists of 1898*, p. 50.

12. Stevens to Foster, Nov. 20, 1892, *House Executive Documents*, 53 Cong., 2 Sess., No. 48, pp. 115, 117. See also Stevens to Blaine, Sept. 5, 1891, April 2, 1892, and Stevens to Foster, Sept. 14, 1892, *ibid.*, pp. 85–86, 90, 95; also Stevens to Foster, Nov. 8, 1892, *Foreign Relations, 1894*, Appendix II, p. 376.

a revolution? Blaine did not say. Did Blaine favor annexation? Absolute silence reigned in Washington. A highly intelligent man, the Secretary obviously saw the drift of his protégé's queries and comments. Had he disapproved he should have sent a strong caution. By not doing so Blaine in particular, but also Foster and President Harrison, incurred a clear responsibility for Stevens's actions when the revolution occurred. Having been orally informed (one may be sure) prior to assuming his post in 1889 of Blaine's convictions regarding Hawaii, having been told to study the Secretary's instruction of 1881, having declared his own advocacy of annexation and asked whether he and the navy should "deviate from established rules and precedents" in the event of the revolution he anticipated, Stevens was justified in interpreting Washington's silence as approval of his implicit recommendations, and therefore in acting as he did when the revolution occurred.

In a later year at least one Congressman could not believe that the minister's dispatches had gone without answer. Representative Isidor Rayner stated in Congress: "I refer to the missing letters of Mr. Blaine. Where are those letters? Does anyone in possession of his reason suppose that there was no correspondence between Mr. Blaine and Mr. Stevens . . . ? Mr. Blaine was an ardent expansionist. . . . Mr. Stevens was the representative of his policy upon these islands. Months before he predicted the very disturbance that took place in January and asked for instructions in case that it should occur. Where are the instructions?"[13] Throughout his official life James G. Blaine was haunted by questions about missing letters—in 1876 and 1884 about the Mulligan letters, in 1882 about alleged correspondence regarding Peru. But the strong probability is that in 1892, at any rate, there were no such letters; there was no need of any, for their absence was almost as meaningful to Minister Stevens, who knew his chief well, as an explicit instruction would have been.

The revolutionary party to which Stevens alluded (the "Annexation Club," it called itself), though small, included several prominent white leaders of American background.[14] The most dynamic of them, a lawyer named Lorrin A. Thurston, arrived in Washington

13. *Congressional Record,* 53 Cong., 2 Sess., p. 1829 (Feb. 3, 1894).
14. For the revolution of 1893 see William A. Russ, Jr., *The Hawaiian Revolution (1893–94)* (Selinsgrove, Pa., 1959).

in May 1892. Carrying a letter of introduction from Minister Stevens, he visited Secretary Blaine, who, according to Thurston, said reassuringly that if Hawaii applied for annexation "he did not see how the application could be rejected." Blaine sent him to Secretary of the Navy Benjamin F. Tracy, who spoke similarly encouraging words. A convinced expansionist, Tracy is supposed to have said at the end of 1892 that the United States would be "very glad to annex Hawaii."[15] Thurston also conferred with Cushman K. Davis, an influential member of the Senate Foreign Relations Committee, and with James H. Blount, chairman of the House Foreign Affairs Committee. He arranged a continuing contact with the administration through Archibald Hopkins, a clerk in the court of claims.[16] Assured of Washington's sympathy, Thurston started back to Honolulu, stopping at San Francisco long enough to write Blaine that the substantial people of Hawaii wanted to be annexed and that if the United States spurned them "a union with England would be preferable to a continuance under existing circumstances."[17] The Secretary, though preoccupied with his impending resignation (in June 1892), could not have missed the barbed reminder that Hawaii had the alternative of turning to Great Britain.

During much of 1892 a deadlock existed between the Hawaiian legislature, supported by American and German elements, and the cabinet, appointed by Queen Liliuokalani. In November the legislature triumphed; a new Cabinet composed of wealthy men, three of American descent, was formed. "I am happy to say that my official and personal relations with this ministry are likely to be most friendly and cordial," Minister Stevens informed Washington.[18] He

15. Pratt, *Expansionists of 1898*, pp. 54–57; Stevens, *American Expansion in Hawaii*, pp. 207–8. Rear Admiral Joseph S. Skerrett, recently appointed to command the Pacific squadron, said that Tracy made the remark about annexing Hawaii to him on Dec. 30, 1892, *House Executive Documents*, 53 Cong., 2 Sess., No. 47 (Serial 3224), p. 10. Despite Tracy's interest in expansion in Hawaii, his papers in the Library of Congress for the crucial period between Dec. 1, 1892, and Feb. 28, 1893, contain no reference to Hawaii. For an argument that President Harrison was only lukewarm about annexation see George W. Baker, Jr., "Benjamin Harrison and Hawaiian Annexation: A Reinterpretation," *Pacific Historical Review*, XXXIII (1964), 295–309.

16. Russ, *Hawaiian Revolution*, pp. 57–59. See also Merze Tate, *The United States and the Hawaiian Kingdom: A Political History* (New Haven, 1965), p. 117; and Lorrin A. Thurston, *Memoirs of the Hawaiian Revolution, Edited by Andrew Farrell* (Honolulu, 1936), pp. 233–34, 235–40.

17. Thurston to Blaine, May 27, 1892, Julius W. Pratt, "The Hawaiian Revolution: A Re-Interpretation," *Pacific Historical Review*, I (1932), 287.

18. Stevens to Foster, Nov. 8, 1892, *Foreign Relations, 1894*, Appendix II, p. 376.

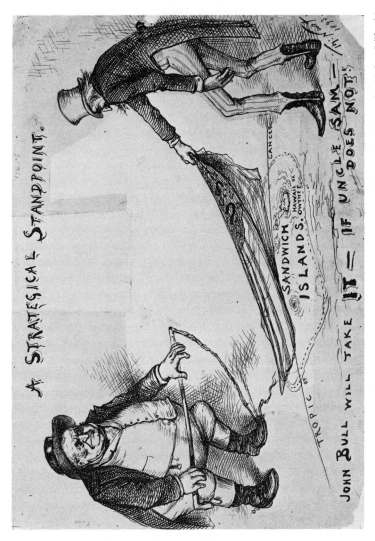

A STRATEGICAL STANDPOINT.

JOHN BULL WILL TAKE IT — IF UNCLE SAM — DOES NOT.

left Honolulu on the U.S.S. *Boston* on January 4, 1893, for a ten-day cruise. During that time the scene changed abruptly. Taking advantage of his absence, the Queen succeeded in removing the Cabinet from office on January 12. Two days later she prorogued the legislature and attempted, but without success, to proclaim a new constitution depriving the wealthy whites of much of the power they had gained in 1887.[19]

The Queen's moves alarmed Thurston and his fellow annexationists. Hopkins had just written Thurston that Secretary of State Foster—he had succeeded Blaine the previous June—thought it too late "to attempt to bring matters to a head during the short time which remains to this administration"; Hopkins added, probably as his own view rather than Foster's, that if "unexpected changes make it seem best for you to act immediately, everything possible to second your plans will be done at this end of the line in the short time that remains." Thurston could not have seen this letter before January 12 at the earliest, a late date to decide for revolutionary action on the sixteenth; and in any case it would seem natural to interpret it as advising delay.[20] However, men in a hurry may have found in the letter sufficient promise of support from Washington to cause them to act. At all events, the Annexation Club immediately organized a Committee of Safety, which on January 16 petitioned Stevens, just back in Honolulu from his trip, for military protection.[21] The minister did not reply; later that day the Committee, concluding that its plans were not sufficiently developed, withdrew the request. It was too late. Captain Gilbert C. Wiltse of the *Boston,* stationed at Honolulu, had already decided, apparently independently of Stevens (though the two may have reached an understanding during the cruise), to order his men ashore. Preparations for the landing were under way. At that juncture Stevens boarded the ship, requested troops for the protection of Americans and their property,

19. Stevens to Foster, Jan. 18, 1893, *House Executive Documents,* 53 Cong., 2 Sess., No. 48, pp. 120–22. See also Wiltse to Tracy, Jan. 18, 1893, *Senate Executive Documents,* 52 Cong., 2 Sess., No. 76 (Serial 3062), p. 25.

20. Hopkins to Thurston, Dec. 29, 1892, Thurston, *Hawaiian Revolution,* pp. 240–43.

21. Committee of Safety to Stevens, Jan. 16, 1893, *House Executive Documents,* 53 Cong., 2 Sess., No. 47, p. 590. For detailed accounts of the revolution see Ralph S. Kuykendall, *The Hawaiian Kingdom . . .* (3 vols., Honolulu, 1938–1967), III, chs. 20–21; Russ, *Hawaiian Revolution;* Tate, *Hawaiian Kingdom,* ch. 5.

and learned approvingly what was afoot.[22] At four thirty on the afternoon of the sixteenth Wiltse ordered a battalion of marines ashore "for the purpose of protecting our legation, consulate, and the lives and property of American citizens, and [here Wiltse was on more dubious grounds] to assist in preserving public order."[23] The Hawaiian government, when asked by Stevens for lodging for the troops, protested against their presence on land.[24] Nevertheless one detachment stationed itself at the American Legation, one at the Consulate, and the main body with two pieces of artillery in a building near the government offices and the royal palace known as Arion Hall.[25]

The next day, January 17, the revolutionary group occupied the principal government buildings, proclaimed a provisional government, and asked Stevens for recognition. The minister complied the same day. Confronted by this fait accompli, Queen Liliuokalani gave way. Ordering her troops to surrender, she proclaimed on January 17 that, to avoid loss of life, she was yielding to American force, until Washington reversed Stevens's action and restored her to power.[26] The new government, whose main reason for existence was to win annexation to the United States, appointed a commission to go to Washington and make overtures. It sailed on January 19. By then the government had also been recognized by the envoys of Germany, Austria-Hungary, Italy, Russia, Spain, Sweden and Norway, Denmark, the Netherlands, Belgium, Mexico, Chile, Peru, and China, and by the next day all the countries represented in Hawaii

22. Majority report of the Senate Foreign Relations Committee, Feb. 26, 1894, *Senate Reports*, 53 Cong., 2 Sess., No. 227 (Serial 3180), p. vii; W. D. Alexander, *History of Later Years of the Hawaiian Monarchy and the Revolution of 1893* (Honolulu, 1896), p. 52; according to Alexander, American Consul General Henry W. Severance sent Wiltse a note on Jan. 16 warning of an outbreak on shore. See also Lucien Young, *The Boston at Hawaii*... (Washington, 1898), pp. 185–86; according to Young (an officer on the *Boston* in 1893), the petition of the Committee of Safety "had nothing to do with the subsequent landing."

23. Wiltse to Lieutenant Commander William T. Swinburne, Jan. 16, 1893, *Senate Reports*, 53 Cong., 2 Sess., No. 227, p. vi.

24. *House Executive Documents*, 53 Cong., 2 Sess., No. 47, pp. 591–93.

25. Wiltse to Tracy, Jan. 18, 1893, *Senate Executive Documents*, 52 Cong., 2 Sess., No. 76, p. 27. According to Young, it was Wiltse who secured the use of Arion Hall. Young, *Boston at Hawaii*, p. 188. Stevens said later that he had not known of the existence of Arion Hall until the evening of Jan. 16. *Congressional Record*, 53 Cong., 2 Sess., p. 193 (Dec. 13, 1893).

26. *House Executive Documents*, 53 Cong., 2 Sess., No. 47, p. 120.

had recognized it.[27] So speedily did revolution become legitimate. But if legitimate, the provisional government did not feel secure. At its request Minister Stevens (with Wiltse's approval) announced an American protectorate on February 1, 1893. "The Hawaiian pear is now fully ripe," he declared exultingly, "and this is the golden hour for the United States to pluck it."[28] Secretary of State Foster had previously commended the minister's role during the revolution; but now he telegraphed that to the extent the protectorate set American authority above that of the Hawaiian government or impaired Hawaii's independence, "it is disavowed."[29] This was the first jolt of many for Stevens.

Arriving in Washington on February 3, 1893, the Hawaiian commissioners started to negotiate a treaty of annexation. They had little time. Grover Cleveland was to become President on March 4, and in view of his moralistic aversion to anything akin to imperialism, his support of annexation would be most unlikely. Even President Harrison at first wanted to get an expression of opinion from the Hawaiians about the revolution's popularity, but he was dissuaded by Foster.[30] In short order the Secretary had a draft treaty ready. It provided for annexation, prohibition of further Chinese immigration, and an annuity for the ex-Queen. Signed on February 14, it was promptly endorsed by the Foreign Relations Committee.[31] Its approval by the Senate depended on the Democrats, who could block a two-thirds majority. On February 22 Cleveland conferred with his future Secretary of State and Secretary of the Treasury, Walter Q. Gresham and John G. Carlisle, respectively. Carlisle then went to Washington and indicated that Cleveland preferred to deal with Hawaii himself. That doomed a vote during the few remaining days of the Republican administration.

Hardly were the Democrats in power on March 4, 1893, when the new President withdrew the treaty from the Senate, pending an investigation, as eight years before he had withdrawn the Freling-

27. China extended recognition on the 19th; all the other countries named, on the 18th. *Foreign Relations, 1894*, Appendix II, pp. 229–32.
28. Stevens to Foster, Feb. 1, 1893, *House Executive Documents*, 53 Cong., 2 Sess., No. 48, p. 136. The text of his announcement is in *Congressional Record*, 53 Cong., 2 Sess., p. 191 (Dec. 13, 1893).
29. Foster to Stevens, Jan. 28, Feb. 14, 1893, *House Executive Documents*, 53 Cong., 2 Sess., No. 48, pp. 133, 140–41, respectively.
30. Pratt, *Expansionists of 1898*, pp. 119–20.
31. *Foreign Relations, 1894*, Appendix II, pp. 197–205.

huysen-Zavala canal treaty; on the eleventh he appointed James H. Blount, who had just resigned as chairman of the House Foreign Affairs Committee, a special commissioner to go to Hawaii. Blount was to investigate the revolution and the Hawaiian people's opinion of the provisional government; his instructions specified that his "authority in all matters touching the relations of this Government to the existing or other government of the islands, and the protection of our citizens therein" was to be "paramount."[32] By the time "Paramount" Blount, as he was called by disgruntled Republicans, reached Honolulu on March 29, Stevens, his hour of triumph supplanted by humiliation, had resigned. Blount, now named minister, added to his predecessor's discomfiture by ordering that the American flag be lowered over the Honolulu government buildings and that the troops be reembarked on the *Boston*.[33]

"Paramount" Blount stayed in Hawaii a little over four months. He interviewed royalists, revolutionary leaders, and businessmen; he received letters, affidavits, and memorials. Listening to all opinions, he expressed none himself. His long report, the main part of it dated July 17, 1893, but not published until November, censured Stevens harshly for his role and concluded: "The undoubted sentiment of the people is for the Queen, against the Provisional Government and against annexation"; the report rashly predicted that the new government would last only a year or two.[34] Both President Cleveland and Secretary of State Gresham, a high-principled, politically independent man who had been Postmaster General under President Arthur, agreed that the revolution was unrepresentative of the people; Gresham's papers are replete with denunciations of it as immoral as well, a sentiment with which the President doubtless agreed.[35]

32. Secretary of State Walter Q. Gresham to Blount, March 11, 1893, *House Executive Documents*, 53 Cong., 2 Sess., No. 47, p. 2.

33. Skerrett to Blount, April 1, 1893, *Foreign Relations, 1894*, Appendix II, pp. 1060–61.

34. Blount to Gresham, July 17 and 31, 1893, *House Executive Documents*, 53 Cong., 2 Sess., No. 47, pp. 133, 164. Julius W. Pratt characterized Blount's report as "more nearly the philippic of a prosecuting attorney than the reasoned conclusion of a judge." *Expansionists of 1898*, p. 134. Regarding Blount's mission see Russ, *Hawaiian Revolution*, ch. 5. Blount left Hawaii on Aug. 8, 1893.

35. Gresham to Bayard, Oct. 29, Dec. 17, 1893; to Noble C. Butler, Nov. 23, 1893; to Edward J. Phelps, Nov. 29, 1893; to John Overmeyer, July 25, 1894; to Thomas G. Sherman, March 5, 1895. Walter Q. Gresham Papers, Library of Congress (Washington), Letterbook.

But most Americans were prepared to let bygones be bygones. The administration was roundly abused for repudiating the Hawaiian republic. Even such Democratic newspapers as the Philadelphia *Record,* the New York *World,* the New York *Sun,* and the independent Democratic New York *Herald* criticized the President; Republican papers were violent in disapproval. "I do not want to comment on Mr. Cleveland's acts," ex-President Harrison declared acidly. "If his policy suits him, mine suits me. . . . the Queen cannot resume her throne, I believe, without bloodshed." And John L. Stevens scored a telling point by insisting that his conduct "was more than covered by Secretary Bayard's instructions [to George W. Merrill, quoted above], approved by Mr. Cleveland, of July 12, 1887."[36] (On a later date he made another pertinent point: that whereas he had asked Captain Wiltse for troops to protect the American Legation and Consulate and American life and property, Wiltse had gone much further when he instructed the marines to protect public order also.)[37] Similar press observations, critical of Cleveland, appeared after the Blount report's publication in November, although most Democratic newspapers contended that Stevens, too, was blameworthy. Cleveland's subsequent unpopularity was due in part to his allegedly weak Hawaiian policy, as well as to his backing of the gold standard; the Detroit *News* sounded a note soon to echo throughout the country when it charged that his actions in Hawaii were "sure to give as much pleasure to England" as did his defense of gold.[38]

Blount's successor as minister at Honolulu, Albert S. Willis, was instructed (October 18, 1893) to tell Liliuokalani that Cleveland regretted the "flagrant wrong" done her by the "reprehensible conduct of the American minister and the unauthorized presence on land of a military force of the United States," that the President wanted her to be reinstated as Queen, but that first she must promise to grant "full amnesty" and to assume the provisional government's obligations. When she did so, Willis was to order the provisional government "to promptly relinquish to her her constitutional

36. *Literary Digest,* VIII (Nov. 18, 1893), 58–60. For a long defense of himself by Stevens see *Congressional Record,* 53 Cong., 2 Sess., pp. 191–94 (Dec. 13, 1893). For the instruction of 1887 see pp. 178–79.

37. *Senate Reports,* 53 Cong., 2 Sess., No. 227, p. 533.

38. *Literary Digest,* VIII (Nov. 25, 1893), 77–78.

authority."[39] Perhaps never before had an American envoy—not even Trescot in Chile in 1882—been assigned a more impossible task. Even the ex-Queen refused to cooperate at first. When Willis told her that she must grant the revolutionists an amnesty, he received a nasty shock. Drawing herself up, she replied in measured tones: "My decision would be, as the law directs, that such persons should be beheaded and their property confiscated to the Government."[40] One can imagine the consternation in Washington. The State Department hastened to tell Willis to stick to the prescribed conditions for the Queen's restoration. But although Liliuokalani retreated slightly at a second interview, she still did not accept the American demands. Only after a third talk did she change her mind, on December 18, and agree to Cleveland's conditions.[41] Her written pledge in hand, Willis proceeded to instruct Sanford B. Dole, President of the republic, to relinquish his authority. The leaders of the tiny republic, who seem to have received no official forewarning, were dismayed; for all they knew, the United States was prepared to use force against them. Courageously Dole refused to yield.[42]

Cleveland had apparently anticipated this outcome and had decided to turn to Congress. In a long special message on December 18, 1893, he submitted the Blount report and announced that, the investigation having been completed, he would abandon Foster's annexation treaty; annexation, he explained, would convict the United States of having employed "unjustifiable methods" and would constitute "a departure from unbroken American tradition in providing for the addition to our territory of islands of the sea more than 2,000 miles removed from our nearest coast." If not annexation, what should occur? Echoing Gresham, the President declared that "the United States, in aiming to maintain itself as one of the most enlightened nations, would do its citizens gross injustice if it

39. Gresham to Willis, Oct. 18, 1893, *Foreign Relations, 1894,* Appendix II, pp. 1189–91. See also Sereno E. Bishop, "The President's Endeavor to Restore the Queen," in Alexander, *Hawaiian Monarchy,* p. 103.

40. Willis to Gresham, Nov. 16, 1893, *House Executive Documents,* 53 Cong., 2 Sess., No. 70 (Serial 3224), p. 2.

41. Gresham to Willis, Dec. 3, 1893, *ibid.,* No. 48, p. 171; Willis to Gresham, Dec. 20, 1893, enclosing a letter and a statement from Liliuokalani, both dated Dec. 18, 1893, *ibid.,* No. 70, p. 29.

42. Willis to Dole, Dec. 19, 1893, *ibid.,* No. 70, p. 35; Dole to Willis, Dec. 23, 1893, *ibid.,* p. 42. Regarding the new government see William A. Russ, Jr., *The Hawaiian Republic (1894–98) and Its Struggle to Win Annexation* (Selinsgrove, Pa., 1961).

applied to its international relations any other than a high standard of honor and morality." He said that he would cooperate in any honorable, moral plan that Congress (then controlled by the Democrats) could devise.[43] In effect he confessed that he himself could think of no solution and was therefore asking Congress to find one.

An angry debate ensued. It was devoted in part to questions of the national interest, to those economic and strategic matters which had become familiar in earlier discussions about Hawaii, and which would be heard again in 1898 when the islands were annexed. Senator Shelby M. Cullom believed that the economic stakes involved in annexation were of "vast importance to the United States"; Senator Joseph N. Dolph stressed the "importance of the islands commercially and as a naval station"; and Senator Henry M. Teller asserted that "this group of islands on the west, looking out upon our Pacific coast, should not be allowed to pass under the control of any other nation," and that "the commercial advantages of those islands are too great to be overlooked."[44] These men were Republicans; some Democrats, though by no means all, disagreed with them. Thus for Senator George G. Vest the "plain issue" was whether the United States should desert her traditional policy and "venture upon the great colonial system of the European powers."[45] The nationwide debate at the end of the century was already taking shape: should the United States abandon her time-tested continental policy, or should she join the great powers of Europe in a scramble for colonies?

But in 1893 and 1894 a surprisingly large part of Congress's attention was occupied not by the national interest but by legal and ethical questions. Republicans were not inclined to accept the depiction of their deeds as morally loathsome, and many of them also thought it quixotic in the extreme to try to overthrow the government of a friendly republic. Eagerly they censured as unconstitutional Blount's appointment without congressional consent and the assignment to him of paramount authority over the American minister and the naval commander. Bitterly they excoriated the President

43. James D. Richardson (ed.), *A Compilation of the Messages and Papers of the Presidents* (10 vols., Washington, 1899), IX, 461, 470–71, 472.

44. *Congressional Record*, 53 Cong., 2 Sess., p. 1234 (Jan. 23, 1894), p. 1312 (Jan. 24, 1894), p. 1578 (Jan. 29, 1894).

45. *Ibid.*, p. 196 (Dec. 13, 1893).

and Secretary Gresham for trying to dislodge a recognized government and to replace it by, of all un-American things, a monarchy, and for hauling down the Stars and Stripes. "The assumption by the President of authority to set up or pull down governments is extraordinary, and unknown before in our history," Representative Robert R. Hitt asserted, and he depicted Liliuokalani as "the Tiger protégé of Mr. Cleveland," who "proposed to celebrate her restoration, with a holocaust, with a St. Bartholomew massacre."[46] Democrats countered. Many precedents existed for the appointment of a commissioner without heed to the Senate, they insisted; and not Cleveland, Gresham, or Blount but John L. Stevens was the culprit who had destroyed a foreign government. But their party was already weakening under the stress of the panic of 1893. Cleveland had called a special session of Congress in the autumn of 1893 and by exerting great pressure had secured the repeal, as we have seen, of part of the Silver Purchase Act of 1890—but at the cost of tremendous bitterness. When the regular session met in December at the time of the Hawaiian message, the wounds had not yet healed; they were never to heal during Cleveland's term of office.

The House acted sooner than the Senate. On February 7, 1894, it adopted resolutions that censured Stevens, approved the principle of noninterference in the domestic affairs of another country, and pronounced against annexation or the assumption of a protectorate by the United States or any other power.[47]

The Senate's plan was incorporated in a voluminous report issued by the Foreign Relations Committee on February 26, 1894. The committee had taken testimony from Lorrin A. Thurston, Blount, Stevens, and many others. John T. Morgan, the committee's expansionist-minded chairman, probably envisaged the report as an answer to Blount, but only Morgan accepted all its conclusions. Unlike the House resolutions, it exonerated Stevens and defended the annexation treaty. But—and here Morgan, a Democrat, departed from Republican expansionists—Cleveland also had acted commendably: he was justified in sending "Paramount" Blount to

46. *Ibid.*, Appendix, p. 445 (Feb. 3, 1894), p. 441 (Feb. 2, 1894); see also *ibid.*, pp. 1836–37 (Feb. 3, 1894).

47. *Ibid.*, p. 1594 (Jan. 29, 1894), pp. 2001, 2007 (Feb. 7, 1894). For the House debate see *ibid.*, pp. 1807–22 (Feb. 2, 1894), pp. 1825–52 (Feb. 3, 1894), pp. 1879–1921 (Feb. 5, 1894), pp. 1942–72 (Feb. 6, 1894).

the islands and in attempting to reinstate Liliuokalani. The Republican committee members accepted Morgan's "essential findings" but censured Cleveland for appointing Blount and giving him paramount authority without the Senate's approval, and for attempting to restore the monarchy.[48] Accompanying the report was a resolution; it was adopted by the Senate on May 31, 1894, 55 to 0 (30 not voting): "*Resolved,* That of right it belongs wholly to the people of the Hawaiian Islands to establish and maintain their own form of government and domestic polity; that the United States ought in no wise to interfere therewith, and that any intervention in the political affairs of these islands by any other government will be regarded as an act unfriendly to the United States."[49]

Both the Senate and the House had agreed on one basic point: the United States should not attempt to undo the Hawaiian revolution. Cleveland and Gresham had no recourse but to accept the recommendation. Consequently the United States now assumed a posture of aloofness toward Hawaii, although commercial reciprocity of course continued. In August 1894 the U.S.S. *Philadelphia* sailed away from Honolulu, and for the first time since 1889 no American warship stood guard over the islands.

In Hawaii royalists plotted to restore the monarchy. Their revolt was precipitated when some armed men were discovered on Waikiki beach in January 1895. Fighting broke out; and for once in a Hawaiian revolution a man was killed. The royalists were quickly captured. Some commotion ensued in Congress as Republicans tried to pin these events—attacks on republicanism, they called them—on the withdrawal of the *Philadelphia.* Shortly before the revolt Senator Henry Cabot Lodge had introduced a resolution deploring the withdrawal and asking for a warship to be permanently stationed at Honolulu. Republicans now made capital of the prescience of their Senator. [50] Cleveland was vulnerable in the *Philadelphia* incident, and the ship was soon ordered back to Honolulu.

The President was vulnerable on other grounds, too, because almost coincidentally with the revolt he had urged Congress to

48. *Senate Reports,* 53 Cong., 2 Sess., No. 227, pp. xxi, xxxiii–iv.
49. *Congressional Record,* 53 Cong., 2 Sess., p. 1220 (Jan. 23, 1894), pp. 5499–5500 (May 31, 1894).
50. Gresham to Willis, May 12, July 22, 1894, Gresham Papers, Letterbook; *Congressional Record,* 53 Cong., 3 Sess., p. 555 (Dec. 22, 1894), p. 1133 (Jan. 19, 1895).

release Hawaii from a clause in the Hawaiian-American reciprocity treaty of 1884 that prevented her from leasing the uninhabited Necker Island to Great Britain for a cable station between Canada and Australia. The low-tariff and gold-standard proclivities that had long since exposed him to charges of being pro-British now added credibility to accusations that he was neglecting American interests in Hawaii in favor of those of Britain. Congress refused to sanction a British cable but instead made some inconclusive moves toward providing for an American one.[51]

During the rest of Cleveland's administration Hawaii slipped into the background. The calamitous economic situation, the Cuban rebellion, the dramatic election of 1896, a clash with Great Britain over Venezuela, these events absorbed American interest. Hawaii settled down and waited for the Republicans to return to power. Only then could she hope to be annexed.

51. *Congressional Record*, 53 Cong., 3 Sess., pp. 1978–86 (Feb. 9, 1895), p. 3126 (March 2, 1895); *House Reports*, 54 Cong., 1 Sess., No. 2092 (Serial 3464).

# CHAPTER 11

# *The Venezuela Boundary Dispute:*
# *A Turning Point*
# *in Anglo-American Relations*

As a result of the Hawaiian Revolution of 1893 circumstances were somewhat more propitious for United States expansion in the Pacific Ocean. On the other hand, an isthmian canal and bases in the Caribbean Sea seemed no nearer realization. As regards the other main theme of foreign policy, that is, relations with Great Britain, there too some progress had been made in the sense that the treaty of Washington, the fisheries *modus vivendi* of 1888, and the Bering Sea arbitration of 1893 had more or less settled the principal altercations; and that basic, long-range forces were working to bring the two English-speaking nations closer together. That these forces were already making themselves felt became evident when the United States in 1895, abruptly and unexpectedly, intervened in an old controversy between Great Britain and Venezuela over the boundary between the latter and British Guiana.

That boundary had never been legally defined. For many years this did not greatly matter because most of the unmapped area was uninhabited jungle. But in time settlers moved there. In 1840 a surveyor commissioned by London, Robert Schomburgk, drew up the so-called Schomburgk line, which Britain, but not Venezuela, accepted as a satisfactory boundary. However, Britain's maximum claims extended considerably west of the line, and Venezuela's claims even farther east of it. In fact, Venezuela asserted title to about two-thirds of British Guiana. Beginning in 1876 she kept the

United States informed of her sporadic negotiations with Britain, and appealed for assistance in the name of the Monroe Doctrine. Gold discoveries in the disputed zone attracted more settlers. When British Guiana, as described in an official British yearbook, grew in area by 40 percent between 1885 and 1886, Washington feared that Britain was expanding in South America, the Monroe Doctrine notwithstanding, as she was doing in other parts of the world. In 1887 Venezuela suspended diplomatic relations with Great Britain.

The Arthur, first Cleveland, and Harrison administrations all informed London, rather mildly, that the United States felt concern about a sister New World republic; Secretary of State Bayard went so far as to remind London that the Monroe Doctrine had lost none of its importance.[1] But nothing came of these overtures. Great Britain had agreed to arbitrate claims west of the Schomburgk line but not east of it, where she believed her title to be incontestable.[2] Venezuela insisted that arbitration must embrace the entire disputed territory, extending eastward all the way to the Essequibo River, far beyond the Schomburgk line.

When Cleveland became President again in 1893 he could be expected to show renewed interest in the altercation. But he was preoccupied with the Hawaiian revolution and the panic of 1893. In his annual messages of 1893 and 1894 he expressed hope that the disputants would arbitrate; and Secretary of State Gresham wrote Bayard (at London since 1893 as the first American with the title of ambassador) that the administration would gladly help arrange an arbitration. When the ambassador mentioned this to the British Foreign Secretary, he received a familiar reply: Britain would arbitrate everything except Venezuela's claims east of the Schomburgk line.[3]

1. Frederick T. Frelinghuysen to James Russell Lowell, July 7, 1884, *Senate Executive Documents*, 50 Cong., 1 Sess., No. 226 (Serial 2514), p. 48; Thomas F. Bayard to Edward J. Phelps, Dec. 30, 1886, *ibid.*, p. 68; Prime Minister Lord Salisbury to Phelps, Feb. 22, 1887, *ibid.*, p. 84; James G. Blaine to Henry White (Secretary of American Legation, London), Dec. 30, 1889, and to Robert T. Lincoln (American minister to Great Britain), May 1 and 6, 1890, *Papers Relating to the Foreign Relations of the United States, 1890* (Washington, 1891), pp. 322, 337, 339, respectively.

2. Salisbury to Lincoln, May 26, 1890, *ibid.*, pp. 340–41.

3. Messages of Dec. 4, 1893, Dec. 3, 1894, James D. Richardson (ed.), *A Compilation of the Messages and Papers of the Presidents, 1789–1897* (10 vols., Washington, 1899), IX, 441, 526, respectively; Gresham to Bayard, July 13, Dec. 1, 1894, *Papers Relating to the Foreign Relations of the United States, 1894* (Washington, 1895), pp. 250–52; minutes by K (Foreign Secretary Lord Kimberley), Jan. 23, Feb. 20, 1895, and memorandum by Kimberley, Jan. 23, 1895, Public Record Office, Foreign Office 80/361.

The
VENEZUELA~BR.GUIANA
BOUNDARY DISPUTE

•••••  Schomburgk Line
▬▬▬  Final Settlement
▦▦  Extreme British claim
▨▨  Extreme Venezuelan claim

Orinoco R.        Pt. Barima

VENEZUELA

Essequibo R.

BRITISH

GUIANA

DUTCH GUIANA

BRAZIL

In 1894 an active propagandist appeared in Washington. William L. Scruggs, a former American minister at Caracas, had been dismissed by the Harrison administration for bribing the Venezuelan President. So resourceful a man deserved employment, and Venezuela appointed him a special agent.[4] He wrote a pamphlet with the accusatory title *British Aggressions in Venezuela, or the Monroe Doctrine on Trial*, which went to influential people in Washington in late 1894. It made a deep impression. One of Scruggs's contacts was Representative Leonidas F. Livingston of Georgia, who on January 10, 1895, introduced a joint resolution in the House, word for word as drafted by Scruggs; a slightly different version passed the House and Senate unanimously on February 20. It proposed that arbitration "be earnestly recommended to the favorable consideration of both parties in interest."[5] This was moderate enough, but the unanimity of the vote was a signal of coming trouble. Another such signal had appeared on January 2, 1895, when Venezuelan police seized two British officers and six constables in a place near the Uruan River that had been tacitly recognized as British. Although they were all soon released, a strong reaction could be expected from London.

Under the combined influence of Scruggs, the resolution, and the Uruan incident, Cleveland and Gresham realized that a somewhat more active American role was called for; the President, in fact, may already have been considering a much stronger policy, although the evidence is sketchy. But Gresham, in a long instruction he was preparing for Bayard, envisaged no more than tactful pressure on the British; he also hoped to persuade Venezuela to restore diplomatic relations and negotiate directly with Great Britain.[6] Whether he would have succeeded with this plan cannot be known, because on May 28, 1895, he died. During his last illness Acting Secretary

4. Theodore D. Jervey, "William Lindsay Scruggs—a Forgotten Diplomat," *South Atlantic Quarterly*, XXVII (1928), 292–309; John A. S. Grenville and George B. Young, *Politics, Strategy, and American Diplomacy: Studies in Foreign Policy, 1873–1917* (New Haven, 1966), pp. 132–33.

5. *Congressional Record*, 53 Cong., 3 Sess., p. 837 (Jan. 10, 1895), p. 2642 (Feb. 23, 1895). Grenville and Young, *American Diplomacy*, pp. 142, 145.

6. Matilda Gresham, *Life of Walter Quintin Gresham, 1832–1895* (2 vols., Chicago, 1919), II, 795; Foreign Minister Lucio Pulido to José Andrade (Venezuelan minister to the United States), April 17, 1895, *Papers Relating to the Foreign Relations of the United States, 1895* (Washington, 1896), II, 1482. Regarding Cleveland's mood see Grenville and Young, *American Diplomacy*, pp. 160–62.

of State Edwin F. Uhl recommended direct negotiations to the Venezuelan minister at Washington.[7] A subordinate official, Uhl would not have taken this step without Cleveland's approval. His cautious approach was entirely different from the violent intervention of Gresham's successor, Richard Olney, a few weeks later; and it suggests that Cleveland's thinking changed under Olney's influence.

Olney moved from the position of Attorney General to the State Department on June 8, 1895. A successful Boston lawyer, he was a strong-willed, intelligent person. He was not a bellicose man; he admired Great Britain and wanted good relations with her. In November 1895 Sir Julian Pauncefote (like Bayard, he had been made an ambassador in 1893, a sign of the importance London now attached to the United States) called Olney "a most able, large minded, and honest negotiator."[8] But he was too brusque, direct, and impatient to be a good Secretary of State. His biographer compared him to "one of those modern wartanks which proceeds across the roughest ground, heedless of opposition, deaf alike to messages between friends and cries from the foe, able to crush every person and every obstacle that gets between it and its chosen objective."[9] During Gresham's illness Attorney General Olney, at Cleveland's request, had studied the State Department records about Venezuela and British Guiana; now, as Secretary of State, he resolved to bring the dragging controversy to a head forthwith. He drafted a long instruction to Ambassador Bayard; needing Cleveland's approval, he took the note on July 2 to the President in Massachusetts, where Mrs. Cleveland was expecting a baby. On the seventh a baby girl was born and the proud father relieved his Secretary's suspense: "I read your deliverance," he wrote archly, "on Venezuelan affairs. . . . It's the best thing of the kind I have ever read. . . ."[10] The instruction, slightly modified, went off to Bayard on July 20, 1895.

Dogmatic and demanding in tone—a "twenty-inch gun," Cleveland called it—the note was calculated to end the years of indecision about the boundary. It included a history of the controversy that did

7. Uhl to Andrade, May 25, 1895, *Foreign Relations, 1895*, II, 1485–86.
8. Quoted in Grenville and Young, *American Diplomacy*, p. 162.
9. Henry James, *Richard Olney and His Public Service* (Boston, 1923), p. 12.
10. Robert McElroy, *Grover Cleveland, the Man and the Statesman: An Authorized Biography* (2 vols., London, 1923), II, 180–81.

A SIMPLE DEFINITION. *(Punch,* November 2, 1895)

MASTER JOHNNY BULL: "Monroe Doctrine! What *is* the 'Monroe Doctrine'?"

MASTER JONATHAN: "Wa-al—guess it's that everything everywhere be-longs to *us!*"

not put Great Britain in a good light. A large part of the note concerned the Monroe Doctrine. Olney called it "a doctrine of American public law, well founded in principle and abundantly sanctioned by precedent, which entitles and requires the United States to treat as an injury to itself the forcible assumption by an European power of political control over an American state." Was the doctrine applicable to the boundary controversy between Great Britain and Venezuela? Britain, Olney argued, would not cede any of the disputed land to Venezuela, and would agree to arbitrate only if Venezuela would first surrender whatever part of the land Britain might designate. Territory acquired by Britain as a result of this unfair attitude would, he asserted, come under British political control exactly as if British troops had seized the area—and consequently the Monroe Doctrine was relevant. Although Olney admitted that the United States did not herself have the right to determine the merits of the controversy, she clearly was entitled to demand that the merits be ascertained; and "there is but one feasible mode of determining them, viz., peaceful arbitration."[11] To this argument Olney added the dubious geographical point that "distance and three thousand miles of intervening ocean make any permanent political union between an European and an American state unnatural and inexpedient. . . ."[12] He ordered Bayard to obtain a "definite decision" from Lord Salisbury, the British Prime Minister and Foreign Secretary, "upon the point whether Great Britain will consent or will decline to submit the Venezuelan boundary question in its entirety to impartial arbitration." Bayard was to ask for a reply in time for the President's annual message to Congress in December —thus allowing plenty of time, so Olney and the President may have supposed, for further negotiations and a settlement before Congress convened in that month. Although the note was anti-British in tone, it did not align the United States with Venezuela, and Olney's foolish boast—"To-day the United States is practically sovereign on this continent, and its fiat is law upon the subjects to which it confines its interposition"—was not calculated to please sensitive Latin Americans.[13]

11. Olney to Bayard, July 20, 1895, *Foreign Relations, 1895,* I, 559–62.
12. *Ibid.,* p. 556.
13. *Ibid.,* pp. 562, 558. See also George B. Young, "Intervention under the Monroe Doctrine: The Olney Corollary," *Political Science Quarterly,* LVII (1942), 251–52.

The twenty-inch gun marked such a break from previous American practice in the boundary dispute that it needs further explanation. Olney's role can be understood well enough in terms of his dogmatic, impatient temperament. But why did Cleveland, normally a deliberate person, approve so abrupt a move? For one thing, presumably he did not want to offend his new Secretary of State at the very beginning of the latter's duties. During his first weeks in the State Department, Olney had worked hard on the Venezuelan note, about which he felt strongly; Cleveland would have hesitated to discourage so dedicated an assistant.

But the President had positive reasons for welcoming the note. It seems to have come to him as a revelation about the Monroe Doctrine, which, he suddenly perceived (or so he thought), Great Britain was flagrantly violating. "You . . . place it [the doctrine] I think on better and more defensible ground than any of your predecessors—*or mine,*" he wrote Olney; and in a later year he attributed his administration's sudden interposition in the controversy to a need "to assert and vindicate a principle distinctively American, and in the maintenance of which the people and Government of the United States were profoundly concerned."[14]

Not only did the President believe that Britain was violating the Monroe Doctrine; he also came to believe that Britain was bullying Venezuela—and brushing off American protests in an intolerable manner. This brings us again to his moralistic hatred of imperialism. By nature Cleveland suspected strong powers of harboring designs on weak ones; he had already tried to protect native Samoans and Hawaiians. About the boundary dispute he was poorly informed. He did not know that Venezuela's claim to territory up to the Essequibo River was untenable, nor did he stop to think that Britain would be no more justified in exposing her subjects living far within British Guiana to the uncertainties of arbitration than she would have been to give the Geneva tribunal unrestricted jurisdiction over the indirect claims in 1872. What he did see, with painful clarity, was a world power browbeating a defenseless, backward country. This aroused his anger. Not only was the Monroe Doctrine at stake but also international morality—and in an area of American influence.

14. McElroy, *Cleveland,* II, 181; Grover Cleveland, *Presidential Problems* (New York, 1904), pp. 278–79. See also his letter to Bayard, Dec. 29, 1895, Charles C. Tansill, *The Foreign Policy of Thomas F. Bayard, 1885–1897* (New York, 1940), pp. 731–32.

Whenever Grover Cleveland became convinced of that, action was not far off.

Was he also moved by political, economic, and strategic considerations? The Democrats had slipped badly in the 1894 elections. Whereas in 1893 they had 44 Senators and 218 Representatives and controlled both houses of Congress, in 1895 they had only 39 Senators and 105 Representatives and had lost both houses. Over the same period Republican Senators increased from 38 to 43, Representatives from 127 to 244. To be sure this Democratic calamity was ascribable mainly to the panic of 1893. But to some extent it resulted from Cleveland's rejection of the new Hawaiian government's plea for annexation in 1893. Republicans were still enraged, and many people denounced Cleveland for conducting a flabby, un-American foreign policy. It is true that during another revolution of 1893 the administration had shown that it could act more strongly. When Brazilian monarchists, seeking to overturn their country's republican government, interfered with an American merchantman trying to land goods, a United States warship fired on the rebels.[15] But although Americans applauded this blow for New World republicanism, the episode was too trivial to silence the clamor over Hawaii.

Soon after the disastrous elections Cleveland found himself exposed to another charge of foreign-policy weakness. For several decades Great Britain had claimed the right to protect the Mosquito Indians on the east coast of Nicaragua. In 1894 Nicaragua, denying the right, extended her sovereignty over the Mosquito Coast; and in doing so she expelled some Americans and Britons, including the British consul at Bluefields. The Americans were permitted to return but not the Britons. Great Britain was incensed. The situation was serious enough to keep Ambassador Pauncefote in Washington during a July hot spell. "Nothing but the great importance of my

15. Regarding United States policy during the revolution see João Pandía Calogeras and Percy A. Martin (ed.), *A History of Brazil* (Chapel Hill, 1939), pp. 291–95; Lawrence F. Hill, *Diplomatic Relations between the United States and Brazil* (Durham, N.C., 1932), pp. 272–80; Walter LaFeber, "United States Depression Diplomacy and the Brazilian Revolution, 1893–1894," *Hispanic American Historical Review*, XL (1960), 107–118, and *The New Empire: An Interpretation of American Expansion, 1860–1898* (Ithaca, 1963), pp. 210–18; John Bassett Moore, *A Digest of International Law . . .* (8 vols., Washington, 1906), II, 1113–20; Charles A. Timm, "The Diplomatic Relations between the United States and Brazil during the Naval Revolt of 1893," *Southwestern Political and Social Science Quarterly*, V (1924), 119–37.

presence here just now would keep me in this fiery furnace," he complained irritably.[16] On February 26, 1895, Great Britain demanded an apology and reparations.[17] Nicaragua refused, and appealed to the United States under the Monroe Doctrine. Secretary Gresham took the position that the doctrine was not involved. But when the British demands were disclosed in March, the news filled American headlines for several weeks; and when British marines seized the Nicaraguan town of Corinto on April 27, 1895, much of the press denounced President Cleveland. It did so even though a settlement was reached on May 2, following which the British immediately withdrew. The President's refusal to oppose the British when they were trampling upon New World soil—and soil close to the potential isthmian canal—moved many Americans (especially Republicans) to transports of anger. To them a nearly treasonable presidential weakness seemed confirmed.[18]

Even though he was not a candidate for a third term, so astute a politician as Cleveland would instantly have perceived that the twenty-inch gun could help the Democrats; it might squelch the talk about flabbiness, cast him in the role of an even more resolute twister of the Lion's tail than had his dismissal of Sackville West in 1888, divert attention from the deplorable economy, and perhaps even draw together the gold and silver wings of his party, thereby undermining the radical forces of Populism and free silver. Surely, in the parlous conditions of 1895 he would not have neglected such an opportunity. Cleveland was an honorable, courageous man; but as the *Nation* said, with reference to Venezuela (and it might have mentioned Sackville West and the Scott immigration act as well), he was "not incapable of using foreign questions to achieve domestic victories."[19]

In sanctioning the twenty-inch gun, the President probably had also in mind economic and strategic matters pertaining to the national interest. So resolute a defender of the gold standard could

16. Gresham to Bayard, May 2, 1894, Walter Q. Gresham Papers, Library of Congress (Washington), Letterbook; Pauncefote to Bertie, July 10, 1894, Foreign Office 5/2234.

17. Gresham, *Gresham*, II, 781–85.

18. *Public Opinion*, XVIII (May 2, 1895), 468–69.

19. *Nation*, LXI (Dec. 19, 1895), 437. For rumors that, in fact, he was a candidate see New York *Tribune*, Dec. 18, 1895, quoting Chauncey M. Depew; *Public Opinion*, XIX (Dec. 26, 1895), 842; *Literary Digest*, XII (Jan. 4, 1896), 277.

not have overlooked the discovery in the disputed area of the largest gold nugget ever found anywhere. But beyond that, businessmen and government officials, attributing the depression to overproduction, attached great hope to a potential Latin American market that could relieve the surplus.[20] Crucial for the United States was the Caribbean Sea, and Americans sometimes envisaged it as about to become a British lake like the Mediterranean. As early as 1883 Britain's island of Antigua was called her "Malta of the West," and in 1895 Senator Henry Cabot Lodge described the West Indies as "studded" with British "strong places."[21] Strangely enough, some of the foreboding focused on the Orinoco River, a fact explainable partly by Scruggs's attention to the river in his *Monroe Doctrine on Trial.* Secretary Olney implied that the Orinoco controlled "the whole river navigation of the interior of South America"; a publicist called the Orinoco "the great commercial artery of South America, running far inland, through Venezuela, Brazil, and other countries"; and the Venezuelan minister at Washington even predicted that British domination of the river would "effectually destroy the celebrated and beneficent Monroe Doctrine."[22] Representative Joseph Wheeler of Alabama was no less extravagant in concluding that such control gave "almost a monopoly of the trade and commerce of nearly a third of the South American continent."[23] Great Britain laid formal claim to Point Barima at the Orinoco's mouth on April 5, 1895, shortly before Olney became Secretary of State.[24] Although no documentary evidence is known to show that this worried him and the President, it would be strange if it did not—given

20. Regarding Venezuelan gold see Ernest R. May, *Imperial Democracy: The Emergence of America as a Great Power* (New York, 1961), p. 34; regarding interest in the market see Walter LaFeber, "The Background of Cleveland's Venezuelan Policy: A Reinterpretation," *American Historical Review,* LXVI (1961), 955, G. H. D. Gossip, "Venezuela before Europe and America: From an American Point of View," *Fortnightly Review,* LIX (1896), 404.

21. *Congressional Record,* 47 Cong., 2 Sess., p. 1559 (Jan. 24, 1883). Representative George M. Robeson so described Antigua; Henry Cabot Lodge, "Our Blundering Foreign Policy," *Forum,* XIX (1895), 17.

22. Olney to Bayard, July 20, 1895, *Foreign Relations, 1895,* Pt. 1, p. 559; G. H. D. Gossip, "England in Nicaragua and Venezuela: From an American Point of View," *Fortnightly Review,* LVIII (1895), 833; Andrade to Gresham, Dec. 19, 1894, *Foreign Relations, 1894,* pp. 842–43.

23. Joseph Wheeler, "Our Duty in the Venezuelan Crisis," *North American Review,* CLXI (1895), 630.

24. LaFeber, "Cleveland's Venezuelan Policy," p. 961.

the depression, the fixation on overproduction, and the conception of the Orinoco as a great commercial artery. "There can be no doubt," Sir Julian Pauncefote reported, "that the desire of the United States to prevent Great Britain from gaining a permanent foothold at the mouth of the Orinoco, is likely to warp the judgment of all Americans. . . ."[25]

At the end of 1893 Cleveland had given his blessing to an isthmian canal constructed under American supervision. Few Americans would have questioned Henry Cabot Lodge's dictum in 1895: "the American people are not ready to abandon the Monroe Doctrine, or give up their rightful supremacy in the Western Hemisphere. . . . They are resolved that the Nicaraguan canal shall be built and absolutely controlled by the United States. . . ."[26] Britain's claim to Point Barima and her seizure of Corinto certainly aroused concern not only for American exports but also for the future canal. This persisting attention to the potential canal and the potential market in Latin America—and also in China—had a profound impact on United States foreign policy. To Americans living during the turbulent 1890s it did not seem ridiculous to visualize British power in the Caribbean as raising a formidable barrier against their indispensable exports to Latin America and the Far East; nor did it seem ridiculous to those who knew that the British navy outnumbered the American by some seven to one to suspect that Britain, with far-sighted intent, was extending her power in Nicaragua and in Venezuela—close to the future canal.

Ambassador Bayard handed Lord Salisbury a copy of the twenty-inch gun on August 7, 1895. After glancing through it the Prime Minister said that so elaborate a statement could not be answered quickly.[27] About four months were to elapse before the reply reached Washington. During most of that time the boundary question disappeared from the newspapers. There was one notable exception. On October 19, 1895, a Boston newspaper reported a rumor that London had sent Venezuela the long-anticipated ultima-

25. Pauncefote to Salisbury, April 24, 1896, Foreign Office 80/370.
26. Annual message, Dec. 4, 1893, Richardson, *Messages and Papers*, IX, 438; Henry Cabot Lodge, "England, Venezuela, and the Monroe Doctrine," *North American Review*, CLX (1895), 658. See also Alfred T. Mahan, "The Isthmus and Sea Power," *Atlantic Monthly*, LXXII (1893), 459–72.
27. Salisbury to Lord Gough (an officer in the British Embassy, Washington), Aug. 7, 1895, Foreign Office 80/362.

tum over the Uruan arrests. The rumor was correct; on the four-teenth Britain had demanded that Venezuela apologize and pay reparations; otherwise, Britain would "adopt other means." Promptly the Venezuelans sent Olney a copy of the ultimatum.[28] The additional indication of British bullying must have confirmed American suspicions. The ever-watchful Senator Lodge predicted: "If we allow England to invade Venezuela nominally for reparation, as at Corinto, really for territory, our supremacy in the Americas is over." Sir Julian Pauncefote thought it fortunate that the fabulous wedding between Consuela Vanderbilt and the Duke of Marl-borough was absorbing the public's interest just then.[29]

It was not Venezuela, however, that preoccupied the British For-eign Office as it prepared a reply to Olney. Two international crises threatened to lead to general war. In 1894 and 1895 some fifty thousand Armenians had been massacred in Turkey. England rang with demands for intervention. Had she used force, war with Russia could have ensued. Even in the United States there was much excite-ment, and Cleveland was mildly criticized for another alleged fo-reign-policy weakness: his failure to help the Armenians.[30] In Octo-ber 1895 the rumor arose that Russia had forced China to cede a naval base at Port Arthur and to let her build a railway through Manchuria. If true, England's position in eastern Asia might be outflanked by her arch-foe, Russia. "Is Europe on the Eve of War?" the *Literary Digest* wondered in November.[31] It was not a time when London could devote much attention to an obscure boundary in a South American jungle, a boundary whose importance to Olney and Cleveland it did not yet appreciate.

As December 2, the day set for Cleveland's annual message, drew near with no sign of a British reply, Olney became impatient. Twice he cabled Ambassador Bayard suggesting that Salisbury be prod-ded. But if Bayard did see the Prime Minister, presumably he spoke

28. Salisbury to Venezuelan Minister for Foreign Affairs, Oct. 14, 1895, *ibid.*; Nelson M. Blake, "Background of Cleveland's Venezuelan Policy," *American Historical Review*, XLVII (1942), 270–71.

29. Lodge to Theodore Roosevelt, Oct. 23, 1895, *Selections from the Correspondence of Theodore Roosevelt and Henry Cabot Lodge, 1884–1918* (2 vols., New York, 1925), I, 193; for press comments see *Literary Digest*, XI (Oct. 26, 1895), 754. Pauncefote to Salisbury, Oct. 19, Nov. 8, 1895, Foreign Office 80/362, and Lord Salisbury Papers, Christ Church Library (Oxford), respectively.

30. May, *Imperial Democracy*, pp. 27–29.

31. *Literary Digest*, XII (Nov. 2, 1895), 3.

softly because he considered Britain's delay justifiable in the tense international circumstances.[32] The Foreign Office finished its reply on November 26 and sent it off by ship the next day. It is strange that the American Embassy, which received a copy, did not cable Washington. Apparently Bayard was away shooting; the First Secretary at the Embassy, asked by a surprised Foreign Office official why no cable had been sent, explained that the ambassador had an understanding with the British to keep the reply confidential until Pauncefote gave it to Olney.[33] Given the known urgency in Washington, however, the Embassy should have cabled to inquire whether Washington wanted a summary at once, or even the full reply. As it was, an annoyed President could only inform Congress in his annual message that no answer had come, that the United States desired a settlement by arbitration which "should include the whole controversy," and that she would not be satisfied "if one of the powers concerned is permitted to draw an arbitrary line through the territory in debate and to declare that it will submit to arbitration only the portion lying on one side of it."[34] His prejudgment of blame is apparent.

A few days later, on December 6, Sir Julian gave Olney Lord Salisbury's answer to the twenty-inch gun. It consisted of two notes, the first dealing with the Monroe Doctrine, the second with the boundary dispute. In the first note the Prime Minister rejected Olney's contention that political union between a European and an American country was unnatural. He denied, rather positively, that the Monroe Doctrine gave the United States the right to intervene —"The disputed frontier of Venezuela has nothing to do with any of the questions dealt with by President Monroe"—or that the doctrine was international law. But he admitted that the United States, like any nation, did have the right to intervene in any dispute that, in her exclusive judgment, touched her interests. In the second note he corrected what he called Olney's inaccurate historical account, and concluded by saying that, although Britain had repeatedly of-

32. Olney to Bayard, Nov. 16 and 20, 1895, Tansill, *Bayard*, p. 713; Bayard to Olney, Nov. 23, 1895, *ibid.*, p. 714; F.B. (Francis Bertie, Assistant Undersecretary of State, Foreign Office) to Salisbury, Nov. 25, 1895, Foreign Office 80/363.

33. F.B. (Francis Bertie) to Salisbury, Nov. 25, 1895, *ibid.*; James R. Roosevelt to Bayard, Nov. 30, 1895, Tansill, *Bayard*, p. 715. See also Grenville and Young, *American Diplomacy*, p. 166.

34. Annual message, Dec. 2, 1895, Richardson, *Messages and Papers*, IX, 632.

fered to arbitrate, she would not agree to an arbitration that could lead to "the transfer of large numbers of British subjects, who have for many years enjoyed the settled rule of a British Colony, to a nation of different race and language, whose political system is subject to frequent disturbance, and whose institutions as yet too often afford very inadequate protection to life and property."[35] Throughout the negotiations the Prime Minister held firm to this resolve not to put settled British districts to the risk of being handed over to Venezuela.

President Cleveland had left Washington on December 5 to shoot ducks in North Carolina. He had shown no feeling of urgency; he had written Secretary Olney with reference to the anticipated communication from London that if, after reading it, Olney considered a message to Congress desirable he could draft one—if he had the time. "If I were here I would not be hurried . . . ," he observed. He did not ask to be kept informed while away.[36] But Olney did not proceed slowly; he decided that the British reply required no less than a special message to Congress, and without consulting anyone in the State Department he drafted one forthwith. Such was his secrecy that he sent the draft to his Boston office to be typed by his confidential clerk of many years, Miss Antoinette M. Straw.[37] Cleveland returned to Washington on Sunday, December 15, and that very evening, tired as he must have been, conferred at length with the Secretary of State and with Secretary of War Daniel S. Lamont. If he had felt no urgency on leaving Washington, he felt a good deal now as he read Salisbury's dismissal of the Monroe Doctrine and the defiant retort Olney had penned. After his two visitors left, the President sat down at his desk and spent most or all of the night reworking the draft message.[38] He had a second conference with

35. Dexter Perkins, *The Monroe Doctrine, 1867–1907* (Baltimore, 1937), p. 173; James, *Olney*, p. 115, says that the reply was delivered to Olney on the seventh. Salisbury to Pauncefote, Nov. 26, 1895, *Foreign Relations, 1895* (Washington, 1896), Pt. 1, pp. 564–65, 566, 575.

36. Cleveland to Olney, Dec. 3, 1895, McElroy, *Cleveland,* II, 183. See also New York *World*, Dec. 6, 1895, cited in Tansill, *Bayard*, p. 724; Pauncefote to Salisbury, Dec. 10, 1895, Foreign Office 80/364.

37. According to H. O. Bax-Ironside (Second Secretary at the British Embassy, Washington), Olney was assisted by a lawyer (James J. Storrow?). Pauncefote to Salisbury, Dec. 20, 1895, enclosing a memorandum by Bax-Ironside, Salisbury Papers; James, *Olney*, p. 119.

38. Young, "Intervention under the Monroe Doctrine," p. 256; James, *Olney*, p. 119; McElroy, *Cleveland*, p. 188.

Olney the next day, and he read the revised message to the Cabinet on the morning of the seventeenth without asking for suggestions. That afternoon it went to Congress.

The message was a sensational one. Contrary to Salisbury, Cleveland insisted that the Monroe Doctrine most certainly was international law and applicable to the boundary dispute. Because Great Britain refused to arbitrate, he asserted, the United States was obliged to determine the true boundary by an impartial examination; and he asked Congress to appropriate money for a commission that would investigate and submit a report. He concluded in words that sent a thrill of excitement through his congressional and world audience: "When such report is made and accepted it will, in my opinion, be the duty of the United States to resist by every means in its power, as a willful aggression upon its rights and interests, the appropriation by Great Britain of any lands or the exercise of governmental jurisdiction over any territory which after investigation we have determined of right belongs to Venezuela." He ended grimly, "In making these recommendations I am fully alive to the responsibility incurred and keenly realize all the consequences that may follow."[39] These were dangerous words and were recognized as such. No country could dictate a British boundary to Queen Victoria's Great Britain without running grave risks of war. Nevertheless, the concluding passage was carefully phrased. The report had to be "accepted"; Cleveland was expressing his "opinion" about American duty; and the United States would resist only "after investigation." The last qualification was crucial; as Pauncefote perceived, the boundary commission would give Washington a "safety valve" enabling it to defer any decisive move for a long time.[40]

The President's stirring message aroused the ugly passions always latent in human beings, and for a dreadful moment war seemed imminent. Unanimously Congress approved Cleveland's boundary commission and appropriated $100,000 for its expenses. The Irish National Alliance offered 100,000 men for the conquest of Canada, and inflammatory talk resounded in other quarters.[41]

39. Message to Congress, Dec. 17, 1895, Richardson, *Messages and Papers*, IX, 656, 656–57, 658.

40. Pauncefote to Salisbury, Jan. 3, 1896, Salisbury Papers. See also Grenville and Young, *American Diplomacy*, pp. 167–68.

41. *Congressional Record*, 54 Cong., 1 Sess., pp. 234–35 (Dec. 18, 1895), pp. 240–47 (Dec. 19, 1895), pp. 256–65 (Dec. 20, 1895); regarding the Irish National Alliance see the New York *Herald*, Dec. 18, 1895.

Always an acute observer, Sir Julian Pauncefote reported an "extraordinary state of excitement into which the Congress of the United States and the whole country were thrown by the warlike Message . . . a condition of mind which can only be described as hysterical."[42] "Hysterical" was too strong, but the country was swept by a real war scare.

"Cleveland in my opinion, by his explicit allusion to war, has committed the biggest political crime I have ever seen here," the famous American philosopher William James wrote a friend.[43] In July the United States had asked London to arbitrate; when Salisbury responded by refusing to arbitrate everything but agreeing to arbitrate something, normal diplomatic procedure would have been to send a second note carrying the argument a step further. Why did Cleveland, usually a cautious, pacific man, throw up his hands, proclaim he was finished with diplomacy, and send a near-war message to Congress?

Undoubtedly the considerations that had influenced him in July were still present; in fact, they had grown stronger as the depression lengthened and the presidential election drew nearer. But the principal explanation of Cleveland's conduct lies elsewhere. Highly significant is the haste with which he rewrote Olney's draft, and then gave it to Congress only two days after returning from North Carolina. One cannot avoid the impression that the President, already annoyed by Salisbury's failure to reply in time for the annual message, was enraged beyond endurance by the sweeping dismissal of the Monroe Doctrine. Why otherwise should he have acted so hurriedly? There was no emergency. "Again and again," so writes the President's biographer, "he endured opposition . . . patiently for a long period, and then suddenly exploded with a force which astonished observers who had not noticed the tokens of rising internal wrath."[44] The message is to be explained in terms of a surge of

42. Pauncefote to Salisbury, Dec. 24, 1895, Foreign Office 80/364.
43. James to F. W. H. Myers, Jan. 1, 1896, Henry James (ed.), *The Letters of William James* (2 vols., Boston, 1920), II, 31.
44. Allan Nevins, *Grover Cleveland: A Study in Courage* (New York, 1932), p. 629. The British ambassador reported a rumor that Cleveland wrote the message "sitting in his shirt sleeves, between two bottles of whiskey," and Henry Adams wrote that "Cleveland was perhaps drunk, as the story goes. . . ." Pauncefote to Salisbury, June 23, 1896, Salisbury Papers, and Adams to Elizabeth Cameron, Feb. 23, 1902, Worthington C. Ford (ed.), *Letters of Henry Adams* (2 vols., Boston, 1930–38), II, 374, respectively. But even if these charges happened to be correct, which seems unlikely,

presidential temper more than in terms of rational calculation of political and national interest.

The excitement subsided as quickly as it had risen. Indeed, even at its height the war scare was limited in scope and intensity. Despite the unanimous vote, Congress witnessed no outburst of jingoism; the few members participating in the debate usually dismissed the possibility of hostilities, and only two days after the President's message the *Congressional Record* printed a memorial sent to Washington the previous January by several hundred members of the British Parliament calling for an arbitration treaty.[45] After a display of banner-waving patriotism on the Wednesday and Thursday following the message's delivery on Tuesday, the country had an unpleasant shock when panic swept Wall Street and prices fell steeply on the New York stock exchange, in part because of British selling of American securities. Agriculture, too, was affected; and Minneapolis wheat interests telegraphed Washington their fears lest flour exports to Britain be affected adversely.[46] Since mid-1894 the economy had been expanding; the expansion ended precisely in December 1895. Contemporaries blamed the war scare; and according to a recent authority on business cycles it may indeed have been responsible for the renewed contraction.[47] The gold reserve fell to $63 million as large shipments of the metal went to Europe. Businessmen denounced the disturber of the precarious economy and demanded a quick settlement. On December 20 the President felt impelled to send Congress another special message, this one dealing with the disastrous financial situation. Pauncefote believed that the initial support for the message had yielded "to consternation at the financial panic which it has caused."[48]

Leaders of thought also helped turn the tide toward peace with speeches condemning the President for his recklessness, and espe-

---

the message was not sent to Congress until Tuesday, and by then a sober Cleveland would have reviewed it.

45. *Congressional Record,* 54 Cong., 1 Sess., p. 245 (Dec. 19, 1895). For evidence of considerable press disapproval of the special message see *Literary Digest,* XII (Dec. 28, 1895), 241–43.

46. *Northwestern Miller* to Attorney General Judson Harmon, Jan. 8, 1896, Richard Olney Papers, Library of Congress (Washington).

47. Rendigs Fels, *American Business Cycles, 1867–1897* (Chapel Hill, 1959), p. 200.

48. Richardson, *Messages and Papers,* IX, 659–60; *Literary Digest,* XII (Dec. 28, 1895), 245; Pauncefote to Salisbury, Dec. 24, 1895, Foreign Office 80/364.

cially for raising the specter of war with America's Anglo-Saxon cousins across the sea.[49] On the Sunday after the message Cleveland, according to the *Nation*, "received the most unanimous and crushing rebuke that the pulpit of this country ever addressed to a President"; two days earlier the Senate chaplain, in the Senate itself, had prayed most fervently for peace.[50] Altogether the possibility of war with Great Britain seems to have engendered something like a feeling of horror in the United States. This strong sense of kinship with the British was a new and immensely significant factor in Anglo-American relations.

British people, also, recoiled from the terrible prospect which, to their utter amazement, had so suddenly appeared over a matter about which they knew nothing. And at that very moment another international incident flared up. On January 3, 1896, following the failure of a raid into the Transvaal by some Britons led by a Dr. Leander Starr Jameson, the German Kaiser publicly congratulated the Boer President. British anger over this impertinence far overshadowed the annoyance with Cleveland; and pressure mounted for a settlement with the United States. All at once the existence of much underlying friendship for that country became evident. Arthur Balfour, Lord Salisbury's nephew and Leader of the House of Commons, speaking at Manchester on January 15, welcomed the approaching time when "some statesman of authority, more fortunate even than President Monroe, will lay down the doctrine that between English-speaking peoples war is impossible"; a few days later Colonial Secretary Joseph Chamberlain made a famous statement at Birmingham: "While I should look with horror upon any-

49. For a protest meeting in New York arranged by Henry George see *Nation*, LXII (Jan. 2, 1896), 1; for statements by John Bassett Moore, Theodore S. Woolsey, Hermann von Holst, and John Bach McMaster (who, however, supported Cleveland) see *Public Opinion*, XIX (Dec. 26, 1895), 840, and *Literary Digest*, XII (Jan. 11, 1896), 306–8. In Feb. 1896 two leading magazines published articles generally condemnatory of the administration: James Bryce, "British Feeling on the Venezuelan Question," *North American Review*, CLXII (1896), 145–53; Andrew Carnegie, "The Venezuelan Question," *ibid.*, pp. 129–44; Charles Eliot Norton, "Some Aspects of Civilization in America," *Forum*, XX (1896), 641–51; Oscar S. Straus, "Lord Salisbury and the Monroe Doctrine," *ibid.*, pp. 713–20; Theodore S. Woolsey, "The President's Monroe Doctrine," *ibid.*, pp. 705–12.

50. *Nation*, LXI (Dec. 26, 1895), 456. *Congressional Record*, 54 Cong., 1 Sess., p. 251 (Dec. 20, 1895). By unanimous consent the prayer was printed in the *Record*. The religious press condemned Cleveland's message. *Literary Digest*, XII (Jan. 4, 1896), 278.

thing in the nature of a fratricidal strife, I should look forward with pleasure to the possibility of the Stars and Stripes and the Union Jack floating together in defence of a common cause sanctioned by humanity and by justice."[51]

Both countries now witnessed an extraordinary outpouring of letters and resolutions demanding that steps be taken to eliminate forever any possibility of a British-American war. In the British archives there is an enormous volume nearly two feet thick containing an "Anglo-American Arbitration Memorial" with thousands of signatures, declaring that "whatever may be the differences between the Governments in the present or in the future, all English-speaking peoples united by race, language, and religion, should regard war as the one absolutely intolerable mode of settling the domestic differences of the Anglo-American family," and urging the establishment of a permanent arbitration tribunal. Another large volume contains a memorial, signed by 5,357 officers of trade and friendly societies, asking for permanent arbitration; and still other memorials pleading for Anglo-American arbitration on a permanent basis can be found elsewhere in the British archives. Two other entire volumes are filled with similar letters and resolutions signed by thousands of Americans, and pro-arbitration meetings were held in many American cities.[52] In this horrified reaction to the prospect of hostilities lies the chief significance of the British-American contention over Venezuela.

Thus the ironical consequence of Cleveland's special message and of the war scare was an upsurge of demand for an Anglo-American general arbitration treaty. Negotiations for one paralleled negotiations to terminate the boundary controversy. In each case they reached a deadlock in early summer, 1896; in each case formal diplomacy was suspended while Pauncefote and Olney were out of Washington; and in each case a settlement was quickly made when

51. The *Times* (London), Jan. 16, 1896, has Balfour's speech; see also Blanche E. C. Dugdale, *Arthur James Balfour, First Earl of Balfour, K.G., O.M., F.R.S., Etc.* (2 vols., London, 1936), I, 226. For Chamberlain's speech see the *Times* (London), Jan. 27, 1896. For a similar utterance by Senator Edward O. Wolcott see *Congressional Record*, 54 Cong., 1 Sess., pp. 856–60 (Jan. 22, 1896).

52. For the "Anglo-American Arbitration Memorial" see Foreign Office 96/200; for the memorial of the trade and friendly societies see Foreign Office 5/2303. See also Foreign Office 80/367 and 5/2010. Regarding American petitions and meetings see Foreign Office 5/2316; *Nation*, LXII (Feb. 27, 1896), 169.

they returned in October. As regards the negotiations for a general arbitration treaty, it is enough to say that they turned on two different approaches: Salisbury, characteristically, wanted to proceed cautiously, first testing a limited arrangement and then, if experience warranted, moving to a broader arrangement; Olney urgently wanted an agreement under which any dispute would be arbitrable and any award final.[53] Although not particularly complicated, the negotiations were concluded only after the signature of the boundary agreement, to a consideration of which we may now turn.

President Cleveland appointed his boundary commission on January 1, 1896.[54] With full British cooperation it started gathering data; and its background labors must have served as a constant prod to London to make a quick settlement. The two countries faced a grave problem as a result of Cleveland's public demand that Great Britain accept a boundary defined by Washington; for Britain could not accept the demand without humiliation, and the United States could not easily withdraw it, particularly in a presidential election year. Olney was in a hurry to get a settlement; Salisbury, who once remarked that "among all the qualities essential to a diplomatist patience is most likely to be of permanent use,"[55] refused to be rushed.

The negotiations proved to be difficult. The reason for this was not that Salisbury denied the right of American intervention. In February 1896 he repeated publicly the sentiment already essentially expressed in his Monroe Doctrine note of the previous November: "I do think the bringing in of the Monroe doctrine was, controversially, quite unnecessary for the United States. Considering the position of Venezuela in the Caribbean Sea, it was no more unnatural that the United States should take an interest in it than that we should feel an interest in Holland and Belgium." Nor did the Prime Minister demand a rigid adherence to the Schomburgk line. According to a later Foreign Office memorandum he "did not

53. See John Bassett Moore, *History and Digest of the International Arbitrations to Which the United States Has Been a Party* (6 vols., Washington, 1898), I, 962–82.

54. Regarding it see *Report and Accompanying Papers of the Commission Appointed by the President of the United States . . .* (9 vols., Washington, 1896–97); Marcus Baker, "The Venezuelan Boundary Commission and Its Work," *National Geographic Magazine*, VIII (1897), 193–201.

55. George W. Smalley, *Anglo-American Memories: Second Series* (London, 1912), p. 76; for a similar observation see Alexander E. Campbell, *Great Britain and the United States, 1895–1903* (London, 1960), p. 17.

originally insist that no portion of territory lying within the Schomburgk line should be submitted to arbitration . . ."; and he told the Cabinet on January 11, 1896, that although he would resign rather than submit unconditionally, he would be willing to arbitrate unsettled areas east of that line.[56] But the Prime Minister adamantly refused to sanction arbitration over settled areas. This was the point he had stressed in his November note, and throughout the controversy he never departed from it. Britain's insistence on protecting her subjects in settled districts was the central issue in the negotiations.

As a stickler for punctilio, Salisbury refused to make any formal diplomatic move until his last two dispatches (those of November 26, 1895) had been answered; the next move, properly, was Olney's. But he had no objection to informal diplomacy, and various official and unofficial persons—the most important of them was a certain Lord Playfair who, with the government's approval, had several talks with Bayard—vainly bestirred themselves to find an agreement.[57] They encountered the same basic difficulty about settled districts. Olney would agree that an arbitral tribunal could give these districts "such weight and effect . . . as reason, justice, the rules of international law, and the equities of the particular case may appear to require." He rejected a suggestion that five years of occupation would justify exclusion from arbitration.[58] But the Prime Minister stuck to his irreducible demand: "When the interests of many thousand British subjects are at stake, we cannot venture to run the risk of exposing them to an *unrestricted* arbitration." "We are contending for men—not for land! for the rights of settlers whom we had encouraged to invest in such property, and tie up their futures to it. . . ."[59]

56. Hansard's *Parliamentary Debates,* Fourth Series, XXXVII, column 52 (Feb. 11, 1896). Foreign Office memorandum, Jan. 17, 1897, Foreign Office 80/379; James L. Garvin, *The Life of Joseph Chamberlain* (3 vols., London, 1932–34), III, 161. See also John A. S. Grenville, *Lord Salisbury and Foreign Policy: The Close of the Nineteenth Century* (London, 1964), pp. 67–69.

57. Joseph J. Mathews, "Informal Diplomacy in the Venezuelan Crisis of 1896," *Mississippi Valley Historical Review,* L (1963), 195–212; (Thomas) Wemyss Reid, *Memoirs and Correspondence of Lyon Playfair, First Lord Playfair of St. Andrews, P.C., G.C.B., LL.D., F.R.S., Ec.* (New York, 1899), pp. 414–26.

58. Olney to Pauncefote, June 12, 1896, *Papers Relating to the Foreign Relations of the United States, 1896* (Washington, 1897), pp. 251–52; Chamberlain to Playfair, Jan. 23, Feb. 1 and 25, 1896, Reid, *Playfair,* pp. 420, 421–22, 423–25, respectively.

59. Salisbury to Pauncefote, Feb. 7, 1896, Salisbury Papers; Salisbury to Chamberlain, Jan. 31, 1896, Mathews, "Informal Diplomacy," p. 202.

Formal diplomacy resumed briefly on February 26 when Olney asked London to begin negotiations in Washington. But the Secretary continued to demand that Venezuela's entire claim, all the way to the Essequibo River, be arbitrated; Salisbury continued to insist on excluding settled districts.[60] The summer of 1896 came. Both informal and formal diplomacy had led to nothing but confusion and disagreement.

As sometimes happens with apparently unsolvable controversies, the Venezuelan impasse broke suddenly in mid-July. On the thirteenth Secretary Olney, abandoning his hitherto unbending refusal to exclude settled districts from arbitration, abruptly inquired whether London would allow unrestricted arbitration—provided that land occupied by either party for a minimum of sixty years was excluded.[61] Why he yielded cannot be established with certainty. No doubt he wanted to wind up the controversy before leaving office in early 1897, but perhaps Sir Julian had a more fundamental explanation. During an April talk he had found the Secretary alarmed over the possibility that the deadlock would not be resolved before the presidential election, which promised to be dangerously embittered.[62] Then, in July, the Democrats, at their Chicago convention, came out for free silver and nominated the "dangerous" William Jennings Bryan. To Grover Cleveland and his Secretary of State these dreadful events portended the doom of their party, and one dared not think what perils for the country. For years silverites had raised an outcry against Great Britain as the citadel of gold. Surely Olney saw the wisdom of making a move that, by pointing to an early resolution of the altercation, would minimize anti-British rhetoric during the campaign.

Yet one cannot be certain about this interpretation. The crucial question is, how much land had been occupied by British subjects for sixty years? To answer this would require a detailed examination of parts of Venezuela and British Guiana, mile by mile, and a study of the history of every settlement; sufficient evidence might well be impossible to find. But if in fact only an insignificant portion of the area had been settled for the minimum period, then Olney had yielded nothing of substance; and the emphasis would be not on the

60. Olney to Bayard, Feb. 26, 1896, Tansill, *Bayard*, p. 759; Pauncefote to Salisbury, April 2, 1896, Foreign Office 5/2290.
61. Olney to Pauncefote, July 13, 1896, *Foreign Relations, 1896*, pp. 253–54.
62. Pauncefote to Salisbury, April 2, 1896, Foreign Office 5/2290.

collapse of his stand but on Britain's retreat from her earlier position that five years of settlement should constitute ground for exclusion from arbitration. It is impossible to believe, however, that Lord Salisbury would have agreed to sacrifice a large number of British subjects, and it is probable that his government had sufficient information to know that this would not happen if he accepted Olney's proposal. Nor is any indication known to exist of large-scale population movements after the new line was drawn under a formula close to that suggested by the Secretary of State. The Foreign Office believed that Salisbury had succeeded in protecting British settlers;[63] and it is reasonable to conclude that he had done so.

With this American retreat an agreement was close. Pauncefote spent the summer in London, where he supported the evolving accord in talks with high government officials, and also with the leader of the Liberal opposition, Sir William Harcourt. After he returned in October, he persuaded Olney to reduce the settlement requirement to fifty years, and the two men quickly came to terms on other details. Now that a procedure for determining the boundary was in sight, Cleveland's boundary commission became redundant; it therefore disbanded.

The Anglo-American agreement of November 12, 1896, gave the terms of a treaty to be concluded by Great Britain and Venezuela. The treaty would provide for an arbitral tribunal to define the boundary, composed of two members nominated by the Supreme Court of the United States, two by the British supreme court of justice, and a fifth selected by the four members or by the King of Sweden and Norway. Fifty years or more of settlement would convey good title; and (paraphrasing Olney's earlier suggestion) in considering territory occupied for less than fifty years, "such effect shall be given to such occupation as reason, justice, the principles of international law, and the equities of the case shall . . . require." The arbitrators could also consider "exclusive political control," whether the area controlled had been actually occupied or not, as sufficient to convey title—a point raised by Joseph Chamberlain during a September visit to the United States.[64]

63. Foreign Office memorandum, Jan. 17, 1897, Foreign Office 80/379.
64. For its terms see *Foreign Relations, 1896*, pp. 254–55. Regarding Chamberlain's visit see Tansill, *Bayard*, pp. 772–73n; Garvin, *Chamberlain*, III, 163–64. See Salisbury's appraisal of the agreement in his Guildhall speech, the *Times* (London), Nov. 10, 1896.

The agreement was popular in the United States, although there was some congressional criticism of the fifty-year rule as unfair to Venezuela.[65] A colleague described Secretary Olney as "much elated" over "a great success."[66] The agreement was popular in Great Britain, too. The *Times* portrayed the outcome as "the original contention of this country in a slightly altered form." Lord Salisbury believed that "in accepting the good offices of the United States as the friend of Venezuela, England has done nothing to accept or to maintain the Monroe doctrine. It stands where it did before the controversy began."[67] His appraisal was correct in a narrow sense; on a broader view, however, the doctrine did not stand where it did before the American intervention: its prestige was enormously greater. So, for that matter, was the prestige of the United States as a result of her dramatic interposition in a British quarrel. All the same, Lord Salisbury had succeeded in his main objective of protecting British settlers.

What about Venezuela, expected to sign the treaty but disregarded ever since Secretary Olney elbowed her aside? Only after the negotiations ended was she told her fate. When the terms became known in Caracas, a storm of indignation burst out; talk of revolution was heard. Apparently Venezuela sounded out London on making a direct settlement that would scrap the treaty. To appease her, Britain and America let her appoint one of the arbitrators (the United States accordingly naming only one), but not a Venezuelan. (She chose the American Chief Justice, Melville W. Fuller.) Even so, it was only under considerable American pressure that Venezuela finally accepted the inevitable and signed the treaty on February 2, 1897—as did also Great Britain.[68]

We may pass over the British-Venezuelan arbitration quickly. As arbitrators Great Britain appointed Lord Chief Justice Russell and Lord Justice Collins; Venezuela appointed Fuller; and the United

65. Pauncefote to Salisbury, Nov. 17, 1896, Salisbury Papers.

66. Diary of Wilson, Nov. 13, 1896, Festus P. Summers (ed.), *The Cabinet Diary of William L. Wilson, 1896–1897* (Chapel Hill, 1957), p. 168.

67. The *Times* (London), Nov. 11, 1896; memorandum by S (Salisbury), Jan. 17, 1897, Foreign Office 80/379. See also Pauncefote to Salisbury, Nov. 13, 1896, Salisbury Papers.

68. For the Venezuelan reaction see Young, "Intervention under the Monroe Doctrine," pp. 276–77. For the treaty see *British and Foreign State Papers, 1896–1897* (London, 1901), LXXXIX, 57–65.

States named Supreme Court Justice David J. Brewer; these four named as the fifth member and president of the tribunal Professor Feodor de Martens, a Russian authority on international law. The tribunal held formal sessions in Paris from June to September 1899. Venezuela was represented exclusively by Americans: James Russell Soley, Assistant Secretary of the Navy under President Benjamin Harrison; Severo Mallet-Prevost, an expert in Spanish law; former Secretary of the Navy Benjamin F. Tracy; and former President Benjamin Harrison, the chief counsel. The tribunal returned a unanimous award on October 3, 1899, giving British Guiana almost all the disputed territory. Venezuela, however, got the mouth of the Orinoco River and about 5,000 square miles in the interior. The Venezuelans were embittered; since the new boundary followed the Schomburgk line fairly closely, the British were pleased.[69]

When Pauncefote returned to Washington in October 1896, he had resumed discussions with Olney about the general arbitration treaty, as well as about Venezuela; and the two men reached agreement about the former almost as expeditiously as about the latter. On January 11, 1897, they signed the arbitration treaty. It provided for arbitration of all disputes, but complicated provisions permitted

69. Clifton J. Child, "The Venezuela-British Guiana Boundary Arbitration of 1899," *American Journal of International Law*, XLIV (1950), 691–92. The award had a strange sequel. Soon after it was made, Mallet-Prevost and Harrison were reported as declaring that the line drawn was one of compromise, diplomatic in nature, not of right. The *Times* (London), Oct. 4, 1899. Years later, in 1944, Mallet-Prevost wrote a memorandum that was published in 1949 after his death. The memorandum is in Otto Schoenrich, "The Venezuela-British Guiana Boundary Dispute," *American Journal of International Law*, XLIII (1949), 523–30. According to it, de Martens told the two American arbitrators in 1899 that he wanted a unanimous award; that he therefore proposed as a compromise the line that was in fact awarded, saying that if the Americans voted for it he and the British arbitrators would do so, but that if they refused he would support the British claim, which would consequently be accepted by majority vote; and that Justices Brewer and Fuller, although believing Venezuela entitled to more land than the compromise gave her, felt obliged to accept de Martens's suggestion as the least of evils. As a result of these allegations Venezuela, on Aug. 18, 1962, asked the United Nations to investigate; eventually she and Great Britain agreed to resume consideration, through regular diplomatic channels, of the troublesome boundary question. Perhaps a new definition of the much-discussed line is in the making. Regarding the appeal to the United Nations see *United Nations, Official Records of the General Assembly, Seventeenth Session, Annexes*, III, 1–15, Agenda Item 88; *ibid., Plenary Meetings*, I, 244–46, III, 1098; *ibid., Special Political Committee*, pp. 119–21. The *Evening Standard* (London), Aug. 13, 1965, reported that on that day over a thousand Venezuelans demonstrated at the British Embassy in Caracas in support of their country's claim to 60,000 square miles of British Guiana.

either country to nullify awards on important matters.[70] Both countries hailed the treaty as epoch-making; arbitration and peace societies, churches, business organizations, universities, newspapers, and a host of prominent people sprang to its enthusiastic support. Grover Cleveland and his successor, William McKinley, strongly backed it.[71] All but universal was the assumption that the Senate would approve it. But on May 5, 1897, that body, after having severely amended the treaty, defeated it by a vote of 43 to 26, three short of the needed two-thirds.[72]

Must one, then, conclude that all the hands-across-the-seas sentiment of 1896 was just as ephemeral as the war scare? Such a verdict would be grossly superficial. The decisive facts are that the densely populated eastern states cast only two votes against the treaty; that seven western silver states with a total population of less than 2,500,000 accounted for no fewer than twelve negative votes; and that southern states, where dislike of Cleveland was rampant, had ten negative votes. A large majority of the Senate approved the treaty, something that could not have happened in a previous decade. To some extent, no doubt, the vote did reflect dislike of Great Britain. Many pockets of anti-British feeling still existed, notably among Irish-Americans and free-silverites; Fourth of July orators still denounced King George. All things considered, however, it is plain that, except for the unrepresentative character of the Senate, the treaty would have been approved. The Chicago *Evening Post* summed up the matter accurately: "Silver, jingoism, antagonism to Cleveland, and hatred of England killed the treaty. The popular will is overborne by a senatorial cabal."[73]

70. Its terms are in *Foreign Relations, 1896*, pp. 237–40; a good analysis is Theodore S. Woolsey, "Some Comment upon the Arbitration Treaty," *Forum*, XXIII (1897), 23–27.

71. *Literary Digest*, XIV (Jan. 23, 1897), 356–58; *Public Opinion*, XXII (Jan. 21, 1897), 68–70; Foreign Office 5/2320 and 115/1072; James D. Richardson (ed.), *A Compilation of the Messages and Papers of the Presidents* . . . (20 vols., New York, 1916), XIV, 6178–79, 6242.

72. *Journal of the Executive Proceedings of the Senate* . . . (Washington, 1909), XXXI, 102–5. Regarding the treaty in the Senate see *Senate Documents*, 58 Cong., 3 Sess., No. 161 (Serial 4766), pp. 8–33; for reports of the Foreign Relations Committee see *ibid.*, 56 Cong., 2 Sess., No. 231 (Serial 4054), pp. 389–425.

73. Quoted in *Literary Digest*, XV (May 15, 1897), 65; see also an analysis of the defeat by the New York *World*, *ibid.*, 64, and another by Senator George F. Hoar in the Boston *Daily Globe*, May 27, 1897. For a broad account see W. Stull Holt, *Treaties Defeated by the Senate: A Study of the Struggle between President and Senate over the Conduct*

More significant than the treaty was the massive revulsion from the prospect of a fratricidal war, and the spontaneous demand that such a dreadful moment must never recur. The public reaction revealed the presence of reciprocal good will in the United States and Great Britain that was much more pervasive and deeply rooted than had been suspected. Evidently basic underlying influences, such powerful influences as the booming Anglo-American commerce and the common heritage, had already had a considerable effect by the mid-1890s. Moreover the public reaction itself undoubtedly deepened the trans-Atlantic good will somewhat. For these reasons the swing from the war scare to the clamor for peace signalized a major turning point in the history of the two English-speaking countries.

It should also be observed that Britain's implicit acceptance of America's right to intervene,[74] and the strengthening of the Monroe Doctrine whether the Salisbury government admitted this or not, signalized the virtual end of any British effort to challenge American predominance in the Caribbean Sea. The British attitude was to pave the way to an Anglo-American agreement early in the twentieth century abrogating the Clayton-Bulwer treaty and permitting the United States to construct her isthmian canal. These developments were of the utmost significance as regards perpetuating the greatly improved trans-Atlantic relations that the Venezuelan boundary dispute had revealed. The new American position in the Caribbean, furthermore, strengthened Washington's hand in dealing with Spain over the Cuban rebellion that, breaking out in 1895, led to the Spanish-American War in 1898.

---

*of Foreign Relations* (Baltimore, 1933), pp. 154–62. See also Robert B. Mowat, *The Life of Lord Pauncefote, First Ambassador to the United States* (Boston, 1929), p. 169.

74. A. E. Campbell, *Great Britain and the United States,* pp. 44–45.

CHAPTER 12

# Stalemate: An American Isthmian Canal and Hawaii

IF State Department officials had paused to survey the world in the mid-1890s, they would have perceived both successes and failures in American foreign policy. On the one hand, by patient diplomacy and a remarkable series of agreements the United States and Great Britain had surmounted many perils and were moving toward a friendship that contrasted sharply with the glowering hostility after the Civil War. But as regards territorial expansion, the other main theme of foreign policy, a Central American canal and acquisitions in the Pacific Ocean and the Caribbean Sea seemed little nearer realization than when William H. Seward was Secretary of State thirty years before. In 1885 President Cleveland had shelved the Frelinghuysen-Zavala treaty, thereby dashing hopes for an American canal in the foreseeable future. Two years later the United States had acquired a potential naval station at Pearl River in Hawaii, and in 1893 the revolution had produced a government at Honolulu that longed for the island republic to be annexed by its great trading partner; but the river's mouth was still blocked by a coral reef, and Cleveland had made it perfectly clear that Hawaii could not hope for annexation soon, if ever. The prospective base at Pago Pago also remained undeveloped. Nor was the outlook any brighter for the acquisition of a Caribbean base. An isthmian canal, Caribbean and Hawaiian naval bases—these were the essential objectives of expansionists such as James G. Blaine and Alfred T. Mahan; they were also the objectives prescribed by considerations of naval strategy and by underlying geographic and economic pressures. If even these vital areas seemed out of reach, it was no wonder that among expansionists a mood of frustration prevailed.

Since that day in 1885 when Cleveland had terminated the Frelinghuysen-Zavala treaty, a number of developments had occurred, some encouraging to American canal aspirations, others most discouraging. Distinctly encouraging were the bankruptcy of the French Panama Canal Company and the formation of a new American concern to replace the Maritime Canal Company that had failed in 1884. As early as January 1885 the American consul general at Panama reported that Ferdinand de Lesseps's company was in trouble;[1] thereafter its fortunes declined from bad to catastrophic. Its frantic attempts to persuade the French government to rescue it led the United States Senate to adopt, all but unanimously, a resolution declaring that the United States would disapprove any connection of a European government with a Central American canal. Although the House did not follow suit, Paris must have taken note of the warning; the French company went bankrupt in December 1888 amid a vast, billowing cloud of scandal.[2]

Two years before, in December 1886, a provisional Nicaragua Canal Association had been founded in the United States.[3] Its most active members were two persistent canal enthusiasts, both of them prominently associated with the old Maritime Canal Company and

1. Consul General Thomas Adamson to William Hunter (Second Assistant Secretary of State), Jan. 31, 1885, Sarah G. Walton, "The Frelinghuysen-Zavala Treaty, 1884–1885" (M.A. thesis, University of Virginia, 1953), pp. 186–87).

2. The resolution is in *Congressional Record*, 50 Cong., 2 Sess., pp. 338 (Dec. 19, 1888), pp. 567–68 (Jan. 7, 1889); see also *Public Opinion*, VI (Jan. 12, 1889), 279; the *Times* (London), Jan. 19, 1889; Dexter Perkins, *The Monroe Doctrine, 1867–1907* (Baltimore, 1937), pp. 105–7. Regarding the company's collapse see Lindley M. Keasbey, *The Nicaragua Canal and the Monroe Doctrine . . .* (New York, 1896), pp. 429–31; Willis F. Johnson, *Four Centuries of the Panama Canal* (New York, 1906), pp. 95–96.

3. Margaret S. Wilkerson, "The Maritime Canal Company of Nicaragua" (M.A. thesis, University of Buffalo, 1932), p. 13; Gerstle Mack, *The Land Divided: A History of the Panama Canal and Other Isthmian Canal Projects* (New York, 1944), p. 217; *Congressional Record*, 53 Cong., 3 Sess., p. 777 (Jan. 9, 1895); Keasbey, *Nicaragua Canal*, p. 438. For a list of some of the original promoters of the company see *Congressional Record*, 53 Cong., 3 Sess., p. 1341 (Jan. 25, 1895); the company's directors, with a short description of each, from 1889 to 1898, are listed in *ibid.*, 55 Cong., 3 Sess., p. 153 (Dec. 13, 1898). For the shareholders in April 1901, see *Senate Documents*, 57 Cong., 1 Sess., No. 253 (Serial 4238), Pt. 1, pp. 347–52.

both advocates of the Nicaragua route that Americans still assumed to be the best: Aniceto G. Menocal and Daniel Ammen (the man who had helped stimulate President Grant's interest in a canal and in Santo Domingo). In the spring of 1887 Menocal obtained a concession from Nicaragua that granted the Canal Association the exclusive right to construct and operate a canal; in return the Association agreed to begin a survey within a year, begin work within two and a half years, spend $2 million during the first year of construction, and complete the canal within ten years.[4] The Association formed a construction company (the Nicaragua Canal Construction Company, chartered in Colorado in 1887) to do the actual building, and transferred to it the rights obtained from Nicaragua; although legally distinct, the two companies were composed with few exceptions of the same persons.[5] In using a construction company, the provisional company imitated the transcontinental railroad concerns; this was to earn it censure from people who recalled the Crédit Mobilier and other railroad scandals.

Like the old canal company, the new company wanted to obtain a federal charter. A bill providing for incorporation was introduced in Congress in January 1888.[6] Quite unlike the early 1880s, when Congress refused to incorporate the previous company, little opposition now manifested itself. It is noteworthy that, with the French firm on the verge of bankruptcy and James B. Eads (the ship-railway advocate) dead, their once formidable opposition to a Nicaragua canal no longer existed. It is noteworthy, too, that Congress received a flood of petitions in favor of incorporation from such prominent business organizations as the Los Angeles Board of Trade, the New Orleans Produce Exchange, the St. Louis Board of Trade, and the Philadelphia Board of Trade.[7] They testified to the desire of many businessmen, now that exports of manufactured goods were about to surpass imports, for the easy access to South

4. The text of the concession is in *Senate Documents,* 58 Cong., 2 Sess., No. 222 (Serial 4609), I, 389–400.

5. *Congressional Record,* 53 Cong., 3 Sess., pp. 777–78 (Jan. 9, 1895); *ibid.,* 51 Cong., 2 Sess., p. 2976 (Feb. 20, 1891).

6. *Ibid.,* 50 Cong., 1 Sess., p. 340 (Jan. 10, 1888), p. 632 (Jan. 23, 1888).

7. *Ibid.,* p. 6039 (July 9, 1888), p. 5342 (June 16, 1888), p. 3435 (April 26, 1888), p. 4613 (May 24, 1888). For other petitions see *ibid.,* pp. 125, 1038, 2637, 2724, 2820, 2824, 2870, 3768, 3798, 4141, 4493, 4534, 4689, 4871, 4935, 4971, 4977, 5378, 5524, 7322; most of them were dated in the first half of 1888.

American and Far Eastern markets that an isthmian canal would provide. The incorporation bill passed both houses by large margins and was approved by President Cleveland, apparently routinely, on February 20, 1889.[8] The Maritime Canal Company of Nicaragua, succeeding the provisional association, was formally organized on May 7; and it soon set to work vigorously in Nicaragua.[9]

So far all had gone well. But now began the company's tribulations. It was strange that this happened when Benjamin Harrison was President and James G. Blaine Secretary of State. As might be expected, these two ardent nationalists backed the American company; indeed, they reverted to the position taken by all administrations since the Civil War save Cleveland's: that the United States needed a national canal under her own control. The difficulty was not the administration but money: construction was proving to be extremely costly, as both the first American company and the French company had already discovered. It became clear that the new Maritime Canal Company could not raise the needed funds without federal assistance. Specifically, it wanted a government guarantee of its bonds as a means of encouraging private investors to buy them. The company could have supposed that a guarantee bill would be certain of enactment; for the general public favored a canal, and a mere guarantee need not cost the government a cent. But when John Sherman, the influential Senator from Ohio, submitted a bill in January 1891 authorizing a guarantee of $100 million worth of the company's bonds, the opposition turned out to be surprisingly powerful and well armed with a miscellany of arguments: by guaranteeing the bonds the government would in effect be taking over the company and therefore violating the Clayton-Bulwer treaty; the government should build the canal itself; the money should be spent on the navy; the project was not practicable;

8. For the text of the bill see *Senate Documents,* 58 Cong., 2 Sess., No. 222, I, 401–2. It passed the Senate on Feb. 27, 1888, *Congressional Record,* 50 Cong., 1 Sess., p. 1498; the House amended the act and passed it on Jan. 4, 1889, *ibid.,* 50 Cong., 2 Sess., pp. 537–38; a joint committee reached a compromise on Feb. 1, 1889, *ibid.,* pp. 1402–4.

9. Statement of Hiram Hitchcock (president of the company), Jan. 28, 1897, *Congressional Record,* 54 Cong., 2 Sess., p. 1309 (Jan. 29, 1897); Nicaragua formally recognized construction as having commenced on Oct. 8, 1889, which met the terms of the concession. *Ibid.* For arrangements between the canal company and the construction company see *ibid.,* 53 Cong., 3 Sess., p. 777 (Jan. 9, 1895). Keasbey, *Nicaragua Canal,* pp. 449–50, has material on the organization of the company.

a Crédit Mobilier type of swindle would result. During the debate the railroads were accused of lobbying against the bill; and one may assume that they were a major factor in its downfall. So great was the antagonism that Sherman withdrew his bill at the end of February.[10] This was the first of many such failures.

Disappointed and faced with growing financial problems, the Maritime Canal Company continued its activities in Nicaragua. In his annual message of 1891 Harrison asked for a guarantee measure; the next year he repeated the request "with great earnestness," calling it "impossible to overstate the value from every standpoint of this great enterprise."[11] Encouragement came from other quarters, too. A national canal convention met in St. Louis in June 1892, and another convention, with hundreds of delegates from every state and territory, met in New Orleans in November; both urged federal help for the Maritime Canal Company.[12] The widespread desire for construction was evident in the Republican and Democratic platforms of 1892, the former calling a Nicaragua canal "of the highest importance" and demanding that it "be controlled by the United States Government," the latter describing "the early construction of the Nicaragua Canal and its protection against foreign control as of great importance to the United States."[13] Senator Sherman introduced another bond-guarantee bill on December 21, 1892. But no more than his measure of 1891 did it make any headway; debate was limited, and the bill disappeared from sight in February 1893.[14]

Among the casualties of the panic of 1893 was the Nicaragua

10. *Congressional Record*, 51 Cong., 2 Sess., p. 1123 (Jan. 10, 1891), p. 3410 (Feb. 27, 1891). For the debate see *ibid.*, pp. 2224–34 (Feb. 6, 1891), pp. 2970–91 (Feb. 20, 1891), pp. 3052–70, 3073–77 (Feb. 21, 1891). For the charges against the railroads see *ibid.*, pp. 3062, 3074 (Feb. 21, 1891). Regarding Sherman's bill see also *Senate Reports*, 51 Cong., 2 Sess., No. 1944 (Serial 2826).

11. Messages to Congress, Dec. 9, 1891, Dec. 6, 1892, James D. Richardson (ed.), *A Compilation of the Messages and Papers of the Presidents . . .* (20 vols., New York, 1916), XIII, 5623–24, 5752, respectively.

12. Mack, *Land Divided*, p. 220.

13. Kirk H. Porter and Donald B. Johnson (eds.), *National Party Platforms, 1840–1960* (Urbana, Ill., 1956), pp. 94, 89.

14. *Congressional Record*, 52 Cong., 2 Sess., p. 260 (Dec. 21, 1892), p. 967 (Jan. 30, 1893), pp. 1486–87 (Feb. 11, 1893), pp. 1513–31 (Feb. 13, 1893), pp. 1569–77 (Feb. 14, 1893), p. 1727 (Feb. 17, 1893). For explanations of the defeat see *Public Opinion*, XIV (Dec. 17, 1892), 259–60; a remark of Senator James H. Kyle, *Congressional Record*, 52 Cong., 2 Sess., p. 1529 (Feb. 13, 1893).

Canal Construction Company, which went bankrupt in August 1893. The Maritime Canal Company itself survived, to be sure, and it even arranged the incorporation in Vermont of a new construction company in 1894;[15] but during years when even the United States government could market its bonds only with great difficulty, the concessionaires had no chance of raising the colossal sums needed for construction. Nicaragua added to their woes by declaring the concession forfeited for nonfulfillment (though she did not formally revoke it), and by virtually confiscating their canal property.[16]

However, reasons for hope still remained. Grover Cleveland, in the White House again in 1893, was expressing sentiments about a canal that were considerably more expansionistic than were his views about Hawaii; and whereas in 1885 he had argued for a canal "removed from the chance of domination by any single power," he now advocated construction "under distinctively American auspices" and pronounced himself "especially interested" in the success of the Maritime Canal Company of Nicaragua.[17] No doubt the evolution of his thinking reflected the current diagnosis of overproduction as the cause of the devastating depression, and the consequent emphasis on a canal as a means of promoting exports to the potential Latin American and Chinese markets. Moreover, the company enjoyed the unlimited backing of Senator John T. Morgan of Alabama, the chairman of the Foreign Relations Committee and an almost fanatical Nicaragua canal enthusiast. In January 1894 he introduced a guarantee bill.[18] The familiar charges were again

15. Wilkerson, "Maritime Canal Company," p. 26; *Congressional Record,* 53 Cong., 3 Sess., p. 443 (Dec. 19, 1894); Mack, *Land Divided,* p. 222.

16. Secretary of State Walter Q. Gresham to Thomas F. Bayard (ambassador to Great Britain), May 2, 1894, Walter Q. Gresham Papers, Library of Congress (Washington), Letterbook; Gresham to Hiram Hitchcock, May 9, 1894, *ibid.*

17. Annual messages of Dec. 8, 1885, Dec. 4, 1893, Richardson, *Messages and Papers,* XI, 4912, and XII, 5870, respectively.

18. *Congressional Record,* 53 Cong., 2 Sess., p. 1165 (Jan. 22, 1894); *ibid.,* 53 Cong., 3 Sess., p. 76 (Dec. 6, 1894), pp. 157–69 (Dec. 10, 1894). The Foreign Relations Committee reported the bill favorably on April 14, 1894, *ibid.,* 53 Cong., 2 Sess., p. 3751; for its report see *Senate Reports,* 53 Cong., 2 Sess., No. 331 (Serial 3183). Morgan's enthusiasm for Nicaragua and for the Maritime Canal Company may have been fanned by, but certainly was not dependent on, such an offer as the following made to him by Hiram Hitchcock, May 19, 1900: "If nothing happens you will get a Third Jersey Charter Sunday morning." John T. Morgan Papers, Library of Congress (Washington), X.

brought forth: another Crédit Mobilier was in the making, the government should build the canal, the Clayton-Bulwer treaty would be violated.[19] There was also a new charge, reflecting the furor over attempts made by Cleveland to replenish the gold reserve by selling bonds: some Senators fought the measure because it contemplated another bond issue. "I am opposed to the issuance and sale of bonds for any purpose," Senator William Peffer, Populist of Kansas, declared roundly.[20] Nevertheless the bill passed the Senate on January 25, 1895, by a vote of 31 to 21, the first such bill to do so. It was not to become law. Little time remained before Congress was to adjourn, and in the closing rush the House declined to act despite the plea of more than 170 Representatives.[21]

One important canal measure did pass that session; and this success, together with the Senate's approval of the Morgan bill, reflected a growing awareness of the military and economic requirements of the mid-1890s: the day was near when the navy's need for greater mobility and the business demand for quicker access to South America and China would overwhelm the opposition to a canal. The Morgan bill included a provision for a survey of the Nicaragua route. When it became evident that the House would not vote on the bill, Senator Samuel Pasco of Florida, probably at Morgan's instigation, submitted an amendment to a civil appropriation bill, providing for a survey; thus amended, the appropriation bill became law on March 2, 1895.[22] Pursuant to it President Cleveland on April 25 commissioned a Nicaragua Canal Board, headed by William Ludlow, a lieutenant colonel in the Army's Corps of Engineers. The Ludlow Board soon left for Central America; on October 31, 1895, it issued a report generally endorsing the Maritime Canal Company's plans, although placing a higher estimate on construction costs and

19. See especially *Congressional Record*, 53 Cong., 3 Sess., p. 287 (Dec. 13, 1894), p. 779 (Jan. 9, 1895), p. 1346 (Jan. 25, 1895), Appendix, p. 79 (Jan. 18, 1895). See also Gresham to Bayard, May 2, 1894, Gresham Papers, Letterbook.

20. *Congressional Record*, 53 Cong., 3 Sess., p. 351 (Dec. 17, 1894).

21. *Ibid.*, p. 1358 (Jan. 25, 1895), p. 1458 (Jan. 28, 1895), p. 1902 (Feb. 7, 1895), p. 2847 (Feb. 27, 1895). For a favorable report by the House Committee on Interstate and Foreign Commerce see *House Reports*, 53 Cong., 3 Sess., No. 1779 (Serial 3346).

22. *Congressional Record*, 53 Cong., 3 Sess., p. 2847 (Feb. 27, 1895), p. 3250 (March 2, 1895).

recommending a more thorough survey of Nicaragua.[23]

Morgan believed that the Senate's action had ensured construction; he had high hopes when he introduced yet another guarantee bill on June 1, 1896. But Congress adjourned ten days later without having acted, and everyone's thoughts turned to the presidential campaign that occupied the rest of the year.[24] After the election the bill, though debated interminably, fared no better. Inhibiting to favorable action was the realization that the formidable Speaker of the House, Thomas B. Reed, who disliked the Nicaragua project, would never allow the bill to pass.[25] (Somewhat later the Speaker called the canal "too difficult a problem to be mastered by enthusiasm alone"—a sardonic reference to Senator Morgan.)[26] Morgan himself lashed out at the railroads: "The railroads in the United States have power enough to break down their great competitor. . . . we are dealing with men of enormous power, who control Presidents, Senates, Houses of Representatives, in respect to the railroads, with an absolute and despotic will which the Government of the United States has not even the ability to resist. . . ."[27] The Senator's bitter appraisal was not greatly exaggerated.

Yet Morgan should have looked elsewhere as well for his culprits. In October 1894 a most important event had occurred: the establishment in France of a New Panama Canal Company to replace the old de Lesseps concern. Its aim was not so much to construct a canal as to sell its Panama concession, and since the United States was the most probable buyer, the New Company had at all costs to forestall an American decision for Nicaragua. In 1896 it appointed a prominent New York law firm, Sullivan and Cromwell, to represent its American interests.[28] William Nelson Cromwell was the partner in

23. The other two members were Mordecai T. Endicott, a Navy engineer, and Alfred Noble, a civil engineer. For the Ludlow report see *House Documents*, 54 Cong., 1 Sess., No. 279 (Serial 3456).

24. *Congressional Record*, 53 Cong., 3 Sess., p. 2847 (Feb. 27, 1895); *ibid.*, 54 Cong., 1 Sess., p. 5928 (June 1, 1896), p. 5980 (June 2, 1896); *ibid.*, 54 Cong., 2 Sess., p. 324 (Dec. 21, 1896); see also *Senate Reports*, 54 Cong., 1 Sess., No. 1109 (Serial 3247).

25. See Sherman's remark, *Congressional Record*, 54 Cong., 2 Sess., p. 1214 (Jan. 27, 1897).

26. Thomas B. Reed, "The Nicaragua Canal," *North American Review*, CLXVIII (1899), 562.

27. *Congressional Record*, 54 Cong., 2 Sess., p. 1698 (Feb. 10, 1897).

28. Dwight C. Miner, *The Fight for the Panama Route: The Story of the Spooner Act and the Hay-Herrán Treaty* (New York, 1940), pp. 30–31, 79.

charge of the French company's affairs; and he later claimed to have had remarkable success. Although no evidence is known to show that the New Company was involved in the defeat of the Morgan bill in 1896, this possibility cannot be precluded.

When William McKinley became President in March 1897, the Maritime Canal Company could glean some hope from his platform's forthright assertion that "the Nicaragua Canal should be built, owned and operated by the United States."[29] But Congress merely implemented the Ludlow Board's recommendation for still another survey of Nicaragua, thus affording a further delay that must have pleased Cromwell and the French. After signing legislation for a Nicaragua Canal Commission, McKinley named Rear Admiral John G. Walker to head it.[30]

In 1897 American attention was increasingly riveted on the growing quarrel with Spain over Cuba. Outright war erupted in April 1898. The moment was therefore most unpropitious when in May 1898 Morgan, yet again, submitted his guarantee bill; yet again, it failed to pass.[31] For years the indomitable Senator and other backers of a Nicaragua canal had pushed with utmost determination to obtain their cherished objective; for years they had obtained nothing but frustration.

At that same time a similar situation existed with respect to the annexation of Hawaii. Spurned by Washington in 1893, the new republic had settled down for an independence of indefinite duration; however, its constitution empowered the government to negotiate a treaty of annexation with the United States whenever it saw fit. The royalists may have been cowed, but perils threatened Hawaii from another quarter—the rising empire of Japan, proud and confident after its easy victory over China in the war of 1894–1895. Americans saw China as a backward country, stubbornly and stu-

29. Porter and Johnson, *National Party Platforms*, p. 108. The Republican platform continued: "And, by the purchase of the Danish Islands we should secure a much needed Naval station in the West Indies," *ibid.* The Democratic platform did not refer to a canal.

30. *Congressional Record*, 55 Cong., 1 Sess., p. 20 (March 15, 1897), pp. 891–93, 899 (May 5, 1897), pp. 929–31 (May 6, 1897), p. 1398 (June 1, 1897), p. 1563 (June 7, 1897). For the commission's report see *Senate Documents*, 57 Cong., 1 Sess., No. 357 (Serial 4245); *ibid.*, 58 Cong., 2 Sess., No. 222, p. 42.

31. *Congressional Record*, 55 Cong., 2 Sess., p. 4603 (May 5, 1898), pp. 4923–25 (May 16, 1898), p. 6140 (June 20, 1898); *Senate Reports*, 55 Cong., 2 Sess., No. 1265 (Serial 3627).

pidly refusing to emulate the West but instead exporting thousands of her degenerate laborers to bedevil California. On the other hand, as the opener of Japan to Western commerce and ways, Americans took pride in their protégé's triumph over the ponderous, inefficient Chinese empire. China, it is true, was still the great potential market of many American dreams, the home of 400 million customers; and her supposed commercial value was rising sharply during the years of severe American depression following the panic of 1893.[32] Japan, with her far smaller population, aroused no such hopes, even though America's exports to her in the late 1890s were greater in value than exports to China. These contrasting commercial expectations probably tempered the American pleasure over the outcome of the Sino-Japanese War. So did the fears, prevalent in the 1890s, that Japan, with her efficient low-paid labor and her speedy industrialization, would soon undersell American exports not only in the Far East but in many other markets as well.

Furthermore Japan's newly demonstrated martial qualities had ominous implications for Americans looking to the future and also for people concerned about immediate prospects for the Hawaiian Islands. In 1883 there had been 116 Japanese in Hawaii. More and more contract labor was needed to produce sugar for the ever expanding American market, and in 1886 Honolulu concluded an immigration convention with Japan. Ten years later 24,407 Japanese had moved to the islands, well over a fifth of the total population.[33] Here was a great population change such as James G. Blaine had anticipated with foreboding in 1881. It was the more dangerous because, unlike the older Oriental immigration into Hawaii, these new immigrants came from a country of proved military power.

Alarmed at the flood, Hawaii imposed restrictions. In March 1897 she turned away 1,174 Japanese immigrants, alleging irregularities. Japan reacted angrily by suspending all emigration of contract laborers to Hawaii. Her warship, the *Naniwa*, sailed into Honolulu on May 5, 1897, shortly after the U.S.S. *Philadelphia* returned there.

32. Regarding Far Eastern developments see Akira Iriye, *Across the Pacific: An Inner History of American–East Asian Relations* (New York, 1967), pp. 62–64; Thomas J. McCormick, *China Market: America's Quest for Informal Empire, 1893–1901* (Chicago, 1967), pp. 54–62; Marilyn B. Young, *The Rhetoric of Empire: American China Policy, 1895–1901* (Cambridge, Mass., 1968), pp. 20–23.

33. Thomas A. Bailey, "Japan's Protest against the Annexation of Hawaii," *Journal of Modern History*, III (1931), 46.

Interviewed by a Honolulu newspaper, the Japanese minister, H. Shimamura, virtually threatened war: "If I cannot get a reasonable answer to my request [that Hawaii admit the Japanese] I may go home, and perhaps someone else will have better success. If I withdraw, you know what follows. I hope it will not reach that point."[34]

These disturbing events greeted the McKinley administration. Although primarily interested in domestic affairs, McKinley was not the man to permit Japan to seize the strategic archipelago; and his Republican party platform had come out for American control of it. When the Hawaiian minister to the United States, Francis M. Hatch, and a colleague named W. O. Smith, who had gone to Washington to promote annexation, called on the new President they were delighted to discover that the difference between him and Cleveland was like "the difference between daylight and darkness" and that McKinley was only waiting for a good opportunity to take the islands. Greatly encouraged, Hatch asked for negotiations to start without delay.[35]

John W. Foster, who had negotiated the abortive annexation treaty of 1893, was assigned the task of drafting a new treaty. He and Hawaiian negotiators soon had one ready. Signed on June 16, 1897, it went to the Senate; but although the Foreign Relations Committee reported it back favorably on July 14, Congress adjourned ten days later without having taken further action.[36]

The treaty was unwelcome to Japan, concerned as she was for the welfare of her many subjects out on the Pacific. Moreover, she was indignant because McKinley's Secretary of State, John Sherman, once an outstanding Senator but now an old man whose frequent memory lapses rendered him unfit for his new duties, had assured the Japanese minister at Washington, Toru Hoshi, that annexation

34. William A. Russ, Jr., *The Hawaiian Republic (1894–98) and Its Struggle to Win Annexation* (Selinsgrove, Pa., 1961), pp. 131, 139.

35. Smith to Hawaiian Minister of Foreign Affairs Henry E. Cooper, March 26, 1897, Julius W. Pratt, *Expansionists of 1898: The Acquisition of Hawaii and the Spanish Islands* (Baltimore, 1936), p. 216; Hatch to Sherman, April 5, 1897, Russ, *Hawaiian Republic*, p. 135. For the Republican platform of 1896 see Porter and Johnson, *National Party Platforms*, p. 108.

36. *Journal of the Executive Proceedings of the Senate* . . . (Washington, 1909), XXXI, Pt. 1, p. 230 (July 14, 1897); John Bassett Moore, *A Digest of International Law* . . . (8 vols., Washington, 1906), I, 503; John W. Foster, *Diplomatic Memoirs* (2 vols., Boston, 1909), II, 173; Pratt, *Expansionists of 1898*, p. 219. The text of the treaty is in *Senate Reports*, 55 Cong., 2 Sess., No. 681 (Serial 3622), pp. 96–97.

was not contemplated. On June 19, 1897, she protested that the treaty changed the status quo in the Pacific, endangered her treaty rights in Hawaii, and might delay a settlement of claims she had advanced in the immigration controversy. Although the Secretary promised that Japan's interests would be respected, Tokyo was not satisfied.[37]

The United States, already deeply involved with Spain over Cuba, felt compelled to take precautions. The navy prepared for an emergency; and Sherman instructed the minister at Honolulu, Harold M. Sewall (the former consul general in Samoa), to be ready, in case Japan used force, to order American troops ashore and declare a protectorate pending annexation.[38] A letter to the Secretary of the Navy, John D. Long, from Captain Albert S. Barker, a highly respected officer who was soon to become one of the three or four members of the key Naval War Board, raised alarming prospects. Barker thought that a Japanese-American war over Hawaii was "almost a probability"; that if the islands fell, part of North America would fall, too; and that the temptation for Japan to resort to force "must be very great."

"Were I the Japanese Admiral with power to act," he continued, "I should get the Japanese vessels ready for service in their respective ports, so as not to attract too much attention, then issue orders to go to sea—to as many as I had concluded to take with me or send across the water. One half of the fleet—or an amply large force— I would have rendezvous on a certain day at the Hawaiian Islands.

"I would arm the adult Japanese population [in Hawaii] to the number of 25,000 or so, hoist the Japanese flag over the Islands, attack and defeat the United States vessels—for all could easily be destroyed, as they would be tied up head and stern in Honolulu harbor. . . .

"For it must be bourne [sic] in mind that if the Japanese mean business they will endeavor to take the Islands and attack the fleet by surprise."

"To me," he wrote the Secretary a fortnight later, "this question seems of very much more importance than the Spanish one; Japan

37. Bailey, "Japan's Protest against Annexation," pp. 51–52, 54–55.
38. Sherman to Sewall, July 10, 1897, Russ, *Hawaiian Republic,* pp. 155–56. Minister Willis had died on Jan. 6, 1897.

could do us very much more *permanent* harm on the Pacific Coast than Spain could do on the Atlantic."[39]

While the navy was taking precautions Sherman was trying to promote an accord between Hawaii and Japan, because certainly the United States did not want to inherit a quarrel with Tokyo if she annexed the islands. He pressed Honolulu to settle the immigration dispute by paying an indemnity.[40] After some three-cornered argument among Washington, Tokyo, and Honolulu, Japan withdrew her protest over the annexation treaty on December 22, and Sherman promised that if Hawaii became American there would be no discrimination against Japanese commerce, navigation, or subjects. During the Spanish-American War, Hawaii, under United States pressure, reluctantly paid Japan $75,000 in reparations.[41]

Meanwhile a public debate over annexation had been taking place in the United States. The strategic and commercial reasons for acquiring Hawaii were well known and, to many, conclusive. On the other hand, antipathy to overseas expansion on grounds of principle, which had frustrated Seward's and Grant's expansionist aspirations, was still extremely strong. Old-fashioned Americans, and others too, dreaded the unbridled colonialism and the undermining of the republic's hallowed traditions that they expected to follow from the acquisition of a mongrel population far out on the Pacific Ocean. Reflecting the current Anglo-Saxonism and antipathy for Orientals, one publicist argued in a leading magazine that annexation would entitle the "detested and dangerous Asiatic" to vote in American elections and would occasion "the writing of an absolutely novel chapter in national and international history, more momentous than the American Civil War and its political, economic, industrial, and social results."[42] Others pointed to the somber lesson of ancient

39. Barker to the Secretary of the Navy, Aug. 30, Sept. 15, 1897, National Archives (Washington), Record Group 45, ON File, Box 3.

40. Sherman to Sewall, Aug. 31, Oct. 20, 1897, Russ, *Hawaiian Republic*, pp. 163, 169.

41. *Ibid.*, pp. 173–74, 362; Bailey, "Japan's Protest against Annexation," p. 59. Japan withdrew the protest on Dec. 22, 1897; Hawaii paid the money on July 27, 1898.

42. Longfield Gorman, "The Administration and Hawaii," *North American Review*, CLXV (1897), 379. Other significant articles were Carl Schurz, "Manifest Destiny," *Harper's New Monthly Magazine*, LXXXVII (1893), 737–46; Stephen M. White, "The Proposed Annexation of Hawaii," *Forum*, XXIII (1897), 723–36; John R. Procter, "Hawaii and the Changing Front of the World," *Forum*, XXIV (1897), 34–45; Daniel Agnew, "Unconstitutionality of the Hawaiian Treaty," *Forum*, XXIV (1897), 461–70; James Bryce, "The Policy of Annexation for America," *ibid.*, 385–95; Arthur C.

Rome, whose republican institutions were undermined when the first colonies were taken.

On September 6, 1897, Hawaii ratified the annexation treaty unanimously. That same month a congressional delegation advocating annexation went to Honolulu; it was composed of Senator John T. Morgan and of Representatives Joseph G. Cannon, James A. Tawney, Henry C. Loudenslager, and Albert S. Berry. Trailing it were two foes of expansion, Senator Richard F. Pettigrew and former Senator Fred T. Dubois.[43] The unusual expeditions aroused American interest and newspaper controversy as to whether the United States should follow Hawaii's example and ratify the treaty. Congress reconvened on December 6. In his first annual message President McKinley made the confident prediction that "the logic of events"—this appeal to the dictates of fate to justify a proposed move was characteristic of him—"required that annexation, heretofore offered but declined, should in the ripeness of time come about as the natural result of the strengthening ties that bind us to those Islands, and be realized by the free will of the Hawaiian State."[44] President Dole made the long trip to Washington to work for the treaty, and McKinley was reported to be rounding up votes.[45] Although Secretary of Agriculture James Wilson gave assurances that Hawaiian sugar would not seriously compete with American, Claus Spreckles (he was now in the California sugar-beet business), sugar-beet producers, the sugar trust, and other sugar interests opposed annexation. Labor interests did likewise, fearing that if Hawaii were taken, her Chinese, Japanese, and Portuguese would flood the mainland.[46] Opposition also came from Hawaiian royalists; and the belief that the island natives did not want to be annexed carried weight in the United States.

The Senate debated the treaty in secret session.[47] A majority

---

James, "Advantages of Hawaiian Annexation," *North American Review*, CLXV (1897), 758–60; John T. Morgan, "The Duty of Annexing Hawaii," *Forum*, XXV (1898), 11–16.

43. Russ, *Hawaiian Republic*, pp. 206, 208.

44. Message of Dec. 6, 1897, Richardson, *Messages and Papers*, XIV, 6263.

45. So said Representative Henry U. Johnson of Indiana, *Congressional Record*, 55 Cong., 2 Sess., p. 2031 (Feb. 22, 1898).

46. Wilson to the Vice-President, Jan. 17, 1898, *Senate Documents*, 55 Cong., 2 Sess., No. 63 (Serial 3592), p. 4; Russ, *Hawaiian Republic*, p. 217; Pratt, *Expansionists of 1898*, p. 225; John C. Appel, "American Labor and the Annexation of Hawaii: A Study in Logic and Economic Interest," *Pacific Historical Review*, XXIII (1954), 1–18.

47. A good account of the debate is in Russ, *Hawaiian Republic*, pp. 199–227.

supported annexation, and apparently a two-thirds vote hung in the balance. No doubt the well-known strategic and economic considerations that had been heard in 1875 and 1876 when the reciprocity treaty was approved, in the 1880s when the treaty's renewal was under consideration, and in 1893 and 1894 after Foster's treaty failed, were again advanced. In the late 1890s the partition of China seemed imminent, and some proponents of Hawaiian annexation hoped that this dread prospect would convince the most diehard American anticolonialist that the acquisition of a position of secure strength in the mid-Pacific was imperative. But some Senators, faithful to traditional ways—such a man, for example, as the aged and respected Justin S. Morrill of Vermont—adamantly opposed overseas expansion in principle; and others heeded the massive lobbying of the sugar interests.[48]

Perhaps the treaty would have succeeded except for the growing controversy with Spain. In not many more months the Spanish-American War would bring Hawaii to the United States; but in early 1898 Senators whose attention was absorbed by events in Cuba were in no mood to struggle for the Hawaiian treaty—if indeed a two-thirds majority could have been acquired even with utmost effort. By mid-March 1898 the second session of the fifty-fifth Congress had been under way for three months. The treaty was no nearer approval than it had been when signed almost a year earlier. The United States was close to war with Spain. Obviously Hawaii was not to be annexed by a treaty for a long time—perhaps never. President Dole returned to Honolulu looking "wholly broken in health"; the most sanguine annexationists were said to have lost hope for 1898, and the royalists to be correspondingly elated.[49] The failure to muster a vote even for Hawaii, so essential for United States security, and begging to be annexed, is impossible to reconcile with the imperialistic mood that is often supposed to have engulfed the American people in the mid-1890s. In fact, this mood did not appear until the war with Spain.

Yet annexation had enthusiastic supporters. Abandoning the treaty as hopeless, they turned to the alternative of a joint resolution of both houses, the procedure that had brought Texas into the

48. Pratt, *Expansionists of 1898,* p. 225.
49. John M. Ellicott, U.S.S. *Baltimore,* Honolulu, to Captain C. G. Fosdick, March 24, 1898, National Archives, Record Group 45, Area 10 file, Box 16.

union half a century earlier. On March 16, 1898, Senator Cushman K. Davis submitted a report, in the form of a joint resolution for annexation, from the Foreign Relations Committee.[50] Signed by Davis, John T. Morgan, and Henry Cabot Lodge, among others, it advanced five reasons for taking Hawaii and refuted (to its authors' satisfaction) twenty current objections to so doing. It hit hard at Japan (and that country formally remonstrated): "JAPAN HAS OPENLY PROTESTED against the annexation of Hawaii to the United States. . . . The policy of Japan toward Hawaii will become aggressive and determined so soon as the United States refuses to annex the islands, and makes the return to monarchy possible. . . . *The conditions are such that the United States must act* NOW *to preserve the results of its past policy, and to prevent the dominancy in Hawaii of a foreign people. . . . It is no longer a question of whether Hawaii shall be controlled by the native Hawaiian or by some foreign people; but the question is, What foreign people shall control Hawaii?*" The report put forward the familiar security argument: "By simply keeping other nations out of Hawaii the United States will thereby secure almost absolute immunity from naval attack on its Pacific coast for the simple reason that their bases are too far away to be made available." As for the objections, only the eighteenth need be mentioned, namely, that the monarchy had been overthrown by American troops; the rejoinder was that even if the charge was true, which was not admitted, it would have no more present weight than the fact that French troops had helped overthrow the British monarchy during the American revolution.[51]

But the crisis with Spain was near its climax. A month before, the American warship *Maine* had sunk in Havana harbor; a month later, war was to be declared. However dramatic the report on Hawaii, with its profusion of capital letters and italics, even the joint resolution for annexation could make no headway.

In the spring of 1898 the United States was utterly unable to resolve the baffling Hawaiian problem. As for an isthmian canal, the

50. *Congressional Record,* 55 Cong., 2 Sess., p. 2853 (March 16, 1898).
51. *Senate Reports,* 55 Cong., 2 Sess., No. 681, pp. 8, 31, 34, 36. Regarding the security argument see also a long report, published in 1898, by Commodore George W. Melville, Chief Engineer of the Navy, *Senate Documents,* 55 Cong., 2 Sess., No. 188 (Serial 3600), especially pp. 12, 25. For the Japanese protest see Hoshi to Sherman, April 11, 1898, Russ, *Hawaiian Republic,* p. 295. The five reasons and twenty objections are in Lorrin A. Thurston, *A Hand-Book on the Annexation of Hawaii* (St. Joseph [?], Mich., 1897[?]).

Maritime Canal Company of Nicaragua could scarcely have been more bogged down. And in the Caribbean Sea, that other area of vital concern, there seemed at the moment little possibility of acquiring a base. In all three places frustration held sway.

But the stalemate was not to last much longer. The now imminent Spanish-American War would break the long impasse: it would give the country Caribbean naval bases, it would precipitate Hawaiian annexation, and it would create an irresistible demand for an American isthmian canal.

CHAPTER 13

# Chronic Rebellion in Cuba

I N February 1895 another rebellion broke out in Cuba. Only seventeen years had elapsed since the previous one ended; little more than three years were to ensue before the United States found herself at war with Spain. The United States unwittingly helped touch off the rebellion by adopting the Wilson-Gorman tariff act of 1894. It imposed a duty on Cuban sugar, which had been made free by the reciprocity agreement with Spain concluded under the McKinley tariff of 1890; thereby it struck a heavy blow at the island's all-important sugar industry. Revolutionary sentiment flared higher; a republican government was established.[1] Spain held Havana, the seaports, and the interior towns. Outside of them roamed bands of insurgents and bandits, pillaging, burning, and killing. Deliberately they embarked upon destruction of crops, buildings, and machinery in order to prevent their use by pro-Spanish elements and to drive the unemployed into their own ranks. Some of the property was American, and the rebels hoped that the disorder they were creating would provoke United States intervention, presumably on their side.

And now history seemed to repeat itself. Just as during the rebellion of 1868 to 1878, so again Cuban Juntas in the United States smuggled weapons to the nearby island and spread propaganda, and again American commerce with Cuba was disrupted and atroc-

1. Martin A. S. Hume, *Modern Spain, 1788–1898* (New York, 1909), p. 554.

ity stories filled the headlines. If a European colony in the New World had seemed anachronistic in the 1870s, how much more so it seemed now; and to Protestant Anglo-Saxons, the proximity of Spanish Catholics was more intolerable than ever.

Significant, too, was the weakening of strong restraints of the 1870s. The opposition on moral grounds to tropical expansion, which had so deeply moved former abolitionists like Charles Sumner, had dwindled by the 1890s. By then, too, a new generation was at hand, one without vivid memories of terrible Civil War years and far more disposed to go to war with Spain than their fathers had been.

Most important of all was the simple fact that this was yet another Cuban rebellion; it was indeed one rebellion too many. The breakdown of law and order, it now seemed clear, had become chronic. Eight revolts had broken out between 1823 and 1853. Fifty Americans had been executed in 1851, and more in 1873 when the *Virginius* was captured. During the 1870s Americans already felt that their patience with Spain was wearing very thin. After the Pact of Zanzón supposedly ushered in peace, banditry continued rife for two years, and the United States had to devote frequent attention to the island. On several occasions in the 1880s Cubans in America tried to organize filibustering raids.[2] In March 1884 a revolutionary named Carlos Agüero led a filibustering expedition from Key West to Cuba. It failed dismally, but the United States sent two warships to Matanzas to protect Americans. The next year the State Department busied itself answering Madrid's frequent complaints about filibusters.[3] When in 1884 and again in 1885 rumors spread that Spain was about to cede Cuba to Germany, Washington warned against such a step.[4] In 1885 and 1886 German moves threatening the Caroline Islands (which Spain claimed) in the Pacific Ocean gave rise to talk of a Spanish-German war and to American apprehension

2. Chester L. Barrow, *William M. Evarts, Lawyer, Diplomat, Statesman* (Chapel Hill, 1941), p. 370; John W. Foster, *Diplomatic Memoirs* (2 vols., Boston, 1909), I, 254.

3. Frelinghuysen to Dwight F. Reed (American chargé d'affaires at Madrid), April 30, 1884, *Papers Relating to the Foreign Relations of the United States, 1884* (Washington, 1885), pp. 493–95; *ibid., 1885* (Washington, 1886), pp. 768–80, 782; David M. Pletcher, *The Awkward Years: American Foreign Relations under Garfield and Arthur* (Columbia, Mo., 1962), p. 292.

4. Charles C. Tansill, *The Foreign Policy of Thomas F. Bayard, 1885–1897* (New York, 1940), pp. 30n, 29–30. For reports regarding Germany and other matters in 1884 see the New York *Herald,* July 9, 24, 25, 1884.

lest Germany seize Cuba as well.[5] In all the Cuban fighting the United States had been closely involved. Filibusters had departed from American shores; exiles had plotted in American cities. Strain, economic loss, and bloodshed had been suffered by Americans during the ten long years of the recent rebellion. If soon after 1878 large-scale fighting should again break out on the island, Spanish-American peace would hang by a thread. There is much truth in the assertion of a contemporary American that "the conflict [with Spain in 1898] had been inevitable ever since the Cubans rose in 1868. . . ."[6]

The excess exports of manufactures, appearing in 1894, directed attention to potential markets in Latin America and the Far East, and therefore to Cuba dominating routes (via a canal) between them and the manufacturing centers in northeastern United States. Inevitably impatience mounted over the chaotic conditions in the European-owned island lying squarely athwart vital lines of communication in the Caribbean Sea. By the mid-1890s that sea had become the focal point of United States foreign policy. United States naval and economic imperatives, as well as American sensibilities, could no longer tolerate the chronic disorder in so vital and nearby an area. If Spain did not quickly restore law and order in Cuba, American intervention could be expected.

At the outset of the rebellion in 1895, Grover Cleveland was President. Although he would soon use strong language against Great Britain over Venezuela, he was more prudent toward Spain, with whom, as he must have realized, a real danger of war could have quickly arisen. In June 1895 the government invoked the neutrality laws, admonishing Americans not to enlist for service against Spain and not to organize military enterprises.[7] But enforcing the laws proved difficult in view of the long coastline, the proximity of Cuba, the resourcefulness of the Juntas, and the pro-rebel atmosphere that made court convictions difficult to obtain. During the early months of the rebellion many men and munitions got through to the rebels, and without them the insurrection would probably

5. Thomas F. Bayard (American ambassador to Great Britain) to Secretary of State Richard Olney, Jan. 15, 1896, Richard Olney Papers, Library of Congress (Washington); Hume, *Modern Spain*, p. 541.

6. Harry T. Peck, *Twenty Years of the Republic, 1885–1905* (New York, 1906), p. 664.

7. James D. Richardson (ed.), *A Compilation of the Messages and Papers of the Presidents* . . . (20 vols., New York, 1916), XIII, 6023–24.

have failed. Spain (recalling the American lapses of 1868 and 1869) was understandably incensed. But she herself failed to maintain an effective patrol along the Cuban coast.[8]

Arrests of Americans in Cuba, most of them native-born Cubans who had been naturalized, constituted another recurring aggravation. The Cuban Junta in New York seized upon these incidents to arouse American anger,[9] members of Congress orated indignantly, the State Department belabored Madrid with demands for the prisoners' release. Spain, on the other hand, denounced her former subjects who plotted against her under the protection of an insincerely assumed nationality, and she denounced the United States for defending them.[10]

More disturbing still were atrocity tales. Spain had sent her most famous soldier to Cuba, the man who had ended the rebellion of 1868–1878, Martínez de Campos. He proved unable to repeat his earlier success, and in February 1896 was replaced as captain general by Valereano Weyler. The new commander, who already had a reputation for harshness, quickly became known in the United States as "Butcher" Weyler. No atrocity was too terrible to be attributed to him and to his armies, though in committing atrocities the rebels probably outdid their antagonists.[11] Weyler played into the hands of his accusers by his reconcentration policy. The Spanish army seldom met the elusive guerrillas in pitched battles as it would have preferred; if hard-pressed, the guerrillas melted away and

8. Regarding the neutrality laws see *Papers Relating to the Foreign Relations of the United States, 1895* (Washington, 1896), Pt. 2, pp. 1187–1209; *Senate Documents,* 55 Cong., 2 Sess., No. 35 (Serial 3590). French E. Chadwick, *The Relations of the United States and Spain, Diplomacy* (New York, 1909), p. 418, estimates that out of 71 filibustering expeditions from the United States one-third reached Cuba. See also Albert G. Robinson, *Cuba, Old and New* (London, 1916), pp. 187–202.

9. Regarding the Juntas see George W. Auxier, "The Propaganda Activities of the Cuban *Junta* in Precipitating the Spanish-American War, 1895–1898," *Hispanic American Historical Review,* XIX (1939), 286–305.

10. The series *Papers Relating to the Foreign Relations of the United States* for the rebellion years has considerable correspondence regarding the arrests. See also *Senate Documents,* 54 Cong., 1 Sess., No. 278 (Serial 3357); *ibid.,* 54 Cong., 2 Sess., No. 39 (Serial 3469), No. 84 (Serial 3469), No. 104 (Serial 3470), No. 119 (Serial 3470), No. 120 (Serial 3470), No. 172 (Serial 3471); *ibid.,* 55 Cong., 1 Sess., No. 47 (Serial 3561); *Senate Reports,* 55 Cong., 1 Sess., No. 377 (Serial 3570); *ibid.,* 55 Cong., 2 Sess., No. 885 (Serial 3624), pp. 319ff.

11. Chadwick, *United States and Spain,* pp. 523–24. A good example of pro-rebel propaganda is Grover Flint, *Marching with Gomez: A War Correspondent's Field Note-Book Kept during Four Months with the Cuban Army* (Boston, 1898), ch. 10; John Fiske wrote an introduction to the book.

resumed their peacetime pursuits. How to identify who was a rebel, who a friendly farmer? Under an order of October 21, 1896, the Spanish segregated Cubans in fortified towns and then treated as a rebel anyone found outside.[12] Reconcentration worked well militarily, and area after area was mopped up, but the uprooted people, crowded together and lacking adequate sanitation, died by the thousands. In Havana, Consul General Fitzhugh Lee apprised Washington in the spring of 1897 that there was "no question but that these people, principally as I say, women, old men and children, are rapidly dying from starvation alone." About 400,000 *reconcentrados*, a quarter of the total Cuban population, were commonly believed to have perished by early 1898.[13] Terrible conditions spread over the island.

The Juntas in America made the most of the golden opportunity for propaganda. Horrifying accounts of starving babies, of piles of unburied corpses, of a whole population being deliberately exterminated, were disseminated. Although the accounts were exaggerated, the truth was bad enough. "It is high time this carnage is put a stop to, and the United States will only be undertaking a necessary public duty if they step in and end this carnival of butchery."[14] This assertion by the Havana correspondent of the London *Times* in 1896 foreshadowed the thinking of increasing numbers of Americans in 1897 and 1898.

Much has been written about the yellow press as a cause of the war.[15] In the United States, as in other countries, newspapers attained in the 1890s a mass circulation, irresponsibility, and vulgarity

12. *Papers Relating to the Foreign Relations of the United States, 1898* (Washington, 1901), p. 739; a less comprehensive concentration order had been issued on Feb. 16, 1896, *Senate Reports*, 55 Cong., 2 Sess., No. 885, p. 549.

13. Lee to Assistant Secretary of State William R. Day, May 29, 1897, National Archives (Washington), Record Group 59, Despatches from United States Consuls in Havana. The figure for the number of Cuban *reconcentrados* who died may have been nearer 100,000; see Ernest R. May, *Imperial Democracy: The Emergence of America as a Great Power* (New York, 1961), p. 127, and Marcus M. Wilkerson, *Public Opinion and the Spanish-American War: A Study in War Propaganda* (Baton Rouge, 1932), p. 40.

14. C. K. Akers to Sir Julian Pauncefote (British ambassador to the United States), Nov. 14, 1896, Lord Salisbury Papers, Christ Church Library (Oxford). For reports from American consuls in Cuba see *Senate Documents*, 55 Cong., 2 Sess., No. 230 (Serial 3610); *Senate Reports*, 55 Cong., 2 Sess., No. 885, *passim.*

15. Wilkerson, *Public Opinion and the Spanish-American War;* Joseph E. Wisan, *The Cuban Crisis as Reflected in the New York Press (1895–1898)* (New York, 1934); George W. Auxier, "Middle Western Newspapers and the Spanish-American War, 1895–1898," *Mississippi Valley Historical Review*, XXVI (1940), 523–34.

never before known. In 1895 William Randolph Hearst purchased the New York *Journal;* speedily he embarked upon a circulation race with Joseph Pulitzer's New York *World.* Atrocity story succeeded atrocity story in the *Journal* and *World,* and other newspapers throughout the country repeated them. In February 1897 a Cuban dentist named Ricardo Ruiz, who had taken out American naturalization papers, was arrested in Cuba and soon afterward was found dead in prison. The *Journal* raised an outcry, asserting that Spanish jailors had murdered him. Congress considered the case; it became famous throughout the nation.[16] More sensational was the story of Evangelina Cisneros, niece of the president of the rebel government. She had been imprisoned in Cuba, according to the *Journal,* for defending her honor against lascivious Spaniards. In issue after issue the *Journal* championed the "Cuban Girl Martyr," enlisting the aid of hundreds of women. The climax came when one of its reporters rescued the girl from her cell on October 6, 1897, and spirited her away to the United States. Hearst's exulting can readily be imagined.[17]

Clearly the press, and notably the New York *Journal,* played a part in fomenting the war with Spain. On the other hand the American people were not a sort of passive receptacle waiting to be filled by whatever material the press magnates selected; their opinions did not automatically sway to the pens of Hearst and Pulitzer. It is highly significant that, as we shall see, the public and Congress were not persuaded to take decisive action until convinced by reports having a sober, judicial character. Three years of sensationalism in the yellow press failed to move them to war. It should also be said that much of the slanted news emanated from the Juntas.

The belligerency of the yellow press manifested itself also in Congress, where jingoistic feelings gathered volume as the fighting continued. Especially among western Democrats and Populists, war hawks abounded. Although for many months the antiwar vote dominated both houses, an ominous sign of legislative restlessness appeared in April 1896 when Congress adopted resolutions calling for the extension of belligerent rights to the rebels and also, going much further, for the tender to Madrid of friendly offices by the

16. Wilkerson, *Public Opinion and the Spanish-American War,* pp. 83–87; Wisan, *Cuban Crisis,* pp. 224ff.; *Congressional Record,* 55 Cong., 1 Sess., p. 119 (March 22, 1897).

17. Wilkerson, *Public Opinion and the Spanish-American War,* pp. 87–91; Walter Millis, *The Martial Spirit: A Study of Our War with Spain* (Boston, 1931), pp. 82–84.

President for the recognition of Cuban independence.[18] But the Cleveland administration had no intention of recognizing even belligerency, congressional advice notwithstanding. No more than Secretary of State Hamilton Fish had done, did it consider recognition legally justified, because the rebels had no fixed seat of government and held no defined territory. The administration correctly believed that recognition would mean taking a long stride toward war, and this it was determined to avoid.

In the presidential election of 1896 the free silver question dominated all others. Cuban policy, however, was much discussed. Both major parties took the side of the rebels. The Democratic platform extended "sympathy to the people of Cuba in their heroic struggle for liberty and independence." The Republican platform, although avowing noninterference, demanded interference: "The government of Spain, having lost control of Cuba, and being unable to protect the property or lives of resident American citizens, or to comply with its Treaty obligations, we believe that the government of the United States should actively use its influence and good offices to restore peace and give independence to the Island."[19] This challenging statement must have alarmed Madrid deeply, especially when the Republican candidate, William McKinley, was elected President.

After the election, during the remaining weeks of Cleveland's term, nothing of note occurred. But in his last annual message the President declared bluntly: "When the inability of Spain to deal successfully with the insurrection has become manifest and it is demonstrated that her sovereignty is extinct in Cuba for all purposes of its rightful existence, and when a hopeless struggle for its re-establishment has degenerated into a strife which means nothing more than the useless sacrifice of human life and the utter destruction of the very subject-matter of the conflict, a situation will be presented in which our obligations to the sovereignty of Spain will be superseded by higher obligations, which we can hardly hesitate to recognize and discharge."[20] This line of thought was remarkably

18. *Congressional Record,* 54 Cong., 1 Sess., pp. 3627–28 (April 6, 1896). For the preceding debate in the House see *ibid.,* pp. 3574–3600 (April 4, 1896).

19. Kirk H. Porter and Donald B. Johnson (eds.), *National Party Platforms, 1840–1960* (Urbana, Ill., 1956), pp. 99–100, 108.

20. Message of Dec. 7, 1896, Richardson, *Messages and Papers,* XIV, 6154; see also Walter LaFeber, *The New Empire: An Interpretation of American Expansion, 1860–1898* (Ithaca, 1963), pp. 295–97.

similar to that soon to be expressed by his Republican successor.

Everyone now marked time until McKinley entered the White House. Cleveland had held firm against the Juntas, the jingo press, and belligerent members of Congress. "The Cuban question is to-day dead in Congress and before the public, and to this is to be attributed the little excitement the matter is creating here," the Spanish minister at Washington, Enrique Dupuy de Lôme, reported complacently in mid-February 1897.[21]

By March 1897, when McKinley took office, the Cuban insurrection had been pursuing its fearful course for more than two years. The disruption of American trade, the devastation of American property, the expense of patrolling American coasts—these were greater than ever. The Juntas continued to stir up sympathy for the rebels. "Butcher" Weyler and the horrors of reconcentration continued to figure in the headlines. And no end was in sight. Chronic disorder loomed ahead as far as one could see. Could the United States again tolerate ten turbulent years like those from 1868 to 1878? As week succeeded week with the fighting apparently deadlocked hopelessly, increasing numbers of people began to ask this question.

Notwithstanding the similarity between Cleveland's final position toward Spain as expressed in his annual message of 1896 and the position soon adopted by President McKinley, one significant difference did exist between the attitudes of the two administrations. McKinley was more solicitous for the Cuban rebels. He would soon insist that Spain moderate her reconcentration methods, and he would show himself reluctant to bypass the rebels and foist upon them a Spanish-American settlement of Cuba unacceptable to them.[22] During his first administration Cleveland had demonstrated a strong moralistic sympathy for the oppressed Samoan natives; but in his second term Richard Olney rather than Thomas F. Bayard was in the State Department, and one has the impression that Olney, at least, would not have hesitated to sacrifice the Cuban natives. McKinley's more pro-Cuban policy, if persisted in, meant that the

21. Dupuy de Lôme to Minister of State, Feb. 13, 1897, *Spanish Diplomatic Correspondence and Documents, 1896–1900, Presented at the Cortes by the Minister of State* (Washington, 1905), p. 24.

22. John A. S. Grenville and George B. Young, *Politics, Strategy, and American Diplomacy: Studies in Foreign Policy, 1873–1917* (New Haven, 1966), pp. 248–49.

rebels could block a settlement they disliked. The problem of finding terms agreeable to the United States and Spain was difficult enough, but if the rebels, too, had to be satisfied, the problem became nearly impossible of solution. Yet McKinley was no jingo. Although resolved to bring peace and stability to Cuba, he did not want to fight Spain. Charles G. Dawes, Comptroller of the Currency, who saw him frequently, wrote on February 21, 1898: "He has withstood all efforts to stampede him. He will endeavor in every possible way consistent with honor to avoid war"; Dawes wrote again on March 9: "The President stands for any course consistent with national honor which will bring peace."[23]

McKinley was confirmed in his peaceful disposition by the attitude of the business community, on whose favors he depended politically. Some special business interests, it is true, may have hoped for hostilities. American exports to Cuba, valued at $18 million in 1892, $24 million in 1893, and $20 million in 1894, fell to $13 million in 1895, $8 million in 1896 and also in 1897, and $10 million in 1898. American imports from Cuba also suffered. Amounting to $78 million in 1892, $79 million in 1893, and $76 million in 1894, they declined to $53 million in 1895, and thereafter dropped steeply to $40 million in 1896, $18 million in 1897, and only $15 million in 1898.[24] Americans who customarily gained their livelihood from commerce with Cuba were hard hit; and they could not have been sorry when war came. Their impatience was expressed by McKinley's first Secretary of State, the elderly John Sherman, who admonished the Spanish in July 1897: "The extraordinary, because direct and not merely theoretical or sentimental, interest of the United States in the Cuban situation can not be ignored."[25] One might also suppose that investors in Cuba, along with many traders, would not have viewed hostilities with displeasure. In 1898 United States investments in the island amounted to about $50 million.[26] This money was mainly in sugar plantations; the most important single business interest in Cuba was the Ameri-

23. Charles G. Dawes, *A Journal of the McKinley Years: Edited, and with a Foreword, by Bascom N. Timmons* (Chicago, 1950), pp. 145, 145–46.

24. U.S. Bureau of the Census, *Historical Statistics of the United States, Colonial Times to 1957* (Washington, 1961), pp. 550, 552.

25. Sherman to Woodford, July 16, 1897, *Foreign Relations, 1898*, p. 560.

26. Samuel F. Bemis, *The Latin American Policy of the United States: An Historical Interpretation* (New York, 1961), p. 137.

can Sugar Refining Company, and this powerful concern, like other investors in Cuba, suffered from the destruction of its holdings. The sugar trust customarily made large election donations and maintained an active lobby in Washington. It is natural to suspect that it meddled with Cuban policy—just as the sugar interests tried to shape policy toward Hawaii and elsewhere. But no evidence of successful meddling about Cuba is known. Indeed, Senators Nelson W. Aldrich and William B. Allison, spokesmen for the trust, were among those who resisted the slide to war.[27]

There can be little doubt that businessmen in general opposed war strongly. The country was climbing out of the depression following the panic of 1893; the last thing businessmen wanted was the uncertainty of warfare. Furthermore they feared that war might usher in free silver (just as some silver zealots welcomed a war, hoping it would lead to free silver).[28] "I have had . . . hundreds of letters from businessmen all over the country . . . protesting against this whole crusade" against Spain, Senator Eugene Hale reported in 1896. "The business interests and the stock market [in opposing war] do not represent the sentiment of 70,000,000 people of our great Republic," Representative Robert Adams, Jr., thought.[29]

> Populists, Democrats, Republicans are we,
> But we are all Americans to make Cubans free.

In such happy vein Senator Benjamin R. Tillman regaled the Senate a week before the war started. But he felt constrained to add: "I feel that I can claim this for the American people with the exception of a few thousand who live within the purview or within the influence of boards of trade and chambers of commerce and banking houses. . . ."[30] The Senator believed that American business interests opposed war. The evidence supports him.

But although not a jingo, McKinley was no extreme devotee of peace either. If hostilities could be avoided only at the cost of Republican party unity, or of harm to the national interest, he would have few qualms about resorting to force. Nor would the President

27. May, *Imperial Democracy*, p. 116.
28. *Congressional Record*, 54 Cong., 1 Sess., p. 2827 (March 16, 1896). Regarding the business attitude see Julius W. Pratt, *Expansionists of 1898: The Acquisition of Hawaii and the Spanish Islands* (Baltimore, 1936), ch. 7.
29. *Congressional Record*, 54 Cong., 1 Sess., p. 3576 (April 4, 1896).
30. *Ibid.*, 55 Cong., 2 Sess., p. 3888 (April 15, 1898).

allow the Cuban suffering, which moved him deeply, to continue indefinitely. He persuaded Congress to appropriate $50,000 for a relief fund for Americans in Cuba; he persuaded Madrid to admit duty-free into Cuba provisions, food, and medicine; and anonymously he contributed $5,000 to a Cuban relief fund.[31] His administration showed itself resolute toward Spain. It continued to register protests about Americans in Cuban jails and about the destruction of American property; at the same time it tightened vigilance over filibustering. And in Secretary Sherman's instructions to the new United States minister to Spain, General Stewart L. Woodford, it took a very strong, even threatening, line. (The similarity of the instructions, however, to the policy foreshadowed in Cleveland's last annual message is apparent.)

To start with, Sherman laid down the principal American grievance: the chronic disorder in nearby Cuba. For thirteen out of the past twenty-nine years, he emphasized, the island had been the scene of sanguinary conflict, and with every passing day it became more evident that Spain could not restore order. Therefore, the United States "must seriously inquire whether the time has not arrived when Spain . . . will put a stop to this destructive war. . . . the chronic condition of trouble and violent derangement in that island constantly causes disturbance in the social and political condition of our own people. . . . Assuredly Spain can not expect this Government to sit idle, letting vast interests suffer, our political elements disturbed, and the country perpetually embroiled, while no progress is being made in the settlement of the Cuban problem. . . ."[32] Woodford read his instructions to the Spanish Foreign Minister at his first interview on September 18, 1897. He stressed the need for speedy action; indeed, since he named a time limit his statement partook of the nature of an ultimatum. He suggested, he wrote Sherman, that either Spain must give satisfactory assurances by November 1, 1897, of an "early and certain peace," or else the United States would feel free to do whatever she "should deem

31. *Ibid.*, 55 Cong., 1 Sess., p. 1122 (May 17, 1897), p. 1214 (May 24, 1897); *Senate Documents*, 58 Cong., 2 Sess., No. 105 (Serial 4597), p. 113; Acting Secretary of State William R. Day to Dupuy de Lôme, Dec. 1, 1897, and Dupuy de Lôme to Day, Dec. 24, 1897, *Papers Relating to the Foreign Relations of the United States, 1897* (Washington, 1898), pp. 511, 512–513, respectively. For McKinley's contribution see Margaret Leech, *In the Days of McKinley* (New York, 1959), p. 150.

32. Sherman to Woodford, July 16, 1897, *Foreign Relations, 1898*, pp. 559–60.

necessary to procure this result."[33] Thus Washington had made clear its insistence that the chronic disorder must be terminated in the very near future. Seven months after Woodford's warning, Spain having failed to meet the demand, the United States declared war.

Why did the United States take so long? On August 8, 1897, the head of the Conservative government, Cánovas del Castillo, was assassinated; on October 4 the Liberals under Prime Minister Praxedes Mateo Sagasta took office. The Liberals had been as critical of the Conservatives as had the United States. Promptly they recalled "Butcher" Weyler and replaced him as captain general with the less rigid Ramón Blanco.[34] Sagasta did not fully meet Woodford's November 1 deadline, but he almost did. On the thirteenth of that month Spain alleviated reconcentration, on the twenty-fifth she adopted a comprehensive scheme of autonomy, and on the twenty-eighth Woodford happily reported the release of all Americans arrested in Cuba.[35] Thus by an accident of history more friendly men had come to power at the critical moment; and the United States paused to see whether they would succeed. Dupuy de Lôme reported optimistically that "the political situation has never been better, nor my mission easier, since May, 1895, and, as I am informed, all motive for irritation has disappeared."[36]

But would Madrid's reforms work out in practice? The next four months were to give the answer. During that period four episodes occurred that convinced Washington and the country at large that Spain had irretrievably lost control of events in Cuba, and that consequently the reforms could not be made effective; "early and certain peace" would not come to Cuba after all. The chronic disorder would continue.

At the beginning of 1898 came the first, tragic indication that Spain could no longer maintain authority in the island. Furious over

33. Woodford to Sherman, Sept. 20, 1897, *ibid.*, p. 567.

34. Willis F. Johnson, *The History of Cuba* (5 vols., New York, 1920), IV, 88. See the Liberal manifesto of June 24, 1897, *Foreign Relations, 1898*, pp. 592–94.

35. Chadwick, *United States and Spain*, p. 522; Woodford to Sherman, Nov. 26, 1897 (enclosing copies of the decrees granting autonomy), and Nov. 28, 1897, *Foreign Relations, 1898*, pp. 616–44, 644, respectively.

36. Dupuy de Lôme to Foreign Minister Pio Gullón, Dec. 2, 1897, *Spanish Diplomatic Correspondence*, p. 43. For Woodford's similar optimism see Woodford to Sherman, Nov. 13, 1897, H. Wayne Morgan, *William McKinley and His America* (Syracuse, 1963), p. 346.

the grant of autonomy, Spanish loyalists rioted in Havana on January 12. "Uncertainty exists whether Blanco can control the situation," Consul General Lee telegraphed the State Department from Havana. Lee heard that the Spanish army had disobeyed orders, and that instead of moving against the rioters, soldiers had shouted, "Death to autonomy! Death to Blanco!"[37] American hope in Sagasta and the Liberals was dealt a heavy blow from which it never recovered. Minister Dupuy de Lôme discarded his recent optimism and on January 16 made the gloomy assessment: "The sensational press is just as it was in the worst period, and the Government and Cabinet, although they have said nothing to me, seem to have lost all faith in Spain's success. . . . At any event, it indicates a state of things that would have been impossible a week ago."[38]

The second incident apparently demonstrating the disintegration of Spanish power was far more dramatic, and inflammatory to an extreme degree. This was the destruction in Havana harbor of the American battleship *Maine*. The loss of the *Maine* was an indirect consequence of the Havana riots. Alarmed by the turmoil, Lee had advised Washington that warships might be needed on short notice to protect Americans; and overhastily the Navy Department ordered the *Maine* to proceed to Havana on January 24. On learning of the order, Lee judged it premature and advised waiting six or seven days. Washington answered that the ship had already been told to sail.[39] The Spanish authorities in Cuba likewise requested a delay; they were rightly alarmed, because the presence of an American battleship at Havana would raise insurgent hopes—just as the appearance of the *Boston* at Honolulu five years earlier had heartened the insurgents there. Nevertheless the *Maine* was not recalled but allowed to tempt fate by lingering on day after day at Havana. Washington should have foreseen the possibility of an incident. In Madrid the Foreign Minister did foresee it: the ship, he thought, "might, through some mischance, bring about a conflict."[40] On

37. Lee to Day, Jan. 13, 1898, *Foreign Relations, 1898,* p. 1025.
38. Dupuy de Lôme to Gullón, Jan. 5, 16, 1898, *Spanish Diplomatic Correspondence,* pp. 62, 64–65.
39. Lee to Day, Jan. 12, 13, 1898, *Foreign Relations, 1898,* pp. 1024–25; Lee to Day, and Day to Lee, Jan. 24, 1898, *Senate Documents,* 55 Cong., 2 Sess., No. 230, p. 84.
40. Gullón to Spanish ambassadors at Paris, Berlin, London, Vienna, Rome, and St. Petersburg, Feb. 8, 1898, *Spanish Diplomatic Correspondence,* p. 80. See also the *Times* (London), Feb. 14, 1898; G. Barclay (British chargé d'affaires at Madrid) to Prime

February 16, 1898, enormous headlines shocked Americans. The *Maine* had sunk in Havana harbor the day before. Out of 350 officers and men, 260 had been lost.

What caused the disaster is still unknown,[41] but interventionists saw a sinister Spanish hand at work. "The *Maine* was sunk by an act of dirty treachery on the part of the Spaniards, *I* believe . . . ," Assistant Secretary of the Navy Theodore Roosevelt exclaimed excitedly. The shrieks of the yellow press can be imagined.[42] Extremists in Congress, too, reacted violently. But the administration moved circumspectly by sending a board of naval officers to Havana to investigate. The Secretary of the Navy, John D. Long, cabled Commodore George Dewey, who had recently taken command of the Pacific squadron, that the *Maine* had been destroyed "by accident," and he reiterated this assertion to the press.[43] President McKinley himself was reported to attribute the disaster to an internal explosion.[44] The general public, too, after the first flash of anger and supposition that Spain was guilty, suspended judgment pending the naval board's report. Edwin L. Godkin, editor of the *Nation*,

---

Minister Lord Salisbury, Jan. 26, 1898, Public Record Office (London), Foreign Office 72/2062. However, Spain decided to send some of her own warships to visit American ports "in return for the demonstrations received and in testimony also of friendly feeling." Gullón to Dupuy de Lôme, Jan. 26, 1898, *Spanish Diplomatic Correspondence*, p. 70.

41. Steel ships were widely regarded as experimental. Senator Eugene Hale, chairman of the Senate Committee on Naval Affairs, believed that a battleship was about as dangerous as a volcano, Leech, *McKinley*, p. 167. Edward Atkinson, a Boston industrialist, attributed the explosion to "gases developed in bituminous coal, coupled with electricity," Harold F. Williamson, *Edward Atkinson: The Biography of an American Liberal, 1827–1905* (Boston, 1934), p. 223. The *Maine* was raised in 1911 and another board of investigation again reported an external explosion; but at least one man on the board believed that an internal explosion could have done the same damage. A Spanish board of investigation of 1898 reported an internal explosion only. See *Senate Documents*, 55 Cong., 2 Sess., Nos. 207, 230, 231 (Serial 3610); *House Documents*, 63 Cong., 2 Sess., No. 480 (Serial 6754); John E. Weems, *The Fate of the Maine* (New York, 1958). For reports that the Junta was involved see Auxier, "Propaganda Activities of the Cuban *Junta*," p. 303.

42. Roosevelt to B. H. Diblee, Feb. 16, 1898, Elting E. Morison and John M. Blum (eds.), *The Letters of Theodore Roosevelt* (8 vols., Cambridge, Mass., 1951–54), I, 775. See also Millis, *Martial Spirit*, p. 110. For the press reaction see *Public Opinion*, XXIV (Feb. 24, 1898), 229–31; *Literary Digest*, XVI (Feb. 26, 1898), 241–44. For Blanco's message of sympathy see Blanco to Lee, Feb. 16, 1898, National Archives, Record Group 59, Despatches from United States Consuls in Havana.

43. Long to Dewey, Feb. 16, 1898, National Archives, Record Group 45, Area 10 File, Box 16; New York *Herald*, Feb. 17, 1898, cited in Wisan, *Cuban Crisis*, p. 390.

44. New York *World*, Feb. 18, 1898, cited in Wisan, *Cuban Crisis*, p. 390. See also Dawes, *McKinley Years*, p. 143.

wrote that although a few newspapers had behaved disgracefully most people did not take them seriously.[45] But Acting Secretary of State William R. Day, who had assumed command of the State Department because of the aged Sherman's incapacity, called the situation "very grave"; he thought that "the highest wisdom and greatest prudence" would be required to avert a crisis.[46]

The impact of the *Maine* tragedy was greater because it occurred just a week after another sensation. This was the publication by the New York *Journal* on February 9 of the facsimile of a private letter written some months earlier by Dupuy de Lôme to a friend in Cuba. The letter had been stolen by a rebel sympathizer, delivered to the *Journal,* and held until Hearst judged its release opportune. In it Dupuy described McKinley as "weak and a bidder for the admiration of the crowd, besides being a would-be politician who tries to leave a door open behind himself while keeping on good terms with the jingoes of his party." That the President should be so libeled by a foreigner—and a Spaniard at that—was bad enough; worse, to reflective Americans, was another passage in which the minister advised: "It would be very advantageous to take up, even if only for effect, the question of commercial relations. . . ."[47] His unwise recommendation pointed beyond the minister to Spain herself: she seemed convicted of a basic insincerity most disheartening to Americans who hoped to avoid war. The yellow press unleashed an all-out attack on the repulsive Spaniard and his perfidious country. Like Sackville West, Dupuy de Lôme had been undone by a private communication. He did not wait to be recalled; he resigned at once.

The publication of the Dupuy de Lôme letter and the sinking of the *Maine,* one hard upon the other in February 1898, boded ill for peace. In the circumstances Congress cannot be censured for appropriating, shortly after the explosion in Havana, a national defense fund of $50 million, the expenditure of which was left to the President's discretion. William Jennings Bryan said that "it might have been better to have made it [the appropriation] $100,000,000. . . ."[48] The appropriation act passed Con-

45. *Nation,* LXVI (Feb. 24, 1898), 139.

46. Day to Woodford, March 3, 1898, *Foreign Relations, 1898,* p. 681.

47. For a copy of the entire letter see John Bassett Moore, *A Digest of International Law* . . . (8 vols., Washington, 1906), VI, 176–77.

48. Washington *Post,* March 10, 1898, quoted in *Congressional Record,* 55 Cong., 2 Sess., p. 4023 (April 18, 1898). For the appropriation act see *ibid.,* pp. 2602–21 (March 8, 1898), 2631–32 (March 9, 1898).

(*Harper's Weekly*, March 19, 1898)

Not One Cent for Bunkum—Fifty Millions for Defence.

gress unanimously in early March, an expression of resolve that "stunned" the Spanish, according to Woodford.[49] The army and navy speeded up war preparations. Press reports of cruisers being purchased, of imports of war materials being exempted from customs duties, of an appropriation by the House of funds for the construction of three battleships and twenty-four torpedo boats,[50] and of other such stirring developments strengthened the impression that war was near. Nor could such news have failed to encourage the rebels. All indications were that the powerful republic would soon be fighting on their side.

In the midst of the excitement Senator Redfield Proctor of Vermont delivered a famous speech. Together with the Havana riots of January and the destruction of the *Maine,* this was the third event attesting that Spain had lost control in Cuba. The Senator was widely recognized as a sober, judicious man opposed to war. Having recently visited Cuba, he was urged by friends to make public his impressions. To the Senate on March 17 he made one of the most effective speeches ever delivered there—according to ex-President Benjamin Harrison, the most effective speech made in any legislature anywhere for fifty years.[51] It was a terrible indictment of Spain, the more persuasive because of Proctor's factual, objective, unemotional tone. With regard to the *reconcentrados,* he said: "Torn from their homes, with foul earth, foul air, foul water, and foul food or none, what wonder that one-half have died and that one-quarter of the living are so diseased that they can not be saved? . . . I went to Cuba with a strong conviction that the picture had been overdrawn. . . . I could not believe that out of a population of 1,600,000, two hundred thousand had died within these Spanish forts. . . . My inquiries were entirely outside of sensational sources . . . every time the answer was that the case had not been overstated."[52]

How could Spain pretend to exercise meaningful sovereignty where such frightful conditions existed? When Proctor finished his address Senator James H. Berry whispered to George G. Vest beside him: "That speech means war; that speech will stir the people of the United States from Maine to California, and no power on

49. Woodford to McKinley, March 9, 1898, *Foreign Relations, 1898,* p. 684.
50. *Congressional Record,* 55 Cong., 2 Sess., pp. 3457–84 (April 1, 1898).
51. Wisan, *Cuban Crisis,* p. 412.
52. *Congressional Record,* 55 Cong., 2 Sess., p. 2917 (March 17, 1898).

earth can longer keep them back." Senator Stephen B. Elkins thought that Proctor "has stirred this nation in a great speech as no other man." And Senator Tillman said that the "calm, dispassionate, and almost judicial statement of facts" had "furnished the bomb" for the fuse ignited by the *Maine*.[53] Senator Proctor owned marble quarries in Vermont—the marble king, he was called. After his speech the Speaker of the House, Thomas B. Reed, remarked sardonically, but unfairly, "A war will make a large market for gravestones."[54]

The naval board's report, dated March 21 and made public a week later, constituted the fourth and final indication that Spanish authority had virtually collapsed. In a special message to Congress on March 28 the President summarized the board's conclusions: "The ship was destroyed by the explosion of a submarine mine, which caused the partial explosion of two or more of her forward magazines; and . . . no evidence has been obtainable fixing the responsibility for the destruction of the *Maine* upon any person or persons."[55] Although McKinley asked Congress for its "deliberate consideration," the report probably clinched Spain's guilt in the eyes of most Americans; for an explosion caused by a submarine mine must be the fault of Spain, and whether the explosion was intentional or due to negligence made no crucial difference.

If any one event was responsible for the Spanish-American War, it was not the mere destruction of the *Maine* but her destruction by an outside explosion as attested by a responsible board of inquiry. No member of the American government is known to have attributed direct responsibility to the Spanish government.[56] One Senator, George L. Wellington, went so far as to ask, "May there not be those who say we are responsible for the defeat of autonomy in Cuba and, by that defeat, indirectly the cause of this disaster?" Consul General Lee said, "I do not think it [a mine] was put there by the Government. . . . I do not think General Blanco gave any order about it." Even Senator William B. Bate, who believed that

53. *Ibid.*, p. 3880 (April 15, 1898), p. 3977 (April 16, 1898), p. 3892 (April 15, 1898). Senator George Frisbie Hoar thought that the speech influenced the outbreak of the war more than the loss of the *Maine*, Wisan, *Cuban Crisis*, p. 412n.
54. Leech, *McKinley*, p. 172.
55. Richardson, *Messages and Papers*, XIV, 6280.
56. Representative Hugh A. Dinsmore came near to doing so, *Congressional Record*, 55 Cong., 2 Sess., p. 3816 (April 13, 1898).

"on no page of history is recorded a parallel act of perfidy and treachery," admitted, "I do not charge the Spanish government was a party. . . ."[57] Nevertheless most certainly Spain was blamed, not because she had ordered the deed, but because her crumbling authority in Cuba had made it possible. No nation had the right to claim sovereignty in an area where its control had disappeared, where disorder had become chronic, where it had no chance of regaining control. Senator Clarence D. Clark charged Spain with "criminal responsibility" on the ground that "the vessel and crew were destroyed either by Spanish authority direct or by Spanish negligence equally criminal."[58] This was the prevalent opinion. Senator John C. Spooner also expressed it: "Acquitting Spain as a sovereignty, and General Blanco as her representative, of any complicity in the destruction of the *Maine,* the fact remains that under circumstances which called for unusual measures of protection, her government in Cuba was at least too weak to prevent her subjects from destroying our battle ship and murdering our sailors." "We can endure it all no longer," he pronounced.[59]

Two reports in the second half of March—Senator Proctor's and the naval board's, each persuasive not because of sensationalism but because of its calm, judicial nature—following upon the Havana riots and the *Maine*'s destruction, convinced Americans that Spanish authority in Cuba had weakened beyond repair. This frightful state of affairs existed in an area vital to the United States. By the spring of 1898 Americans could no longer tolerate the chronic turmoil there. If Spain could not exercise control, either she must sever her ties with Cuba in short order or forceful intervention by the United States would become inevitable.

57. *Ibid.,* p. 3953 (April 16, 1898), p. 3966 (April 16, 1898).
58. *Ibid.,* p. 3967 (April 16, 1898).
59. *Ibid.,* Appendix, pp. 300–1 (April 15, 1898).

# CHAPTER 14

# *War with Spain*

I N late March 1898 the United States and Spain were on the verge of hostilities. As a result of the Havana riots, the sinking of the *Maine,* and the dispassionate reports of Senator Proctor and the naval board, the American people and the administration had become convinced that Spain could no longer control Cuba. American opinion was near the breaking point; unless Spain departed in the very near future from the Ever-Faithful Isle, the United States could be expected to intervene by force of arms. The next few weeks witnessed a race between the strongly gathering pressures for war in the United States and the dawning realization by the Spanish that they must leave their old colony. Could Spain make the tremendous decision to depart before American war fever mounted irresistibly? On that hung war or peace.

One conceivable resolution of the crisis was for the United States to buy Cuba. President McKinley toyed with this idea, discussing it at different times in 1898 with a Junta representative, with Prince Albert of Belgium, and with the Archbishop of St. Paul, Minnesota, John Ireland. But in the unlikely event that Spain would have agreed to sell, Congress might well have refused to appropriate the millions of dollars needed.[1] In any event the rebels would have opposed an

1. Ernest R. May, *Imperial Democracy: The Emergence of America as a Great Power* (New York, 1961), pp. 149–50; Minister Woodford favored purchasing Cuba. Regarding a plan for Americans to finance the purchase of Cuba by the rebels see David F. Healy, *The United States in Cuba, 1898–1902: Generals, Politicians, and the Search for Policy* (Madison, 1963), pp. 14–16, 25–27.

American ownership blocking their independence.

If Cuba was not to be purchased, could Spain be persuaded, short of war, to leave the island? Not later than March 20 the administration had been informed confidentially that the naval board attributed the *Maine*'s explosion to a submarine mine. A report so eagerly awaited by the general public could not be suppressed, and the inflammatory effect its ominous finding would produce was easy to foresee. In late March a crisis, therefore, was suddenly at hand, and the administration had to find a solution quickly if hostilities were to be averted. From that time on, diplomatic negotiations became furiously active. Letters and telegrams streamed back and forth between Washington and Madrid; frequently Minister Woodford closeted himself with Spanish officials, and Minister Luis Polo de Bernabé (Dupuy de Lôme's successor) conferred with Acting Secretary of State William R. Day (he would become Secretary of State in name as well as in fact in April). The State Department pushed Spain hard to make radical changes in her colony. What changes did it want? Day dispatched three major telegrams to Woodford on March 20, 26, and 27 that set forth the demands, but failed to make them precise.

On the twentieth Day cabled the minister the naval board's finding about a submarine mine. The *Maine* incident, he said, need not lead to hostilities if Spain agreed to make reparations. More dangerous were the "general conditions in Cuba which can not be longer endured." Spain must restore peace, and "April 15 is none too early" for that.[2] To tell Madrid to restore peace in less than a month was to make a virtually impossible demand.

In Washington the Cabinet met all day March 25. The day before, the President had conferred for the first time with leading Democrats. He was reported to have asked them for thirty days in which to prepare the country for war, but to have obtained no satisfactory assurances.[3] After the Cabinet meeting, at ten minutes past midnight on the twenty-sixth, Day sent Woodford his second major telegram: "For your own guidance, the President suggests that if

2. Day to Woodford, March 20, 1898, *Papers Relating to the Foreign Relations of the United States, 1898* (Washington, 1901), p. 692.

3. James H. Wilson to John J. McCook, March 18, 1898, James Harrison Wilson Papers, Library of Congress (Washington), Letterbook. Sam H. Acheson, *Joe Bailey: The Last Democrat* (New York, 1932), pp. 98–99; Charles G. Dawes, *A Journal of the McKinley Years, Edited, and with a Foreword, by Bascom N. Timmons* (Chicago, 1950), pp. 147–48.

Spain will revoke the reconcentration order and maintain the people until they can support themselves and offer to the Cubans full self-government, with reasonable indemnity, the President will gladly assist in its consummation. If Spain should invite the United States to mediate for peace and the insurgents would make like request, the President might undertake such office of friendship." What did "full self-government, with reasonable indemnity" mean? Woodford asked Day to elucidate. The Acting Secretary replied: "Full self-government with indemnity would mean Cuban independence."[4] One may wonder why Day, if he intended to make so crucial a demand as independence, had not said so outright before being questioned.

Day's third telegram, dated March 27, was also unclear. "See if the following can be done," he told Woodford: first, an armistice lasting until October 1, and peace negotiations between Spain and the rebels under McKinley's good offices; second, an immediate end of reconcentration. To this, "Add, if possible: Third. If terms of peace not satisfactorily settled by October 1, President of the United States to be final arbiter between Spain and insurgents."[5] The meaning of the first two points is reasonably clear. But were they demands? And what was the meaning of the third? Was it a demand? If so, why was it prefaced, "Add, if possible"? Did it mean that the President as "final arbiter" could decree Cuban independence if he so desired? Apparently it did. A few days later Woodford promised that, if given time, he could get peace; thereupon Day inquired: Would this "mean the independence of Cuba?"[6] Interpreting the phrase "final arbiter" in the light of this query and of Day's previous explanation that self-government with indemnity meant "Cuban independence," one must conclude that the administration had decided that Cuban independence was indispensable.

Yet, as far as the record shows, Washington never explicitly informed Madrid of this *sine qua non* of independence.[7] For the inept

4. Day to Woodford, March 26, 1898, *Foreign Relations, 1898,* p. 704; Woodford to Day, March 27, 1898, and Day to Woodford, March 28, 1898, *ibid.,* p. 713.

5. Day to Woodford, March 27, 1898, *ibid.,* pp. 711–12.

6. Woodford to McKinley, April 3, 1898, *ibid.,* p. 732; Day to Woodford, April 3, 1898, *ibid.,* p. 733.

7. May, *Imperial Democracy,* p. 154, says that the administration could not be explicit about a demand for independence, of which conservative Senators would have disapproved, because it was afraid the demand would leak out. This is not convincing, if

diplomacy the administration was most blameworthy. If its minimum demands included Cuban independence, it should have driven this point home and not required Madrid to read between the lines. Moreover, it should have made the demand at an early date, not in late March 1898, when events were escalating dangerously. In this matter one can see a consequence of McKinley's naming of the nearly senile John Sherman to head the State Department (a move made in large part to vacate Sherman's Senate seat for the President's indispensable supporter, Marcus A. Hanna). Sherman would retire a month after the three-point message went off to Madrid. Day, though Acting Secretary, did not have full authority. Charles G. Dawes observed the difficult situation: "As Assistant Secretary of State, William R. Day has proved as great a diplomat in handling the situation within the Department as the International situation without. Upon Day has fallen everything of trouble from without and within. He has been compelled to watch the venerable Secretary and guard the country from his mistakes."[8] Unfortunately Day was no great diplomat at all, though more proficient than McKinley had any right to expect of a man with no adequate training for the position. The President was grievously at fault for entrusting the country's foreign affairs at a critical time to men unequal to the task. Imprecise diplomacy inevitably resulted.

Nevertheless it must be admitted that more praiseworthy appointments probably would not have altered the main events. No Spanish government could have granted Cuban independence no matter how clearly Washington's demands were formulated. How could the proud Spaniards, who had ruled the Ever-Faithful Isle for centuries before the United States was even born, have meekly departed at Yankee behest? The government would have been swept from office; even the monarchy might have fallen, and Spain been rent by civil war.

By the end of March events were fast taking over control from governments. On March 29 Woodford presented Prime Minister Sagasta with the terms of the telegram of the twenty-seventh. However, he did not convey Washington's apparent sense that the three-

only because on March 28 and April 3 the administration did suggest to Woodford outright that it wanted independence.
8. Dawes, *McKinley Years*, p. 156, entry for April 24, 1898.

point message constituted a demand rather than a suggestion, nor the resolve that the President must be allowed to declare Cuba independent if he wished. He said nothing at all about independence. This reticence was not his fault; for he had been instructed only to "see if the following can be done," and "add, if possible." He was not reprimanded when he sent Washington the exact words —containing no mention of independence—he had read to Sagasta.[9] Nor is there evidence that Day himself raised the matter with Minister Polo in Washington.

Spain replied on March 31. She agreed to arbitrate any differences regarding the *Maine;* she said that Captain General Blanco had been ordered to revoke reconcentration;[10] and she declared that she would not "find it inconvenient to accept at once a suspension of hostilities asked for by the insurgents from the general in chief, to whom it will belong in this case to determine the duration and the conditions of the suspension."[11] These were major concessions, and the political and psychological difficulties of making them should not be underrated. Nevertheless they fell far short of Day's terms of March 27. An armistice was ruled out: not the slightest chance existed that the insurgents would request one when effective American intervention was increasingly likely; and even if, almost miraculously, they should make the request, an armistice subject to Spanish definition was not what Washington wanted. Nor did Spain agree to peace negotiations under the President's supervision. Neither did she accept McKinley as "final arbiter" free to declare Cuba independent; but since Woodford had never made the request, her silence was hardly surprising. Despondently, Woodford telegraphed that the Spanish offer meant not peace but "continuation of this destructive, cruel, and now needless war."[12]

9. For the exact words see Woodford to Day, April 1, 1898, *Foreign Relations, 1898,* p. 730.

10. The statement to Woodford was that reconstruction had been revoked in the western provinces. However, Blanco's order of March 30, revoking reconcentration, applied to "the entire island," *ibid.,* p. 738. See correspondence between Polo de Bernabé and Day, *ibid.,* pp. 725, 737.

11. Woodford to Day, March 31, 1898, *ibid.,* pp. 726–27; Woodford translated the Spanish note, and the Minister for Colonies approved his translation. The translation in *Spanish Diplomatic Correspondence and Documents, 1896–1900, Presented at the Cortes by the Minister of State* (Washington, 1905), pp. 107–8, is slightly but not significantly different.

12. Woodford to Day, March 31, 1898, *Foreign Relations, 1898,* p. 727; see also Woodford to McKinley, March 31, 1898, *ibid.*

In all probability Madrid's reply was the spark that made McKinley decide to ask Congress for authority to use force—and once he had turned to Congress war was very nearly, though not quite, inevitable. On April 2, not long after the reply reached Washington late on March 31, Dawes met Secretary of the Treasury Lyman J. Gage following a Cabinet meeting. "He [Gage] is making the argument for peace," Dawes wrote, "but the President does not accord with all his views."[13] McKinley, in fact, had just started to write a special message to Congress.

One chance for peace remained, a very poor one. This was for Spain herself to take the initiative and declare an armistice, not wait for the rebels to request one. Woodford thought that pride would prevent her making so humiliating a move; and he feared that if she did, revolution might result.[14] He might have been correct, had an unexpected development not occurred.

To the great powers of Europe the prospect of Spanish-American hostilities was dismaying. No European government wanted ancient, monarchical Spain, whose Queen Regent was closely related to the British and Austrian royal families, to be humbled by the pushing New World republic. Especially on the Continent sympathy for Spain was strong and widespread. Financial considerations, too, were present. French and other holders of Spanish bonds feared for their investments if war came. Germany took the lead by persuading Austria-Hungary to request Pope Leo XIII to mediate.[15] The Pope asked Archbishop Ireland to see McKinley. After interviews with the President on April 3 and 4, Ireland reported that McKinley wanted peace; and in talks with Polo de Bernabé the Archbishop urged acceptance of the American demands.[16] The Pope also inquired whether Spain would accept his mediation.[17] Spanish pride would weigh much less heavily if she could couch a surrender in religious

13. Dawes, *McKinley Years*, p. 151.

14. Woodford to McKinley, March 31, 1898, *Foreign Relations, 1898*, p. 727.

15. The complicated maneuverings in Europe are described in May, *Imperial Democracy*, chs. 14, 15; and Lester B. Shippee, "Germany and the Spanish-American War," *American Historical Review*, XXX (1925), 754–77.

16. Polo de Bernabé to Foreign Minister Pio Gullon, April 4 and 6, 1898, *Spanish Diplomatic Correspondence*, pp. 111, 112–13; Orestes Ferrara, *The Last Spanish War: Revelations in "Diplomacy"* (New York, 1937), pp. 119–20; Frank T. Reuter, *Catholic Influence on American Colonial Policies, 1898–1904* (Austin, Tex., 1967), pp. 8–11.

17. Merry del Val (Spanish ambassador near the Holy See) to Gullón, April 2, 1898, and Gullón to Merry del Val, April 3, 1898, *Spanish Diplomatic Correspondence*, pp. 109, 110, respectively.

guise; Leo's intervention was therefore welcome at Madrid.

The upshot of considerable diplomatic maneuvering was a Spanish proposal, sent to Washington on April 5, to issue on the sixth "at the request of the Holy Father" an "immediate and unconditional suspension of hostilities," which would be effective when accepted by the rebels and would last until October 5.[18] Day replied rather coldly that McKinley greatly appreciated the Queen's desire for peace, that the United States needed "peace and stable government in Cuba," and that the President would inform Congress, in his message due to be delivered the next day (the sixth), of any Spanish armistice offer.[19] On April 4 Woodford had been told to prepare to leave Spain, and Lee to prepare to leave Cuba; on the fifth the Navy Department issued contingency plans for waging war.[20] All signs pointed to the meaninglessness of the armistice moves.

But McKinley's message did not go to Congress on the sixth after all; at Lee's request he postponed it five days in order to give time to evacuate Americans from Cuba.[21] And Madrid, despite the absence of assurances from Washington, proceeded with the armistice, ordering Blanco to suspend hostilities immediately "for such length of time as he may think prudent." The captain general carried out the order on April 7; and the news was given Woodford officially on the ninth.[22] It was nearly certain that an effective armistice would terminate Spanish sovereignty in Cuba because never, after a long truce, could Spain regain the impetus to fight; and Woodford now advised that an armistice would bring peace.[23] All the American demands, one could maintain, had substantially been met. According to reports, the President considered altering his special message, which had been basically completed by April 4 or 5, so as to bring it into conformity with the new situation, but was

18. Woodford to McKinley, April 5, 1898, *Foreign Relations, 1898*, pp. 734–35.
19. Day to Woodford, April 5, 1898, midnight, *ibid.*, p. 735.
20. Sherman to Woodford, April 4, 1898, *ibid.*, p. 733; Day to Lee, April 4, 1898, National Archives (Washington), Record Group 59, Despatches from United States Consuls in Havana, Roll No. 132; Rear Admiral Montgomery Sicard to Secretary of the Navy John D. Long, Aug. 24, 1898, National Archives, Record Group 45, "A," Naval War Board, I, 1898, Entry 371, p. 356.
21. Day to Woodford, April 6, 1898, *Foreign Relations, 1898*, p. 743.
22. The quoted words come from Woodford's translation of a memorandum given him by Gullón on April 9, 1898, and cabled that same day by Woodford to Day, *ibid.*, p. 746. For the date of April 7 see *ibid.*, p. 750.
23. Woodford to McKinley, April 5, 1898, *ibid.*, p. 735.

strongly advised by congressional leaders not to revise it.[24] He decided to deliver the message as written, except for the addition of a short reference to the armistice.

His decision was made easier by a manifestation of British support. On April 7 the Washington representatives of the six great European powers handed the President a collective note expressing their hope that the United States would act moderately and with regard for the interests of humanity. McKinley replied calmly that he shared their wish "for the re-establishment of order in the island, so terminating the chronic condition of disturbance there."[25] The reference to the "chronic" disturbance was significant, as pointing to the basic American grievance. But much more significant was the role of the British government in the preparation of the note. When it was still under consideration, the Foreign Office had instructed Ambassador Pauncefote to ascertain the views of the American government. Accordingly, Sir Julian had shown Acting Secretary Day a draft of the note; and when Day disapproved of it, Pauncefote had secured the consent of the other envoys to an amended version. Consequently, the note, as presented to McKinley, was worded to meet American wishes.[26] This British solicitude was most reassuring to Washington. We have seen that the Continental powers sympathized with Spain. The key to their possible intervention to save that country lay in London, because British naval power would be decisive in 1898 (as it had been in 1823 when a European move on behalf of Spain was contemplated). Any apprehensions felt by Washington that Spain might not stand alone in the event of war must have been removed by Britain's considerate attitude at a critical moment.

The President's decision to turn to Congress was also made easier

24. Washington *Post,* April 10, 1898, quoted in *Congressional Record,* 55 Cong., 2 Sess., p. 3765 (April 12, 1898); May, *Imperial Democracy,* p. 157.

25. The collective note (dated April 6, 1898) and the President's reply are in *Foreign Relations, 1898,* pp. 740–41.

26. Foreign Office to Pauncefote, March 28, 1898, Public Record Office (London), Foreign Office 115/1087; John Hay (American ambassador to Great Britain) to Sherman, April 6, 1898, National Archives, Record Group 59, Great Britain, Despatches. See also Charles S. Campbell, *Anglo-American Understanding, 1898–1903* (Baltimore, 1957), pp. 31–32; Robert G. Neale, *Great Britain and United States Expansion: 1898–1900* (East Lansing, 1966), pp. 14–15. Regarding Pauncefote's less friendly position of April 14 see Campbell, *Anglo-American Understanding,* pp. 32–36, 244–53; Alexander E. Campbell, *Great Britain and the United States, 1895–1903* (Glasgow, 1960), pp. 142–46; and Neale, *Great Britain and United States Expansion,* pp. 15–30.

by a modification in the attitude of businessmen. The outlook of so diverse a group is difficult to assess, but the evidence indicates that the business community, on the whole, opposed hostilities almost to the end. We find, for example, that when a rumor of an armistice reached Wall Street on March 28, stock prices instantly rose. We find, further, the Boston Chamber of Commerce lauding McKinley on March 31 for withstanding war pressures, and the Trades League of Philadelphia appealing to Congress on April 5 to cooperate with the President in seeking peace. As late as April 7 the New York Chamber of Commerce unanimously passed a resolution applauding "the pacific policy so wisely, patiently and nobly pursued by the President."[27] On the twelfth, Representative Jeremiah D. Botkin complained that Congress was being "flooded" with telegrams from business interests in favor of peace. Pauncefote, too, noted that influential members of Congress were being "earnestly canvassed" by New York financial circles to work for peace.[28]

As the days passed, however, an atmosphere of the inevitability of conflict settled upon the country. Suspense mounted; business planning became difficult. Near the end of March an administration consultant found that the big corporations would welcome war "as a relief to suspense."[29] And on April 13, as hostilities drew near, Senator Henry Cabot Lodge observed: "All men in this country are agreed to-day . . . that this situation must end. We can not go on indefinitely with this strain, this suspense, and this uncertainty, this tottering upon the verge of war. It is killing to business."[30] Ideally,

27. The *Times* (London), March 29, 1898. Joseph R. Leeson, president of the Boston Chamber of Commerce, to Secretary of the Navy Long, March 31, 1898, Gardner W. Allen (ed.), *Papers of John Davis Long, 1897–1904* (Boston, 1939), p. 81; the resolution of the Trades League is in *Congressional Record*, 55 Cong., 2 Sess., p. 3698 (April 11, 1898); regarding the New York Chamber see New York *Herald*, April 8, 1898, and the *Times* (London), April 8, 1898. For differing views on the attitude of businessmen see Julius W. Pratt, "American Business and the Spanish-American War," *Hispanic American Historical Review*, XIV (1934), 163–201; Nancy L. O'Connor, "The Influence of Populist Legislators upon American Foreign Policy, 1892–1898" (Master of Science thesis, University of Oregon, 1958).

28. *Congressional Record*, 55 Cong., 2 Sess., p. 3746 (April 12, 1898); Pauncefote to Salisbury, April 12, 1898, Foreign Office 5/2517.

29. William C. Reick to John Russell Young, March 25, 1898, "The Spanish American War: Business Recovery, and the China Market: Selected Documents and Commentary," *Studies on the Left*, I (1960), 59. See also William A. Williams, *The Tragedy of American Diplomacy* (Cleveland, 1959), p. 34.

30. *Congressional Record*, 55 Cong., 2 Sess., p. 3781 (April 13, 1898).

the business world preferred peace; but if war was fated to come, the sooner it came the better. The relaxation of business opposition to war facilitated McKinley's difficult decision to appeal to Congress.

The message went to Congress on April 11. Describing the rebellion as "the successor of other similar insurrections which have occurred in Cuba against the dominion of Spain, extending over a period of nearly half a century," the President requested authority "to take measures to secure a full and final termination of hostilities between the Government of Spain and the people of Cuba, and to secure in the island the establishment of a stable government, capable of maintaining order and observing its international obligations." He expressed strong opposition to recognition of the rebels. In two brief terminal paragraphs he mentioned the armistice, and said he was sure Congress would give it "just and careful attention." He concluded, "The issue is now with Congress."[31]

McKinley was blamed by some people at the time, and has been blamed by many more subsequently, for not stressing the armistice. The message has come to be considered a war message. But in 1898 warmongers denounced it angrily, whereas peace lovers heaved a sigh of relief. Pauncefote believed that "war is certainly less imminent since the delivery of the President's Message, which is said to have gravely disappointed the War Party."[32] James H. Wilson, a prominent businessman, thought the message "too ethical, in short too nice."[33] Gamaliel Bradford, the well-known author, who opposed war, could scarcely wait to express his pleasure to Secretary of the Navy Long: "You can hardly imagine the faint and trembling eagerness with which I seized the President's message and the infinite relief and gratitude which followed from reading it. It is all that could possibly be expected."[34] The message was well received in European capitals. London considered it "on the whole, temperate and fair," and Berlin as "warranting a somewhat more hopeful view"; even Madrid thought its "spirit admittedly moderate and as

31. James D. Richardson (ed.), *A Compilation of the Messages and Papers of the Presidents* . . . (20 vols., New York, 1916), XIV, 6281, 6292, 6286–89.
32. Pauncefote to Salisbury, April 12, 1898, Foreign Office 115/1079.
33. Wilson to Senator William P. Frye, April 11, 1898, Wilson Papers, Letterbook. Regarding Wilson see David F. Healy, *US Expansionism: The Imperialist Urge in the 1890s* (Madison, 1970), ch. 4.
34. Bradford to Long, April 11, 1898, Allen, *Papers of Long*, p. 92.

conciliatory as circumstances permit, while Spain's concession in the matter of the armistice finds due acknowledgement." A Havana newspaper was reported to believe that the message made war unlikely.[35]

All this, however, did not justify the appeal to Congress. McKinley was running the gravest risk of ensuring hostilities. In his annual message of 1897 he had asserted that intervention should not occur at a time of "hopeful change" in Spanish policy. (He was referring to the reforms just made by the Liberals.) Why then, four months later, did he request authority to intervene when another hopeful change—nothing less than an armistice declaration—had appeared? The easiest explanation is that he caved in under pressure. McKinley has been depicted as well-intentioned but spineless—"a victim of . . . amiable weakness," according to Grover Cleveland[36] —a man who capitulated under fire from Congress. But the truth is not so simple as that.

In appraising the President's fateful decision to turn to Congress, several points need consideration. First, one wonders what would have happened had McKinley been informed of an armistice declaration soon after Woodford's interview with Sagasta on March 31. Might he not have prepared an altogether different message, and might not hostilities, just possibly, have been averted? But as things were, the President, learning on about the thirty-first that the armistice he wanted was not forthcoming, steeled himself to ask Congress for authority to use force. Thereafter the pressure on him became extreme. He found it difficult to sleep, even with drugs. Secretary Long noted on April 4: "He has been robbed of sleep, overworked, and I fancy that I can see that his mind does not work as clearly and as self-reliantly as it otherwise would." His private secretary wrote a few days later: "The President does not look well at all. . . . His haggard face and anxious inquiry for news . . . tell of

35. The *Times* (London), April 12, 13, 1898; New York *Herald,* April 13, 1898. But the British chargé d'affaires at Madrid reported that the Spanish ministry viewed the message as a step toward Cuban annexation. G. Barclay to Salisbury, April 16, 1898, Foreign Office 72/2062.

36. Walter Millis, *The Martial Spirit; A Study of Our War with Spain* (Cambridge, Mass., 1931), p. 161; Theodore Roosevelt's observation about McKinley is well known: he "has no more backbone than a chocolate eclair." Henry F. Pringle, *Theodore Roosevelt* (New York, 1931), p. 178.

the sense of tremendous responsibility." Adding to his worry was his wife, who was in very poor health.[37] Amid these manifold strains, McKinley lacked the stamina to make another agonizing readjustment when he heard of the armistice declaration. Spain had delayed too long. The psychological moment had passed.

Another point to be considered in judging the message is whether the armistice had any chance of becoming effective. There is considerable evidence that it would not even have gone into effect, none that it would have. On several occasions the Juntas and the insurgents themselves had expressed opposition to an armistice without a guarantee of Cuban independence.[38] Calixto García, a rebel leader, had issued orders on November 6, 1897, not to accept autonomy; and on March 9, 1898, Máximo Gómez, the commander in chief, had demanded "absolute independence."[39] Other rebels insisted that they would continue to fight unless Spain agreed to leave the island. "Nobody wants an armistice here" in Havana, a reporter of the New York *Sun* asserted.[40]

Nor would Spanish loyalists in Cuba be likely to accept an armistice. If they had rioted in January over autonomy, would they not sooner or later react more violently against this enormously larger capitulation of April? The "great majority" of the army and navy in Cuba were described as being "most decidedly in favour of a war with the United States."[41]

Finally, an armistice was not certain to be accepted even in Spain. An editorial in the London *Times* on April 11 warned that an armistice might mean a Spanish civil war. And in fact the armistice news brought turmoil to Madrid. "It is not too much to say," the *Times* reported on the fourteenth, "that ever since the armistice was made

37. Margaret Leech, *In the Days of McKinley* (New York, 1959), p. 181; Herman H. Kohlsaat, *From McKinley to Harding: Personal Recollections of Our Presidents* (New York, 1923), pp. 66–67.

38. George W. Auxier, "The Propaganda Activities of the Cuban *Junta* in Precipitating the Spanish-American War, 1895–1898," *Hispanic American Historical Review*, XIX (1939), 304; the *Times* (London), April 7, 1898.

39. *Congressional Record*, 55 Cong., 2 Sess., p. 3957 (April 16, 1898), p. 3975 (April 16, 1898); the *Times* (London), April 12, 1898; see also Joseph E. Wisan, *The Cuban Crisis as Reflected in the New York Press (1895–1898)* (New York, 1934), p. 189.

40. The *Times* (London), April 7 and 22, 1898; New York *Sun*, April 11, 1898, quoted in *Congressional Record*, 55 Cong., 2 Sess., p. 3884 (April 15, 1898).

41. The *Times* (London), April 14, 1898; the article was dated Havana, April 2.

public on Saturday afternoon [April 9] this city has been under martial law."[42] A similar description came from the American naval attaché in Madrid: "There was . . . for two days, considerable danger of a mob riot in Madrid after the announcement of the proclamation of the armistice in Cuba."[43]

If the armistice did not become effective, prolonged chaos in Cuba could be expected—unless the United States acted to stop it. Chronic turmoil in so strategic an area was the one thing that Americans, by April 1898, would no longer tolerate. The Republican platform of 1896 had stated that the United States should control Hawaii; build, own, and operate an isthmian canal; and bring independence to Cuba. In his most recent annual message the President, after recounting events in Cuba, had turned to the two other foreign-policy objectives stressed in that platform: Hawaii and a Central American canal. Regarding Hawaii he argued that annexation was fated to take place before much longer. Then, with reference to a canal, he said: "A subject of large importance to our country, and increasing appreciation on the part of the people, is the completion of the great highway of trade between the Atlantic and Pacific. . . ."[44] For years the Republican party had asserted the need to build a canal and to acquire bases in Hawaii and the Caribbean. So had A. T. Mahan and other expansionists, persuaded as they were that geographic and economic forces prescribed these objectives; and by the late 1890s their message was receiving considerable public approval. The long island of Cuba dominated routes between American ports and the prospective waterway. McKinley supported this basic three-cornered objective of foreign policy—an isthmian canal, control of Hawaii, a Caribbean base. He could not have overlooked Cuba's importance for American vital interests.

In the absence of an effective armistice, authorization to intervene forcibly appeared necessary for two other reasons besides that of the national interest: one humanitarian, the other political. The recent indications that Spain had lost her grip on Cuba meant that only the United States could terminate the horrible strife so near

42. *Ibid.*, April 11 and 14, 1898.
43. Lieutenant G. L. Dyer to Chief Intelligence Officer, Navy Department, Washington, April 16, 1898, National Archives, Record Group 45, Strategy Board, No. 1, Entry 372, pp. 31–32.
44. Message of Dec. 6, 1897, Richardson, *Messages and Papers*, XIV, 6263, 6265.

her shores. The beautiful island seemed to be foundering in a welter of bloodshed. The London *Times* correspondent in Cuba had written: "I see no way out of this terrible mess in Cuba, unless the United States intervenes. . . . The Spaniards seems [*sic*] unable to do anything towards crushing the rebellion. . . ."[45] A limited war for humanitarian ends could make sense in those years. William James expressed the idealistic motive to a French friend: "The European nations of the Continent cannot believe that our pretense of humanity, and our disclaiming of all ideas of conquest, is sincere. It has been *absolutely* sincere! The self-conscious feeling of our people has been entirely based in a sense of philanthropic duty, without which not a step would have been taken."[46]

We come now to the political situation. The Republicans had won the presidency in 1896 only after the fright of their lives. The free-silver heresy still divided the country; radical Populism was not entirely dead. Congressional elections in 1898 loomed ahead. At the end of March that dangerous Democratic firebrand, as Republicans considered Bryan, visited Washington. "Yes," he told reporters, "the time for intervention has arrived. Humanity demands that we shall act. Cuba lies almost within sight of our shores and the sufferings of her people can not be ignored unless we, as a nation, have become so engrossed in money making as to be indifferent to distress."[47] Republicans felt obliged to reply in kind. In April 1898 congressional excitement reached a pitch that McKinley could ignore only at great peril to himself and his party. He could not have forgotten how Grover Cleveland had split the Democrats over the silver question—and seen the Democratic party fall to pieces. Senator Lodge had warned McKinley on March 21 that if the Cuban fighting dragged on all summer without action from Washington, the Republicans would suffer a stunning defeat in the November elections. Senators and Representatives were reported to be pre-

45. Pauncefote to Salisbury, May 19, 1896, enclosing a letter to himself from the correspondent dated May 13, 1896, Lord Salisbury Papers, Christ Church Library (Oxford).

46. James to François Pillon, June 15, 1898, Henry James (ed.), *The Letters of William James* (2 vols., Boston, 1920), II, 74; see also James to Professor Theodore Flournoy, June 17, 1898, Ralph B. Perry, *The Thought and Character of William James* (2 vols., Boston, 1935), II, 307.

47. Washington *Post*, April 1, 1898, quoted in *Congressional Record*, 55 Cong., 2 Sess., p. 4023 (April 18, 1898).

dicting that Congress would "run away" from the President and declare for Cuban independence unless he took strong steps at once.[48]

It may well be wondered, granting that the armistice would in all likelihood fail, why McKinley did not wait two or three weeks to test it. Perhaps he could not have endured, psychologically, such a delay himself. In any case he had strained congressional patience nearly to the breaking point; a further postponement of his message would have entailed the gravest risk of provoking such an explosion in Congress as to endanger party unity. On the other hand, a delay was by no means certain to head off war.

In addition to these points—Spain's lateness in declaring the armistice, the strong probability that the armistice would not prove effective, humanitarian sentiment, and the delicate political situation—another point should be considered in appraising the President's famous message of April 11. It was an unusual sort of intervention for which he requested authority, unusual in two ways. First, he did not ask for war, but for authorization to use force if sometime in the future that should appear desirable to him. Second, assuming that he should one day resort to force, it would not necessarily be applied against Spain alone. Specifically, he asked Congress to authorize him to intervene "as an *impartial neutral,* by imposing a rational compromise between the contestants." He explained: "The forcible intervention of the United States *as a neutral to stop the war* . . . is justifiable on rational grounds. It involves, however, hostile constraint upon *both* the parties to the contest, as well *to enforce a truce* as to guide the eventual settlement."[49] By the plain meaning of these words the President's plan was this: holding in reserve the discretionary power to use force, he would continue negotiations; if he still could not obtain a peaceful solution, he would then use force against both Spain and the rebels to compel them to stop fighting and to make a lasting settlement. No wonder that many members of Congress were amazed. Senator Marion Butler exclaimed, "That message does not mean the independence of Cuba. The message means, if it means anything, that the President asks Congress to authorize him to make the Cubans stop fighting for

48. Lodge to McKinley, March 21, 1898, quoted in May, *Imperial Democracy,* p. 146; New York *Herald,* April 4, 1898. See also Wisan, *Cuban Crisis,* p. 428.
49. Richardson, *Messages and Papers,* XIV, 6289; italics inserted.

their liberty. . . ." Senator Edmund W. Pettus observed correctly: "We are advised to delegate to the President the power to intervene between Spain and Cuba for the purpose of putting an end to the war, and to use the Army and Navy at his discretion and force both parties to keep the peace. . . ." Other Senators were shocked that the President did not want an independent Cuba but only a "stable government."[50]

Was McKinley sincere in proposing impartial intervention? Could he really have believed it possible that Congress would efface itself to the extent of giving him the discretionary powers requested, and (if it should do so) that proud Spain would meekly accept his tutelage? The probability is that he did. Congress *might* vote the discretionary powers, as it had done with the $50 million the previous month; Spain, having conceded so much, *might* permit impartial intervention. No doubt the chances were slim, but what alternative procedure had any chance at all of ending the intolerable disorder peaceably, without splitting the Republicans and opening the way to Bryan and the radicals?

The President must be blamed, however, because of the phraseology of his message. He should have given Madrid full credit for the armistice, while at the same time elucidating the tragic circumstances involving Spain, the insurgents, and the United States that made implementing it next to impossible. Possibly he should have counseled a delay of a week or two in order to give the armistice move a trial. He should have been more candid about the legitimate American interests involved. To have done all this would probably not have altered the main developments one iota. The Spanish-American War still, almost certainly, would have occurred. But McKinley would have delivered a dignified, intelligent paper that would have enhanced his and the country's reputation in the eyes of contemporary and future critics. His fault lay not so much in mistaking realities as in neglecting appearances—which should never be discounted.

Ideally, Spain should have faced facts and yielded. Her whole past history and her present political situation made this impossible. If

50. *Congressional Record,* 55 Cong., 2 Sess., p. 3703 (April 11, 1898), p. 3731 (April 12, 1898), p. 4074 (April 19, 1898), pp. 4096–97 (April 20, 1898). See also Sam Acheson, "Joseph W. Bailey and the Spanish War," *Southwest Review,* XVII (1932), 157–58.

by mid-April 1898 American politics made it virtually impossible for Washington to delay, Spanish politics made it altogether impossible for Madrid to set Cuba free. By then both countries were caught up in forces making hostilities nearly inevitable.

With the delivery of the message war became probable, but a slight chance existed that Congress would adopt a resolution along the lines requested by the President. If so, hostilities could, conceivably, still be avoided. The House of Representatives was the first to act. On April 13 it adopted, 325 to 19, a resolution much to McKinley's liking that directed him to intervene to stop the Cuban fighting, but only "authorized and empowered" him (thus giving him the discretion) to use armed force. Yet the vote reflected not so much the House's true feeling, which was swinging strongly toward war, as it did administration pressure and the firm grip of Speaker Reed, who still hoped for peace; it was significant that another resolution, *directing* the use of force, had failed earlier on that same day by the much narrower margin of 190 to 150.[51]

The Senate Foreign Relations Committee reported three resolutions that were distinctly unwelcome to the President. They recommended that "the people of the Island of Cuba are, and of right ought to be, free and independent"; that the United States demand that Spain evacuate Cuba; and that the President be "directed and empowered," not simply authorized, to use force if necessary to make the resolutions effective. A minority resolution, known as the Turpie amendment (to the first resolution), demanded also "the immediate recognition of the Republic of Cuba."[52]

McKinley was so opposed to recognition that he would have vetoed a measure providing for it. He did not want his hands to be tied, nor did he consider the rebels yet worthy of recognition.[53] But Populists and some Democrats and Silver Republicans were convinced that his real motive was to retain the bargaining power to compel a rebel government to honor the hundreds of millions of dollars' worth of Cuban bonds issued by Spain. As Senator William M. Stewart, Silver Republican of Nevada, asserted, the President

51. *Congressional Record,* 55 Cong., 2 Sess., pp. 3820–21, 3819–20 (April 13, 1898).

52. *Ibid.,* pp. 3773, 3776 (April 13, 1898); Paul S. Holbo, "Presidential Leadership in Foreign Affairs: William McKinley and the Turpie-Foraker Amendment," *American Historical Review,* LXXII (1967), 1321–35.

53. Dawes, *McKinley Years,* p. 154, entry of April 17, 1898; Holbo, "Presidential Leadership," p. 1324.

wanted Cuba to be "liable for the payment of the $400,000,000 of Spanish debt secured on that island."[54]

A vehement argument developed over the Turpie recognition amendment, which monopolized attention to the extent that the distinction between authorizing and directing the use of force was largely lost sight of. The President and his Senate supporters became preoccupied with combating the amendment. Their strategy was to defeat it, and then persuade the Senate to adopt the House resolution. But on April 16 the Senate passed the amendment, 51 to 37.[55] Five Democrats and 32 Republicans voted against it; 28 Democrats, 5 Populists, 4 Silver Republicans, and 1 Independent joined 13 regular Republicans to pass it. Seven of these 13 Republicans came from west of the Mississippi River and 1 from Minnesota. Thus a coalition of Democrats, Populists, and western Republicans defied the President. The nearly solid Democratic vote undoubtedly owed something to the presence in Washington of the party's leader, Bryan, who on April 13 pronounced himself in favor of recognizing Cuba.[56]

The Senate proceeded to pass, 67 to 21, the three resolutions reported by the Foreign Relations Committee, together with the Turpie amendment. In addition it adopted another amendment, the Teller amendment, proposed by Senator Henry M. Teller of Colorado (in the end it was given the status of a fourth resolution). The Teller amendment disclaimed "any disposition or intention to exercise sovereignty, jurisdiction, or control over" Cuba except to pacify it, and announced American intent "to leave the government and control of the island to its people."[57] With its vote to recognize the republic of Cuba and to direct the President to intervene, the Senate stood in solid opposition to the House.

Each branch of Congress refused to yield. If the House had its way

54. *Congressional Record,* 55 Cong., 2 Sess., p. 3901 (April 15, 1898). A large number of similar assertions is in the *Congressional Record* for April, 1898. See also O'Connor, "Influence of Populist Legislators," ch. 5; Senator William E. Chandler to Paul Dana (editor of the New York *Sun*), April 5, 17, 1898, William E. Chandler Papers, Library of Congress (Washington).

55. *Congressional Record,* 55 Cong., 2 Sess., p. 3988 (April 16, 1898).

56. See the statement of Senator Eugene Hale, *ibid.,* p. 3990 (April 16, 1898).

57. *Ibid.,* p. 3993 (April 16, 1898). Auxier, "Propaganda Activities of the Cuban *Junta,"* p. 304, thinks that the United States sugar-beet industry was probably behind the amendment; for other possible explanations see Healy, *United States in Cuba,* pp. 24–27.

war might, just possibly, still be averted. The climax came on April 18. In an effort to resolve the impasse a House-Senate committee of six was appointed. Twice it met on the eighteenth; twice it reported back its failure to each branch, and twice each branch refused to compromise. At one time that hectic day Senator Cushman K. Davis, chairman of the Foreign Relations Committee, moved that the Senate concur in House amendments of its resolutions that would have given the President substantially what he wanted. The motion was defeated 46 to 32,[58] an outcome that would have been reversed if only 7 of the 14 Republicans voting nay had changed their minds. But as things were, a deadlock existed. Would Congress really have to advise the President that it could not agree and that he would have to reassume the task of dealing with Spain? (Could it even be that McKinley had anticipated disagreement, as a means of regaining control of events, when on April 11 he made his unusual recommendations to Congress?) The deadlock was not to endure. War fever was sweeping the country, and members of Congress could not help but catch the heady infection. "Sir, this country appears to be swept from its feet by a perfect cyclone of passion," Senator Donelson Caffery of Louisiana had exclaimed on April 16.[59] By the eighteenth the administration and Speaker Reed could hold the House no longer. Reed faced a revolt, as emotionalism and the martial spirit engulfed the chamber; he knew that he must compromise, and his decision was to accept the Senate resolutions except for the recognition of Cuba.[60]

Late on the same day, April 18, the House-Senate committee met a third time. At 1:15 A.M. on Tuesday, April 19, its report went to the Senate. This time the committee had been able to compromise

58. *Congressional Record*, 55 Cong., 2 Sess., pp. 4017–18, 4033, 4060 (April 18, 1898).

59. *Ibid.*, 3958 (April 16, 1898). See also Edward Atkinson, "Jingoes and Silverites," *North American Review*, CLXI (1895), 558; Henry S. Pritchett, "Some Recollections of President McKinley and the Cuban Intervention," *ibid.*, CLXXXIX (1909), 397–403; May, *Imperial Democracy*, ch. 11.

60. New York *Herald*, April 18 and 19, 1898. Senator Chandler, who wanted war, wrote Paul Dana, April 19, 1898: "If it had not been for the *Ten* [presumably ten Senators who agreed with Chandler] and for *organized* action on the part of the Ten we would have had the House resolutions accepted by the Senate; and they were little more than authority to continue negotiations. . . . we should have been compelled to accept the House action at the dictation of Aldrich, Hale, spooner [*sic*] *et al* if it had not been for our radical movement. But when Reed & Co. decided to accept the Senate amendment without recognition the *main battle was won.*" Chandler Papers.

on a joint resolution: the House conferees had agreed that the people of Cuba were free and independent (hitherto they had agreed only that they ought to be free and independent), and the Senate conferees had accepted that the republic of Cuba was not to be recognized. The President was to be directed, not simply authorized, to use force. The weary Senators voted on the resolution; the result was close. Forty-two favored the compromise; thirty-five did not. Rather than yield their stubbornly contested point that the Cuban government must be recognized, all the Populists in effect voted against war by opposing the compromise; so did all the Silver Republicans and many southern and western Democrats. Not a single northeastern Democrat and not a single regular Republican voted against the compromise.[61] The resolution then went to the House, which approved it, 311 to 6.[62]

President McKinley signed the joint resolution on April 20, 1898. The people of Cuba were declared independent; Spain was to evacuate the island; the President was directed to use force; and the United States was not to exercise permanent sovereignty over Cuba. Immediately an ultimatum was sent to Spain: unless by noon April 23 she agreed to relinquish her authority in Cuba, the United States would use force to carry out the terms of the resolution. It was politically and psychologically impossible for Spain to accept this dictation, and she broke off diplomatic relations.[63] On April 25, 1898, Congress declared that a state of war had been in effect since and including the twenty-first.[64] After so many months of tension and uncertainty, of alternating hope for peace and gloomy foreboding, of pressure by war hawks, Juntas, and journalists, the conflict had come.

The United States, it is clear, had ample justification to intervene. She could not have been expected to endure much longer the

61. *Congressional Record*, 55 Cong., 2 Sess., pp. 4040–41 (April 18, 1898). Turpie from Indiana was, geographically, the nearest to being a northeastern Democrat who voted against the compromise; Mitchell was a Democrat from Wisconsin. Cannon, Jones of Nevada, and Pettigrew were Republicans voting against the compromise. Cannon was to affiliate himself with the Democrats in 1900; Jones probably should not be termed a regular Republican; Pettigrew had voted for Bryan in 1896.

62. *Ibid.*, pp. 4063–64 (April 18, 1898).

63. Sherman to Woodford, April 20, 1898, *Foreign Relations, 1898*, pp. 762–63; Polo de Bernabé to Sherman, April 20, 1898, and Woodford to Sherman, April 21, 1898, *ibid.*, pp. 765, 766, respectively.

64. *Congressional Record*, 55 Cong., 2 Sess., p. 4244 (April 25, 1898).

chronic disorder in a vital area, an area soon to come into the greatest prominence with the decision to construct the Panama canal. Nor could the American people have been expected to endure much longer the horrible slaughter just off their shores. For too many years Spain had failed to fulfill a government's primary obligation: to provide orderly conditions. Judging by his last annual message, President Cleveland had drawn this conclusion, and certainly McKinley did so.

But granted the justification, could not the United States have limited herself to diplomatic intervention? Once President McKinley had made up his mind to accept no settlement short of early Cuban independence from Spain, war became extremely difficult, perhaps impossible, to avoid. Could McKinley have stopped short of demanding independence? His administration was more pro-rebel than Cleveland's had been, and by April 1898 the American Congress and people probably would have insisted on Spanish withdrawal from the distressed island, and that meant Cuban independence. Was the war, then, inevitable by the spring of 1898? Very likely it was. But both Washington and Madrid should have done more than they did to test the matter. McKinley should have made his demand for independence perfectly clear to Spain; and, if possible, he should have delayed his message of April 11 to Congress and waited to see whether the armistice, by some miracle, would be effective. Madrid should, if possible, have faced reality and made concessions earlier. The chances are strong, as we have seen, that these steps—if indeed they could have been taken at all—would not have stopped the drift to war. But every government confronting a probable catastrophe has the obligation to do its utmost to avoid it, no matter how hopeless the situation may appear. Human judgment is fallible; seemingly hopeless action may succeed.

In a larger perspective, the Spanish-American War, like the Mexican War, was a consequence of the disintegration of the Spanish empire. Few are the great empires of history that have broken up without forceful intervention from outside; and the Spanish empire furnished no exception. In 1898 Cuba and Puerto Rico alone remained to Spain. She had held on to them too long, through too many years of disorder. Perhaps a peaceful separation could have been arranged at an earlier date. But in April 1898, in the last agony of the old empire, the United States and Spain could no longer handle the situation rationally and not lapse into warfare.

CHAPTER 15

# Fait Accompli at Manila Bay

THE Spanish-American War had scarcely begun when a surprising event occurred. News reached the United States, not of fighting in nearby Cuba, but of a victory by Commodore George Dewey over the Spanish fleet at Manila Bay, about as far from the Caribbean as possible. Momentous consequences were to follow.

At the beginning of a war focused on Cuba how did an American naval squadron happen to find itself in the Philippines? The telegram that Assistant Secretary of the Navy Theodore Roosevelt sent on February 25, 1898, to Commodore Dewey, who was in command of the Asiatic squadron at Nagasaki, Japan, is well known: "Order the squadron except *Monocacy* to Hong Kong. Keep full of coal. In the event of declaration war Spain, your duty will be to see that the Spanish squadron does not leave the Asiatic coast, and then offensive operations in Philippine Islands." As instructed, Dewey did move his little fleet to Hong Kong, where it stood poised to attack the Spanish in the nearby islands.

Roosevelt's telegram expressed no brilliant new idea. For years Washington had considered attacking the Philippines in the event of war. As early as 1876 an American naval officer, disguised as a civilian, had investigated Manila's defenses.[1] In 1896 a naval intelligence officer, Lieutenant William M. Kimball, had devised a plan to seize Manila; and before the outbreak of hostilities the American

1. Notes of a report of April 1876 by Lieutenant Royal R. Ingersoll, George Dewey Papers, Library of Congress (Washington), Box 56.

consul at Manila, Oscar F. Williams, had been forwarding Dewey military information about that Spanish base.[2] Roosevelt himself had advised McKinley in September 1897 that the Asiatic squadron should attack Manila if war came, and the President approved Roosevelt's order of February 25, 1898.[3] It made sense to strike at Spain wherever she was vulnerable; and a loss in the Philippines would weaken her in Cuba as well. Moreover, Spanish warships, left unchecked in the islands, could prey upon American commerce and threaten the west coast of the United States. In the first days of the war, insurance rates on Pacific shipping rose, and Dewey's victory relieved Americans of the need to pay excessive premiums.[4] If only to safeguard American commerce, a move against the Spanish ships was called for.

Just after the war started, Washington sent Dewey another message, dated April 24, 1898: "Proceed at once to the Philippine Islands. Commence operations at once, particularly against the Spanish fleet. You must capture vessels or destroy. Use utmost endeavors."[5] Unlike the February order, which could have been countermanded by Roosevelt's superiors had they disapproved of it, this April order did ensure an attack on the Spanish; however, had their warships been dispersed among the islands no dramatic victory would have occurred to electrify Americans. As it was, the ships were concentrated in Manila Bay; and on May 2 there reached the United States an unofficial report of a triumph in the Far East, of all places. "Great Victory at Manila," the New York *Tribune* excit-

2. William R. Braisted, *The United States Navy in the Pacific, 1897–1909* (Austin, Tex., 1958), pp. 21–22; Williams to Thomas W. Cridler (Third Assistant Secretary of State), March 27, 1898, *Correspondence Relating to the War with Spain . . . from April 15, 1898, to July 30, 1902* (Washington, 1902), p. 652; memorandum of Captain Arent S. Crowninshield for the Office of Naval Intelligence, March 10, 1898, National Archives (Washington), Record Group 45, Area 10 File, Box 16. For an account of the Kimball plan see John A. S. Grenville and George B. Young, *Politics, Strategy, and American Diplomacy: Studies in Foreign Policy, 1873–1917* (New Haven, 1966), pp. 270–76.

3. Paolo E. Coletta, "McKinley, the Peace Negotiations, and the Acquisition of the Philippines," *Pacific Historical Review*, XXX (1961), 342; Charles A. Beard, *The Idea of National Interest: An Analytical Study in American Foreign Policy* (New York, 1934), p. 80.

4. Everett Frazar (an American with business interests in China) to McKinley, Nov. 11, 1898, National Archives, Record Group 59, Miscellaneous Letters.

5. Ernest R. May, *Imperial Democracy: The Emergence of America as a Great Power* (New York, 1961), p. 244.

edly announced, and the *Herald* declared, "Spain's Asiatic Fleet Destroyed by Dewey." This wonderful news, too good to be unreservedly accepted at once, seemed to be confirmed on the third, and Secretary of the Navy Long cabled congratulations to the new American hero.[6]

But thereafter, for several days, the rejoicing gave way to gnawing anxiety. A report from Dewey himself was expected imminently, but none came. News did arrive on May 3 that the cable line between Manila and Hong Kong, the only one out of the Philippines, had been cut on the day of the battle—by Dewey's own orders, as it turned out.[7] The supposition then was that the commodore had sent the revenue cutter *McCulloch* to Hong Kong after the battle, and that a cable from there would reach Washington on the third or fourth. But the third and fourth and even the fifth passed, still without official word. "No Fears About Commodore Dewey," the New York *Herald* bravely assured its readers on the sixth, and Secretary Long expressed his own confidence. Fears were felt, however. What dreadful thing might have happened in that remote and silent bay? The suspense was terrible. In London on the seventh anxiety was reflected in the lobbies of Parliament, where "Sinister speculations were indulged in. . . ."[8]

On that very day, May 7, Thomas W. Cridler, Third Assistant Secretary of State, whose turn it was to sleep overnight at the State Department, was awakened at four forty in the morning by a messenger with a three-word cable just received from Consul Edwin Wildman at Hong Kong: "Hong Kong, McCulloch, Wildman."[9] Here was the thrilling news that the *McCulloch* had at length arrived —Dewey had not bothered to dispatch her from Manila until four days after the battle—and hard upon it came the eagerly awaited report from the commodore. He had destroyed the Spanish squadron with no American loss.

At the tremendous news, the more welcome because it ended

6. New York *Tribune* and New York *Herald*, May 2, 1898; Charles G. Dawes, *A Journal of the McKinley Years, Edited, and with a Foreword, by Bascom N. Timmons* (Chicago, 1950), p. 158, wrote on May 3 that the news was "confirmed."

7. New York *Tribune*, May 4, 1898, citing news from London that the cable had been cut at 10 A.M., May 2, 50 miles from Manila. W. Cameron Forbes, *The Philippine Islands* (2 vols., Boston, 1928), I, 63.

8. New York *Herald*, May 6, 1898; New York *Tribune*, May 7, 1898.

9. New York *Tribune*, May 8, 1898.

such suspense, paeans of exultation broke forth across the United States. Overnight Dewey became a national hero. Pictures of his handsome countenance appeared everywhere; babies, streets, hotels—the list was endless—were named for him; manufacturers capitalized on his rapidly growing legend; reporters rushed to his flagship to write rapturous articles. The Philippine Islands, up to then virtually unknown to Americans, became a focal point of interest; and the longer Dewey stayed at Manila Bay, the less preposterous did it seem that the United States might be there for good. May 1, 1898, was a fateful date in American history.

A few people quickly realized the possibilities opened up by the brilliant triumph. "We hold the other side of the Pacific and the value to this country is almost beyond imagination," Senator Henry Cabot Lodge rejoiced.[10] For years the Navy had been urging that a base be acquired in the Far East; and in February 1898 Secretary Long has asked Dewey to advise on the best available port in China.[11] Although ideally the navy would have preferred a base north of the Philippines, it welcomed the opportunity now handed to it; and in August 1898 the Naval War Board (the Navy Department's central advisory body, then comprised of Captains Alfred T. Mahan and Arent S. Crowninshield, and Rear Admiral Montgomery Sicard) formally recommended taking a base in the Philippines. Perhaps the Board did not know that at least as early as June 3, 1898, McKinley had already decided he wanted a port there.[12]

A related consideration was also present. In early 1898, as the United States was moving to war, the storm center of international affairs lay not in the Caribbean but in the Far East. China's danger-

10. Lodge to Henry White, May 5, 1898, quoted in May, *Imperial Democracy*, p. 245.
11. Memorandum for the Bureau of Navigation by Secretary Long, Feb. 1, 1898, National Archives, Record Group 45, Area 10 File, Box 16. See also *Report of the Secretary of the Navy, 1899* (Washington, 1899), p. 25.
12. Sicard, Mahan, and Crowninshield to Secretary of the Navy, undated but Aug. 22, 23, or 24, 1898, National Archives, Record Group 45, Naval Records Collections of the Office of Naval Records and Library, Naval War Board, I, "A," Entry 371, pp. 338–39; William R. Braisted, "The Philippine Naval Base Problem, 1898–1909," *Mississippi Valley Historical Review*, XLI (1954), 22, refers to the communication. Regarding McKinley's decision see Day to Hay, June 3, 1898, Alfred L. P. Dennis, *Adventures in American Diplomacy, 1896–1906* (New York, 1928), p. 99. Regarding the navy's desires for a base see Seward W. Livermore, "American Naval Base Policy in the Far East, 1850–1914," *Pacific Historical Review*, XIII (1944), pp. 113–35; James K. Eyre, Jr., "Japan and the American Annexation of the Philippines," *ibid.*, XI (1942), p. 71.

## THE PRIZE BRAND.

(*Punch*, May 14, 1898)

COUSIN JONATHAN: "These look very nice! Wonder if they'll be the better for *keeping!*"

ous weakness had recently been exposed. In 1894 she had felt obliged to sign the treaty with the United States prohibiting the immigration of Chinese laborers for ten years. In 1895 she had lost the Sino-Japanese War; Tokyo had insisted upon harsh peace terms, including the cession of Formosa, the Pescadores Islands, and the strategically situated Liaotung Peninsula in southern Manchuria; but a joint French-German-Russian intervention had forced Japan to relinquish the Liaotung Peninsula. Moreover, the great European powers, which had almost finished parceling out Africa among themselves, now swooped down upon prostrate China, and her partition seemed imminent. In 1897 France extorted valuable privileges in southern China; Germany landed troops at Kiaochow in Shantung province, close to Peking; and a Russian fleet sailed into Port Arthur, at the tip of the Liaotung Peninsula. Soon an alarmed Great Britain leased the seaport of Weihaiwei, confronting the nearby Russians. Other leased territories and spheres of influence threatened China and nondiscriminatory commerce with her.

Many American businesses viewed these developments most apprehensively. At the beginning of 1898 a group of businessmen founded a Committee on American Interests in China; its purpose was to persuade Washington to support American economic expansion in China, the great potential market for agricultural goods and especially for the industrial surplus that had first appeared in 1894, a market greater, it was believed, even than Latin America. The Committee addressed petitions to the chambers of commerce of New York, Boston, San Francisco, and Cleveland, and to the Philadelphia Board of Trade, suggesting that, in view of the threatened partition, they urge the State Department to safeguard American interests in China. The petitions touched off a spate of memorials that reached Washington in February, March, and early April, 1898, just when relations with Spain were deteriorating rapidly.[13] An administration so closely allied to business as McKinley's could not fail to heed this concentrated campaign by the country's most important commercial associations; and a letter to Congress from Secretary of State William R. Day (he had succeeded John Sherman on April 28), requesting an appropriation for a commercial commission to China, indicated that the administration was responsive to

13. Charles S. Campbell, *Special Business Interests and the Open Door Policy* (New Haven, 1951), pp. 30, 34–37.

their views. Dated June 9, 1898, soon after the battle of Manila Bay made a strong American role in the Far East feasible, the letter stated: "The fact has become more and more apparent that the output of the United States manufacturers . . . has reached the point of large excess above the demands of home consumption. . . . the United States has important interests at stake in the partition of commercial facilities in regions which are likely to offer developing markets for its goods. Nowhere is this consideration of more interest than in its relation to the Chinese Empire."[14]

Against this background came the thrilling news that Spanish naval power in the Far East had been smashed. All at once people awoke to the possibility that Manila could be a base for safeguarding the potential Chinese market. Germany had her Kiaochow, Russia her Port Arthur, Great Britain her Weihaiwei. And here was the United States, by a providential stroke it might seem, suddenly presented with a chance to acquire a magnificent base of her own. Of course she was not going to muff the opportunity; she was going to take Manila, and also Hawaii, so that a long American finger, sticking out across the Pacific Ocean, would point menacingly at any nation endangering United States interests in China. In all parts of the country people saw the connection between the Philippines and the potential market. In the West the San Francisco Chamber of Commerce petitioned the President to keep the islands "with a view to strengthening our trade relations with the Orient."[15] Southern states were reported to believe that "profit and progress will come to this nation from safeguarding the Philippines; the islands are already the indispensable base of a profitable trade with the whole Orient."[16] On the east coast the *United States Investor* admonished its readers: "Our interests in China are great enough to demand careful protection. And the way to protect them is to supply ourselves with a base of operations in the East. That desideratum the Philippine Islands are capable of supplying."[17] Similarly at a meeting of the Connecticut State Board of Trade a speaker prophesied that a strong position in the Philippines would bring "unparalleled

14. Day to Secretary of the Treasury Lyman J. Gage (for submission to Congress), June 9, 1898, *House Documents*, 55 Cong., 2 Sess., No. 536 (Serial 3692), pp. 1–3.

15. San Francisco Chamber of Commerce, *Forty-Ninth Annual Report*, pp. 23–24; the petition was dated July 29, 1898.

16. Chattanooga *Tradesman*, quoted in *Literary Digest*, XVII (Sept. 24, 1898), 361.

17. *United States Investor*, IX (Aug. 13, 1898), 1145.

benefits" to American industries; and that in China "the future looks bright for our manufacturing industries to find a market for their surplus goods."[18]

At least two very important Senators agreed with these views. "The time has come when we must take our place in the Orient," asserted Senator Marcus A. Hanna, the President's close adviser and spokesman for big business; ". . . with a strong foothold in the Philippine Islands and the occupancy of a well-fortified harbor and a limitless anchorage for the ships of trade, we can and will take a large slice of the commerce of Asia. That is what we want. We are bound to share in the commerce of the Far East, and it is better to strike for it while the iron is hot." And Cushman K. Davis, chairman of the Foreign Relations Committee, declared: "China is the coveted part of the earth's surface to-day. . . . Providence has stepped in to point the future course for us. We must police the Pacific Ocean!"[19] At the end of the year President McKinley himself, heedful as usual of business opinion, told Congress that the administration was keeping close watch on events in China and that "it will be my aim to subserve our large interests in that quarter by all means appropriate to the constant policy of our Government." The base in the Philippines that he already wanted to acquire would provide one such means.[20]

Thus the fait accompli of Dewey's great victory, a victory coming against the background of the navy's desire for a Far Eastern naval base and of the ominous developments in China, foreshadowed the acquisition of at least a base in the Philippines. There was another, closely associated fait accompli at Manila Bay—the arrival of an army there; and if the victory made the retention of a base highly probable, the army's presence made it virtually certain.

The decision to send the soldiers came hard upon the naval battle. In early 1898 the thoughts of American military leaders were on Cuba; on April 15, about a week before war was declared, the commanding general, Major General Nelson A. Miles, recom-

18. Annual meeting, Oct. 19, 1898, *Proceedings of the Connecticut State Board of Trade, 1891–1906*, p. 24.

19. New York *World*, Aug. 29, 1898, quoting Hanna and Davis.

20. Annual message, Dec. 5, 1898, James D. Richardson (ed.), *A Compilation of the Messages and Papers of the Presidents* . . . (20 vols., New York, 1916), XIV, 6327, 6328; *Literary Digest*, XVII (Dec. 17, 1898), 710.

mended that the army be mobilized on the Gulf of Mexico.[21] Neither he nor any other top official was dreaming of dispatching troops to any place overseas except the Caribbean, certainly not to the far distant Philippine Islands. As Major General Elwell S. Otis explained later: "The supply departments, not anticipating any concentration of forces on the Pacific coast, had made no provisions for furnishing arms, ammunition, clothing, subsistence, or other war material with which an army about to operate 7,000 miles from its base must necessarily be supplied. Indeed . . . such property, usually kept in moderate quantities on the Pacific coast, had been sent to the East [coast] for the army destined to invade Cuba and Puerto Rico."[22]

In this situation, with all eyes on the Caribbean, there came on May 2 the rumor of a victory at Manila Bay. This exciting news at hand, several conferences were held in the White House that same day, attended by the President, Major Generals Miles and Wesley Merritt, Rear Admiral Montgomery Sicard, Secretary of the Navy Long, and Secretary of War Russell A. Alger; and the decision was taken to postpone the expedition to Cuba. One reason for this was the uncertainty as to the whereabouts, somewhere out on the Atlantic, of a Spanish squadron under Admiral Pascual Cervera; but no doubt the officials at the meeting gave consideration also to Dewey's situation. The American ships could not long remain off Manila without a base on land, and to obtain one an army was needed. Consequently on the third Major General Miles formally recommended that troops be diverted from the Gulf to the west coast for the succor of the commodore in case he should want them. On May 4 President McKinley approved the recommendation, and a steamer, the *City of Peking*, was chartered.[23] The President's ap-

21. Miles to Secretary of War, April 15, 1898, *Annual Reports of the War Department for the Fiscal Year Ended June 30, 1898: Report of the Major General Commanding the Army* (Washington, 1898), pp. 5–6.

22. *Annual Reports of the War Department for the Fiscal Year Ended June 30, 1899: Report of the Major General Commanding the Army* (Washington, 1899), I, Pt. 4, p. 2. In his book *The Spanish-American War* (New York, 1901), p. 326, Secretary of War Russell A. Alger wrote that "the determination to send an army of occupation to the Philippines was reached before Dewey's victory occurred. . . ." Alger's meaning of "determination" is obscure; if he meant that the decision to send an army was made before May 1, he was almost certainly wrong.

23. Miles to Secretary of War, May 3, 1898, and McKinley to Secretary of War, May 4, 1898, *Correspondence Relating to the War with Spain*, II, 635; New York *Tribune*, May 5, 1898; see also Miles's report of Nov. 5, 1898, *Annual Reports of the War Department, 1898*, p. 6.

proval was apparently routine, without consideration of long-range consequences. He did, however, receive a letter, dated the twelfth, from Oscar S. Straus, a New York businessman and a former minister to Turkey, warning that "entanglement and embarrassment" would result from sending soldiers to the Philippines, and that they could not be withdrawn "without turning over the islands to anarchy and slaughter."[24]

Since confirmation of a victory at Manila Bay was lacking before May 7, these decisions were taken tentatively, subject to cancellation. But after Dewey's report finally arrived, definitive preparations were hurriedly made. On May 14 Major General Otis was told to be ready to sail from San Francisco with 1,200 soldiers; on the twenty-fifth the *City of Peking* weighed anchor, and the first expedition was off for the relief of Dewey, now a rear admiral.[25]

Some people have regretted that the Pacific squadron, having destroyed the Spanish fleet, did not sail away. President McKinley is supposed to have exclaimed: "If old Dewey had just sailed away when he smashed that Spanish fleet, what a lot of trouble he would have saved us."[26] The implication was that if he had "just sailed away," Washington would not have sent the troops, and the Philippines would not have been annexed. If the President did make the remark, he had forgotten the circumstances of that spring of 1898. The fact is that it never entered anyone's head to order the commodore to leave; it was simply taken for granted that he would stay. As for Dewey himself, the victor of Manila Bay had no intention of quitting the scene of his glory. Furthermore the government knew that a Spanish squadron under Rear Admiral Eduardo de la Cámara y Livermoore was being readied to leave Cádiz for the Philippines. As early as May 7 ominous headlines in the New York *Herald* read, "Suez Canal Open to War Vessels," and in June the Spanish squadron set sail; it proceeded eastward at a speed calculated to bring it to Manila Bay in early August.[27] Dewey would then need all his ships

24. Straus to McKinley, May 12, 1898, May, *Imperial Democracy,* p. 246.

25. Adjutant General Henry C. Corbin to Otis, May 14, 1898, *Correspondence Relating to the War with Spain,* II, 639; *Annual Reports of the War Department, 1898,* p. 393. See also Commissary General to Secretary of War, May 9, 1898, National Archives, Record Group 107, Document 3103, Box 18.

26. Herman H. Kohlsaat, *From McKinley to Harding: Personal Recollections of Our Presidents* (New York, 1923), p. 68.

27. New York *Herald,* May 7, 1898; Secretary of War to Major General Wesley Merritt, undated but June 1898, National Archives, Record Group 45, Strategy Board, No. 1, Entry 372, p. 137.

and perhaps more. With this threat hanging over the Philippines, it was reasonable for him to remain where he was. He had been sent there in the first place partly to safeguard American commerce on the Pacific Ocean, and to have sailed away and permitted another Spanish fleet to replace the one he had destroyed would have been an act of folly.

Not until July 11, 1898, almost two and a half months after the battle of Manila Bay, did Washington learn that Cámara had abandoned his eastward course and was returning to Spain.[28] By then three expeditionary forces had sailed to Dewey's aid, a fourth was about to depart, and thousands of American troops had disembarked near Manila (which they occupied on August 13). Moreover, insurgent Filipino bands were increasingly active. When American soldiers first landed in the Philippines on June 30, Dewey said of rebel leader Emilio Aguinaldo, whom the Americans themselves had brought to the islands: *"He is sorry our troops are here, I think"*; and a month later he cabled Washington that the insurgents were acting menacingly.[29] If the American army withdrew under such a threat, would not chaos ensue on the islands, as Straus had warned, chaos for which the United States would bear responsibility since she had broken Spanish power there and fanned the flames of rebellion?

Another complication resulted from the presence at Manila Bay of German, British, French, and Japanese warships. The German ships had arrived there on June 17, 1898, and the others followed soon afterward. During the war Great Britain let it be known that she would be willing to annex the islands if the United States did not want them; Germany said that she would like to have at least a base; Japan that she would be willing to participate in a joint or tripartite protectorate.[30] Did not these dangerous circumstances make an American withdrawal virtually unthinkable? If the United

28. Sicard to Secretary Long, July 11, 1898, National Archives, Record Group 45, Naval War Board, I, "A," Entry 371.

29. Dewey to Edwin Wildman (American consul at Hong Kong), July 1, 1898, Edwin Wildman, "What Dewey Feared in Manila Bay, as Revealed by His Letters," *Forum*, LIX (1918), 526; for the cable of July 30 see May, *Imperial Democracy*, p. 250.

30. Julius W. Pratt, *Expansionists of 1898: The Acquisition of Hawaii and the Spanish Islands* (Baltimore, 1936), p. 333. See also Thomas A. Bailey, "Dewey and the Germans at Manila Bay," *American Historical Review*, XLV (1939), 59–81; Lester B. Shippee, "Germany and the Spanish-American War," *ibid.*, XXX (1925), 754–77; James K. Eyre, Jr., "Russia and the American Acquisition of the Philippines," *Mississippi Valley Historical Review*, XXVIII (1942), 539–62, and "Japan and the American Annexation of the Philippines," pp. 55–71.

States committed so irresponsible an act, a scramble among the powers to grab the spoils of Spanish empire could be expected; and this might touch off the world war that had been feared ever since the breakup of China seemed imminent.

Thus Dewey's presence in Manila Bay, and the consequent dispatch of an army, had resulted by mid-July 1898 in a thoroughly entangling situation from which no ready escape existed. The United States, who had entered the islands so blithely, found that, as Mr. Dooley put it, "We've got the Ph'lippeens, Hinnissy; we've got thim the way Casey got the bulldog—be th' teeth."[31] At the very least a naval base was going to be kept—that seemed clear.

The fait accompli at Manila Bay—Dewey's victory and the arrival of the army—led not only to a decision to retain a base in the Philippines; it clinched the annexation of the Hawaiian Islands. In the spring of 1898 the long-sustained move to annex Hawaii had fizzled out. But Manila Bay broke the stalemate; and annexation followed forthwith. Hawaii was one of the three basic objectives so long and ardently desired by expansionists; but curiously enough the United States had to reach the Philippines before she could consummate Hawaiian annexation.

To support the troops far across the wide Pacific was a difficult task; the convenience of the Hawaiian Islands was obvious. As a supposed neutral, Hawaii should have closed her ports to war uses; and indeed she hesitated about keeping them open to Americans until Dewey's victory made her safe from Spanish attack. Thereafter she cooperated wholeheartedly with the United States. She refueled American ships, she suggested an alliance, she placed her resources unreservedly at American disposal—and confidently awaited the annexation she had earned.[32] The United States could hardly deny her suit. Representative John M. Mitchell expressed the prevailing view: "The Hawaiian Government has tendered to us the hospitality of its shores and harbors when we most needed them, even to the extent of violating for our benefit the rules of international law. We owe the most solemn duty to reciprocate this friendly spirit and see

31. May, *Imperial Democracy*, p. 257.

32. Thomas A. Bailey, "The United States and Hawaii During the Spanish-American War," *American Historical Review*, XXXVI (1931), 554–56; William A. Russ, Jr., *The Hawaiian Republic (1894–98) and Its Struggle to Win Annexation* (Selinsgrove, Pa., 1961), pp. 287–88.

that no possible harm shall come to them by reason of it."[33]

Moreover, the war dramatized the security argument. If Admiral Cervera could threaten the east coast, could not a naval power endanger California—unless Hawaii was firmly American? Then, too, the rise of sentiment to keep the Philippines and to pursue an active role in China affected thinking about Hawaii. Thus the Baltimore *American* proclaimed: ". . . Hawaii is coming under our flag, and nothing can stop it. . . . The stepping-stones to the Philippines and to the great trade of the East will be ours, and in that fact is real good fortune for the country."[34] Similarly the Cincinnati *Enquirer* remarked: "Aside from the natural reasons why the Hawaiian republic should become a part of the United States there suddenly comes upon us the necessity for a half-way station to the Philippine islands." The *Enquirer* expressed, too, another thought frequently being heard: "A scheme of empire has come upon the country in spite of our extraordinary conservatism. . . . Opposition to the annexation of the Hawaiian group is merely another fight against destiny. These islands belong to us in the coming general distribution of the world among a few strong nations."[35]

It was not the joint resolution proposed in March 1898 that finally brought Hawaii into the union; that resolution was abandoned forever on July 7, 1898. Only after the battle of Manila Bay, that catalyst in American history, did the decisive joint resolution for annexation make its appearance. It was introduced in the House by Representative Francis G. Newlands on May 4, 1898 (just three days after the battle), and the Foreign Affairs Committee reported it favorably on the seventeenth.[36] The long majority report repeated word for word the Senate report of March 16: its five reasons for annexation, twenty objections, capital letters, and italics. The report reflected the new urgency imparted by the war: that conflict, it asserted correctly, had "called public attention to . . . the inestimable importance to the United States of possessing the Hawaiian Islands in case of war with any strong naval power." Pearl Harbor alone was inadequate; it could not be defended without the whole

33. *Congressional Record*, 55 Cong., 2 Sess., Appendix, p. 580 (June 15, 1898). See also *Review of Reviews*, XVIII (1898), 124; New York *Tribune*, May 5 and 6, 1898.

34. *Literary Digest*, XVI (June 25, 1898), 752.

35. *Public Opinion*, XXIV (June 9, 1898), 707.

36. *Congressional Record*, 55 Cong., 2 Sess., p. 6743 (July 7, 1898), p. 4600 (May 4, 1898), p. 4989 (May 17, 1898).

archipelago. Besides, an independent, perhaps orientalized Hawaii might some day terminate the treaty of 1884 (as amended), which gave the United States the right to use the base.[37] Here again was the security argument, heightened by the recent scare over Japanese immigration into Hawaii and by the Spanish war; its widespread appreciation in 1898 was a major factor in bringing Hawaii to the United States.

A minority report, offering a substitute resolution, opposed the Newlands resolution, maintaining that annexation would be unconstitutional, that the Hawaiian population could not be assimilated into the American, and that United States interests could be protected by a guarantee of Hawaiian independence.[38] The powerful Speaker of the House, Thomas B. Reed, who shared these views, prevented consideration of the majority resolution for over three weeks. But even "Czar" Reed could not block it indefinitely, now that the American people had become engulfed in the intoxication of war. President McKinley, of course, had long favored annexation; not later than June 3 he decided to work hard for the Newlands resolution.[39]

Debate commenced in the House on the eleventh. For four days it proceeded. Page after page of the *Congressional Record* is filled with impassioned oratory. The arguments had been heard before. Defense, duty, destiny, commerce, sugar, security, Japan—all these and other themes were rung. Opening the debate, Robert R. Hitt made a compelling point: "There is no one in our country so recreant in his duty as an American that he would refuse to support the President in succoring Dewey after his magnificent victory. . . . Yet it is not possible to send support to Dewey to-day without taking on coal and supplies at Honolulu in the Hawaiian Islands—a neutral power."[40] Several speakers placed Hawaii in the context of the "rapidly growing trade" with China and Japan across the Pacific Ocean, "destined to be the theater of the world's struggle for the rich commerce of the East." "As a government we must either advance or recede," Michael Griffin, evidently a good Social Darwin-

37. *House Reports*, 55 Cong., 2 Sess., No. 1355 (Serial 3721), pp. 2, 3, 4, 6. For the Senate report see p. 237.
38. *House Reports*, 55 Cong., 2 Sess., No. 1355, Pt. 2, pp. 1–2.
39. Dennis, *Adventures in American Diplomacy*, p. 99.
40. *Congressional Record*, 55 Cong., 2 Sess., p. 5772 (June 11, 1898). The debate is in *ibid.*, June 11 through 15, and Appendix, *passim.*

ist, advised, "for no nation can long remain stationary."[41] Outside
Congress Herbert Myrick, claiming to represent almost a million
farmers (he was an editor of several agricultural journals), protested
against annexation because "the cooly labor of these tropical colonies, directed by capable overseers, and their products manipulated
by world-wide trusts, would close up every beet-sugar proposition
and cane-sugar mill in the United States"; tobacco manufacture
would "be annihilated"; and as regards rice, cotton, hemp, and all
fiber crops a "death knell" would toll.[42] And Samuel Gompers,
speaking for the American Federation of Labor, held up the bogey
that annexation "would threaten an inundation of Mongolians to
overwhelm the free laborers of our country."[43] Myrick and especially Gompers were powerful men, but they could not sway the
result. The House voted on June 15, mainly on party lines. The
substitute resolution was first swept aside: 96 in favor, 204 against.
Then came the test on the Newlands resolution; it passed decisively,
209 to 91.[44]

The resolution now moved to the Senate. Despite the fervor of
the antiexpansionists it was riding an irresistible wave. ". . . I do not
believe the Senate can hold out for long," Henry Cabot Lodge
gleefully told Theodore Roosevelt, "for the President has been very
firm about it and means to annex the Islands any way."[45] For fifteen
days the debate went on. An eager listener in the gallery was the
Hawaiian leader of 1893, Lorrin A. Thurston, his great design near
fulfillment.[46] Long, often emotional addresses rang through the
chamber as old-fashioned Senators made their final stand to save
the republic from the evils of imperialism and the fate of republican
Rome.[47] In one of the last efforts of his career Justin S. Morrill, now
in his eighty-eighth year, pleaded fervently against annexation as
violating the republic's tested principles. "Has the country ever

41. *Ibid.*, Appendix, p. 587 (June 15, 1898); for the remarks about Pacific Ocean
trade see *ibid.*, p. 566 (June 11, 1898), p. 669 (June 13, 1898).
42. *Ibid.*, p. 6270 (June 23, 1898).
43. Gompers to Reed, June 11, 1898, *ibid.*
44. *Ibid.*, pp. 6018, 6019 (June 15, 1898).
45. Lodge to Roosevelt, June 15, 1898, *Selections from the Correspondence of Theodore
Roosevelt and Henry Cabot Lodge, 1884–1918* (2 vols., New York, 1925), I, 311.
46. Russ, *Hawaiian Republic*, p. 352.
47. For the debate see *Congressional Record*, 55 Cong., 2 Sess., June 16 through July
6, 1898, *passim;* Pratt, *Expansionists of 1898*, pp. 323–26, has a good summary of the
debate.

lamented the rejection of Santo Domingo?" he inquired, harking back to another stormy controversy.[48] Perhaps the most moving speech was delivered by George Frisbie Hoar, like Morrill near the end of a long career. Reluctantly he came out for annexation. "It is not a question of empire in the Pacific, small or great. It is a question of . . . whether we shall be there forever in a strait-waistcoat and within stone walls, or whether we shall have about our walls a little breathing room and a little elbow room." But he warned: "If this be the first step in the acquisition of dominion over barbarous archipelagoes in distant seas; . . . if we are to govern subject and vassal states, trampling as we do it on our own great charter which recognizes alike the liberty and the dignity of individual manhood, then let us resist this thing in the beginning, and let us resist it to the death."[49] Already Hoar anticipated with dread the acquisition of the Philippine Islands.

The vote came on July 6. Forty-two Senators approved the resolution; 21 opposed it. As in the House, the vote divided on party lines with few exceptions, Republicans favoring annexation, Democrats opposing it. Morrill, a Republican, voted no, and the Democrat John T. Morgan voted yes, each man thus maintaining his consistent position of many years. Although a two-thirds majority was obtained, this would not necessarily have happened had a treaty rather than a resolution been at issue, because a large number of Senators (twenty-six) did not vote. President McKinley signed the joint resolution the next day.[50] The islands were formally annexed on August 12, 1898. After so many years of indecision, Commodore Dewey's momentous victory and the sending of an army to Manila had clinched the matter. Through the back door of the distant Philippines, the Hawaiian Islands had come to the United States.

In Hawaii the ruling classes hailed the news enthusiastically, but a league of natives, how representative of their compatriots it is hard to say, filed a solemn "protest against annexation . . . without refer-

48. *Congressional Record*, 55 Cong., 2 Sess., p. 6142 (June 20, 1898); for a comparison with Rome see *ibid.*, p. 6229 (June 22, 1898).

49. *Ibid.*, p. 6661 (July 5, 1898); see also George Frisbie Hoar, *Autobiography of Seventy Years* (2 vols., New York, 1903), II, 307–11.

50. *Congressional Record*, 55 Cong., 2 Sess., p. 6712 (July 6, 1898), p. 6806 (July 8, 1898). For an analysis of the annexation and its implications see *Review of Reviews*, XVIII (1898), 123–27.

ence to the consent of the people of the Hawaiian Islands."[51]

Thus the fait accompli at Manila Bay made the retention of at least a naval base in the Philippines nearly certain, and it precipitated the annexation of Hawaii. As a matter of fact, the presence of an American army at Manila suggested that more than a base would be taken: it strongly encouraged the acquisition of the entire archipelago. Moreover, just as Manila Bay broke the indecision over Hawaii, so the war as a whole served as a catalyst that ended the stalemate over an isthmian canal and over a Caribbean base. To this climax of expansion we must now turn.

51. Harold M. Sewall (American minister to Hawaii) to Day, Aug. 6, 1898, Russ, *Hawaiian Republic,* pp. 364–65.

# CHAPTER 16

## *Territorial Expansion*

THE annexation of the Philippine Islands in 1899 represented a departure from American traditions. United States history may have been characterized by steady commercial and territorial expansion, but never before had land thousands of miles away and inhabited by millions of people been acquired. Americans realized that they were contemplating an unprecedented step, and passionately they debated the wisdom of extending their rule to the immense archipelago off the shores of Asia. It should be added, however, that had annexation been limited to a naval base, no such departure from past practices would have occurred, because the acquisition of a Philippine base would have fitted into the pattern of privileges in Pago Pago, and of old pressures to obtain bases in the Caribbean Sea and the Pacific Ocean. Taking the archipelago was an aberration; taking a base was not.[1]

The decision regarding the Philippines was crucial for the entire Pacific expansion. We have already observed the connection between the events at Manila Bay and the annexation of Hawaii. Wake and Guam were stepping stones to the Philippines; if the latter were to be taken, Wake and Guam, or islands similarly located, would follow almost as a matter of course. Moreover, an example would

1. Frederick Merk, *Manifest Destiny and Mission in American History: A Reinterpretation* (New York, 1963), pp. 251, 256–57; Samuel F. Bemis, *A Diplomatic History of the United States* (New York, 1955), ch. 26; Richard W. Van Alstyne, *The Rising American Empire* (New York, 1960), ch. 8.

be set for acquiring Samoa. To explain the annexation of the Philippines, therefore, is to explain in large measure the annexation of several other islands as well.

The fait accompli at Manila Bay goes far to explain the decision to annex at least a base in the Philippines. But it does not explain why the decision was subsequently broadened: on September 16 to a demand that Spain cede the island of Luzon, and on October 28[2] to a demand that she cede the entire archipelago. To elucidate this we must consider further the sending of the army, and must examine two additional factors: the emergence of a popular relish for colonialism, and military advice that a base alone or Luzon alone would not be defensible.

As regards the army, little need be added. Its presence in the Philippines greatly facilitated the Senate's approval in early 1899 of the treaty with Spain, which provided for annexation. Had the troops not been there already, approval would have been tantamount to telling the American people, during the psychological letdown after the war, to raise fresh armies, send them to a remote land of no obvious significance to the national interest, and suppress a native people ready to fight for independence. It is altogether possible that Congress would have refused to allow this. But the troops were there already. Furthermore, as President McKinley stated in September 1898, "Without any original thought of complete or even partial acquisition, the presence and success of our arms at Manila imposes upon us obligations which we can not disregard."[3] He had in mind the assumption in Washington that the Filipinos could not govern themselves, and the possibility that a great struggle for the islands would break out among the powers should the United States withdraw. Even while Dewey was still at Manila Bay, Aguinaldo had arrived, and the foreign warships had gathered ominously there. In short, the President had come to realize that, as Oscar S. Straus had foreseen, the presence of the army had thoroughly entangled the United States in the Philippine Islands. There seemed no alternative to annexation.

2. This demand has usually been dated Oct. 26; Richard Leopold, "The *Foreign Relations* Series: A Centennial Estimate," *Mississippi Valley Historical Review*, XLIX (1963), 598, shows that a telegram of Oct. 26 was never sent, but that a longer one dated Oct. 28 was sent. For both telegrams see *Papers Relating to the Foreign Relations of the United States, 1898* (Washington, 1901), pp. 935, 937–38.

3. McKinley to peace commissioners, Sept. 16, 1898, *ibid.*, p. 907.

The upsurge of sentiment in favor of colonialism was another development inclining the United States to take all the Philippines. We have seen that the ground had been well prepared for such a conversion. The longstanding propaganda for an isthmian canal, the industrial surplus, Social Darwinism and Anglo-Saxonism, the major shift in European thinking and practices about colonialism, the teachings of such publicists as Alfred T. Mahan—all these and other factors working away over many years had undermined the traditional American hostility to colonialism. And now in the spring of 1898 the glorious triumph at Manila Bay exhilarated the government and the American people. The brilliant success made it easier for them to countenance further adventurous steps. Hardly had official news of the battle reached Washington when the Naval War Board persuaded Secretary of the Navy John D. Long to order the seizure of Guam, conveniently situated between the Hawaiian and Philippine islands.[4] Captain Henry Glass of the cruiser *Charleston* was given sealed orders on May 10, 1898, to proceed to Guam, and on June 20 he took the island from the weak Spanish garrison.[5] On May 19 the President intimated that his own aspirations were broadening when he referred to the approaching end of Spain's political tie with the Philippines; on the twenty-fourth an exultant Senator Henry Cabot Lodge left a meeting with the President convinced that McKinley now shared his own expansionist outlook.[6] On June 3 the President expressed his desire to annex an island in the Ladrones (presumably Guam); we have seen that that same day he indicated his decision to take a harbor in the Philippines and to push hard for the annexation of the Hawaiian Islands.[7] Just when he resolved to annex the uninhabited and unclaimed Wake Islands is not known,

4. Rear Admiral Montgomery Sicard to Long, May 9, 1898, National Archives (Washington), Record Group 45, Naval Records Collections of the Office of Naval Records and Library, OC File; memorandum for the Secretary of the Navy by Sicard, June 3, 1898, *ibid.*, Naval War Board, I, "A," Entry 371. For the Naval War Board see Jarvis Butler, "The General Board of the Navy," *United States Naval Institute Proceedings*, LVI (1930), 701.

5. Leslie W. Walker, "Guam's Seizure by the United States in 1898," *Pacific Historical Review*, XIV (1945), 1–12.

6.McKinley to Secretary of War, May 19, 1898, Louis J. Halle, *Dream and Reality: Aspects of American Foreign Policy* (New York, 1959), p. 186; Lodge to Theodore Roosevelt, May 24, 1898, *Selections from the Correspondence of Theodore Roosevelt and Henry Cabot Lodge, 1884–1918* (2 vols., New York, 1925), I, 299–300.

7. Day to Hay, June 3, 1898, Alfred L. P. Dennis, *Adventures in American Diplomacy, 1896–1906* (New York, 1928), p. 99.

but on January 17, 1899, Commander Edward D. Taussig, U.S.S. *Bennington,* took possession of them. Hawaii, the Midway Islands (acquired in 1867), Wake, Guam, a base in the Philippines—these would provide a chain of conveniently spaced coaling stations right across the Pacific Ocean; and within little more than a month of the outbreak of war McKinley had decided (except perhaps as regards Wake) to take or keep them all.

In like manner success whetted the public's appetite for colonialism. As a contemporary wrote: "The brilliancy of their [the American people's] achievements in the war had quickened their imaginations, and greatly broadened out their aspirations and ambitions. To rule distant lands, to hold colonies and dependencies, to have their country figure largely on the vast stage of international affairs, appealed to their national love of bigness."[8] In distant Athens the wife of the American minister, William W. Rockhill, was near death. "The day before she died," her husband wrote a friend, "she was . . . expressing her pride and delight at what our country has done to take its place among nations within the last three months."[9] Millions of her compatriots back home felt a similar exaltation. It influenced some church groups, which believed that the United States had a duty—the "white man's burden," they called it—to keep the islands, so that she could uplift the natives and save them from Spanish misrule and their own supposed ineptitude for self-government.

This lure of distant lands that animated the American people as a consequence of the drama of Manila Bay helps explain why the administration expanded its demands from a base, first to Luzon, and then to the whole archipelago. Another influence was present. Hard at work in Washington on a special study of the Philippines was Commander Royal B. Bradford, chief of the Bureau of Equipment. Facing one of the most perplexing decisions in American history, President McKinley needed expert advice; but scarcely anyone available had ever visited the Philippines. Bradford was exceptional in having been there three times, and it would be surprising

8. Harry Thurston Peck, *Twenty Years of the Republic, 1885–1905* (New York, 1906), pp. 608–9.
9. Rockhill to James H. Wilson, Aug. 17, 1898, James Harrison Wilson Papers, Library of Congress (Washington), Box 21. See also Ernest R. May, *Imperial Democracy: The Emergence of America as a Great Power* (New York, 1961), pp. 248–49, 255–56.

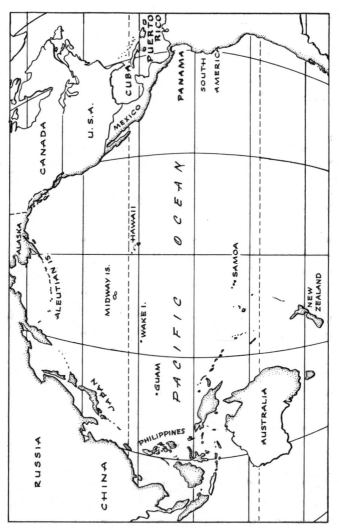

if the President did not pay careful heed to him. The commander argued that Manila without all of Luzon would be difficult to defend, but he also contended that it made little sense to take Luzon alone without the adjacent islands—and then, step by step, all the islands.

During the crucial period between September 16 and October 28 another knowledgeable figure appeared in the capital. General Francis V. Greene was the first person to arrive fresh from the great events at Manila. On September 30 he gave the President a long memorandum recommending the annexation of the whole archipelago. McKinley studied it carefully and talked with Greene several times. His decision to take the archipelago was made at the time he was hearing the general's arguments, and it is reasonable to believe he was influenced by them.[10]

For several days in mid-October McKinley was on a trip that took him as far west as Omaha. He delivered a number of speeches about the Philippines, and whenever he alluded to annexation the crowd responded with an enthusiastic roar of approval. The President's decision, expressed October 28, to acquire the entire archipelago has often been depicted as a response to the public's imperialistic mood demonstrated during the Omaha trip. But more significant, in all probability, was the testimony of Bradford and Greene. McKinley knew their views before he headed west; probably he had already made up his mind about the Philippines. The Omaha trip confirmed; it did not inspire.

A protectorate, rather than outright annexation, might have met many American requirements. But Washington did not seriously consider this alternative, under which it could anticipate frequent bickering with a native government. Difficulties in Samoa did not dispose it to establish another complicated regime in the Pacific.

Such were the reasons that persuaded the administration to demand the Philippine Islands. We may now turn to the peace treaty in which Spain accepted the demand and also ceded territory elsewhere in the Pacific Ocean, as well as in the Caribbean Sea.

Spain was no match for the United States; on July 19, 1898, she asked France to mediate. A week later the French ambassador at

---

10. Regarding Bradford and Greene see Margaret Leech, *In the Days of McKinley* (New York, 1959), pp. 327, 334–36. McKinley wrote Day, Sept. 28, 1898, that he had just had a long talk with Greene, who was thoroughly informed, *Senate Documents*, 56 Cong., 2 Sess., No. 148 (Serial 4039), p. 14.

Washington, Jules Cambon, brought to the White House a Spanish invitation to negotiate for peace. The result was an armistice on August 12. Spain yielded Cuba and agreed to cede Puerto Rico and an island in the Ladrones; the fate of the Philippines was to be decided at a peace conference to convene in Paris not later than October 1, 1898; meanwhile the United States was to hold the city, bay, and harbor of Manila.

President McKinley selected a peace commission of five, three of them from the Senate: Cushman K. Davis, chairman of the Foreign Relations Committee; William P. Frye, another committee member; and George Gray, also a member and the commission's only Democrat. The other commissioners were William R. Day (replaced on September 30 as Secretary of State by John Hay) and Whitelaw Reid, owner of the New York *Tribune* and influential in high Republican circles. John Bassett Moore, the eminent international lawyer and occasional State Department official over many years, was the commission's secretary. These men held their first meeting with their Spanish counterparts on October 1 at the Quai d'Orsay Palace in Paris. For more than two months they deliberated.[11]

Yet only two questions had not been settled by the armistice: what country was to be responsible for the Cuban debt of about $400 million (in Spanish bonds), and what was to be done with the Philippine Islands. Spain insisted that the United States assume the debt; the American commissioners refused. When the Americans rejected the counterproposal of arbitration, the Spanish threatened to break off negotiations. But in the end they yielded, and the United States had her way.

The American commissioners did not agree among themselves about the Philippines. In Paris they heard the testimony of Major General Merritt, fresh from Manila, and of John Foreman, an Englishman long resident in the islands, whose recent article denying the natives' capacity for self-government the President himself studied.[12] McKinley's instruction of October 28 demanding the entire archipelago worried Senator Frye; he cabled that if Washington did

11. Regarding the peace conference see *Senate Documents*, 55 Cong., 3 Sess., No. 62 (Serial 3732), Pt. 1; H. Wayne Morgan (ed.), *Making Peace with Spain: The Diary of Whitelaw Reid, September–December, 1898* (Austin, Tex., 1965).

12. John Foreman, "Spain and the Philippine Islands," *Contemporary Review*, LXXIV (1898), 20–33; Leech, *McKinley*, p. 328.

not compromise, fighting would recommence, and that the United States should pay Spain $10 million or $20 million to get a treaty. Reid, too, favored compromise: either let Spain keep Mindanao Island and the Sulu islands, and in their place cede to the United States all the Carolines and Ladrones; or let her cede all the Carolines and all the Philippines but be paid $12 million to $15 million —and he added that to save the treaty he would not insist on Mindanao and the Sulu group. Only Davis stood firm against any concession; he recommended an ultimatum, which he predicted would bring Madrid to terms. Gray opposed taking even part of the archipelago as contrary to the "accepted continental policy."[13]

Spain did her best to prolong negotiations in the desperate hope that a Democratic victory in the congressional elections would soften the American stand, or that the great powers would intervene; but she yielded in late November after the United States agreed to buy all the Philippines for $20 million. The treaty of Paris was signed on December 10, 1898. Spain renounced all claim to Cuba and assumed its debt. The United States got the Philippines, Guam, and Puerto Rico.[14] Although Americans had shown little desire for Puerto Rico before the war, they could hardly have permitted Spain, after all their denunciations of her misrule in Cuba, to remain there. Moreover, the United States needed naval bases in the Caribbean, and had pledged herself in the Teller amendment not to annex Cuba—but she soon acquired a Cuban base at Guantánamo Bay; Puerto Rico was well situated to guard the approaches to an isthmian canal.

Already in the United States the wartime intoxication was beginning to give way to sober reflection. The thrill of being a big imperialistic world power was all very well, but did Americans really want to take over the enormous archipelago across the wide Pacific, inhabited by millions of strange people who would never be American citizens? Did the tobacco, sugar-cane, and sugar-beet interests want to admit a competitor inside the American tariff wall? Did the labor leaders want cheap Oriental labor to drive down American wages?

13. Reid to Hay, Nov. 11, 1898, *Senate Documents*, 56 Cong., 2 Sess., No. 148, pp. 46–48; Frye to Second Assistant Secretary of State Alvey A. Adee (for McKinley), Oct. 30, 1898, *ibid.*, pp. 38–39; Gray to Hay, Oct. 25, 1898, *ibid.*, p. 34.
14. William M. Malloy (ed.), *Treaties, Conventions, International Acts, Protocols and Agreements between the United States of America and Other Powers, 1776–1909* (2 vols., Washington, 1910), II, 1690–95.

The arguments that had been advanced against Hawaiian annexation were brought forth once again, and again anxious men predicted the republic's doom, like that of republican Rome, if it succumbed to the lure of empire. An Anti-Imperialist League was founded in Boston on November 19, 1898. Soon other anti-imperialist leagues sprang up in a dozen other cities; and in October 1899 a national Anti-Imperialist League was established at a conference attended by delegates from thirty states. Among the members were such men as former Presidents Grover Cleveland and Benjamin Harrison; George S. Boutwell, Grant's Secretary of the Treasury; George Frisbie Hoar; Andrew Carnegie; and a host of others—over 30,000 of them in the Boston League alone.[15] Thus the opposition was strongly organized. The League made little objection to acquiring nearby Puerto Rico, but most adamantly it opposed taking the exposed and distant Philippines Islands. The ensuing great national debate over the Philippines was the climax of the intermittent debate of the last three decades over territorial expansion, the debates over Alaska, Santo Domingo, Cuba, Samoa, and Hawaii; and emotions ran high.

Yet the opposition had no chance to prevail. The great majority of the Senators favored taking the Philippines, and the nearer islands also. With the splendidly successful war behind him, President McKinley's prestige stood high; if he wanted the Philippines, his party would go along. Persuasive, too, was the fact that an American army was already there; it was even under attack—since February 4, 1899—by Filipino insurgents. Withdrawal would seem dishonorable, even worse than Grover Cleveland's hauling down of the flag in Hawaii in 1893. Furthermore the vision of Far Eastern rule still gripped much of the population, and business interests continued to appreciate the importance of a Philippine springboard into the potential Chinese market.

The peace treaty went to the Senate on January 4, 1899. The

15. Fred H. Harrington, "The Anti-Imperialist Movement in the United States, 1898–1900," *Mississippi Valley Historical Review*, XXII (1935), 211–30; Richard E. Welch, Jr., "Motives and Policy Objectives of Anti-Imperialists, 1898," *Mid-America*, LI (1969), 119–29; Robert L. Beisner, *Twelve against Empire: The Anti-Imperialists, 1898–1900* (New York, 1971). For an argument that many anti-imperialists, while opposing territorial expansion, favored what was crucial, namely, economic expansion, see John W. Rollins, "The Anti-Imperialists and American Foreign Policy: A Reappraisal" (Master of Science thesis, University of Wisconsin, 1961).

fervent debate that followed turned almost entirely on the momentous annexation question. Undoubtedly the strong, almost instinctive feeling that the United States should not depart from tradition and acquire these tropical islands, far away off the shores of Asia, furnished the principal reason for voting against annexation. One can only speculate as to the influence of economic interests, such as Louisiana sugar, which feared Philippine competition.[16] Without the annexation question, the treaty would have gone through easily because its other provision aroused little or no controversy and everyone wanted peace. Similarly, if the Philippines could have been separated from the treaty and considered alone, annexation might have been defeated.

The treaty was debated mainly in executive session, where no doubt the Senators gave due attention to the economic and strategic advantages that the islands would confer, in particular the value to the United States of having a base off the coast of Asia which would serve as an entry into the huge, and endangered, Chinese market. A number of resolutions, however, came up for public consideration in the Senate; the long debates over them were devoted almost exclusively to constitutional and ethical questions.[17]

Much the most significant and time-consuming of these resolutions had been introduced as early as December 6, 1898, by George G. Vest, a Democrat from Missouri; it declared: "That under the Constitution of the United States, no power is given to the Federal Government to acquire territory to be held and governed permanently as colonies." Since (as he apparently took for granted) incorporation of the remote archipelago into the union as one or more states was unthinkable, Vest contended that its acquisition would clearly be unconstitutional. Many pages of the *Congressional Record* are filled with speeches supporting this resolution; comparatively few Senators spoke against it.[18] The support came overwhelmingly

16. See Senator Hoar's remark that the attitude of the Louisiana Senators was determined by the Louisiana sugar planters' fear of Philippine competition, *Congressional Record*, 55 Cong., 3 Sess., p. 1840 (Feb. 14, 1899).

17. For the secret sessions see *Journal of the Executive Proceedings of the Senate of the United States of America* (Washington, 1909), XXXI, Pt. 2, pp. 1161, 1283–84; for a summary of the whole debate see Julius W. Pratt, *Expansionists of 1898: The Acquisition of Hawaii and the Spanish Islands* (Baltimore, 1936), pp. 345–60.

18. The Vest resolution is in *Congressional Record*, 55 Cong., 3 Sess., p. 20 (Dec. 6, 1898); his supporting speech is in *ibid.*, pp. 93–97 (Dec. 12, 1898). For other speeches by opponents of annexation see *ibid.*, pp. 432–39 (Jan. 6, 1899), pp. 783–92

from Democrats and Populists, but no one backed it so emotionally as did a Republican, the venerable senior Senator from Massachusetts, George Frisbie Hoar. The fear he had earlier expressed, that the acquisition of Hawaii would be the prelude to more distant acquisitions, seemed on the verge of realization. To Hoar annexation brought up "the greatest question, this question of the power and authority of our Constitution in this matter, I had almost said, that had been discussed among mankind from the beginning of time." The Constitution, he argued, did not give the authority to take the Philippines. "The power to conquer alien people and hold them in subjugation is nowhere expressly granted" to the federal government by the Constitution, and "is nowhere implied." Our fathers, he declared, "meant to send abroad the American flag bearing upon its folds, invisible perhaps to the bodily eye, but visible to the spiritual discernment, the legend of the dignity of pure mankind." But if the United States went ahead with annexation, then "no longer, as the flag floats over distant seas, shall it bear on its folds to the downtrodden and oppressed among men the glad tidings that there is at least one spot where that beautiful dream is a living reality."[19] Such sentiments, however grandiloquent, impressed many who heard them.

Senator Orville H. Platt, Republican from Connecticut, delivered the strongest attack on the Vest resolution. He put forward what Hoar called the "astonishing" constitutional argument that the United States "as a nation . . . possesses every sovereign power not reserved in the Constitution to the States or the people; that the right to acquire territory was not reserved"; and that therefore she could hold the Philippines without being obligated to make states of them.[20] In a short speech Henry Cabot Lodge, the junior Senator to Hoar, appealed to common sense: "Suppose we reject the treaty; what follows? Let us look at it practically. We continue the state of war, and every sensible man in the country, every business interest, desires the reestablishment of peace in law as well as in fact." Rather

(Jan. 19, 1899), pp. 921–28, 930–31 (Jan. 23, 1899), pp. 1067–71 (Jan. 26, 1899), pp. 1296–99 (Jan. 31, 1899), pp. 1343–49 (Feb. 1, 1899), pp. 1416–32 (Feb. 3, 1899), pp. 1445–51 (Feb. 4, 1899).

19. *Ibid.*, pp. 494, 496, 501 (Jan. 9, 1899).

20. *Ibid.*, pp. 287–97 (Dec. 19, 1898). Hoar's characterization is in *ibid.*, p. 494 (Jan. 9, 1899).

slyly he observed that he "had not touched upon the commercial advantages to the country . . . or the far greater question of the markets of China, of which we must have our share for the benefit of our workingmen."[21]

The debate on the Vest resolution went on interminably through December 1898 and January 1899. The resolution never came to a vote. Perhaps the frequent interruptions for the executive sessions prevented that. In any event, Vest and his supporters realized, no doubt, that they did not constitute a majority. The treaty was going to pass; that became increasingly evident.

Only two Republicans opposed the treaty: Hoar and Eugene Hale of Maine. But many conservatives, pillars of the party who had resisted the slide to war, were very dubious about taking the remote archipelago, such Senators as Stephen B. Elkins, Nelson W. Aldrich, Marcus A. Hanna, Charles W. Fairbanks, William B. Allison, John C. Spooner. In the end they could not desert their leader, the man who had brought the country safely through the war, and the close friend of some of them. It may be, too, that secret promises and bargains secured some votes.[22] One may be sure that many Republicans, and some Democrats too, accepted the economic and strategic arguments for acquiring a Far Eastern base, close to China. Perhaps most persuasive was the lack of a convincing alternative: as McKinley said, the army's presence imposed obligations; the United States *had* to take the islands; later on, she could decide what to do with them. Most Democrats opposed the treaty: 22 voted against it, 10 for it. William Jennings Bryan wanted the United States to annex the Philippines and then declare them independent; probably this swayed some Democratic Senators to favor the treaty. It passed on February 6, 1899, by a vote of 57 to 27, one more than the needed two-thirds.[23] A few days later Senator Augustus O. Bacon, Democrat from Georgia, offered an amendment promising the Filipinos independence as soon as they set up a stable government. It was

21. *Ibid.,* pp. 959, 960 (Jan. 24, 1899).
22. May, *Imperial Democracy,* p. 261; Richard F. Pettigrew also voted against the treaty; he was elected as a Republican but supported Bryan.
23. *Executive Proceedings,* XXXI, Pt. 2, p. 1284. Regarding Bryan's role see Paolo E. Coletta, "Bryan, McKinley, and the Treaty of Paris," *Pacific Historical Review,* XXVI (1957), 131–46, and "Bryan, Anti-Imperialism, and Missionary Diplomacy," *Nebraska History,* XLIV (1963), 167–87; Merle E. Curti, "Bryan and World Peace," Smith College *Studies in History,* XVI (1931), 125.

defeated by the Vice-President's casting vote.[24]

But even had the treaty failed in February, it would have passed soon afterward. The new Senate elected in 1898 could have been called into special session; it lacked seven men who opposed the treaty in February, and its more favorable composition would have assured an affirmative vote. Despite the break with tradition represented by colonial rule over millions of people across the Pacific Ocean, annexation was bound to occur, given all the circumstances, once Old Dewey had not just sailed away and General Merritt had planted his standard firmly at Manila.

One reason for the decision to take at least a Philippine base was that it would serve as a vestibule to the Chinese market. But once the vestibule had been acquired, it constituted, in its turn, an argument for a stronger Chinese policy. For the vestibule would lose its value with a partitioned market behind it. That China was in grave danger there could be no doubt. The Germans at Kiaochow, the Russians at Port Arthur, the leased territories and spheres of influence, all these developments threatening the great potential market worried American business leaders. Business pressure, which had been exerted upon Washington just before the Spanish war, continued to be felt during the conflict; and in the new Secretary of State, John Hay, businessmen found a man long convinced of the need for a larger American role in China.[25]

Hay had had a remarkable career, both in the government and as a fairly distinguished man of letters. When a young man, he had been Abraham Lincoln's private secretary; later he had been Secretary of the American Legation at Madrid (in 1870), and Assistant Secretary of State (1879 to 1881). He was ambassador to Great Britain in 1897 and 1898. Thus he had had considerable experience in diplomacy. He was a person of refined taste, cultivated, and something of an intellectual. Married to a woman with a great fortune, he had no financial worries. But Hay was too gentle, too sensitive, for the rough-and-tumble of American politics. All too

24. *Congressional Record,* 55 Cong., 3 Sess., pp. 1845–46 (Feb. 14, 1899). A similar resolution passed the Senate but not the House, *ibid.,* p. 1479 (Feb. 6, 1899), p. 1529 (Feb. 7, 1899), p. 1847 (Feb. 14, 1899).

25. The best biography of Hay is Tyler Dennett, *John Hay: From Poetry to Politics* (New York, 1933). Regarding Hay's view on Far Eastern Policy see Charles S. Campbell, *Special Business Interests and the Open Door Policy* (New Haven, 1951), chs. 7, 8; and *Anglo-American Understanding, 1898–1903* (Baltimore, 1957), pp. 161–63.

aware of his intellectual and moral qualities, he did not conceal his contempt for most members of Congress. They, in turn, naturally had little love for him. "It is rather sad . . . ," Whitelaw Reid (on whose New York *Tribune* Hay had once worked) observed, "to see how completely he got the Senate on the brain in his later years."[26] The new Secretary would have accomplished more, and with less wear and tear on his delicate nervous system, if he had been able to get along better with Congress. All the same, Hay was an outstanding Secretary of State. In other circumstances he might not have been; but his pro-British, Anglo-Saxon, and expansionist prejudices disposed him to policies that happened to fit American needs around the turn of the century.

In his annual message of 1898, delivered after Hay's return to Washington, President McKinley stated firmly that he would "subserve our large interests" in China "by all means appropriate to the constant policy of our Government."[27] Hay, who presumably wrote this passage, was worried about the German and Russian moves at Kiaochow and Port Arthur. While in London he had urged a stronger Far Eastern policy; now in the State Department he was in a position to push vigorously for one.

The story of the background of the Open Door notes is too well known to need detailed repetition here. Suffice it to say that the European threats to China continued through 1899, and that American business interests continued to agitate for action by Washington.[28] Hay's adviser on Far Eastern policy was William W. Rockhill, back from his post in Athens; Rockhill was another advocate of a more active role in China. During the summer of 1899 he had been corresponding at length about the Far Eastern situation with an old friend, Alfred E. Hippisley, a British subject and an employee of the Chinese customs service, who was visiting the United States. In August, Hippisley urged that the time had come for a decisive American *démarche*. Rockhill agreed; and he told Hay so. The Secretary, who needed little prompting but feared to provoke public and senatorial opposition, decided to delay no longer.

26. John A. Garraty, *Henry Cabot Lodge: A Biography* (New York, 1953), p. 212.
27. Message of Dec. 5, 1898, James D. Richardson (ed.), *A Compilation of the Messages and Papers of the Presidents* . . . (20 vols., New York, 1916), XIV, 6328.
28. Regarding business pressure see Campbell, *Special Business Interests*, chs. 4–8.

He requested Rockhill to draw up a memorandum on the subject of commercial freedom in China.[29]

On September 6, 1899, Secretary Hay dispatched the famous Open Door instructions—they were based on Rockhill's memorandum—to the American ambassadors in London, Berlin, and St. Petersburg; and on later dates, ending November 21, essentially the same instructions to France, Italy, and Japan. The September notes (as they may conveniently be called) asked each country addressed to declare that, within any sphere of influence or leased territory it might have in China, it would not interfere with any treaty port or vested interest, would permit the tariff to be levied and collected by China, and would not impose higher harbor dues or railway charges on foreign nationals than on its own nationals. No country accepted outright; Russia replied evasively. But on March 20, 1900, Hay blandly announced that all had replied satisfactorily.[30]

The Open Door policy, as formally expressed in September 1899, although of tremendous significance for United States foreign policy in the twentieth century, had little immediate importance. The administration itself did not view the notes as formulating a major policy. Rockhill described his memorandum as indicating "the main points of the negotiations for a kind of *modus vivendi* in China"; and the evidence suggests that Hay envisaged the notes as a mild response to a temporary situation.[31] All the same, was it not a fact that the United States had taken a long step toward acquiring a sort of informal commercial empire, one no less the product of imperialism than is a territorial empire? Some writers have so argued.[32] It is certainly true that Washington had, in effect, acted to ensure the expansion of American trade with an underdeveloped country, while at the same time avoiding the hazards of colonial rule. In a

---

29. Regarding Rockhill and Hippisley see A. Whitney Griswold, *The Far Eastern Policy of the United States* (New York, 1938), ch. 2; Marilyn B. Young, *The Rhetoric of Empire: American China Policy, 1895–1901* (Cambridge, Mass., 1968), pp. 123–31.

30. Hay to Joseph H. Choate (American ambassador to Great Britain), Sept. 6, 1899, *Papers Relating to the Foreign Relations of the United States, 1899* (Washington, 1901), pp. 131–33; Hay's declaration of March 20, 1900, is in *ibid.,* p. 142.

31. Rockhill to Hay, Aug. 28, 1899, Paul A. Varg, *Open Door Diplomat: The Life of W. W. Rockhill* (Urbana, Ill., 1952), p. 36. Akira Iriye, *Across the Pacific: The Inner History of American-East Asian Relations* (New York, 1967), pp. 80–82.

32. See William A. Williams, *The Tragedy of American Diplomacy* (Cleveland, 1959); regarding Britain's informal empire see Kenneth Bourne, *The Foreign Policy of Victorian England, 1830–1902* (Oxford, 1970), pp. 3–5.

carefully restricted sense this kind of activity may be considered imperialistic; and Hay's Open Door policy may therefore be associated with the outburst of expansion at the century's close. But one must always remember the administration's scant regard, in 1899, for its September notes; the administration would have been astonished to know that its *modus vivendi* would some day be seen, by some writers, as partaking of the pure essence of imperialism.

Two other matters remain to be considered, Samoa and an isthmian canal; of these the latter was of course much the more important, because a firm decision to build a canal, supplementing the acquisition of Hawaii and Caribbean bases, would mean the virtual realization of the basic trinity of objectives long sought by expansionists.

The governmental structure established in Samoa by the Berlin conference of 1889, with its complicated administrative arrangements, had worked reasonably well, but irritations had inevitably developed among the American, British, and German officials on the islands. Moreover, the chronic civil wars had not been stamped out. Consequently, Washington, London, and Berlin began to wonder whether the clean-cut solution of partition was not called for.[33]

A sudden crisis brought matters to a head. In August 1898, the month when Hawaii was annexed, King Malietoa Laupepa died, and a struggle for the succession got under way. The contenders for the throne were Mataafa, the able chief who had so enraged Germany in 1888, and Malietoa Laupepa's son, Malietoa Tanu. Britons and Americans on the islands favored Malietoa; Germans, overlooking their former dislike of him, backed Mataafa. According to the General Act of Berlin, the Samoan Supreme Court had the duty to decide a contested royal election, and on December 31, 1898, Chief Justice William L. Chambers, an American, pronounced for Malietoa Tanu. Another petty civil war convulsed the islands. Mataafa defeated Malietoa, who with some of his followers and the Chief Justice fled to a British warship. The three consuls appointed a provisional government on January 4, 1899, headed by Mataafa and

33. Regarding events in Samoa from 1889 through 1899 see George H. Ryden, *The Foreign Policy of the United States in Relation to Samoa* (New Haven, 1933), chs. 14, 15; Alfred Vagts, *Deutschland und die Vereinigten Staaten in der Weltpolitik* (2 vols., New York, 1935), I, ch. 10; John Bassett Moore, *A Digest of International Law . . .* (8 vols., Washington, 1906), I, 548–52.

the German president of the municipal council, Dr. Raffel. Chambers refused to recognize it. Raffel then closed the Supreme Court, but the British and American consuls and the commander of the British warship reopened it on January 7. Disorder gripped the islands. Increasingly, partition seemed the only solution.

On March 6, 1899, one month after the annexation of the Philippines had demonstrated that the United States would extend her sway even to distant Pacific islands, an American rear admiral, Albert Kautz, U.S.S. *Philadelphia,* dropped anchor at Apia; on the eleventh he proclaimed the provisional government deposed. In mid-March, British and American marines landed; and their warships bombarded areas held by Mataafa, accidentally damaging the German Consulate. Sporadic fighting continued for days. On the twenty-third Malietoa Tanu was crowned King. Germany was outraged over the damage to her property and over the apparently concerted Anglo-American action against her. Once again, as eleven years before, the state of affairs in Samoa was critical.

At Berlin's suggestion, Germany, Great Britain, and the United States agreed in April to send commissioners to Samoa to investigate. The three commissioners found a grim situation when they arrived on May 13. After establishing themselves as a provisional government and disarming both warring factions, they unanimously reported that Chambers had decided correctly in favor of Malietoa Tanu but that the office of King should be abolished. Malietoa abdicated on June 10, 1899. Peace returned to the islands.

Reporting to Secretary Hay, the American commissioner, Bartlett Tripp, recommended that the arrangement of 1889 be terminated. Germany and Great Britain favored partition, and agreed that the United States should have the island of Tutuila, the site of Pago Pago (where the United States still had not built a base). This was acceptable to Washington.[34] The difficulty was to satisfy the two European powers. Eventually Britain and Germany concluded a treaty on November 14, 1899, by which Britain renounced all her Samoan rights in favor of Germany and the United States, and

34. Tripp to Hay, Aug. 7, 1899, *Foreign Relations, 1899,* p. 659; Hay to Choate, Sept. 7, Nov. 3, 1899, *ibid.,* pp. 663–64, 664–65. Tripp's full report is in *Senate Documents,* 56 Cong., 1 Sess., No. 51 (Serial 3848). Regarding a Pago Pago base see annual report of Secretary of the Navy John D. Long, Nov. 22, 1899, *House Documents,* 56 Cong., 1 Sess., No. 3 (Serial 3912), p. 27.

received from Germany compensation in the Pacific Ocean and Africa.[35] By a British-German-American treaty, concluded December 2, 1899, the Berlin General Act was annulled; Germany and Great Britain renounced, in favor of the United States, all Samoan land east of the 171st longitude (consisting of Tutuila and some islets); and the United States renounced, in favor of Germany, all islands west of that longitude.[36] Germany had raised the question of compensation for the damage inflicted during the British-American bombardment. Under a convention signed on November 7, 1899, the three countries asked King Oscar of Sweden and Norway to arbitrate claims arising from the military action.[37] On October 14, 1902, the King found the two English-speaking countries at fault. The United States later paid $20,000 to German claimants and smaller amounts to some other claimants.[38]

The American readiness to partition the islands was another consequence of the expansionistic mood at the century's end. Samoa stood in about the same relation to American power in the South Pacific and potential American trade with Australia and New Zealand as the Philippines did to American power in the China Sea and potential American trade with China. In both cases the acquisition of a naval base—Pago Pago or Manila—fitted in with traditional policy, whereas the acquisition of far-distant native populations (small in American Samoa, large in the Philippines) did not.

The failure in May 1898 of Senator John T. Morgan's bond-guarantee bill for a Nicaragua canal will be recalled; the canal stalemate still existed even at that late date. But during the course of the year the situation changed drastically. By August the United States had annexed the Hawaiian Islands, invaded Puerto Rico and Cuba, and smashed Spanish power in the Philippines. With Hawaii taken and Caribbean bases occupied, two of the main goals of expansionists had been virtually attained. A canal remained to be built. One

35. *Foreign Relations, 1899*, pp. 665–66.

36. Malloy, *Treaties*, II, 1595–97; the Senate approved the treaty on Jan. 16, 1900.

37. *Ibid.*, pp. 1589–90; the Senate approved the convention on Feb. 21, 1900.

38. *Ibid.*, pp. 1591–95; for the later developments see Walter S. Penfield, "The Settlement of the Samoan Cases," *American Journal of International Law*, VII (1913), 767–773. According to the Swedish minister to the United States, Hay attributed the decision to German influence over Sweden. Sir Michael Herbert (British ambassador to the United States) to Foreign Secretary Lord Lansdowne, Oct. 27, 1902, Public Record Office (London), Foreign Office 5/2488. See also *Literary Digest*, XXV (Nov. 1, 1902), 543.

could feel in the nationalistic air that it would not long be delayed.

During a worrisome period of the hostilities the warship *Oregon,* summoned urgently from the Pacific Ocean, had raced 10,000 miles around Cape Horn to the Atlantic. Millions of Americans followed the vessel's progress; bitterly they lamented the lack of an isthmian waterway. "The voyage of the *Oregon* was an argument, ten thousand arguments, I think, in favor of the building of this canal, and it is that kind of thing that actuates the American people," Senator William A. Harris asserted truly.[39] Important business interests, too, were urging action. A committee of the National Board of Trade resolved in December 1898 that a canal was "an imperative economic factor" and asked Congress for immediate steps to construct a Nicaragua waterway; it recommended that the Maritime Canal Company do the actual building.[40] The industrial surplus that had appeared in 1894 was presenting an irresistible argument for quicker access to the markets on the west coast of Latin America and to the great potential market of China. "All these circumstances," President McKinley declared in his annual message of December 1898, "suggest the urgency of some definite action by the Congress. . . ." He described a canal, presumably through Nicaragua, as "now more than ever indispensable to that intimate and ready intercommunication between our eastern and western seaboards demanded by the annexation of the Hawaiian Islands and the prospective expansion of our influence and commerce in the Pacific," and he concluded "that our national policy now more imperatively than ever calls for its control by this Government."[41]

Two days after the message the indefatigable Morgan submitted yet another guarantee bill in the Senate, where a powerful Nicaraguan bloc existed. But the familiar bickering began again. The French New Panama Canal Company of course bitterly opposed any move favoring the Nicaragua route. Party politics, too, complicated the picture; for Morgan was a Democrat, and the Republican administration did not want to give him the credit for a canal. Moreover, some Senators believed that the governmental control over the Maritime Canal Company provided for by Morgan's bill would, in effect, violate the Clayton-Bulwer treaty, a telling consideration in view of Britain's sympathy with America at the time of the Spanish

39. *Congressional Record,* 55 Cong., 3 Sess., p. 180 (Dec. 14, 1898).
40. *Ibid.,* p. 207; the resolution was dated Dec. 15, 1898.
41. Message of Dec. 5, 1898, Richardson, *Messages and Papers,* XIV, 6327.

war.[42] Other Senators argued that the Maritime Canal Company was an unworthy instrument for what should be a great national enterprise.[43] But the feeling was strong that construction must be delayed no longer and that the bill, however imperfect, offered the best hope for getting it started. On January 21, 1899, in the midst of the debate over the peace treaty with Spain, the Senate passed the bill overwhelmingly, 48 to 6.[44]

In the House it met trouble. On February 13, 1899, William P. Hepburn, chairman of the Committee on Interstate and Foreign Commerce, to which the measure had been referred, reported it back with a recommendation that it be replaced by a measure he himself had introduced in December. The Hepburn bill, in outright disregard of the Clayton-Bulwer treaty, provided that the United States government, instead of acting through the Maritime Canal Company, itself build a canal through Nicaragua, and that $115 million be appropriated for this purpose.[45] Hepburn succeeded in shelving Morgan's bill but could not get a vote on his own measure.

It was now, again, the turn of the Senate. Realizing that agreement with the House on a separate canal bill could not be reached before the session's adjournment on March 3, Senator William P. Frye on February 17 amended a Rivers and Harbors bill so as to provide for a Nicaragua canal—a shrewd maneuver because a Rivers and Harbors bill contains items desired by every member of Congress, and its defeat cannot be contemplated. Like the Hepburn bill, the amendment specified that the government build the canal and appropriate $115 million; unlike the Hepburn bill, the amendment provided for possible compensation for the Maritime Canal Company (an important point for Morgan and other friends of the company). The Rivers and Harbors bill, with the canal proviso, passed the Senate on February 24, and then went to the House Committee on Rivers and Harbors.[46] A victory for Nicara-

42. *Congressional Record,* 55 Cong., 3 Sess., p. 29 (Dec. 7, 1898); see also *Senate Reports,* 55 Cong., 3 Sess., No. 1418 (Serial 3739).

43. See the statements of Senator John C. Spooner, *Congressional Record,* 55 Cong., 3 Sess., p. 691 (Jan. 17, 1899); and of Senator Charles W. Fairbanks, *ibid.,* p. 845 (Jan. 20, 1899). See also *ibid.,* p. 143 (Dec. 13, 1898), p. 799 (Jan. 19, 1899).

44. *Ibid.,* p. 911 (Jan. 21, 1899).

45. *Ibid.,* p. 1829 (Feb. 13, 1899); see also *House Reports,* 55 Cong., 3 Sess., No. 2104 (Serial 3841).

46. *Congressional Record,* 55 Cong., 3 Sess., pp. 2296, 2302; the vote was 50 to 3. Regarding the Maritime Canal Company see the assertions of Pettigrew and Rawlins, *ibid.,* pp. 2290, 2293–94 (Feb. 24, 1899).

gua over Panama and the French company appeared imminent. At this climactic juncture Maurice Hutin, director general of the New Panama Canal Company, arrived in the United States. On February 27 William Nelson Cromwell, the company's American attorney, testified before a House committee that two-fifths of the Panama canal had been completed; and he offered to reincorporate the French company in an American state so as to afford the United States the maximum control possible under the terms of the concession from Colombia. Hutin and Cromwell repeated the offer to McKinley the next day. The proposed American participation in the French venture raised doubts, among some government officials, as to the wisdom of deciding irrevocably for Nicaragua before making a fresh examination of Panama.[47]

Impressed by the French offer, and perhaps responsive to intense lobbying by Cromwell, the House refused to accept Frye's Nicaragua amendment. During the closing three days of the session a House-Senate committee conferred hastily to save the Rivers and Harbors bill. It reached a decision on the last day of the session: Frye's amendment was scrapped in favor of an amendment providing for a new commission to investigate all routes (not merely those through Nicaragua, to which the recent commissions had confined their attention). No time limit was set, and $1 million was appropriated for expenses; the measure envisaged compensation for the Maritime Canal Company.[48] The Rivers and Harbors bill thus amended became law on March 3, 1899.[49] A reprieve had been granted the New Company—in the nick of time.

This was a remarkable story of maneuver and countermaneuver, first between friends and foes of the Maritime Canal Company, and then between backers of Nicaragua on the one hand and the New Panama Canal Company on the other. Why did Cromwell and the French win out? Speaker Reed, a consistent opponent of the Nicaragua project, was undoubtedly somewhat responsible; it is possible, also, that Congress was influenced by engineering opinion, because

47. *The Story of Panama: Hearings on the Rainey Resolution before the Committee on Foreign Affairs of the House of Representatives* (Washington, 1913), pp. 225–26; *Senate Reports,* 56 Cong., 1 Sess., No. 1337 (Serial 3894), Pt. 1, p. 7; see also Sullivan and Cromwell's letter to McKinley, March 11, 1899, *ibid.,* p. 8.
48. *Congressional Record,* 55 Cong., 3 Sess., pp. 2815–16 (March 3, 1899).
49. For the final phase of the legislating see *ibid.,* pp. 2622, 2663 (March 1, 1899), pp. 2814–16, 2818–43, 2923–25 (March 3, 1899).

some engineers were swinging over to Panama as the better route.[50] However, one must agree with Cromwell that he was justified in taking upon himself a large part of the credit. According to him, he had persuaded Reed, Joseph G. Cannon (Republican leader in the House and chairman of the Ways and Means Committee), Theodore E. Burton (chairman of the Committee on Rivers and Harbors), and other powerful Representatives that before deciding for Nicaragua the United States should make a survey of all the routes, including those across the Panama. "We think that we are justified in stating," he boasted, "that without our efforts the . . . Nicaragua bill would . . . have been passed."[51]

One must also agree with the astute attorney that the decision to investigate all the routes "entirely changed the situation."[52] The Maritime Canal Company never resumed its activities in Nicaragua, and before long the United States shifted her attention to Panama. (It should be noted, however, that Representative Hepburn reintroduced his Nicaragua bill in December 1899; it was not shelved until a year later, and even after then its revival occasionally seemed possible.) In accordance with the law of March 3, McKinley dissolved the Nicaragua Canal Commission of 1897 (whose report, submitted May 9, 1899, recommended a Nicaragua canal) and on June 10, 1899, named an Isthmian Canal Commission, headed, like the former commission, by Rear Admiral John G. Walker. This change between May 9 and June 10 from Nicaragua to the entire isthmus presaged the future Panama canal. Although the Walker commission reported for Nicaragua on November 16, 1901, it immediately changed to Panama after the French company, now facing ruin, drastically lowered the selling price for its concession.[53] Thereafter a definitive American decision in favor of Panama was not long in the making.

In 1899 there still remained, it is true, one major obstacle to an American canal: the Clayton-Bulwer treaty. But Anglo-American negotiations to terminate that treaty had already commenced in 1898, and although serious difficulties were to be encountered, the

50. *Engineering Magazine*, XIX (1900), 107.
51. *Story of Panama*, pp. 224–27; Dwight C. Miner, *The Fight for the Panama Route: The Story of the Spooner Act and the Hay-Herrán Treaty* (New York, 1940), p. 90n.
52. *Story of Panama*, p. 229 (misprint for p. 227).
53. *Senate Documents*, 58 Cong., 2 Sess., No. 222 (Serial 4609).

Hay-Pauncefote treaty of November 18, 1901, finally abrogated the detested restrictions of 1850.[54]

Thus by the summer of 1899 the United States had taken an enormous stride toward her isthmian canal. She had also annexed the Hawaiian Islands and bases in the Caribbean Sea. These were the goals toward which geographic and economic pressures, together with the teachings of James G. Blaine, Alfred T. Mahan, and others, and the whole Social Darwinian climate of the time, had been urging the country for years. The war with Spain and the stirring events at Manila Bay had precipitated these developments; they had precipitated, further, the much less deep-rooted but momentous acquisition of the Philippines, as well as the acquisition of Wake, Guam, and Samoa.

What of the other principal theme of the country's foreign policy during the last decades of the century, that is, relations with Great Britain? There, too, by that same summer of 1899, conditions had changed enormously: the emotional hostility of the post–Civil War years had dwindled out of all recognition. Just as the Spanish-American War was a catalyst for territorial expansion, so it occasioned a rise of British-American friendship much more effusive than the display of friendship during the Venezuela boundary controversy. This is the final matter we must examine.

54. Campbell, *Anglo-American Understanding*, chs. 9, 11; the text of the treaty is in Malloy, *Treaties*, I, 782–84.

# CHAPTER 17

# Anglo-American Amity

THE Spanish-American War was the occasion not only of territorial expansion but of an outpouring of expressions of friendship between Great Britain and the United States.[1] Remembering the bitterness of the late sixties, Americans might well have been surprised when the British government and people, quite unlike those of the Continent, sided with the United States. Although Queen Victoria, Prime Minister Salisbury, and many other aristocrats and upper-class Britons sympathized instinctively with monarchical Spain rather than republican America, they did not permit sentiment to blur their perception that the national interest demanded support of the United States. As for the British people in general, they strongly favored Anglo-Saxon America rather than Catholic Spain, the oppressor of Cuba and the former inveterate enemy of Great Britain.

Even before the war Britain's pro-American feelings were evident. One might have expected her to defend Minister Dupuy de

1. This chapter is based, to a considerable extent, on Charles S. Campbell, *Anglo-American Understanding, 1898–1903* (Baltimore, 1957), ch. 1; *From Revolution to Rapprochement: The United States and Great Britain, 1783–1900* (New York, 1974), ch. 14; and "Anglo-American Relations, 1897–1901," in Paolo E. Coletta (ed.), *Threshold to American Internationalism: Essays on the Foreign Policies of William McKinley* (New York, 1970), pp. 221–55. See also Harry C. Allen, *Great Britain and the United States: A History of Anglo-American Relations (1783–1952)* (New York, 1955), Pt. 1; and Bradford Perkins, *The Great Rapprochement: England and the United States, 1895–1914* (New York, 1968), chs. 5 and 6.

Lôme when his private letter was published, if only because his hasty departure from Washington was reminiscent of Sackville West's fate a decade earlier. But, instead, she blamed the chagrined diplomat and scarcely criticized the yellow press or the excessive American reaction. And when the *Maine* plunged to the bottom of Havana harbor, the outburst of grief in Britain was extraordinary. "With the community of race between our people and the sufferers," the London *Daily News* said, "the calamity will send a pang through every British heart."[2] While regretting the prospect of hostilities, the London *Times* predicted that "should the worst come to the worst, we shall not of course forget, whilst maintaining the duties of neutrality towards both, that one of them is knitted to us yet more closely by the ties of blood."[3]

We have seen how Ambassador Pauncefote consulted Acting Secretary William R. Day about the collective note, drawn up by the Washington envoys of the great powers, before it was presented to McKinley on April 7, 1898. London was just as considerate a week later when a stronger mediation step was contemplated. It arose in consequence of the Spanish armistice declaration. This time the European envoys at Washington, including Pauncefote, advised their governments to warn the McKinley administration that the Spanish retreat removed all justification for the use of force by the United States. But London immediately concluded that Pauncefote had made a mistake, and it rejected his advice. Without British cooperation, the Continental governments were unwilling to act; and the mediation move collapsed.[4] Americans did not doubt that except for Britain's stand a damaging intervention would have occurred.

During the conflict Great Britain observed strict neutrality,[5] but her sympathies were clear. "We are glad to feel sure," the Men's Sunday Union declared in a unanimous resolution of May 3, 1898, addressed to the American people, "from your close kinship with ourselves, that you will go resolutely on till you have established good government in the Spanish West Indies; and we hope you will

2. The *Daily News* (London), Feb. 17, 1898. See also the *Standard* (London), Feb. 11, 1898; Campbell, *Anglo-American Understanding*, pp. 28–30.

3. The *Times* (London), March 28, 1898.

4. Campbell, *Anglo-American Understanding*, pp. 32–36.

5. Regarding the problems she faced see Robert G. Neale, *Great Britain and United States Expansion: 1898–1900* (East Lansing, 1966), ch. 2.

see that the Philippines get nothing less."[6] A prominent journalist, Henry Norman, asserted extravagantly but, one suspects, with a measure of truth: "If a combination of European powers should be formed to crush the United States . . . they would have to crush the British fleet as well. That this is the view of those at present responsible for British policy, *I know*. . . . we should never stand idly by and see a hundred millions of people who speak English trampled on by people who speak Russian or French or German."[7] Many such utterances circulated in the United States; they were heard with deep gratitude by Americans, who had entered the conflict with some trepidation and realized that the Continent befriended Spain. Especially appreciated was a report that the British squadron at Manila Bay had maneuvered in a manner to prevent the German warships there from blocking an American naval attack on Manila. Although false, the exciting story became legendary, and it added immeasurably to the friendly sentiment felt for Britain. A later report, in this case true, that London had encouraged Washington to annex the Hawaiian and Philippine Islands, increased Britain's popularity.[8]

The consequence was an upsurge of what Pauncefote called "the most exuberant affection for England & 'Britishers' in general"; or, to quote the London *Times*, "a revolution in American sentiment which even the most sanguine believed would require a generation to accomplish."[9] To a considerable extent the friendliness was reciprocated in Great Britain; John Hay, as ambassador, was delighted to discover that the state of feeling in Britain was the best he had ever known.[10] So fervent was the new mood that a secret Anglo-American alliance was speculated about in coffee houses and foreign offices around the world. The speculation was nourished by

6. John Hay (American ambassador to Great Britain) to Secretary of State William R. Day, May 4, 1898, National Archives (Washington), Record Group 59, Despatches from the American Embassy, London. See also Campbell, *Anglo-American Understanding*, pp. 39–49.

7. *Literary Digest*, XVI (May 7, 1898), 562.

8. Regarding Manila Bay see Thomas A. Bailey, "Dewey and the Germans at Manila Bay," *American Historical Review*, XLV (1939), 59–81; Admiral von Diederichs, "A Statement of Events in Manila Bay, May–October, 1898," *Journal of the Royal United Service Institution*, LIX (1914), 421–46. Regarding the Philippines see Campbell, *Anglo-American Understanding*, pp. 41–42.

9. Pauncefote to Salisbury, May 26, 1898, Lord Salisbury Papers, Christ Church Library (Oxford); the *Times* (London), Jan. 17, 1899.

10. Hay to Senator Henry Cabot Lodge, May 25, 1898, William R. Thayer, *The Life and Letters of John Hay* (2 vols., Boston, 1915), II, 168.

Colonial Secretary Joseph Chamberlain, who in a speech at Birmingham on May 13, 1898, declared: "And I even go so far as to say that, terrible as war may be, even war itself would be cheaply purchased if in a great and noble cause the Stars and Stripes and the Union Jack should wave together over an Anglo-Saxon Alliance."[11] In an earlier day Chamberlain's surprising remark would have evoked a chorus of denunciation in the United States, but the British Embassy reported that hardly an American objected to the proposed alliance, while a number of editorials supported it.[12] Several months later President McKinley mentioned "the remarkable enthusiasm all over the country at any reference to the Union Jack and the Stars and Stripes flying together"; and at the annual dinner of the New York Chamber of Commerce a close British-American union "of heart and purpose" was the theme.[13] As late as December 1901, according to the British ambassador at Madrid, the belief was widespread in Spain that the two English-speaking nations had concluded "an alliance of some kind."[14] The belief, of course, was false; neither country was yet prepared for such a departure from traditional policies.

Both countries perceived that the trans-Atlantic euphoria offered an opportunity to settle their controversies, one that might not long outlive the war. Previous pages have dealt with the northeastern fisheries, where peace continued to be dependent on a periodic British renewal of the *modus vivendi* of 1888, and with the Bering Sea fur seals, a subject of dispute considerably eased but not completely settled by the arbitration of 1893. But in 1898 the two most pressing issues concerned the Clayton-Bulwer treaty of 1850 and the boundary between Alaska and the Dominion of Canada. In the strongly nationalistic temper attendant upon the Spanish war, the American people, as we have seen, would not brook much more delay in acquiring their canal. As for the Alaska boundary, its southern part,

11. The *Times* (London), May 14, 1898.
12. Pauncefote to Salisbury, May 27, 1898, Public Record Office (London), Foreign Office 5/2362, enclosing a memorandum by Second Secretary Reginald T. Tower, also dated May 27.
13. Pauncefote to Salisbury, Nov. 17, 1898, Foreign Office 5/2363; New York *Tribune*, Nov. 16, 1898.
14. Henry Durand to Foreign Secretary Lord Lansdowne, Dec. 14, 1901, Foreign Office 115/1238. See also Campbell, *Anglo-American Understanding*, pp. 47–49; Lionel M. Gelber, *The Rise of Anglo-American Friendship: A Study in World Politics, 1898–1906* (London, 1938), pp. 11–13, 21–23, 29.

the panhandle, had long been uncertain, but this did not matter very much when hardly a person was in the area. In the 1890s, however, gold was discovered in the Yukon, and by 1898 some 50,000 miners had moved across the panhandle.[15] Both a boundary delineation and a revision or termination of the Clayton-Bulwer treaty had suddenly become urgent.

Soon after the Spanish war started, Pauncefote and the Canadian Minister of Marine and Fisheries, Sir Louis Davies, met several times with State Department officials, and with little difficulty they agreed to establish a Joint High Commission that would consider the various Canadian-American issues (not including, of course, the Clayton-Bulwer treaty). This new Joint High Commission was in session from August 23, 1898, to February 20, 1899, first in Quebec, then in Washington.[16] Unfortunately it settled nothing at all. The principal difficulty was the Alaska boundary. The American commissioners refused to accept a line giving Canada access to the open sea; the Canadians would not settle for less. Agreement was reached, or was close, on all the other points under negotiation, but London and Ottawa refused to conclude anything unless all the controversies, including that over the boundary, were disposed of. Unlike the Washington commission of 1871 or the Halifax fisheries commission of 1877, the Joint High Commission of 1898–1899 broke up in complete failure. This was a curious accompaniment of the exuberant affection; and it makes one wonder how deep-rooted the affection was.

The failure could have had disastrous consequences in Alaska had it not, together with some angry quarreling between American and Canadian prospectors, virtually compelled London, Ottawa, and Washington to lay down provisional lines in the most dangerous areas. The emergency *modus vivendi* of October 20, 1899, facilitated adequate policing and helped stave off further confrontations.[17]

Sustained negotiations over the Clayton-Bulwer treaty commenced soon after John Hay replaced Day as Secretary of State in September 1898. Strongly Anglophile, the new Secretary had publicly expressed his faith that "a sanction like that of religion" bound Britain and America together as "joint ministers of the same sacred

15. Campbell, *Anglo-American Understanding,* pp. 62–76.
16. *Ibid.,* pp. 86–87, ch. 4.
17. *Ibid.,* ch. 6.

mission of liberty and progress."[18] Hay asked Pauncefote, another strong proponent of British-American friendship and an authority on legal matters relating to canals, to draft a modification of the unpopular 1850 treaty. This Sir Julian did; Hay accepted the draft with minor alterations, and it went to London on January 12, 1899, for Prime Minister Salisbury's perusal. But the Prime Minister asked for Canada's opinion. Ottawa strongly opposed a canal settlement unless the United States yielded over Alaska.[19] Accordingly Salisbury refused to proceed with Pauncefote's treaty. All Anglo-American negotiations, those over the canal as well as those directly involving the Dominion, ground to a full stop in early 1899, enmeshed in the intractable problems of Alaska.

Unlike the boundary controversy, softened by the *modus vivendi*, the canal dispute was eased by no such accord. On the contrary, the United States, in spite of Britain's support during America's troubles with Spain, took advantage of Great Britain's involvement in the Boer War, which broke out in October 1899, to threaten her with virtual blackmail. It was on December 7, 1899, two days before the beginning of "Black Week," during which Great Britain suffered one military disaster after another, that Representative William P. Hepburn, still disregarding Clayton-Bulwer obligations, reintroduced his Nicaragua canal bill.[20] Thereupon Great Britain, bogged down in South Africa and confronting an outburst of hostility on the Continent, as well as much criticism by the American public (though not by the administration), felt obliged to accept Pauncefote's canal treaty early in 1900, Canada's apprehensions about Alaska notwithstanding. The chances are strong that had she not done so, the United States would have soon started to construct a canal anyway; and Anglo-American animosity, not amity, would have been the turn-of-the-century theme. With a treaty in prospect, the Hepburn bill was put aside; and although it remained a latent threat, it never

18. John Hay, *Addresses of John Hay* (New York, 1906), pp. 78–79.

19. Lord Minto (Governor General of Canada) to Colonial Secretary Joseph Chamberlain, telegram received April 10, 1899, Foreign Office 5/2416.

20. *Congressional Record,* 56 Cong., 1 Sess., p. 151 (Dec. 7, 1899); Hay to Joseph H. Choate (Hay's successor as ambassador to Great Britain), Jan. 15, 1900, Tyler Dennett, *John Hay: From Poetry to Politics* (New York, 1933), p. 251. Regarding British–American relations during the Boer War (almost all of which, however, took place in the twentieth century and therefore outside the time period of this book), see Campbell, *Anglo-American Understanding,* ch. 8; regarding general American policy see John H. Ferguson, *American Diplomacy and the Boer War* (Philadelphia, 1939).

became law. But the treaty, too, encountered difficulty, because the Senate introduced amendments unacceptable to Britain; and not until November 1901 did the Hay-Pauncefote treaty bring a settlement. That agreement was the consequence not of Anglo-American friendship but of Britain's continuing involvement with the Boers and of America's continuing manifest resolve to violate the commitments of 1850, if necessary to get her way. As for the Alaska boundary, it was not drawn until 1903, and the manner of its drawing was no more friendly than was the canal agreement.[21]

"The present honeymoon will not last," Lord Salisbury had predicted in June 1898.[22] Perhaps he recalled the remark sardonically in early 1899, when the Canadian and canal negotiations collapsed, and at the year's end when Congress rattled the Hepburn bill menacingly. All the hands-across-the-seas talk notwithstanding, Great Britain and the United States had come to terms on nothing whatsoever except a *modus vivendi* relating to a small part of the Alaska boundary. Evidently Sir Julian's "most exuberant affection" of May 1898 was not strong enough to produce a reconciliation of conflicting British and American interests.[23]

On the other hand, during that same year of 1899, the two English-speaking countries collaborated, or appeared to collaborate, in three far-flung places—in Samoa, The Hague, and China; and this mitigated the disappointment and vexation caused by the Joint High Commission's failure. In Samoa, it will be remembered, British and American soldiers fought side by side against the German-backed chieftain, Mataafa. Viewing this common front against his own country, the German Foreign Minister, Bernhard von Bülow, ruefully concluded that despite the canal and boundary difficulties the Anglo-American rapprochement still existed.[24] No doubt he was correct; it was indeed remarkable for British and American troops to be acting together on a South Sea island, a joint action that would have astonished earlier generations in Britain and America. But although the affair created an impression of Anglo-American unity,

21. For the Hay-Pauncefote treaty see Campbell, *Anglo-American Understanding*, ch. 11; regarding Alaska see *ibid.*, ch. 15, and Norman Penlington, *The Alaska Boundary Dispute: A Critical Reappraisal* (Toronto, 1972), ch. 6.
22. Salisbury to Pauncefote, June 14, 1898, Salisbury Papers.
23. Campbell, "Anglo-American Relations, 1897–1901," pp. 221–55.
24. Memorandum of von Bülow, March 14, 1899, Edgard T. S. Dugdale (ed.), *German Diplomatic Documents, 1871–1914* (4 vols., London, 1928–31), III, 53.

it was too trivial to have more than passing consequence. A measure of cooperation occurred also in Europe. In response to an appeal by the Czar of Russia, twenty-six nations met at The Hague from May 18 through July 29, 1899, to discuss armament limitation, the amelioration of the rules of war, and the peaceful settlement of international disputes.[25] Andrew D. White, ambassador to Germany, headed the American delegation; Alfred T. Mahan was another member. Sir Julian Pauncefote headed the British delegation. The conference failed to reduce armaments but did provide for some improvement in the laws of war. Its most significant achievement related to arbitration. The United States, Great Britain, and Russia all came to The Hague with plans for an arbitral tribunal. It was basically the British scheme that was adopted; but White worked closely with Sir Julian to achieve this result. Furthermore, when Germany opposed the arbitration scheme as an insidious device to offset her ability to mobilize speedily, the American delegation was instrumental in persuading her to change her mind. Under the final agreement a Permanent Court of Arbitration was established at The Hague, to which any country so inclined could refer a dispute with another country.[26]

Neither Washington nor London put many hopes in the innocuous court, and some people considered it positively dangerous, as well as foolish. However, in each country a broad vein of humanitarian sentiment hailed the arbitration plan, as it had the abortive Olney-Pauncefote treaty of 1897, as a historic step toward abolishing war. Both governments supported the court, which bound them to nothing and attracted popular acclaim; and the United States Senate voted approval of American membership in it.[27]

A certain warm glow of self-satisfaction was felt among English-speaking people over this crusade for the right. But obviously the Permanent Court fell far short of being a major common interest; and partly because of British objection, the Hague conference failed to adopt one proposal dear to American hearts—that the capture of private property at sea be made illegal. Altogether the conference

25. Calvin DeA. Davis, *The United States and the First Hague Peace Conference* (Ithaca, 1962); Campbell, *Anglo-American Understanding,* pp. 157–59.

26. James B. Scott (ed.), *The Proceedings of the Hague Peace Conferences . . .* (5 vols., New York, 1920–21).

27. *Journal of the Executive Proceedings of the Senate . . .* (Washington, 1909), XXXII, 375; the Senate approved membership on Feb. 5, 1900.

did little to bring the two English-speaking countries together. All one can say is that, like the joint action in Samoa, it fostered an impression of Anglo-American cooperation and thereby contributed somewhat to the rapprochement.

Of greater significance, it might be thought, were the developments regarding the decaying empire of China that contributed to the Open Door policy of 1899. Britain and America were reputed to share interests of great consequence in that Far Eastern country. According to the London *Times* in early 1898, the conviction was "general in the United States, that . . . in the Far East England and the United States have vast interests in common."[28] No less a person than Richard Olney, who had so belabored Great Britain in 1895, asserted in 1898 that "the present crying need of our commercial interests . . . is more markets and larger markets for the consumption of the products of the industry and inventive genius of the American people"; and he asked, "through what agency are we so likely to gain new outlets for our products as through that of a Power [that is, Great Britain] whose possessions girdle the earth and in whose ports equal privileges and facilities of trade are accorded to the flags of all nations?" The former Secretary of State thought that "there could not be two opinions" as to the propriety of making an alliance with Britain that would hold open the door in China.[29] Many British people held a similar view. Joseph Chamberlain believed that as regards the fate of China the "interest of the United States in the decision is the same as that of Great Britain"; and the London *Times* declared that the two countries had "immense, permanent, and increasing interests in common" in the Far East.[30] This was also the message of a dynamic Englishman, Lord Charles Beresford, who in a series of speeches in the United States in February 1899 enthusiastically drove home the necessity of British-American cooperation to preserve the Chinese market.[31]

Would not this shared anxiety over China lead to a common

28. The *Times* (London), March 16, 1898.
29. Richard Olney, "International Isolation of the United States," *Atlantic Monthly*, LXXXI (1898), 588, 580.
30. Joseph Chamberlain, "Recent Developments of Policy in the United States and Their Relation to an Anglo-American Alliance," *Scribner's Magazine*, XXIV (1898), 678; the *Times* (London), March 29, 1898.
31. Neale, *Great Britain and United States Expansion*, pp. 169–97; Charles S. Campbell, *Special Business Interests and the Open Door Policy* (New Haven, 1951), pp. 50–51.

policy? Some members of the British government hoped so. On March 7, 1898, London directed Pauncefote to inquire whether the United States would cooperate "in opposing any action by foreign Powers which could tend to restrict the opening of China to the commerce of all nations."[32] But hostilities with Spain were near; and Washington, even had it been inclined, which it was not, to go along with Britain on so far-reaching a move, had no option except to decline the suggestion. John Hay, then still in London, wrote a personal letter to McKinley in June asking him to reconsider; but the President turned him down.[33] Early the next year France, the holder of a territorial concession in Shanghai, asked China for permission to enlarge it. The British were disturbed; Pauncefote asked whether the United States would agree to "conjoint action" warning China not to yield to the French. However, the American Minister at Peking had already filed a separate protest; and in any event the United States was not yet ready for such a departure from traditional practice as Sir Julian had requested.[34]

But did not Hay's September notes represent, in effect, the kind of conjoint action envisaged by London? At first glance one might conclude that they did. The two English-speaking countries both viewed the Chinese market as enormously important for their exports, and they both feared Russian, German, and French encroachments on it. Beresford had stressed Anglo-American action, and William W. Rockhill had incorporated some of the ideas and even the language of his English friend, Alfred E. Hippisley, in his open-door memorandum on which the notes were based. Thus the Open Door notes were, in a sense, a British-American product.[35]

It is apparent, however, that a shared Anglo-American major

32. Foreign Office to Pauncefote, March 7, 1898, Foreign Office 5/2364. See also Blanche E. C. Dugdale, *Arthur James Balfour, First Earl of Balfour, K.G., O.M., F.R.S., Etc.* (2 vols., London, 1936), I, 252–53; Campbell, *Anglo-American Understanding,* pp. 17–20.

33. Tyler Dennett, "The Open Door Policy as Intervention," *Annals of the American Academy of Political and Social Science,* CLXVIII (1933), 79; Campbell, *Anglo-American Understanding,* pp. 20–21.

34. Pauncefote to Hay, Jan. 8, 1899, John Hay Papers, Library of Congress (Washington), Box 21; the minister's protest was dated Jan. 5, 1899, *Papers Relating to the Foreign Relations of the United States, 1899* (Washington, 1901), p. 144.

35. A. Whitney Griswold, *The Far Eastern Policy of the United States* (New York, 1938), ch. 11, pp. 475–91. Regarding Beresford see Campbell, *Special Business Interests,* pp. 50–51.

interest in the Far East is a myth. In 1898 American exports to China were valued at $10 million, as compared with total American exports of $1,231,000,000; the next year the figures were $14 million and $1,227,000,000.[36] The much touted exports to the great potential market hovered around a mere one percent of American exports; and however high the expectations for the future, the Chinese market had little importance for the United States in 1899. In marked contrast, about one sixth of Great Britain's foreign commerce was with China alone; and she controlled over 70 percent of that country's trade. Americans hoped, of course, that partition could be avoided and the open door perpetuated. But as late as 1903 Hay still thought that "concerted action" with Great Britain was "out of the question."[37] As for the September notes, although welcome on balance in Whitehall, they were not what Britain really wanted. She wanted conjoint action, but instead Washington had acted alone and had not distinguished between Britain and the "bad" Continental countries. Hippisley was not a British agent, and Beresford had little influence in Washington; Rockhill believed that ". . . England is as great an offender in China as Russia itself," and he assured the Russian ambassador at Washington that no administration "would adopt an English policy."[38] It is true, however, that the notes, like the cooperation in Samoa and (such as it was) at The Hague, were popularly viewed as demonstrating close friendship, and consequently they helped prolong wartime sentiments a little.

Exuberant wartime affection, failure by the Joint High Commission of 1898–1899, American readiness to take advantage of Britain's South African plight and violate the Clayton-Bulwer treaty, minor collaboration in Samoa and at The Hague, and an appearance of cooperation in China—what is one to make of this miscellany of developments? The wartime affection was short-lived, and

36. U.S. Bureau of the Census, *Historical Statistics of the United States, Colonial Times to 1957* (Washington, 1961), p. 550. See also Paul A. Varg, "The Myth of the China Market, 1890–1914," *American Historical Review*, LXXIII (1968), 742–58.

37. Griswold, *Far Eastern Policy*, p. 88. See a similar statement by Hay, Feb. 1, 1901, Edward H. Zabriskie, *American-Russian Rivalry in the Far East: A Study in Diplomacy and Power Politics, 1895–1914* (Philadelphia, 1946), p. 69.

38. Rockhill to Hay, Aug. 28, 1899, Alfred L. P. Dennis, *Adventures in American Diplomacy, 1896–1906* (New York, 1928), p. 186; Rockhill memorandum, Dec. 1, 1899, William W. Rockhill Papers, Harvard University Library (Cambridge). Regarding Rockhill see Paul A. Varg, *Open Door Diplomat: The Life of W. W. Rockhill* (Urbana, Ill., 1952), p. 29; Neale, *Great Britain and United States Expansion*, pp. 197–200.

bound to be so; it was a hothouse growth that largely withered away once the war, whose emotions had engendered it, came to an end. The collapse of the Joint High Commission, and the American people's reaction to the Boer War, indicated hostility rather than amity. Nor did the other occurrences of 1899 indicate deep friendship.

Nevertheless it scarcely need be argued that Anglo-American relations had improved out of all recognition since the post–Civil War years. Other developments of the 1890s, more fundamental than those just described, bore witness to the great change. The revulsion in Britain and America from the prospect of fratricidal war in 1895, the British sympathy for the United States in 1898, the warmth of the American feeling for Great Britain (even though the wartime exuberance could not last), these showed beyond doubt that a genuine friendship had come to fruition at the end of the century. People around the world did not doubt the existence of trans-Atlantic amity when they speculated that even a secret alliance had been concluded. Although the exuberant affection was transient, the Anglo-American friendship was real and enduring.

Neither the Venezuela controversy nor the Spanish war caused the friendship, although they both, and more particularly the war, deepened it somewhat and made people aware that it existed. How, then, can its rise be explained?

In previous chapters we have considered many subjects of serious contention between the United States and Great Britain: the neutrality proclamation during the Civil War, the *Alabama* claims, the San Juan boundary, the problems bequeathed by the treaty of Washington, the Fortune Bay affair, the northeastern fisheries, the Bering Sea fur seals, the Venezuela boundary. They had all been settled, or greatly eased. We have examined the treaty of Washington, the Bering Sea treaty, and the Venezuela agreement, as well as joint commissions, *modi vivendi*, and no less than six arbitrations— over the *Alabama* claims, the San Juan boundary, the routine Civil War claims, the fishery articles of the treaty of Washington, the fur seals, and the Venezuela boundary (the arbitration of which was between Britain and Venezuela but with considerable American participation). This was a most remarkable record of diplomacy and arbitration, one no other two nations could come close to matching. Because of it more than three decades had passed without a major collision. To be sure, armed encounters had disturbed the Canadian-American border, the northeastern fishing grounds, the fog-enshrouded waters of the Bering Sea, and remote Alaska mining areas. But war and (once the *Alabama* claims were disposed of) even dangerous friction had been staved off. The absence of hostilities provided the indispensable element of time—time for the Civil War rancor to die down.

But time alone, however essential, would not have produced the new amity. For that, the presence of more positive influences was required. Such influences existed (and they, in turn, help account for the diplomatic and arbitral successes). Some of them had been present for decades; others were of more recent appearance. Basic and deep-rooted, these influences had, slowly, imperceptibly, and almost irresistibly, been preparing the ground for better relations between the two countries. They may be compared roughly with the geographic, economic, strategic, and ideological forces that, in the same nearly ineluctable manner, had been turning the United States toward overseas expansion. But whereas these latter forces had had a marked effect on American policy for many years, the underlying influences shaping relations between Britain and America had little impact before the Venezuela boundary dispute and became strongly evident only at the time of the Spanish-American War. What were these influences? We must limit ourselves to a short account.

The United States and Great Britain had a common heritage in language, literature, and many legal concepts and governmental institutions. Such a heritage, it is true, does not automatically produce amity. It had not prevented two wars, and there is an element of truth in the remark of the American poet and minister to Great Britain in the 1880s, James Russell Lowell: "The common blood, and still more the common language, are fatal instruments of misapprehension."[39] All the same, the common heritage did much in the long run to bring the two peoples and their countries closer together. Its basic importance can hardly be overstated.

During the 1890s another kind of sharing became evident. Many

39. James Russell Lowell, "On a Certain Condescension in Foreigners," *Atlantic Monthly*, XXIII (1869), 94. According to Winston Churchill, on the other hand, "Bismarck once said that the supreme fact of the nineteenth century was that Britain and the United States spoke the same language." Allen, *Great Britain and the United States*, p. 983.

Americans took great pride in their Anglo-Saxonism. So did the British. The belief in a common race accounted for much of the horror felt during the Venezuela war scare of 1895, and it helps explain Britain's support of the United States in 1898. At the beginning of 1896 Arthur Balfour had hailed the "Anglo-Saxon patriotism which embraces within its ample folds the whole of that great race which has done so much in every branch of human effort"; and in 1898 Richard Olney told Harvard students: "There is a patriotism of race as well as of country. . . . Family quarrels there have been heretofore and doubtless will be again, and the two peoples, at the safe distance which the broad Atlantic interposes, take with each other liberties of speech which only the fondest and dearest relatives indulge in. Nevertheless, that they would be found standing together against any alien foe by whom either was menaced with destruction or irreparable calamity, it is not permissible to doubt."[40] The effect of such views, which were widely held, was tremendous. It was all the greater because, to a very considerable extent, not only British but also American leaders in many pursuits were Anglo-Saxons.

Over the years multifarious trans-Atlantic links had been established. Hundreds of thousands of personal ties resulted from the fact that more immigrants had come to the United States from Great Britain than from almost any other country; they left behind their mothers, fathers, sisters, and brothers. Trans-Atlantic family links helped to bring the two countries together. Furthermore, people of British background were prominent in all walks of American life. As for British leaders, a surprising number of them had American wives, often from families of great wealth. In 1895 the Duke of Marlborough; Lord Randolph Churchill, a former Chancellor of the Exchequer and Winston Churchill's father; George Curzon, Undersecretary of State for Foreign Affairs and a future Foreign Secretary; Sir Michael Herbert, Pauncefote's successor at Washington in 1902; Sir William Harcourt; Lord Playfair; and Joseph Chamberlain, all were married to Americans. Who can say that the marriages of Chamberlain, Playfair, and Harcourt played no part in the settlement of the Venezuela boundary dispute that erupted in 1895?

40. The *Times* (London), Jan. 16, 1896; Olney, "International Isolation of the United States," p. 588. For the reaction to Olney's remarks see *Public Opinion*, XXIV (May 19, 1898), 613–17.

Lower down the economic scale were the American labor union leaders, several of them British born; close links existed between the unions of the two countries.[41]

No other foreign country attracted so many American intellectuals as did England. A considerable number of Americans, it is true, went to Germany for their higher education; Paris was a Mecca for aspiring American architects and painters, notably Mary Cassatt and, for a while, James A. McNeill Whistler and John Singer Sargent; and Italy cast a spell over some, including William Dean Howells, the well-known author and editor of the *Atlantic Monthly,* who lived in that country several years and made it the setting for some of his novels.[42] But Whistler and Sargent soon left Paris to make London their permanent home. Bret Harte, too, lived in England. So did Henry James, who abandoned his native land at an early age.[43] John Hay, Henry Adams, James Russell Lowell, and a host of other American writers and artists visited England frequently and felt drawn to her culture. ". . . I have never seen civilization at so high a level in some respects as here," Lowell reflected.[44]

Ever since the reform bills of 1867 and 1884 had generated an increasingly vigorous democracy in Great Britain, the traditional American stereotype of that country as archaic, hopelessly feudal, and aristocratic had become untenable. Similarly, respect for the United States as a stronghold of stability in a chaotic world, with her

41. Henry Pelling, *America and the British Left, from Bright to Bevan* (London, 1956), chs. 1–4; Clifton K. Yearley, Jr., *Britons in American Labor: A History of the Influence of the United Kingdom Immigrants on American Labor, 1820–1914* (Baltimore, 1957), pp. 51–302.

42. Regarding relations with Germany see Milton Plesur, *America's Outward Thrust: Approaches to Foreign Affairs, 1865–1890* (DeKalb, Ill., 1971), p. 112. See also Thomas N. Bonner, *American Doctors and German Universities: A Chapter in International Intellectual Relations, 1870–1914* (Lincoln, 1963); Jurgen F. H. Herbst, *The German Historical School in American Scholarship* (Ithaca, 1965); John A. Walz, *German Influence in American Education and Culture* (Philadelphia, 1936); Foster R. Dulles, *Americans Abroad: Two Centuries of European Travel* (Ann Arbor, 1964). Regarding relations with France and Italy see, respectively, Elizabeth B. White, *American Opinion of France from Lafayette to Poincaré* (New York, 1927); Alexander DeConde, *Half Bitter, Half Sweet: An Excursion into Italian-American History* (New York, 1971).

43. Van Wyck Brooks, *The Pilgrimage of Henry James* (London, 1928); Christof Wegelin, *The Image of Europe in Henry James* (Dallas, 1958); Cushing Strout, *The American Image of the Old World* (New York, 1963), pp. 119–31.

44. Lowell to Charles Eliot Norton, April 22, 1883, Charles Eliot Norton (ed.), *Letters of James Russell Lowell* (3 vols., New York, 1904), III, 105.

written constitution, powerful executive, and Supreme Court, had increased in conservative British quarters. Nor were Irish-Americans the disturbing force they once had been. A Fenian raid was scarcely imaginable in the 1890s as a new generation of Irish-Americans turned to their American home instead of to the ancestral land across the waters.[45] Moreover, another anti-British group, the free-silver crusaders, headed rapidly for extinction after the election of 1896.

The venerable Queen Victoria also created a bond, and the older she became the more deeply Americans admired her. Her seventy-ninth birthday fell on May 24, 1898, at the height of the emotionalism accompanying the war with Spain. The New York *Tribune* greeted her as "a Queen of our own race and blood, the head of a sister nation, the titular ruler of the elder half of our own people, who are one with us in spirit, in sympathy, in ambition, and in destiny"; and even the characteristically anti-British Far West celebrated the occasion. Sir Julian was pleased to hear of "the warmth of the feeling" for her there.[46]

In the 1890s Great Britain was by all odds the leading market for American exports, and the chief source of imports and supplier of capital. In 1893, for example, $421 million worth of American goods went to that country, as compared with $84 million worth to Germany, the second most important market; in 1899, $512 million went to Great Britain and $156 million to Germany, still in second place. As regards imports, in 1893, $183 million worth came from Great Britain and $96 million worth from Germany, the second most important supplier; in 1899 the corresponding figures were $118 million (an unusually low figure) and $84 million.[47] Bankers, financiers, and businessmen moved easily from one country to the other, sometimes maintaining homes in both. Such men as Sir John Rose and, later on, J. P. Morgan and others had large financial stakes on both sides of the Atlantic. As early as 1871 the American business community had put pressure on the Grant administration to come to terms with the British; and twenty-four years later, when

45. But the Irish remained a disturbing factor in Anglo-American relations for many years. Alan J. Ward, *Ireland and Anglo-American Relations, 1899–1921* (Toronto, 1969).

46. New York *Tribune*, May 26, 1898; Pauncefote to Salisbury, July 1, 1898, Foreign Office 5/2363.

47. *Historical Statistics*, pp. 550, 552.

British holders of American shares unloaded millions of dollars' worth of them during the Venezuela war scare, American business interests again saw the wisdom of reaching a settlement. Although British jealousy of America's economic progress certainly existed, it did not offset the effect of the commercial and financial interdependence. Nor did Britain and America compete with each other in third countries on a scale to engender much ill will, except possibly in a few Latin American areas.

In the last years of the century a worried Great Britain perceived that her strength was declining. No longer could she maintain her extended position around the world in splendid isolation. Russia, Germany, and France threatened her. Where could she turn for help? The United States, though strong, did not pose the menace that the Continental countries did; nor did her vital interests clash with those of Great Britain. Consequently the British encouraged American expansion in the Caribbean and the Pacific, where the powerful republic could buttress positions Britain could no longer defend alone. No more than London did Washington want German incursions into Latin America, and Russian ones into the Far East. The persisting legend about the Czar's fleets during the Civil War had kept America's friendship for Russia alive for many years, but in the 1890s the friendship dwindled as a result of Russia's expansion in China and her pogroms of Jews. Whereas in 1865 American affection for Russia had been strong and dislike of Great Britain equally intense, American attitudes toward these two countries had become reversed a generation later. To a limited extent a common British-American dislike of Russia, and also of Germany, created a tie. It was more than sentiment that caused a nationalist like Henry Cabot Lodge to believe that "the downfall of the British Empire is something which no rational American could regard as anything but a misfortune to the United States."[48]

The common heritage and conception of race patriotism; the trans-Atlantic family ties, including marriages between important families; the social and political changes; the weakening of Irish-American and free-silver hostility to Britain; the respect felt for the Queen; the intertwining of the two economies; the decline of British power and the sharing of some Caribbean and Far Eastern interests

48. Lodge to Roosevelt, Feb. 2, 1900, *Selections from the Correspondence of Theodore Roosevelt and Henry Cabot Lodge, 1884–1918* (2 vols., New York, 1925), I, 446.

—these were the principal positive influences shaping Anglo-American relations. During the years of peace secured by treaties, *modi vivendi,* and arbitrations, these influences had been working, below the level of governmental action, to draw the two English-speaking countries closer together. At the end of the nineteenth century no one who had observed the revulsion from war in 1895 and the friendliness of 1898 could doubt that the United States had achieved not only her overseas territorial expansion but also an abiding rapprochement with Great Britain.

Overseas expansion and relations with Great Britain—these, as we have seen, were the principal themes of American foreign policy from 1865 to the end of the century. As regards both of them something approaching a reversal had occurred. Whereas for many years after the Civil War the United States, despite the zeal of such men as Secretary of State Seward and President Grant, had not expanded outside North America (except for the Midway Islands), by 1900 she had taken decisive steps toward her isthmian canal and had acquired a galaxy of colonies including even several thousand islands in the distant Philippines. Similarly, in 1865 and for several years thereafter Anglo-American relations were severely strained, but by the end of the century a sentimental but nonetheless real friendship suffused the trans-Atlantic scene.

Geographical and economic impulses contributed to the expansion—such impulses as the west coast settlement, the favorable balance of trade beginning in 1876, and the swelling industrial surplus beginning in 1894. The trade balances directed attention to commercial expansion in general and specifically to a canal as required for shipping the surplus to potential markets in Latin America and China. And if a canal was to be built, bases in Hawaii and the Caribbean Sea would be needed. New ideas—Social Darwinism, Anglo-Saxonism, the influence of sea power—stimulated and supported the developing expansion. Secretary of State Frelinghuysen put the emphasis on commercial expansion, but in the 1890s territorial expansion came to be considered essential, not only to get a canal and the supporting naval stations, but also to provide bases for the new steam navy and for holding open large markets in nearby countries. Prophets of expansion like Alfred T. Mahan and practitioners like William H. Seward, James G. Blaine, and John Hay related these impulses and ideas to the particular needs of the

United States in the post–Civil War decades. The expansion, it is true, was too exuberant; for by annexing the Philippine Islands the United States went beyond her fundamental requirements of a canal and bases in Hawaii and the Caribbean. But annexing the Philippines was a mistake hard to avoid; and on the whole America's territorial expansion fitted her needs.

In Anglo-American relations, too, underlying forces made themselves felt. Given the years of peace provided by the extraordinary series of treaties, *modi vivendi,* and arbitrations, such basic influences as the common heritage and the enmeshing of the two economies were bound to bring the two English-speaking countries closer together. That this had indeed occurred became plain for the first time during the dispute over the Venezuela boundary. Like the expansion, the rapprochement was overly exuberant, at least on the American side. Nevertheless a genuine amity remained after the excessive emotionalism subsided.

The Spanish-American War catalyzed the slowly maturing forces promoting expansion and friendship with Britain. Both the expansion and the friendship would have come to pass without that conflict, but at later dates and in more moderate measure—and greater moderation might well have served America better. As it was, seldom has a country not under duress experienced, in so short a time, so radical a transformation of its relations with the rest of the world as did the United States in the years between 1865 and 1900.

# Bibliographical Essay

## Bibliographies and General Works

The bibliographies of books concerning general United States history from 1865 to 1900 are pertinent for the study of foreign relations during those years. For a voluminous bibliography dealing directly with foreign relations see Samuel F. Bemis and Grace G. Griffin, *Guide to the Diplomatic History of the United States, 1775–1921* (Washington, 1935). The most convenient place for finding the extensive material published since the Bemis and Griffin *Guide* is the bibliographical sections in Thomas A. Bailey, *A Diplomatic History of the American People* (9th ed., New York, 1974).

There is no book, other than the present one, that attempts to give a thorough coverage of United States foreign relations from 1865 to 1900. The general diplomatic histories deal with the period, of course; but none of them treats it at length. There are several fine special studies, most of which deal only with expansion. Walter LaFeber, *The New Empire: An Interpretation of American Expansion, 1860–1898* (Ithaca, 1963), is primarily interpretive and is limited to foreign policy and expansion. William A. Williams, *The Roots of the Modern American Empire: A Study of the Growth and Shaping of Social Consciousness in a Marketplace Society* (New York, 1969), concentrates on overseas commercial expansion, particularly as promoted by agricultural interests. The LaFeber and Williams books largely neglect the role of diplomacy in favor of giving predominantly economic explanations. Williams in particular, in this as in other writings, emphasizes what he believes to be a vital American concern for the open door, that is, a world open to American exports; the desire to achieve this he depicts as essentially equivalent to traditional imperialistic aspirations. Milton Plesur, *America's Outward*

*Thrust: Approaches to Foreign Affairs, 1865–1890* (DeKalb, Ill., 1971), also emphasizes expansion and does not attempt to include all subjects of importance even under that heading. Another study of expansion, from the point of view indicated by its title, is Howard B. Schonberger, *Transportation to the Seaboard: The "Communication Revolution" and American Foreign Policy, 1860–1900* (Westport, Conn., 1971).

Regarding the other main theme of American foreign policy in the latter decades of the nineteenth century, that is, Anglo-American relations, the only fairly long general account is Charles S. Campbell, *From Revolution to Rapprochement: The United States and Great Britain, 1783–1900* (New York, 1974). Harry C. Allen's large history, *Great Britain and the United States: A History of Anglo-American Relations (1783–1952)* (New York, 1955), has a short chronological account of the period 1865–1900 and is particularly valuable for an analytical section dealing with such topics as social contacts and cultural and emotional bonds over the whole period, 1783–1952.

## Published Primary Material

Much information about varied topics is contained in the United States Congress's Serial Set. The congressional debates, in the *Congressional Globe* (before 1874) and the *Congressional Record,* are useful. An extremely helpful guide is *General Index to the Published Volumes of the Diplomatic Correspondence and Foreign Relations of the United States, 1861–1899* (Washington, 1902). Useful, too, is *Senate Documents,* 56 Cong., 2 Sess., No. 231 (Serials 4047–4054), which lists reports of the Committee on Foreign Relations. The State Department series, *Papers Relating to the Foreign Relations of the United States. . . ,* was published in most of the years from 1865 to 1900, each volume containing selections of American diplomatic correspondence with different countries during the year concerned. James D. Richardson (ed.), *A Compilation of the Messages and Papers of the Presidents, 1789–1897* (10 vols., Washington, 1899), has the Presidents' inaugural addresses, proclamations, and messages to Congress. Two authoritative multivolume works, containing a great deal of primary material, by John Bassett Moore are *A Digest of International Law . . .* (8 vols., Washington, 1906) and *History and Digest of the International Arbitrations to Which the United States Has Been a Party . . .* (6 vols., Washington, 1898). For the text of United States treaties and other international agreements see William M. Malloy (ed.), *Treaties, Conventions, International Acts, Protocols and Agreements between the United States of America and Other Powers, 1776–1909* (2 vols., Washington, 1910). For letters written by several important government officials see Albert T. Volwiler (ed.), *The Correspondence between Benjamin Harrison and James G. Blaine, 1882–1893,* (Philadelphia, 1940); *Selections from the Correspondence of Theodore Roosevelt and Henry Cabot Lodge, 1884–1918* (2 vols., New York, 1925); and Elting

E. Morison, John Blum, and John J. Buckley (eds.), *The Letters of Theodore Roosevelt* (8 vols., Cambridge, Mass., 1951–54).

Most foreign countries have official publications giving the text of legislative debates and of treaties, and also statistical and other pertinent information. Particularly relevant to American history, and readily available, are two British series: Hansard's *Parliamentary Debates* and the Foreign Office's annual publication, *British and Foreign State Papers.* The British, French, German, and Austrian governments have published large collections of documents concerning the background of World War I, which have some use for the study of United States foreign relations during the last three or four decades of the nineteenth century. Regarding these collections see Samuel F. Bemis and Grace G. Griffin, *Guide to the Diplomatic History of the United States, 1775–1921* (Washington, 1935), pp. 850–52.

## Documentary Material

The Manuscript Division of the Library of Congress has an enormous collection of the papers of Presidents, Secretaries of State, and other individuals. The official diplomatic correspondence of the Department of State and also the Department's unofficial correspondence with private individuals and concerns are in the National Archives in Washington. The records of the Army and Navy Departments are also in the National Archives. Many libraries around the country have the papers of various persons important in the history of American foreign relations. For the papers of the Presidents, Secretaries of State, and American diplomats see Samuel F. Bemis and Grace G. Griffin, *Guide to the Diplomatic History of the United States, 1775–1921* (Washington, 1935), pp. 862–83. For other personal papers see *ibid.,* pp. 943–45.

Because such a large part of United States foreign relations was with Great Britain, British documentary material is of particular importance. The Public Record Office in London has a vast amount of manuscript information that illuminates almost all the topics considered in the present volume. Especially pertinent to United States history are the Foreign Office 5 and Foreign Office 115 series. A good deal of additional information can be found in the British Museum. Many of the controversies with Great Britain were about Canadian matters; for these the Public Archives of Canada, at Ottawa, have much material. Additional documentary information is available in the French, Spanish, and German archives; although generally less useful for United States history, such information can also be found in the archives of several other foreign countries. An invaluable help in the use of foreign archives is the Bemis and Griffin *Guide,* pp. 836–49, 890–943.

## Anglo-American Relations, 1865–1885

There is an extensive literature on the Anglo-American contention in the post–Civil War years. For the general background see Allan Nevins, *Hamilton Fish: The Inner History of the Grant Administration* (New York, 1936), an outstanding biography though overly laudatory of the Secretary of State; and Charles S. Campbell, *From Revolution to Rapprochement: The United States and Great Britain, 1783–1900* (New York, 1974). For the *Alabama* claims see *Papers Relating to the Foreign Relations of the United States, 1872, Part II, Papers Relating to the Treaty of Washington* (5 vols., Washington, 1872–73), Vols. I–IV. Adrian Cook, *The Alabama Claims, American Politics and Anglo-American Relations, 1865–1872* (Ithaca, 1975), is a well-researched straightforward account; a helpful article is Maureen M. Robson, "The *Alabama* Claims and the Anglo-American Reconciliation, 1865–71," *Canadian Historical Review,* XLII (1961), 1–22.

A competent survey of the Fenians is William D'Arcy, *The Fenian Movement in the United States: 1858–1886* (Washington, 1947). More immediately relevant are Brian Jenkins, *Fenians and Anglo-American Relations during Reconstruction* (Ithaca, 1969); Leon Ó Broin, *Fenian Fever: An Anglo-American Dilemma* (New York, 1971); and Arthur H. DeRosier, Jr., "Importance in Failure: The Fenian Raids of 1866–1871," *Southern Quarterly,* III (1965), 181–97.

A thorough study of the northwest boundary controversy centering on San Juan Island is James O. McCabe, *The San Juan Water Boundary Question* (Toronto, 1964). See also *Senate Executive Documents,* 40 Cong., 2 Sess., No. 29 (Serial 1316); and Hunter Miller, *San Juan Archipelago: Study of the Joint Occupation of San Juan Island* (Bellows Falls, Vt., 1943). For the arbitration by the German Emperor see Miller, *Northwest Water Boundary: Report of the Experts Summoned by the German Emperor . . .* (Seattle, 1942); and John Bassett Moore, *History and Digest of the International Arbitrations to Which the United States Has Been a Party . . .* (6 vols., Washington, 1898), I, 196–235. Useful articles are Alfred Tunem, "The Dispute over the San Juan Island Water Boundary," *Washington Historical Quarterly,* XXIII (1932), 38–46, 133–37, 196–204, 286–300; and Arthur H. DeRosier, Jr., "The Settlement of the San Juan Controversy, *Southern Quarterly,* IV (1965), 74–88.

Regarding the northeastern fisheries and other controversies directly affecting Canada see two general studies: Lester B. Shippee, *Canadian-American Relations, 1849–1874* (New Haven, 1939); and James M. Callahan, *American Foreign Policy in Canadian Relations* (New York, 1937). More specific are Joe P. Smith, *The Republican Expansionists of the Early Reconstruction Era* (Chicago, 1933); and Donald F. Warner, *The Idea of Continental Union: Agitation for the Annexation of Canada to the United States, 1849–1893* (Lexington, Ky., 1960). A useful congressional publication is *Senate Executive Documents,*

39 Cong., 2 Sess., No. 30 (Serial 1277). Good for background information is C. P. Stacey, "Britain's Withdrawal from North America, 1864–1871," *Canadian Historical Review*, XXXVI (1955), 185–98. Donald G. Creighton, "The United States and Canadian Confederation," *ibid.*, XXXIX (1958), 209–22, shows the effect of the Civil War on confederation. Regarding a rebellion that encouraged American expansionists see Donald F. Warner, "Drang nach Norden: The United States and the Riel Rebellion," *Mississippi Valley Historical Review*, XXXIX (1953), 693–712; and Alvin C. Gluek, Jr., "The Riel Rebellion and Canadian-American Relations," *Canadian Historical Review*, XXXVI (1955), 199–221.

The best articles on the John Rose missions are A. H. U. Colquhoun, "The Reciprocity Negotiations with the United States in 1869," *ibid.*, VIII (1927), pp. 233–42; and Robert C. Clark, "The Diplomatic Mission of Sir John Rose, 1871," *Pacific Northwest Quarterly*, XXVII (1936), 227–42. David H. Donald's fine biography, *Charles Sumner and the Rights of Man* (New York, 1970), is enlightening on the Senator and the Johnson-Clarendon convention.

There is a great deal of material about the treaty of Washington. A voluminous source is *Papers Relating to the Foreign Relations of the United States, 1872, Part II, Papers Relating to the Treaty of Washington; Parliamentary Debates,* Third Series, especially Vols. CXCVI, CXCVII, CCIV, and CCVI, has frequent references to the treaty. Goldwin Smith, *The Treaty of Washington, 1871: A Study in Imperial History* (Ithaca, 1941), as the subtitle suggests, is primarily concerned with British imperial matters; Charles Francis Adams, *Lee at Appomattox and Other Papers* (Boston, 1902), also has some general material. More specialized on the British side are James P. Baxter 3d, "The British High Commissioners at Washington in 1871," *Proceedings of the Massachusetts Historical Society*, LXV (1934), 334–57; and Paul Knaplund, *Gladstone and Britain's Imperial Policy* (New York, 1927). Two early books are important because of the authors' personal roles: Caleb Cushing, *The Treaty of Washington: Its Negotiation, Execution, and the Discussions Relating Thereto* (New York, 1873); and John C. Bancroft Davis, *Mr. Fish and the Alabama Claims: A Chapter in Diplomatic History* (Boston, 1893). The standard biography of the great English Prime Minister, the main author of the treaty, is John Morley, *The Life of William Ewart Gladstone* (3 vols., New York, 1903). Biographies of two other Englishmen who made important contributions are Lord Edmond Fitzmaurice, *The Life of Granville, George Leveson Gower, Second Earl Granville, K.G., 1815–1891* (2 vols., London, 1905); and T. Wemyss Reid, *Life of the Right Honourable William Edward Forster* (2 vols., London, 1888). Nevins, *Hamilton Fish*, gives a good account of the Secretary of State's role at the Washington conference. There are good biographies of two of the English commissioners and the Canadian commissioner:

Lucien Wolf, *Life of the First Marquess of Ripon, K.G., P.C., G.C.S.I., D.C.L., Etc.* (2 vols., London, 1921); Andrew Lang, *Life, Letters, and Diaries of Sir Stafford Northcote, First Earl of Iddesleigh* (2 vols., Edinburgh, 1890); and Donald G. Creighton, *John A. Macdonald: The Old Chieftain* (Toronto, 1955). Regarding efforts to save the treaty see George S. Boutwell, *Reminiscences of Sixty Years in Public Affairs* (2 vols., New York, 1902).

Some of the titles mentioned in connection with the treaty of Washington are useful also for the Geneva arbitration. The easiest place to find the documentary material regarding the arbitration is in *Papers Relating to the Foreign Relations of the United States, 1872, Part II, Papers Relating to the Treaty of Washington,* Vols. I–IV. An excellent survey of the arbitration, with documentary material, is Moore, *International Arbitrations,* ch. 14; another good account is Frank W. Hackett, *Reminiscences of the Geneva Tribunal of Arbitration, 1872, the Alabama Claims* (Boston, 1911). Campbell, *From Revolution to Rapprochement,* has material on how the arbitration was saved after the treaty of Washington came under attack. See also Cook, *Alabama Claims.* Bancroft Davis, *Mr. Fish and the Alabama Claims,* is important because written by the American agent at Geneva. A fine biography, although giving too much credit to Adams's role at Geneva, is Martin B. Duberman, *Charles Francis Adams, 1807–1886* (Boston, 1961). Biographies of two of the American counsel are Claude M. Feuss, *The Life of Caleb Cushing* (2 vols., New York, 1923); Chester L. Barrows, *William M. Evarts: Lawyer, Diplomat, Statesman* (Chapel Hill, 1941); and Brainerd Dyer, *The Public Career of William M. Evarts* (Berkeley, 1933). The memoirs of a British counsel are Roundell Palmer, Earl of Selborne, *Memorials, Part II, Personal and Political, 1865–1895* (2 vols., London, 1898).

For the abortive reciprocity of 1874 with Canada, and the contention over the appointment of a third commissioner to the Halifax commission, see Nevins, *Hamilton Fish,* and Campbell, *From Revolution to Rapprochement.* See also James M. S. Careless, *Brown of the Globe* (2 vols., Toronto, 1960–63); and Oscar D. Skelton, "General Economic History, 1867–1912," in Adam Shortt and Arthur G. Doughty (eds.), *Canada and Its Provinces: A History of the Canadian People and Their Institutions by One Hundred Associates* (23 vols., Toronto, 1914–17), IX, 95–274. Two useful congressional publications are *Senate Executive Documents,* 45 Cong., 2 Sess., Nos. 44 and 100 (Serial 1781).

On the Halifax commission, the charges of Hind, and the Fortune Bay affair see Campbell, *From Revolution to Rapprochement.* Biographies of the American Secretary of State at the time of the award are Barrows, *Evarts,* and Dyer, *Public Career of Evarts.* A revealing contemporary article by an influential Senator is George F. Edmunds, "The Fishery Award," *North American Review,* CXXVIII (1879), 1–14. Detailed information about the arbitration can be found in John Bassett Moore, *History and Digest of the International Arbitrations to Which the United States Has Been a Party* . . . (6 vols., Washington, 1898); and in *House Executive Documents,* 45 Cong., 2 Sess., No. 89 (Serials 1810, 1811, 1812). Additional documentary material is in *House Reports,* 46 Cong., 3 Sess., No. 329 (Serial 1982); *Senate Executive Documents,* 45 Cong., 2 Sess., Nos. 44 and 100 (Serial 1781); *Senate Reports,* 45 Cong., 2 Sess., No. 439 (Serial 1790); and *Congressional Record,* 46 Cong., 3 Sess., pp. 421–42 (Jan. 7, 1881). On the Fortune Bay affair see *Congressional Record,* 50 Cong., 1 Sess., pp. 7344–54 (Aug. 8, 1888); and *House Executive Documents,* 46 Cong., 2 Sess., No. 84 (Serial 1925). On the termination of the fishery articles see *House Reports,* 46 Cong., 2 Sess., No. 1275 (Serial 1937); and *ibid.,* 47 Cong., 1 Sess., No. 235 (Serial 2065).

## Attempts at Territorial Expansion in the Late 1860s and the 1870s

The best general account of the great would-be expansionist is Glyndon G. Van Deusen, *William Henry Seward* (New York, 1967). A stimulating book about Seward's foreign policy is Ernest N. Paolino, *The Foundations of the American Empire: William Henry Seward and U.S. Foreign Policy* (Ithaca, 1973); the book perhaps exaggerates the extent to which Seward developed a comprehensive, systematic philosophy of American foreign policy. The Secretary of State's son, Frederick W. Seward, wrote, concerning himself, *Reminiscences of a War-Time Statesman and Diplomat, 1830–1915* (New York, 1916), which is occasionally illuminating. Two complementary articles are Theodore C. Smith, "Expansion after the Civil War, 1865–71," *Political Science Quarterly,* XVI (1901), 412–36; and Donald M. Dozer, "Anti-Expansionism during the Johnson Administration," *Pacific Historical Review,* XII (1943), 253–75. A more comprehensive study is Joe P. Smith, *The Republican Expansionists of the Early Reconstruction Era* (Chicago, 1933). The best study of expansion under the Grant administration is Allan Nevins, *Hamilton Fish: The Inner History of the Grant Administration* (New York, 1936). For expansion as viewed by the censorious editor of the New York *Evening Post* and the *Nation,* see William M. Armstrong, *E. L. Godkin and American Foreign Policy, 1865–1900* (New York, 1957).

In addition to these more general studies, there is a good deal of material concerning specific objectives of expansionists. For the acquisition of the Midway Islands see *Senate Executive Documents,* 40 Cong., 2 Sess., No. 79 (Serial 1317); and *Senate Reports,* 40 Cong., 3 Sess., No. 194 (Serial 1362). The most detailed treatment of Seward's attempt to buy the Danish West Indies is Charles C. Tansill, *The Purchase of the Danish West Indies* (Baltimore, 1932). Halvdan Koht, "The Origin of Seward's Plan to Purchase the Danish West Indies," *American Historical Review,* L (1945), 762–67, is interesting about a smaller point. Good on Seward's Far Eastern aspirations is Tyler Dennett, "Seward's Far Eastern Policy," *American Historical Review,* XXVIII (1922), 45–62. The standard books on Seward and Alaska are Victor J. Farrar, *The Purchase of Alaska* (Washington, 1934) and *The Annexation of Russian America to the United States* (Washington, 1937). A penetrating article is Thomas A. Bailey, "Why the United States Purchased Alaska," *Pacific Historical Review,* III (1934), 39–49. James G. Blaine, *Twenty Years of Congress: from Lincoln to Garfield* . . . (Norwich, Conn., 1884–86), gives the views of a prominent politician about the Alaska purchase. Next to Seward, the most influential American in the purchase was Charles Sumner, whose role may be studied in David H. Donald, *Charles Sumner and the Rights of Man* (New York, 1970); and Edward L. Pierce, *Memoir and Letters of Charles Sumner* (4 vols., Boston, 1878–93). Regarding the possible bribery of some Congressmen there are three good articles: William A. Dunning, "Paying for Alaska: Some Unfamiliar Incidents in the Process," *Political Science Quarterly,* XXVII (1912), 385–98; Frank A. Golder, "The Purchase of Alaska," *American Historical Review,* XXV (1920), 411–25; and Reinhard H. Luthin, "The Sale of Alaska," *Slavonic Review,* XVI (1937), 168–82. See also *House Reports,* 40 Cong., 3 Sess., No. 35 (Serial 1388). Good studies of public opinion are Richard E. Welch, Jr., "American Public Opinion and the Purchase of Russian America," *American Slavic and East European Review,* XVII (1958), 481–94; and Hunter Miller, "Russian Opinion on the Cession of Alaska," *American Historical Review,* XLVIII (1943), 521–31. Farrar, *Annexation of Russian America,* pp. 132–33, has a list of Serial Set references.

The story about the Civil War visits of the Russian squadrons is in Albert A. Woldman, *Lincoln and the Russians* (Cleveland, 1952); Frank A. Golder's revealing article, "The Russian Fleet and the Civil War," *American Historical Review,* XX (1915), 801–12; and Thomas A. Bailey's reassessment, "The Russian Fleet Myth Re-Examined," *Mississippi Valley Historical Review,* XXXVIII (1951), 81–90.

A thorough study of Seward's and Grant's attempts to acquire Santo Domingo is Charles C. Tansill, *The United States and Santo Domingo, 1798–1873: A Chapter in Caribbean Diplomacy* (Baltimore, 1938); less detailed is Sumner Welles, *Naboth's Vineyard: The Dominican Republic, 1844–1924* (2 vols., New York, 1928). Nevins, *Hamilton Fish,* is perceptive on this subject. Regarding an influential Senator and his sponsorship of annexation see Cornelius Cole, *Memoirs of Cornelius Cole, Ex-Senator of the United States from California* (New York, 1908).

Although the United States never expanded into Cuba (except for Guantánamo Bay), the island was a perennial goal of expansionists, and the Cuban civil war of 1868–1878 indirectly influenced American expansion. The best book on United States relations with Spain during the Cuban troubles is Nevins, *Hamilton Fish*. An old, detailed study concentrating on diplomacy is French E. Chadwick, *The Relations of the United States and Spain: Diplomacy* (New York, 1909). Much other material regarding Cuba can best be found in the Serial Set. *House Executive Documents*, 41 Cong., 2 Sess., No. 160 (Serial 1418), has general diplomatic correspondence. *Senate Executive Documents*, 41 Cong., 2 Sess., No. 108 (Serial 1407), has material (up to July 1870) about Americans executed in Cuba, and about Americans whose property was confiscated. For the *Virginius* affair see *House Executive Documents*, 43 Cong., 1 Sess., No. 30 (Serial 1606); *ibid.,* 44 Cong., 1 Sess., No. 90 (Serial 1689); *ibid.,* 45 Cong., 2 Sess., No. 72 (Serial 1806); and *Senate Executive Documents*, 54 Cong., 1 Sess., No. 165 (Serial 3353).

### Mexico, the Caribbean, and South America, 1877–1900

Giving general coverage of relations with Latin America is Samuel F. Bemis, *The Latin American Policy of the United States: An Historical Interpretation* (New York, 1943). David M. Pletcher's authoritative and detailed work, *The Awkward Years: American Foreign Relations under Garfield and Arthur* (Columbia, Mo., 1962), although dealing with a short period, has much information that cannot be obtained elsewhere. Because James G. Blaine was the Secretary of State at the times when the United States had her most critical encounters with South America, general works concerning him are relevant to the present topic. The best biography is David S. Muzzey, *James G. Blaine: A Political Idol of Other Days* (New York, 1934). Alice F. Tyler, *The Foreign Policy of James G. Blaine* (Minneapolis, 1927), deals specifically with Blaine as Secretary of State. Blaine's own *Political Discussions, Legislative, Diplomatic, and Popular, 1856–1886* (Norwich, Conn., 1887), has a section on "The Foreign Policy of the Garfield Administration." A useful collection of letters written after Blaine's first term as secretary is Albert T. Volwiler (ed.), *The Correspondence between Benjamin Harrison and James G. Blaine, 1882–1893* (Philadelphia, 1940); see also Volwiler, "Harrison, Blaine, and American Foreign Policy, 1889–1893," *Proceedings of the American Philosophical Society*, LXXIX (1938), 637–48.

A perceptive book dealing specifically with Mexico is J. Fred Rippy, *The United States and Mexico* (New York, 1931). James M. Callahan, *American Foreign Policy in Mexican Relations* (New York, 1932), is detailed and emphasizes diplomacy. Two books by Mexicans are enlightening: Matías Romero (a Mexican minister to the United States), *Mexico and the United States . . .* (New York, 1898); and Daniel Cosío Villegas, *The United States versus Porfirio Díaz* (Lincoln, Neb., 1963). A comprehensive biography of the Secretary of State during the border-crossing dispute is Chester L. Barrows, *William M. Evarts: Lawyer, Diplomat, Statesman* (Chapel Hill, 1941); Brainerd Dyer, *The*

*Public Career of William M. Evarts* (Berkeley, 1933), is also worth consulting. An important work is John W. Foster (the American minister to Mexico at the time), *Diplomatic Memoirs* (2 vols., Boston, 1909). Although dealing with a larger period, Robert D. Gregg, *The Influence of Border Troubles on Relations between the United States and Mexico, 1876–1910* (Baltimore, 1937), is useful for the 1870s and early 1880s. David M. Pletcher, *Rails, Mines, and Progress: Seven American Promoters in Mexico, 1867–1911* (Ithaca, 1958), and "Mexico Opens the Door to American Capital, 1877–1880," *The Americas,* XVI (1959), 1–14, gives insight into the growing economic relations, as does also Osgood Hardy, "Ulysses S. Grant, President of the Mexican Southern Railroad," *Pacific Historical Review,* XXIV (1955), 111–20. An article dealing with political matters is Charles W. Hackett, "The Recognition of the Díaz Government by the United States," *Southwestern Historical Quarterly,* XXVIII (1924), 34–55. From the many government documents the following may be selected for their broad coverage of the border-crossing dispute: *Senate Reports,* 42 Cong., 3 Sess., No. 39 (Serial 1565); *House Executive Documents,* 45 Cong., 1 Sess., No. 13 (Serial 1773); *House Reports,* 44 Cong., 1 Sess., No. 343 (Serial 1709); *ibid.,* 45 Cong., 2 Sess., No. 701 (Serial 1824); *House Miscellaneous Documents,* 45 Cong., 2 Sess., No. 64 (Serial 1820).

America's role in the Mexican-Guatemalan boundary dispute has produced a fairly extensive literature. A general survey is Leon F. Sensabaugh, *American Interest in the Mexican-Guatemalan Boundary Dispute,* Birmingham-Southern College Bulletin, XXXIII (Birmingham, Ala., 1940). Regarding the Guatemalan dictator see Paul Burgess, *Justo Rufino Barrios: A Biography* (Philadelphia, 1926). Important articles, because written by the Mexican minister at Washington during the dispute, are Matías Romero, "Mr. Blaine and the Boundary Question between Mexico and Guatemala," *Journal of the American Geographical Society of New York,* XXIX (1897), 281–330; and "Settlement of the Mexico-Guatemala Boundary Question," *ibid.,* pp. 123–59. See also J. Fred Rippy, "Relations of the United States and Guatemala during the Epoch of Justo Rufino Barrios," *Hispanic American Historical Review,* XXII (1942), 595–605; and "Justo Rufino Barrios and the Nicaraguan Canal," *ibid.,* XX (1940), 190–97. Some of the diplomatic correspondence is in *Senate Executive Documents,* 47 Cong., 1 Sess., No. 156 (Serial 1990); and *House Executive Documents,* 48 Cong., 1 Sess., No. 154 (Serial 2207).

For the Caribbean see Ludwell L. Montague, *Haiti and the United States, 1714–1938* (Durham, N.C., 1940); Rayford W. Logan, *The Diplomatic Relations of the United States with Haiti, 1776–1891* (Chapel Hill, 1941); Sumner Welles, *Naboth's Vineyard: The Dominican Republic, 1844–1924* (2 vols., New York, 1928); and Frederick Douglass, "Haiti and the United States: Inside History of the Negotiations for the Môle St. Nicolas," *North American Review,* CLIII (1891), 337–45.

Good on Frelinghuysen's reciprocity aspirations is David M. Pletcher, *The Awkward Years: American Foreign Relations under Garfield and Arthur* (Columbia, Mo., 1962). For a broad coverage see Tom E. Terrill, *The Tariff, Politics, and American Foreign Policy, 1874–1901* (Westport, Conn., 1973). An interesting article that corrects overemphasis on the surplus is Paul S. Holbo, "Economics, Emotion, and Expansion: An Emerging Foreign Policy," in H. Wayne Morgan (ed.), *The Gilded Age* (2d ed., Syracuse, 1970), pp. 199–221. *House Reports*, 48 Cong., 1 Sess., No. 2615 (Serial 2443), is informative on the Grant-Romero treaty.

Cleveland's attitude toward reciprocity and other tariff matters is capably handled in Allan Nevins, *Grover Cleveland: A Study in Courage* (New York, 1932). See also William L. Wilson, "The Republican Policy of Reciprocity," *Forum*, XIV (1892), 255–64; Roger Q. Mills, "The Wilson Bill," *North American Review*, CLVIII (1894), 235–44; and George R. Dulebohn, *Principles of Foreign Policy under the Cleveland Administrations* (Philadelphia, 1941).

There is considerable literature on the United States and Chile during the War of the Pacific. General books dealing with a long period, but giving some attention to the war years, are William R. Sherman, *The Diplomatic and Commercial Relations of the United States and Chile, 1820–1914* (Boston, 1926); Henry C. Evans, Jr., *Chile and Its Relations with the United States* (Durham, N.C., 1927); and William J. Dennis, *Tacna and Arica: An Account of the Chile-Peru Boundary Dispute and of the Arbitrations by the United States* (New Haven, 1931). The only work dealing exclusively with the United States and the war is Herbert Millington, *American Diplomacy and the War of the Pacific* (New York, 1948); but Pletcher, *Awkward Years*, has a good deal of material, and Tyler, *Foreign Policy of Blaine*, has some. Russell H. Bastert has written two important articles: "Diplomatic Reversal: Frelinghuysen's Opposition to Blaine's Pan-American Policy in 1882," *Mississippi Valley Historical Review*, XLII (1956), 653–71; and "A New Approach to the Origins of Blaine's Pan-American Policy," *Hispanic American Historical Review*, XXXIX (1959), 375–412. Perry Belmont, *An American Democrat: The Recollections of Perry Belmont* (New York, 1941), has information about the accusations against Blaine regarding his policy toward Chile and Peru. Indispensable are *Senate Executive Documents*, 47 Cong., 1 Sess., No. 79 (Serial 1989); and *House Reports*, 47 Cong., 1 Sess., No. 1790 (Serial 2070). Useful, too, are *Senate Executive Documents*, 47 Cong., 1 Sess., Nos. 181 and 194 (Serial 1991); and *House Executive Documents*, 47 Cong., 1 Sess., No. 68 (Serial 2027), Pt. 2 and *ibid.*, No. 142 (Serial 2030).

Three previously cited books are useful for the Chilean revolution of 1891: Evans, *Chile and the United States;* Sherman, *Relations of the United States and Chile;* and Tyler, *Foreign Policy of Blaine.* See also Frederick B. Pike, *Chile and the United States, 1880–1962: The Emergence of Chile's Social Crisis and the*

*Challenge to United States Diplomacy* (South Bend, 1963). Osgood Hardy, "The Itata Incident," *Hispanic American Historical Review*, V (1922), 195–226, is the best source of information about the incident, and Hardy, "Was Patrick Egan a 'Blundering Minister'?," *ibid.*, VIII (1928), 65–81, is good on the aggressive diplomat. For a colorful and partial account of the Baltimore incident by the person in charge of the ship see Robley D. Evans, *A Sailor's Log: Recollections of Forty Years of Naval Life* (New York, 1907). Walter R. Herrick, Jr., *The American Naval Revolution* (Baton Rouge, 1966), gives much attention to Secretary of the Navy Tracy. Hundreds of pages of diplomatic correspondence are in *House Executive Documents*, 52 Cong., 1 Sess., No. 91 (Serial 2954), Pts. 1 and 2.

Information about James G. Blaine's move to convene an inter-American peace conference can be found in the general books about the Secretary of State; in Bastert, "Diplomatic Reversal," and "Origins of Blaine's Pan-American Policy" (both cited above); and in A. Curtis Wilgus, "James G. Blaine and the Pan American Movement," *Hispanic American Historical Review*, V (1922), 662–708. A valuable source of information about trade with Latin America is a long, contemporary report by William E. Curtis in *Senate Executive Documents*, 51 Cong., 1 Sess., No. 54 (Serial 2685). A good introduction to the inter-American conference is Arthur P. Whitaker, *The Western Hemisphere Idea: Its Rise and Decline* (Ithaca, 1954). Thomas F. McGann, *Argentina, the United States, and the Inter-American System, 1880–1914* (Cambridge, Mass., 1957), devotes more than 30 pages to the conference. See also the contemporary account by a participant, Matías Romero, "The Pan-American Conference," *North American Review*, CLI (1890), 354–66, 407–21; the just-cited Wilgus article; and Tyler, *Foreign Policy of Blaine*. The official records of the conference are in the United States governmental publication *International American Conference . . .* (4 vols., Washington, 1890). Regarding Blaine, reciprocity, and the McKinley tariff act see Tyler, *Foreign Policy of Blaine;* William L. Wilson, "The Republican Policy of Reciprocity," *Forum*, XIV (1892), 255–64; and Edward Stanwood, *American Tariff Controversies in the Nineteenth Century* (2 vols., Boston, 1903).

Regarding the American role in the Brazilian revolution of 1893 see, mainly for background, João Pandiá Cologeras, *A History of Brazil*, trans. and ed. by Percy A. Martin (Chapel Hill, 1939), and Lawrence F. Hill, *Diplomatic Relations between the United States and Brazil* (Durham, N.C., 1932). Charles A. Timm, "The Diplomatic Relations between the United States and Brazil during the Naval Revolt of 1893," *Southwestern Political and Social Science Quarterly*, V (1924), 119–38, is more specific. Emphasizing economic motives is Walter LaFeber, "United States Depression Diplomacy and the Brazilian Revolution, 1893–1894," *Hispanic American Historical Review*, XL (1960), 107–18, and *The New Empire: An Interpretation of American Expansion, 1860–1898* (Ithaca, 1963).

## The New Orleans Riot of 1891

See Alice F. Tyler, *The Foreign Policy of James G. Blaine* (Minneapolis, 1927); John E. Coxe, "The New Orleans Mafia Incident," *Louisiana Historical Quarterly*, XX (1937), 1067–1110; and two articles by J. Alexander Karlin: "The Italo-American Incident of 1891 and the Road to Reunion," *Journal of Southern History*, VIII (1942), 242–46, and "The Indemnification of Aliens Injured by Mob Violence," *Southwestern Social Science Quarterly*, XXV (1945), 235–46.

## An American Isthmian Canal

The number of books, articles, and documents regarding a canal is enormous. Dexter Perkins's classic study, *The Monroe Doctrine, 1867–1907* (Baltimore, 1937), contains some pertinent material, as does another basic study, Mary W. Williams, *Anglo-American Isthmian Diplomacy, 1815–1915* (Washington, 1916). A survey useful for Panama is E. Taylor Parks, *Colombia and the United States, 1765–1934* (Durham, N.C., 1935). General studies more directly concerned with a waterway are Miles P. DuVal, Jr., *Cadiz to Cathay: The Story of the Long Struggle for a Waterway across the American Isthmus* (Stanford, 1940); Lindley M. Keasbey, *The Nicaragua Canal and the Monroe Doctrine . . .* (New York, 1896); and Willis F. Johnson, *Four Centuries of the Panama Canal* (New York, 1906). Very useful is Gerstle Mack, *The Land Divided: A History of the Panama Canal and Other Isthmian Canal Projects* (New York, 1944). Philippe Bunau-Varilla, *Panama: The Creation, Destruction, and Resurrection* (London, 1913), is a colorful account by an important participant. Scholarly and objective, but mainly concerned with the twentieth century, is Dwight C. Miner, *The Fight for the Panama Route: The Story of the Spooner Act and the Hay-Herrán Treaty* (New York, 1940). Regarding the Frelinghuysen-Zavala treaty see David M. Pletcher, *The Awkward Years: American Foreign Relations under Garfield and Arthur* (Columbia, Mo., 1962). From the great number of periodical articles the following are selected as expressing the views of protagonists: Ferdinand de Lesseps, "The Interoceanic Canal," *North American Review*, CXXX (1880), 1–15, and "The Panama Canal," *ibid.*, CXXXI (1880), 75–78; Daniel Ammen's reply to the first de Lesseps article, "M. de Lesseps and His Canal," *ibid.*, CXXX (1880), 130–43; James B. Eads, "The Isthmian Ship-Railway," *ibid.*, CXXXII (1881), 223–38; Ulysses S. Grant, "The Nicaragua Canal," *ibid.*, pp. 107–16; John T. Morgan, "Government Aid to the Nicaragua Canal," *ibid.*, CLVI (1893), 195–203; Thomas B. Reed, "The Nicaragua Canal," *ibid.*, CLXVIII (1899), 552–62; William P. Hepburn, "The Nicaragua Canal," *Independent*, LII (1900), 294–96. In the Congressional Serial Set there are scores of items about a canal. *Senate Documents*, 55 Cong., 3 Sess., No. 26 (Serial 3725), lists all items through 55 Cong., 2 Sess. Later items include: *Senate Reports*, 56 Cong., 1 Sess., No. 1337 (Serial 3894), Pts. 1 and 2; *ibid.*, 56 Cong., 2 Sess., No. 1337 (Serial 4063); *ibid.*, 57 Cong., 1 Sess., No. 1 (Serial 4256); *Senate Executive Documents*, 56 Cong., 2 Sess., No. 231 (Serial 4050); *Senate Documents*, 58 Cong., 2 Sess., No. 222 (Serial 4609); and (enlightening on William Nelson Cromwell) *The Story of Panama: Hearings on the Rainey Resolution before the Committee on Foreign Affairs of the House of Representatives* (Washington, 1913).

## Hawaii and Samoa

Ralph S. Kuykendall, *The Hawaiian Kingdom . . .* (3 vols., Honolulu, 1938–67), Vols. I and II, describes the setting of Hawaiian-American relations. For the influential sugar producer see Jacob Adler, *Claus Spreckels: The Sugar King in Hawaii* (Honolulu, 1966), and Spreckels's article "The Future of the Sandwich Islands," *North American Review*, CLII (1891), 287–91. Essential books are Sylvester K. Stevens, *American Expansion in Hawaii, 1842–1898* (Harrisburg, Pa., 1945); and, with new material, Merze Tate, *Hawaii: Reciprocity or Annexation* (East Lansing, 1968), and *The United States and the Hawaiian Kingdom: A Political History* (New Haven, 1965). John Patterson, "The United States and Hawaiian Reciprocity, 1867–1870," *Pacific Historical Review*, VII (1938), 14–26, and Donald M. Dozer, "The Opposition to Hawaiian Reciprocity, 1876–1888," *Pacific Historical Review*, XIV (1945), 157–83, should be consulted on the 1875 reciprocity treaty. See also Dozer, "Anti-Expansionism during the Johnson Administration," *ibid.*, XII (1943), 253–75. *House Executive Documents*, 53 Cong., 2 Sess., No. 47 (Serial 3224), pp. 303–11, has interesting material on the decline of the native population.

An abundance of material exists about the revolution of 1893 and its aftermath. Allan Nevins, *Grover Cleveland: A Study in Courage* (New York, 1932), considers the President who opposed annexation; John W. Foster, *Diplomatic Memoirs* (2 vols., Boston, 1909), recounts his own role in drafting the abortive treaties of 1893 and 1898. An outstanding work is Julius W. Pratt, *Expansionists of 1898: The Acquisition of Hawaii and the Spanish Islands* (Baltimore, 1936). Stephens, *American Expansion in Hawaii*, and Kuykendall, *Hawaiian Kingdom*, may be consulted on the revolution, but more thorough are William A. Russ, Jr., *The Hawaiian Revolution (1893–94)* (Selinsgrove, Pa., 1959), and Tate, *United States and the Hawaiian Kingdom*. William A. Russ, Jr., *The Hawaiian Republic (1894–98) and Its Struggle to Win Annexation* (Selinsgrove, Pa., 1961), is the standard work. See also the two previously noted books by Tate, and Francis H. Conroy, *The Japanese Frontier in Hawaii, 1868–1898* (Berkeley, 1953). There are many accounts of the events of 1893 and later, written by contemporary participants, which are well worth examining: William D. Alexander, *History of Later Years of the Hawaiian Mon-

*archy and the Revolution of 1893* (Honolulu, 1896); Lorrin A. Thurston, *A Hand-Book on the Annexation of Hawaii* (St. Joseph[?], Mich., 1897[?]), *Memoirs of the Hawaiian Revolution,* ed. by Andrew Farrell (Honolulu, 1936), and "The Sandwich Islands: I. The Advantages of Annexation," *North American Review,* CLVI (1893), 265–81; Sanford B. Dole, *Memoirs of the Hawaiian Revolution,* ed. by Andrew Farrell (Honolulu, 1936); Queen Liliuokalani, *Hawaii's Story by Hawaii's Queen* (Boston, 1898); Lucien Young, *The Boston at Hawaii . . .* (Washington, 1898); and John L. Stevens, "A Plea for Annexation," *North American Review,* CLVII (1893), 736–45. In addition to the Thurston and Stevens articles, the following may be mentioned from the large number of contemporary articles: Sereno E. Bishop, "The Hawaiian Queen and Her Kingdom," *Review of Reviews,* IV (1891), 147–63; George Ticknor Curtis, "Is It Constitutional?" *North American Review,* CLVI (1893), 282–86; Alfred T. Mahan, "Hawaii and Our Future Sea-Power," *Forum,* XV (1893), 1–11; and Henry Cabot Lodge's influential denunciation of the Cleveland administration, "Our Blundering Foreign Policy," *Forum,* XIX (1895), 8–17. Recent, scholarly articles include two interesting reinterpretations and two analyzing the role of the sugar interests: Julius W. Pratt, "The Hawaiian Revolution: A Re-Interpretation," *Pacific Historical Review,* I (1932), 273–94; George W. Baker, Jr., "Benjamin Harrison and Hawaiian Annexation: A Reinterpretation," *ibid.,* XXXIII (1964), 295–309 (minimizing the President's role); William A. Russ, Jr., "The Role of Sugar in Hawaiian Annexation," *ibid.,* XII (1943), 339–50; and Richard D. Weigle, "Sugar and the Hawaiian Revolution," *ibid.,* XVI (1947), 41–58. Among the many government documents two are indispensable: *Papers Relating to the Foreign Relations of the United States, 1894* (Washington, 1895), Appendix II; and *Senate Reports,* 53 Cong., 2 Sess., No. 227 (Serial 3180), vol. 2 of which is incorporated in the just-cited Appendix II of *Foreign Relations, 1894.* In addition see *House Reports,* 53 Cong., 2 Sess., No. 243 (Serial 3269); *Senate Documents,* 54 Cong., 1 Sess., No. 194 (Serial 3353); and *Senate Reports,* 55 Cong., 2 Sess., No. 681 (Serial 3622).

With respect to the annexation of Hawaii in 1898 see the previously noted books by Stevens, Russ, Kuykendall, Tate, Pratt, and Foster. Regarding Japan and Hawaii see Payson J. Treat, *Diplomatic Relations between the United States and Japan, 1853–1905* (3 vols., Stanford, 1932–38); and Thomas A. Bailey, "Japan's Protest against the Annexation of Hawaii," *Journal of Modern History,* III (1931), 46–61. Other important scholarly articles are Bailey, "The United States and Hawaii during the Spanish-American War," *American Historical Review,* XXXVI (1931), 552–60; John C. Appel, "American Labor and the Annexation of Hawaii: A Study in Logic and Economic Interest," *Pacific Historical Review,* XXIII (1954), 1–18; and Donald Rowland, "The United States and the Contract Labor Question in

Hawaii, 1862–1900," *ibid.*, II (1933), 249–69. Significant contemporary articles include: John R. Procter, "Hawaii and the Changing Front of the World," *Forum*, XXIV (1897), 34–45; James Bryce, "The Policy of Annexation for America," *ibid.*, pp. 385–95; Daniel Agnew, "Unconstitutionality of the Hawaiian Treaty," *ibid.*, pp. 461–70; and John T. Morgan, "The Duty of Annexing Hawaii," *ibid.*, XXV (1898), 11–16. Important documentary material is in *House Reports*, 55 Cong., 2 Sess., No. 1355 (Serial 3721), Pts. 1 and 2; and *Senate Documents*, 55 Cong., 3 Sess., No. 16 (Serial 3727).

The standard work on relations with Samoa is George H. Ryden, *The Foreign Policy of the United States in Relation to Samoa* (New Haven, 1933). For background, consult Foster R. Dulles, *America in the Pacific: A Century of Expansion* (Boston, 1932); Sylvia Masterman, *The Origins of International Rivalry in Samoa, 1845–1884* (Stanford, 1934); and Richard P. Gilson, *Samoa, 1830–1900: The Politics of A Multi-Cultural Community* (Melbourne, 1970). Gilson also has some valuable material on the 1870s and 1880s. The later international rivalry is examined in Paul M. Kennedy, *The Samoan Tangle: A Study in Anglo-German-American Relations, 1878–1900* (New York, 1974). For the two American Secretaries of State most involved in the altercation with Germany see Charles C. Tansill's detailed *The Foreign Policy of Thomas F. Bayard, 1885–1897* (New York, 1940); and Alice F. Tyler, *The Foreign Policy of James G. Blaine* (Minneapolis, 1927). Charles O. Paullin, *Diplomatic Negotiations of American Naval Officers, 1778–1883* (Baltimore, 1912), is a good general study; more pertinent to Samoa is an early report by a participant: Edgar Wakeman, *Report of Capt. E. Wakeman, to W. H. Webb, on the Islands of the Samoa Group . . .* (New York, 1872). Robert Louis Stevenson, *A Foot-Note to History: Eight Years of Trouble in Samoa* (New York, 1897), is a fascinating account. There are several good studies of general relations between the United States and Germany: Jeannette Keim, *Forty Years of German-American Political Relations* (Philadelphia, 1919); Clara E. Schieber, *The Transformation of American Sentiment toward Germany, 1870–1914* (Boston, 1923); Otto zu Stolberg-Wernigerode, *Germany and the United States of America during the Era of Bismarck* (Reading, Pa., 1937); and the detailed work by Alfred Vagts, *Deutschland und die Vereinigten Staaten in der Weltpolitik* (2 vols., New York, 1935). Vagts has also written "Hopes and Fears of an American-German War, 1870–1915," *Political Science Quarterly*, LIV (1939), 514–35. Joseph W. Ellison, "The Adventures of an American Premier in Samoa, 1874–1876," *Pacific Northwest Quarterly*, XXVII (1936), 311–46, describes the Steinberger mission; and J. A. C. Gray, "The Apia Hurricane of 1889," *United States Naval Institute Proceedings*, LXXXVI (1960), 34–39, gives an account of the great storm. Joseph W. Ellison, "The Partition of Samoa: A Study in Imperialism and Diplomacy," *Pacific Historical Review*, VIII (1939), 259–88, and Walter S. Penfield, "The Settlement of the Samoan Cases," *American Journal of International Law,* VII (1913), 767–73, are good articles about these later events. Important documentary material is in *Papers Relating to the Foreign Relations of the United States, 1894* (Washington, 1895), Appendix I; *House Executive Documents,* 44 Cong., 1 Sess., No. 161 (Serial 1691); *ibid.,* 44 Cong., 2 Sess., No. 44 (Serial 1755); *ibid.,* 50 Cong., 1 Sess., No. 238 (Serial 2560); *Senate Executive Documents,* 50 Cong., 2 Sess., No. 31 (Serial 2610); *ibid.,* No. 102 (Serial 2612); and *Senate Miscellaneous Documents,* 51 Cong., 1 Sess., No. 81 (Serial 2698).

## The Congo

Clarence Clendenen, Robert Collins, and Peter Duignan, *Americans in Africa, 1865–1890* (Palo Alto, 1966), give the background of the Congo conference. For the conference in its world setting see Sybil E. Crowe, *The Berlin West African Conference, 1884–1885* (London, 1942); for United States participation see David M. Pletcher, *The Awkward Years: American Foreign Relations under Garfield and Arthur* (Columbia, Mo., 1962). Frank Hird, *H. M. Stanley: The Authorized Life . . .* (London, 1935), and Byron Farwell, *The Man Who Presumed: A Biography of Henry M. Stanley* (New York, 1957), write about the famous explorer; and Henry M. Stanley himself wrote *The Congo and the Founding of Its Free State: A Story of Work and Exploration* (2 vols., New York, 1885). For the views of the other American closely associated with the Congo see Henry S. Sanford, "American Interests in Africa," *Forum,* IX (1890), 409–29. A good account of the chief American delegate to the Berlin conference is Edward Younger, *John A. Kasson: Politics and Diplomacy from Lincoln to McKinley* (Iowa City, 1955); see Kasson's indignant article, "The Congo Conference and the President's Message," *North American Review,* CXLII (1886), 119–33. Extensive documentary material is in *House Executive Documents,* 48 Cong., 2 Sess., No. 247 (Serial 2304); and *Senate Executive Documents,* 49 Cong., 1 Sess., No. 196 (Serial 2341).

## The Pork Dispute

For the setting of the pork dispute see Jeannette Keim, *Forty Years of German-American Political Relations* (Philadelphia, 1919); Alfred Vagts, *Deutschland und die Vereinigten Staaten in der Weltpolitik* (2 vols., New York, 1935); and Otto zu Stolberg-Wernigerode, *Germany and the United States of America during the Era of Bismarck* (Reading, Pa., 1937). David M. Pletcher, *The Awkward Years: American Foreign Relations under Garfield and Arthur* (Columbia, Mo., 1962); and Alice F. Tyler, *The Foreign Policy of James G. Blaine* (Minneapolis, 1927), have material on different phases of the dispute; and John L. Gignilliat, "Pigs, Politics, and Protection: The European Boycott of American Pork, 1879–1891," *Agricultural History*, XXXV (1961), 3–12, gives a general coverage. Louis L. Snyder, "The American-German Pork Dispute, 1879–1891," *Journal of Modern History*, XVII (1945), 16–28, is good on Germany; and Bingham Duncan, "Protectionism and Pork: Whitelaw Reid as Diplomat: 1889–1891," *Agricultural History*, XXXIII (1959), 190–95, deals with the altercation with France. For documentary material see *House Executive Documents*, 48 Cong., 1 Sess., No. 70 (Serial 2200), and *ibid.*, No. 106 (Serial 2206).

## Chinese Immigration

The standard work is Mary R. Coolidge, *Chinese Immigration* (New York, 1909); it may be supplemented by Stuart C. Miller, *The Unwelcome Immigrant: The American Image of the Chinese, 1785–1882* (Berkeley, 1969). Gunther Barth, *Bitter Strength: A History of the Chinese in the United States, 1850–1870* (Cambridge, Mass., 1964), though mainly treating the years before 1865, is useful for background. George F. Seward, *Chinese Immigration, in Its Social and Economical Aspects* (New York, 1881), and "Mongolian Immigration," *North American Review*, CXXXIV (1882), 562–77, gives the opinions of an important State Department official involved in the controversy with China. For another contemporary opinion see John H. Durst, "The Exclusion of the Chinese," *ibid.*, CXXXIX (1884), 256–73. James B. Angell, *The Reminiscences of James Burrill Angell* (New York, 1912), has a long chapter on his mission to China; regarding the mission one should also consult Shirley W. Smith, *James Burrill Angell: An American Influence* (Ann Arbor, 1954). The most thorough account of the Chinese issue in California is Elmer C. Sandmeyer, *The Anti-Chinese Movement in California* (Urbana, Ill., 1939), which has also a valuable bibliography. Articles describing the issue in particular localities are: Rodman W. Paul, "The Origin of the Chinese Issue in California," *Mississippi Valley Historical Review*, XXV (1938), 181–96; Robert Seager II, "Some Denominational Reactions to Chinese Immigration to California, 1856–1892," *Pacific Historical Review*, XXVIII (1959), 49–66; Jules Karlin, "The Anti-Chinese Outbreak in Tacoma, 1885," *ibid.*, XXIII (1954), 271–83, and "The Anti-Chinese Outbreaks in Seattle, 1885–1886," *Pacific Northwest Quarterly*, XXXIX (1948), 103–30. The many Serial Set publications include: *House Executive Documents*, 49 Cong., 1 Sess., No. 102 (Serial 2398); *House Reports*, 45 Cong., 3 Sess., No. 62 (Serial 1866); *ibid.*, 51 Cong., 2 Sess., No. 4048 (Serial 2890); *Senate Reports*, 44 Cong., 2 Sess., No. 689 (Serial 1734); *ibid.*, 57 Cong., 1 Sess., No. 776 (Serial 4265), Pt. 2; *Senate Executive Documents*, 47 Cong., 1 Sess., No. 148 (Serial 1990); *ibid.*, 50 Cong., 1 Sess., No. 272 (Serial 2514); *ibid.*, 51 Cong., 1 Sess., No. 41 (Serial 2682); *ibid.*, 52 Cong., 2 Sess., No. 54 (Serial 3056).

## Korea

Early relations with Korea are put in perspective by Tyler Dennett, *Americans in Eastern Asia: A Critical Study of United States' Policy in the Far East in the Nineteenth Century* (New York, 1922); and by Charles O. Paullin, *Diplomatic Negotiations of American Naval Officers, 1778–1883* (Baltimore, 1912). A good general study is M. Frederick Nelson, *Korea and the Old Orders in Eastern Asia* (Baton Rouge, 1945). Yur-Bok Lee, *Diplomatic Relations between the United States and Korea, 1866–1887* (New York, 1970), surveys an important era. More specific are three articles: Charles O. Paullin, "The Opening of Korea by Commodore Shufeldt," *Political Science Quarterly*, XXV (1910), 470–99; Tyler Dennett, "Early American Policy in Korea, 1883–7: The Services of Lieutenant George C. Foulk," *ibid.*, XXXVIII (1923), 82–103; and Harold J. Noble, "The U.S. and Sino-Korean Relations, 1885–1887," *Pacific Historical Review*, II (1933), 292–304. A fine biography of a leading American resident of Korea is Fred H. Harrington, *God, Mammon, and the Japanese: Dr. Horace N. Allen and Korean-American Relations, 1884–1905* (Madison, 1944). For documents consult George M. McCune and John A. Harrison (eds.), *Korean-American Relations, Documents Pertaining to the Far Eastern Diplomacy of the United States*. Vol. I: *The Initial Period, 1883–1886* (Berkeley, 1951); and Spencer J. Palmer (ed.), *Korean-American Relations, Documents Pertaining to the Far Eastern Diplomacy of the United States*. Vol. II: *The Period of Growing Influence, 1887–1895* (Berkeley, 1963).

## Fish and Fur Seals, and Sackville West

Regarding both the fishing and the fur seals controversies see Charles C. Tansill, *Canadian-American Relations, 1875–1911* (New Haven, 1943), and his voluminous and detailed *The Foreign Policy of Thomas F. Bayard, 1885–1897* (New York, 1940). Robert C. Brown's excellent monograph, *Canada's National Policy, 1883–1900: A Study in Canadian-American Relations* (Princeton, 1964), considers the controversies mainly in relation to Canada; and Charles S. Campbell, *From Revolution to Rapprochement: The United States and Great Britain, 1783–1900* (New York, 1974), considers them mainly in relation to Great Britain. Fine biographies of statesmen involved are: Allan Nevins, *Grover Cleveland: A Study in Courage* (New York, 1932); John Morley, *The Life of William Ewart Gladstone* (3 vols., New York, 1903); William F. Monypenny and George E. Buckle, *The Life of Benjamin Disraeli, Earl of Beaconsfield* (6 vols., New York, 1910–20); and Gwendolen Cecil, *Life of Robert, Marquis of Salisbury* (4 vols., London, 1922–33). There are also good biographies of the Canadian Prime Ministers chiefly involved in the dispute: Donald G. Creighton, *John A. Macdonald: The Old Chieftain* (Toronto, 1955);

and Dale C. Thomson, *Alexander Mackenzie: Clear Grit* (Toronto, 1960). On the termination of the Marcy-Elgin treaty of 1854 and its aftermath see Lester B. Shippee, *Canadian-American Relations, 1849–1874* (New Haven, 1939). The following documents have much helpful material: *House Executive Documents,* 39 Cong., 2 Sess., No. 78 (Serial 1293); *ibid.,* 40 Cong., 3 Sess., No. 75 (Serial 1374); *Senate Executive Documents,* 39 Cong., 2 Sess., No. 30 (Serial 1277); and *Senate Miscellaneous Documents,* 50 Cong., 1 Sess., No. 109 (Serial 2517).

Regarding the Bayard-Chamberlain treaty and its background, the general works noted at the beginning of this section should be consulted. An old study is still of value: Charles Isham, *The Fishery Question: Its Origin, History, and Present Situation . . .* (New York, 1887). James L. Garvin's fine biography, *The Life of Joseph Chamberlain* (3 vols., London, 1932–34), is informative about the chief British negotiator; Edward M. Saunders (ed.), *The Life and Letters of the Rt. Hon. Sir Charles Tupper, Bart., K.C.M.G.* (2 vols., London, 1916), has material about the Canadian negotiator. For a leading critic of the treaty see George F. Hoar, *Autobiography of Seventy Years* (2 vols., New York, 1906). Charles S. Campbell, "American Tariff Interests and the Northeastern Fisheries, 1883–1888," *Canadian Historical Review,* XLV (1964), 212–28, deals with the influence of some special interests. See also Campbell, "Edward J. Phelps and Anglo-American Relations," in Harry C. Allen and Roger F. Thompson (eds.), *Contrast and Connection: Bicentennial Essays in Anglo-American History* (London, 1976), pp. 210–24, which examines Phelps's role as minister. A very large number of congressional reports and documents includes: *House Reports,* 49 Cong., 2 Sess., No. 3648 (Serial 2500); *ibid.,* No. 4087 (Serial 2501); *Senate Documents,* 56 Cong., 2 Sess., No. 231 (Serial 4054), Pt. 8; *Senate Executive Documents,* 50 Cong., 1 Sess., No. 113 (Serial 2512); *Senate Miscellaneous Documents,* 50 Cong., 1 Sess., No. 109 (Serial 2517); *Senate Reports,* 51 Cong., 1 Sess., No. 1530 (Serial 2712).

The Sackville West affair was closely connected with the fishery dispute. General treatment of the incident is in Tansill, *Foreign Policy of Bayard;* and Campbell, *From Revolution to Rapprochement.* Charles S. Campbell, "The Dismissal of Lord Sackville," *Mississippi Valley Historical Review,* XLIV (1958), 635–48, analyzes the propriety of the dismissal. See also *House Executive Documents,* 50 Cong., 2 Sess., No. 150 (Serial 2652).

For the background of the fur seals controversy see the able study by H. F. Angus (ed.), F. W. Howay, and W. N. Sage, *British Columbia and the United States: The North Pacific Slope from Fur Trade to Aviation* (Toronto, 1942). Other general books, but more closely related to the controversy, are: David S. Jordan, *The Fur Seals and Fur-Seal Islands of the North Pacific Ocean* (Washington, 1898); Samuel P. Johnston (ed.), *Alaska Commercial Company, 1868–1940 . . .* (San Francisco, 1940); L. D. Kitchener, *Flag over the North: The Story of the Northern Commercial Company* (Seattle, 1954); and Fredericka Martin, *The Hunting of the Silver Fleece: Epic of the Fur Seal* (New York, 1946). On Bayard's diplomacy see Charles C. Tansill, *The Foreign Policy of Thomas F. Bayard, 1885–1897* (New York, 1940). For Blaine's diplomacy there are three general works: Alice F. Tyler, *The Foreign Policy of James G. Blaine* (Minneapolis, 1927); Albert T. Volwiler (ed.), *The Correspondence between Benjamin Harrison and James G. Blaine, 1882–1893* (Philadelphia, 1940); and the same author's "Harrison, Blaine, and American Foreign Policy, 1889–1893," *Proceedings of the American Philosophical Society,* LXXIX (1938), 637–48. In addition to Campbell, *From Revolution to Rapprochement,* see also Charles S. Campbell, "The Anglo-American Crisis in the Bering Sea, 1890–1891," *Mississippi Valley Historical Review,* XLVIII (1961), 393–414, and "The Bering Sea Settlements of 1892," *Pacific Historical Review,* XXXII (1963), 347–67. Important contemporary articles are: Edward J. Phelps, "The Behring Sea Controversy," *Harper's New Monthly Magazine,* LXXXII (1891), 766–74; Benjamin F. Tracy, "The Behring Sea Question," *North American Review,* CLVI (1893), 513–42; John W. Foster, "Results of the Bering Sea Arbitration," *ibid.,* CLXI (1895), 693–702; and William Williams (a member of the American delegation at Paris), "Reminiscences of the Bering Sea Arbitration," *American Journal of International Law,* XXXVII (1943), 562–84. For the arbitration see *Fur Seal Arbitration: Proceedings of the Tribunal of Arbitration Convened at Paris . . .* (16 vols., Washington, 1895); and Moore, *International Arbitrations.*

Among the many documents in the Serial Set the following are especially important: *House Executive Documents,* 44 Cong., 1 Sess., No. 83 (Serial 1687); *House Documents,* 54 Cong., 1 Sess., No. 175 (Serial 3421); *House Reports,* 44 Cong., 1 Sess., No. 623 (Serial 1712); *ibid.,* 50 Cong., 2 Sess., No. 3883 (Serial 2674); *Senate Executive Documents,* 50 Cong., 2 Sess., No. 106 (Serial 2612); and *ibid.,* 52 Cong., 1 Sess., No. 55 (Serial 2900).

## Economics and Foreign Policy

The literature of the influence of economic factors on foreign policy is enormous. Two general works emphasizing the economic influence on American foreign policy are Walter LaFeber, *The New Empire: An Interpretation of American Expansion, 1860–1898* (Ithaca, 1963); and William A. Williams, *The Roots of the Modern American Empire: A Study of the Growth and Shaping of Social Consciousness in a Marketplace Society* (New York, 1969). Milton Plesur, *America's Outward Thrust: Approaches to Foreign Affairs, 1865–1890* (DeKalb, Ill., 1971), has a broader approach but gives considerable attention to economics. Alfred Vagts, *Deutschland und die Vereinigten Staaten in der Weltpolitik* (2 vols., New York, 1935), although limited to relations with one country and to a shorter time period, deals exhaustively with many aspects of American foreign policy. An invaluable publication is United States Bureau of the Census, *Historical Statistics of the United States, Colonial Times to 1957* (Washington, 1960). For investments see also Paul D. Dickens, *American Direct Investments in Foreign Countries* (Washington, 1930); Cleona Lewis, *America's Stake in International Investments* (Washington, 1938).

The literature on economic conditions during the 1890s, on the panic of 1893, and on overproduction and the surplus is so vast that the bibliographies in the general books listed in the first paragraph of this section should be consulted. The following books and articles are especially significant. Rendigs Fels, *American Business Cycles, 1865–1897* (Chapel Hill, 1959), is good on the economic fluctuations. For the depression see Charles Hoffmann, *The Depression of the Nineties: An Economic History* (Westport, Conn., 1970), and "The Depression of the Nineties," *Journal of Economic History*, XVI (1956), 137–64. The previously cited books by Williams and LaFeber emphasize the surplus and the consequent desire to find overseas markets. A book that stresses this thesis heavily, mainly with reference to the twentieth century, is William A. Williams, *The Tragedy of American Diplomacy* (Cleveland, 1959). Charles S. Campbell, *Special Business Interests and the Open Door Policy* (New Haven, 1951), applies the idea of the surplus to policy toward China. William Trimble, "Historical Aspects of the Surplus Food Production of the United States, 1862–1902," *Annual Report of the American Historical Association* (2 vols., Washington, 1918), I, 223–39, is an excellent introduction; and a fine, more narrowly conceived, article is Morton Rothstein, "America in the International Rivalry for the British Wheat Market, 1870–1914," *Mississippi Valley Historical Review*, XLVII (1960), 401–18. Significant contemporary articles include John R. Procter, "America's Battle for Commercial Supremacy," *Forum*, XVI (1893), 315–24; and Worthington C. Ford, "Commercial Superiority of the United States," *North American Review*, CLXVI (1898), 75–84.

A valuable source of information about silver and foreign policy is Henry B. Russell, *International Monetary Conferences . . .* (New York, 1898). Jeannette P. Nichols has written two informative articles: "Silver Diplomacy," *Political Science Quarterly*, XLVIII (1933), 565–88; and "A Painful Lesson in Silver Diplomacy," *South Atlantic Quarterly*, XXXV (1936), 251–72. Among the many contemporary articles are Andrew Carnegie, "The Silver Problem: A Word to Wage Earners," *North American Review*, CLVII (1893), 354–70; and Edward Atkinson, "Jingoes and Silverites," *ibid.*, CLXI (1895), 554–60.

## Ideology and Foreign Policy

Ideological factors, as well as economic factors, have had an enormous impact on American foreign policy. An excellent study, including material on the last two decades of the nineteenth century, is Henry S. Commager, *The American Mind: An Interpretation of American Thought and Character since the 1880's* (New Haven, 1950); it has a useful bibliography. See also David W. Noble, *The Progressive Mind, 1890–1917* (Chicago, 1970). Dealing with topics more specifically concerning foreign relations are Philip Rahv (ed.), *Discovery of Europe: The Story of American Experiences in the Old World* (Boston, 1947); Foster R. Dulles, *Americans Abroad: Two Centuries of European Travel* (Ann Arbor, 1964); Mark Twain, *The Innocents Abroad . . .* (2 vols., New York, 1911); and Cushing Strout, *The American Image of the Old World* (New York, 1963), which ably describes American attitudes toward Europe. Milton Plesur, *America's Outward Thrust: Approaches to Foreign Affairs, 1865–1890* (De-Kalb, Ill., 1971), is enlightening as regards attitudes toward several areas and countries, and has a bibliography giving information not easily obtainable elsewhere.

For attitudes toward Great Britain see Harry C. Allen, *Great Britain and the United States: A History of Anglo-American Relations (1783–1952)* (New York, 1955); Charles S. Campbell, *Anglo-American Understanding, 1898–1903* (Baltimore, 1957), and *From Revolution to Rapprochement: The United States and Great Britain, 1783–1900* (New York, 1974); and Bradford Perkins, *The Great Rapprochement: England and the United States, 1895–1914* (New York, 1968). John B. Brebner, *North Atlantic Triangle: The Interplay of Canada, the United States and Great Britain* (New Haven, 1945), though only incidentally dealing with ideology, is suggestive. On a narrower but important topic see J. G. Cook, *Anglophobia: An Analysis of Anti-British Prejudice in the United States* (Boston, 1919). From the many contemporary articles three may be selected as illuminating and as written by influential men: James Russell Lowell, "On a Certain Condescension in Foreigners," *Atlantic Monthly*, XXIII (1869), 82–94; Edwin L. Godkin, "American Hatred of England," *Nation*, LXII (1896), 46–47; Andrew Carnegie, "Does America Hate England?" *Contemporary Review*, LXXII (1897), 660–68.

The following books are enlightening as regards American attitudes toward other countries and areas: Elizabeth B. White, *American Opinion of France, from Lafayette to Poincaré* (New York, 1927); Alexander DeConde, *Half Bitter, Half Sweet: An Excursion into Italian-American History* (New York, 1971); John G. Gazley, *American Opinion of German Unification, 1848–1871* (New York, 1926); Clara E. Schieber, *The Transformation of American Sentiment toward Germany, 1870–1914* (Boston, 1923); Jurgen F. H. Herbst, *The German Historical School in American Scholarship* (Ithaca, 1965); James A. Field, Jr., *America and the Mediterranean World, 1776–1882* (Princeton, 1969); and William L. Neumann, *America Encounters Japan: From Perry to MacArthur* (Baltimore, 1963). A valuable study of missionary influence is Paul A. Varg, *Missionaries, Chinese, and Diplomats: The American Protestant Missionary Movement in China, 1890–1952* (Princeton, 1958). The following are all good studies of Americans who influenced their countrymen's opinions of Europe, especially of Great Britain: Robert C. Le Clair, *Three American Travellers in England: James Russell Lowell, Henry Adams, Henry James* (Philadelphia, 1945); Martin B. Duberman, *James Russell Lowell* (Boston, 1966); Van Wyck Brooks, *The Pilgrimage of Henry James* (New York, 1925); Christof Wegelin, *The Image of Europe in Henry James* (Dallas, 1958); Harold D. Cater, *Henry Adams and His Friends: A Collection of His Unpublished Letters* (Boston, 1947); Timothy P. Donovan, *Henry Adams and Brooks Adams: The Education of Two American Historians* (Norman, Okla., 1961); James T. Adams, *Henry Adams* (New York, 1933); Worthington C. Ford (ed.), *Letters of Henry Adams . . .* (2 vols., Boston, 1930–38); Oscar Cargill, *Intellectual America: Ideas on the March* (New York, 1941); and Tyler Dennett, *John Hay: From Poetry to Politics* (New York, 1933). See also Matthew Josephson, *The President Makers: The Culture of Politics and Leadership in an Age of Enlightenment, 1896–1919* (New York, 1940).

The classic treatment of Social Darwinism is Richard Hofstadter, *Social Darwinism in American Thought* (New York, 1959). Bert J. Loewenberg, "Darwinism Comes to America, 1859–1900," *Mississippi Valley Historical Review,* XXVIII (1941), 339–68, is also helpful. The famous philosopher Herbert Spencer had much influence in the United States through his book *The Man versus the State* (New York, 1892), which argued, in Social Darwinian terms, for a minimal governmental role. An article that typically applied Darwinism to United States foreign policy is John Barrett, "The Problem of the Philippines," *North American Review,* CLXVII (1898), 257–67. Related to Social Darwinism was the manifest destiny outlook of the 1890s. Albert K. Weinberg, *Manifest Destiny: A Study of Nationalist Expansionism in American History* (Baltimore, 1935), is an able survey; a more judicious interpretation is Frederick Merk, *Manifest Destiny and Mission in American History: A Reinterpretation* (New York, 1963). Another good analysis is Edward McN. Burns, *The American Idea of Mission: Concepts of National Purpose and Destiny* (New Brunswick, 1957). A pertinent biography of the best-known advocate of these ideas is Milton Berman, *John Fiske: The Evolution of a Popularizer* (Cambridge, Mass., 1961); see Fiske's famous "Manifest Destiny," *Harper's New Monthly Magazine,* LXX (1885), 578–90. For a penetrating analysis see Henry S. Commager, "John Fiske: An Interpretation," *Proceedings of the Massachusetts Historical Society,* LXVI (1940), 332–45. For another related idea, Anglo-Saxonism, see below, "The Anglo-American Rapprochement and Related Developments."

The best general studies of the great exponent of sea power are William D. Puleston, *Mahan: The Life and Work of Captain Alfred Thayer Mahan, U.S.N.* (New Haven, 1939); and William E. Livezey, *Mahan on Sea Power* (Norman, Okla., 1947). A thoughtful article is Walter LaFeber, "A Note on the 'Mercantilistic Imperialism' of Alfred Thayer Mahan," *Mississippi Valley Historical*

*Review,* XLVIII (1962), 674–85. Mahan's most famous book is *The Influence of Sea Power upon History, 1660–1783* (Boston, 1898), but more directly related to United States foreign policy is *The Interest of America in Sea Power, Present and Future* (Boston, 1898). Out of his numerous articles the following should be noted: "The United States Looking Outward," *Atlantic Monthly,* LXVI (1890), 816–24; "The Isthmus and Sea Power," *ibid.,* LXXII (1893), 459–72; "Possibilities of an Anglo-American Reunion," *North American Review,* CLIX (1894), 551–63; and "Preparedness for Naval War," *Harper's New Monthly Magazine,* XCIV (1897), 579–88. A convenient collection of articles is his *Lessons of the War with Spain and Other Articles* (Boston, 1899).

Regarding Brooks Adams see, for general information, two biographies: Thornton Anderson, *Brooks Adams, Constructive Conservative* (Ithaca, 1951), and Arthur F. Beringause, *Brooks Adams: A Biography* (New York, 1955); see also Adams's best-known work, *The Law of Civilization and Decay: An Essay on History* (London, 1895), and Theodore Roosevelt's review of *The Law,* "The Law of Civilization and Decay," *Forum,* XXII (1897), 575–89. Adams wrote three provocative articles before 1900: "The Spanish War and the Equilibrium of the World," *ibid.,* XXV (1898), 641–51; "England's Decadence in the West Indies," *ibid.,* XXVII (1899), 464–78; and "The Commercial Future: I. The New Struggle for Life among Nations (From an American Standpoint)," *Fortnightly Review,* LXV (1899), 274–83. Interesting interpretations are Daniel Aaron, "The Unusable Man: An Essay on the Mind of Brooks Adams," *New England Quarterly,* XXI (1948), 3–33; Charles Vevier, "Brooks Adams and the Ambivalence of American Foreign Policy," *World Affairs Quarterly,* XXX (1959), 3–18; and William A. Williams, "Brooks Adams and American Expansion," *New England Quarterly,* XXV (1952), 217–32.

Frederick Jackson Turner's famous essay "The Significance of the Frontier in American History" is in his *The Frontier in American History* (New York, 1921). For earlier warnings of a closing frontier see Herman C. Nixon, "The Precursors of Turner in the Interpretation of the America Frontier," *South Atlantic Quarterly,* XXVIII (1929), 83–89; and Lee Benson, "The Historical Background of Turner's Frontier Essay," *Agricultural History,* XXV (1951), 59–82. Two interesting essays consider Turner's influence on overseas expansion: Lawrence S. Kaplan, "Frederick Jackson Turner and Imperialism," *Social Sciences,* XXVII (1952), 12–16; and William A. Williams, "The Frontier Thesis and American Foreign Policy," *Pacific Historical Review,* XXIV (1955), 379–95. On the same point see Walter LaFeber, *The New Empire: An Interpretation of American Expansion, 1860–1898* (Ithaca, 1963).

Richard Hofstadter's "Manifest Destiny and the Philippines," in Daniel Aaron (ed.), *America in Crisis . . .* (New York, 1952), is a provocative essay about a possible psychic crisis in the 1890s; a revision of the essay is in

Hofstadter, *The Paranoid Style in American Politics, and Other Essays* (New York, 1965). Relevant to the theory of social psychology advanced in the essay are John Dollard et al., *Frustration and Aggression* (New Haven, 1939), a classic work; and John F. Hall, *Psychology of Motivation* (Chicago, 1961). There is no book exclusively devoted to American jingoism. Walter Millis, *The Martial Spirit: A Study of Our War with Spain* (Boston, 1931), emphasizes, and probably exaggerates, the extent and virulence of jingoism; the same observation may be made of Ernest R. May's penetrating *Imperial Democracy: The Emergence of America as a Great Power* (New York, 1961). The pages of the *Nation*, especially at the time of the Venezuela boundary crisis in late 1895 and early 1896, abound in denunciations of jingoism.

On a miscellany of more or less influential ideas current in the 1890s see the valuable book by Julius W. Pratt, *Expansionists of 1898: The Acquisition of Hawaii and the Spanish Islands* (Baltimore, 1936); the stimulating study by Ernest R. May, *American Imperialism: A Speculative Essay* (New York, 1968); and Merk, *Manifest Destiny.* Other influential contemporary books are Josiah Strong, *Our Country: Its Possible Future and Its Present Crisis* (New York, 1885); and John Burgess, *Political Science and Comparative Constitutional Law* (2 vols., Boston, 1890).

## The Navy

A standard account of the American navy is John R. Spears, *The History of Our Navy: From Its Origin to the End of the War with Spain, 1775–1898* (5 vols., New York, 1902). For more recent times consult Donald W. Mitchell, *History of the Modern American Navy, from 1883 through Pearl Harbor* (New York, 1946). For naval expansion see Harold and Margaret Sprout, *The Rise of American Naval Power, 1776–1918* (Princeton, 1939). Walter R. Herrick, Jr., *The American Naval Revolution* (Baton Rouge, 1966), and Peter Karsten, *The Naval Aristocracy: The Golden Age of Annapolis and the Emergence of Modern American Navalism* (New York, 1972), are concerned particularly with the late nineteenth century. David M. Pletcher, *The Awkward Years: American Foreign Relations under Garfield and Arthur* (Columbia, Mo., 1962), and Milton Plesur, *America's Outward Thrust: Approaches to Foreign Policy, 1865–1890* (De-Kalb, Ill., 1971), are good on the naval reforms of the early 1880s; and John A. S. Grenville and George B. Young, *Politics, Strategy, and American Diplomacy: Studies in Foreign Policy, 1873–1917* (New Haven, 1966), are informative about Rear Admiral Stephen B. Luce. Another valuable account of early steps toward rebuilding the navy is Robert Seager II, "Ten Years before Mahan: The Unofficial Case for the New Navy, 1880–1890," *Mississippi Valley Historical Review*, XL (1953), 491–512. *House Executive Documents,* 51 Cong., 1 Sess., No. 1 (Serial 2721), Pt. 3, has Secretary of the Navy

Benjamin F. Tracy's famous annual report of 1889. Regarding the navy and the acquisition of overseas bases see Charles O. Paullin, *Diplomatic Negotiations of American Naval Officers, 1778–1883* (Baltimore, 1912); Kenneth J. Hagan, *American Gunboat Diplomacy and the Old Navy, 1877–1889* (Westport, Conn., 1973); Richard S. West, Jr., *Admirals of American Empire: The Combined Story of George Dewey, Alfred Thayer Mahan, Winfield Scott Schley, and William Thomas Sampson* (Indianapolis, 1948); David N. Leff, *Uncle Sam's Pacific Islets* (Stanford, 1940); William R. Braisted, *The United States Navy in the Pacific, 1897–1909* (Austin, 1958); and Seward W. Livermore, "American Naval-Base Policy in the Far East, 1850–1914," *Pacific Historical Review*, XIII (1944), 113–35.

### The Venezuela Boundary Dispute

The British intervention at Corinto affected the Venezuela dispute. See editorial comment (presumably by Albert Shaw), *Review of Reviews*, XI (1895), 620–22; G. H. D. Gossip, "England in Nicaragua and Venezuela: From an American Point of View," *Fortnightly Review*, LVIII (1895), 829–42; and the lengthy *Senate Executive Documents*, 53 Cong., 3 Sess., No. 20 (Serial 3275).

The best sources of information about United States policy toward the Venezuela boundary question before the altercation with Great Britain are: Paul R. Fossum, "The Anglo-Venezuelan Boundary Controversy," *Hispanic American Historical Review*, VIII (1928), 299–329; and *Senate Executive Documents*, 50 Cong., 1 Sess., No. 226 (Serial 2514).

As regards the clash with Britain, Cleveland himself, retrospectively, gave his own views: *Presidential Problems* (New York, 1904), and *The Venezuelan Boundary Controversy* (Princeton, 1913). The following are competent scholarly works, not exclusively concerned with the controversy but contributing to an understanding of it: Alfred L. P. Dennis, *Adventures in American Diplomacy, 1896–1906* (New York, 1928); Dexter Perkins, *The Monroe Doctrine, 1867–1907* (Baltimore, 1937); Alexander E. Campbell, *Great Britain and the United States 1895–1903* (London, 1960); Ernest R. May, *Imperial Democracy: The Emergence of America as a Great Power* (New York, 1961); LaFeber, *New Empire;* John A. S. Grenville, *Lord Salisbury and Foreign Policy: The Close of the Nineteenth Century* (London, 1964); John A. S. Grenville and George B. Young, *Politics, Strategy, and American Diplomacy: Studies in Foreign Policy, 1873–1917* (New Haven, 1966); Charles S. Campbell, *From Revolution to Rapprochement: The United States and Great Britain, 1783–1900* (New York, 1974). There are several excellent biographies of statesmen who were involved in the controversy. On the British side see: Gwendolen Cecil, *Life of Robert, Marquis of Salisbury* (4 vols., London, 1922–32); James L. Garvin, *The Life of*

*Joseph Chamberlain* (3 vols., London, 1932–34); (Thomas) Wemyss Reid, *Memoirs and Correspondence of Lyon Playfair, First Lord Playfair of St. Andrews, P.C., G.C.B., LL.D., F.R.S., Ec.* (New York, 1899); and Alfred G. Gardiner, *The Life of Sir William Harcourt* (2 vols., London, 1923). See also Robert B. Mowat, *The Life of Lord Pauncefote, First Ambassador to the United States* (Boston, 1929). Except for Allan Nevins's book on Cleveland, the biographies of the American statesmen are less distinguished than most of the British biographies, but are nevertheless indispensable: Robert M. McElroy, *Grover Cleveland, the Man and the Statesman: An Authorized Biography* (2 vols., New York, 1923); Allan Nevins, *Grover Cleveland, A Study in Courage* (New York, 1932), and *Henry White: Thirty Years of American Diplomacy* (New York, 1930); Matilda Gresham, *Life of Walter Quintin Gresham, 1832–1895* (2 vols., Chicago, 1919); and Henry James, *Richard Olney and His Public Service* (Boston, 1923). Charles C. Tansill, *The Foreign Policy of Thomas F. Bayard, 1885–1897* (New York, 1940), has less information on the controversy than on matters in which Bayard was involved when Secretary of State. George W. Smalley, *Anglo-American Memories: Second Series* (London, 1912), has some information about his own role. See also William L. Scruggs's famous pamphlet, *British Aggressions in Venezuela; or, The Monroe Doctrine on Trial* (Atlanta, 1895), and his "The Monroe Doctrine—Its Origins and Import," *North American Review*, CLXXVI (1903), 185–99.

Festus P. Summers (ed.), *The Cabinet Diary of William L. Wilson, 1896–1897* (Chapel Hill, 1957), has some interesting points of detail; as does George R. Dulebohn, *Principles of Foreign Policy under the Cleveland Administrations* . . . (Philadelphia, 1941).

Most of the many contemporary articles censured Cleveland's policy; the following are a good sample: Oscar S. Straus, "Lord Salisbury and the Monroe Doctrine," *Forum*, XX (1896), 713–20; Theodore S. Woolsey, "The President's Monroe Doctrine," *ibid.*, pp. 705–12; Charles Eliot Norton, "Some Aspects of Civilization in America," *ibid.*, pp. 641–51; Henry Cabot Lodge, "England, Venezuela, and the Monroe Doctrine," *North American Review*, CLX (1895), 651–58; Andrew Carnegie, "The Venezuelan Question," *ibid.*, CLXII (1896), 129–44; and James Bryce, "British Feeling on the Venezuelan Question," *ibid.*, pp. 145–53. G. H. D. Gossip wrote two thoughtful articles: "England in Nicaragua and Venezuela" (cited above), and "Venezuela before Europe and America: From an American Point of View," *Fortnightly Review*, LIX (1896), 397–411. Marcus Baker, "The Venezuelan Boundary Commission and Its Work," *National Geographic Magazine*, VIII (1897), 193–201, remains the best article on the commission. Each of the following is the best article on the topic indicated by its title: Nelson M. Blake, "Background of Cleveland's Venezuelan Policy," *American Historical Review*, XLVII (1942), 259–77; Walter LaFeber, "The Background of

Cleveland's Venezuelan Policy: A Reinterpretation," *ibid.,* LXVI (1961), 947–67; Theodore D. Jervey, "William Lindsay Scruggs—A Forgotten Diplomat," *South Atlantic Quarterly,* XXVII (1928), 292–309; Joseph J. Mathews, "Informal Diplomacy in the Venezuelan Crisis of 1896," *Mississippi Valley Historical Review,* L (1963), 195–212; George B. Young, "Intervention under the Monroe Doctrine: The Olney Corollary," *Political Science Quarterly,* LVII (1942), 247–80; Theodore C. Smith, "Secretary Olney's Real Credit in the Venezuelan Affair," *Proceedings of the Massachusetts Historical Society,* LXV (1933), 112–47; Jennie A. Sloan, "Anglo-American Relations and the Venezuelan Boundary Dispute," *Hispanic American Historical Review,* XVIII (1938), 486–506; and P. F. Fenton, "Diplomatic Relations of the United States and Venezuela, 1880–1915," *ibid.,* VIII (1928), 330–56.

The controversy, at its height, was too unexpected and short-lived to engender much congressional investigation. However, *House Executive Documents,* 49 Cong., 1 Sess., No. 50 (Serial 2392), pp. 95–125, has material on the Orinoco River; *Senate Documents,* 54 Cong., 1 Sess., No. 31 (Serial 3347), has diplomatic correspondence; and *Senate Documents,* 55 Cong., 2 Sess., No. 91 (Serials 3595–3598), Pts. 1–4, has the report of the Venezuela Boundary Commission.

Regarding the arbitration between Venezuela and Great Britain, and related developments, see John Bassett Moore, *A Digest of International Law* . . . (8 vols., Washington, 1906), VI, 580–82; Otto Schoenrich, "The Venezuela-British Guiana Boundary Dispute," *American Journal of International Law,* XLIII (1949), 523–30; Clifton J. Child, "The Venezuela-British Guiana Boundary Arbitration of 1899," *ibid.,* XLIV (1950), 682–93; and William C. Dennis, "The Venezuela-British Guiana Boundary Arbitration of 1899," *ibid.,* pp. 720–27.

Some of the previously mentioned general works have material about the abortive general arbitration treaty. Campbell, *From Revolution to Rapprochement,* has a short account of the treaty; and W. Stull Holt, *Treaties Defeated by the Senate: A Study of the Struggle between President and Senate on the Conduct of Foreign Relations* (Baltimore, 1933), analyzes its defeat. See also John Bassett Moore, *History and Digest of the International Arbitrations to Which the United States Has Been a Party* . . . (6 vols., Washington, 1898), I, 962–82; and Mowat, *Life of Pauncefote.* The best scholarly article is Nelson M. Blake, "The Olney-Pauncefote Treaty of 1897," *American Historical Review,* L (1945), 228–43. Significant contemporary articles include: Edward J. Phelps, "Arbitration and Our Relations with England," *Atlantic Monthly,* LXXVIII (1896), 26–34; Frederic R. Coudert, "The Anglo-American Arbitration Treaty," *Forum,* XXIII (1897), 13–22; and Theodore S. Woolsey, "Some Comment upon the Arbitration Treaty," *ibid.,* pp. 23–27. The Senate's careful, if prejudiced, examination of the treaty is indicated by the large amount of material it collected, the most enlightening parts of which are: *Senate Documents*, 54 Cong., 2 Sess., No. 63 (Serial 3469); *ibid.*, 55 Cong., 1 Sess., No. 63 (Serial 3561); *ibid.*, 56 Cong., 2 Sess., No. 231 (Serial 4054), Pt. 8, pp. 389–425; and *ibid.*, 58 Cong., 3 Sess., No. 161 (Serial 4766).

## The Spanish-American War

This conflict has given rise to a great mass of literature, both contemporary comment and later scholarly work. An early book worth perusal because written by McKinley's Secretary of War is Russell A. Alger, *The Spanish-American War* (New York, 1901). Three early, scholarly books still of value are: Horace E. Flack, *Spanish-American Diplomatic Relations Preceding the War of 1898* (Baltimore, 1906); Elbert J. Benton, *International Law and Diplomacy of the Spanish-American War* (Baltimore, 1908); and French E. Chadwick, *The Relations of the United States and Spain: Diplomacy* (New York, 1909). Well written and entertaining books, primarily concerned with military history, are Walter Millis, *The Martial Spirit: A Study of Our War with Spain* (Boston, 1931); and Frank B. Freidel, *The Splendid Little War* (Boston, 1958). A recent short survey is H. Wayne Morgan, *America's Road to Empire: The War with Spain and Overseas Expansion* (New York, 1965). Several books deal with particular aspects of the war. Two good studies of public opinion are Marcus M. Wilkerson, *Public Opinion and the Spanish-American War: A Study in War Propaganda* (Baton Rouge, 1932); and Joseph E. Wisan, *The Cuban Crisis as Reflected in the New York Press (1895–1898)* (New York, 1934). See also a magazine article: George W. Auxier, "Middle Western Newspapers and the Spanish-American War, 1895–1898," *Mississippi Valley Historical Review*, XXVI (1940), 523–34. Useful for the topics their titles indicate are Orestes Ferrara, *The Last Spanish War: Revelations in "Diplomacy"* (New York, 1937); John E. Weems, *The Fate of the Maine* (New York, 1958); and George F. Linderman, *The Mirrors of War: American Society and the Spanish-American War* (Ann Arbor, 1974). An interesting work by an intelligent contemporary is Harry T. Peck, *Twenty Years of the Republic, 1885–1905* (New York, 1906). More recent, broad studies that have perceptive sections on the conflict are: Alfred L. P. Dennis, *Adventures in American Diplomacy, 1896–1906* (New York, 1928); Julius W. Pratt, *Expansionists of 1898: The Acquisition of Hawaii and the Spanish Islands* (Baltimore, 1936); Foster R. Dulles, *The Imperial Years* (New York, 1956); Ernest R. May, *Imperial Democracy: The Emergence of America as a Great Power* (New York, 1961); Walter LaFeber, *The New Empire: An Interpretation of American Expansion, 1860–1898* (Ithaca, 1963); John A. S. Grenville and George B. Young, *Politics, Strategy, and American Diplomacy: Studies in Foreign Policy, 1873–1917* (New Haven, 1966); Richard Hofstadter, *The Paranoid Style in American Politics, and Other Essays* (New York, 1965); Philip S.

Foner, *The Spanish-Cuban-American War and the Birth of American Imperialism, 1895–1902* (2 vols., New York, 1972), a large, detailed work, abandoning many generally accepted opinions and emphasizing economic factors and the role of the Cuban rebels; and Foner, *A History of Cuba and Its Relations with the United States* (2 vols., New York, 1962–63). Dealing mainly with postwar years is David F. Healy, *The United States in Cuba, 1898–1902: Generals, Politicians, and the Search for Policy* (Madison, 1963).

Books have been written about many of the American protagonists; although depicting their subjects against a broad background, all the books throw light on the coming of the war. Allan Nevins's fine biography *Grover Cleveland: A Study in Courage* (New York, 1932) describes the President's attempts to avoid hostilities. For Cleveland's Secretary of State see Henry James, *Richard Olney and His Public Service* (Boston, 1923). A major biography is Margaret Leech, *In the Days of McKinley* (New York, 1959); a little shorter but perceptive is H. Wayne Morgan, *William McKinley and His America* (Syracuse, 1963). Giving revealing sidelights are Charles G. Dawes, *A Journal of the McKinley Years, Edited, and with a Foreword, by Bascom N. Timmons* (Chicago, 1950); and Herman H. Kohlsaat, *From McKinley to Harding: Personal Recollections of Our Presidents* (New York, 1923). Gardner W. Allen (ed.), *Papers of John Davis Long, 1897–1904* (Boston, 1939), has material on the Secretary of the Navy; and Laurin Healy and Luis Kutner, *The Admiral* (Chicago, 1944), describe the hero of Manila Bay. For the great newspaper magnate see John K. Winkler, *W. R. Hearst: An American Phenomenon* (New York, 1928), and *William Randolph Hearst: A New Appraisal* (New York, 1955). Interesting about yellow journalism is W. A. Swanberg, *Citizen Hearst: A Biography of William Randolph Hearst* (New York, 1961).

From the large number of contemporary periodical articles a few may be mentioned as especially significant. Able discussions of debated legal issues are John Bassett Moore, "The Question of Cuban Belligerency," *Forum*, XXI (1896), 288–300; and Amos S. Hershey, "The Recognition of Cuban Belligerency," *Annals of the American Academy of Political and Social Science*, VII (1896), 450–61, and "Intervention and the Recognition of Cuban Independence," *ibid.*, XI (1898), 353–81. Interesting because of their well-known authors are: Clarence King, "Shall Cuba be Free?" *Forum*, XX (1895), 50–65; and Henry Cabot Lodge, "Our Duty to Cuba," *ibid.*, XXI (1896), 278–87. Brooks Adams, "The Spanish War and the Equilibrium of the World," *ibid.*, XXV (1898), 641–51, views the conflict from a lofty perspective. A retrospective look by a contemporary is Henry S. Pritchett, "Some Recollections of President McKinley and the Cuban Intervention," *North American Review*, CLXXXIX (1909), 397–403. More recent, scholarly articles include: Julius W. Pratt, "American Business and the Spanish-American War," *Hispanic American Historical Review*, XIV (1934), 163–201 (minimizing the role of business); Nancy L. O'Connor, "The Spanish-American War: A Reevaluation of Its Causes," *Science and Society,* XXII (1958), 129–43 (disagreeing with Pratt); Philip S. Foner, "Why The United States Went to War with Spain in 1898," *ibid.,* XXXII (1968), 39–65; John A. S. Grenville, "American Naval Preparations for War with Spain, 1896–1898," *Journal of American Studies,* II (1968), 33–47; George W. Auxier, "The Propaganda Activities of the Cuban *Junta* in Precipitating the Spanish-American War, 1895–1898," *Hispanic American Historical Review,* XIX (1939), 286–305; Gerald G. Eggert, "Our Man in Havana: Fitzhugh Lee," *ibid.,* XLVII (1967), 463–85; Paul S. Holbo, "The Convergence of Moods and the Cuban-Bond 'Conspiracy' of 1898," *Journal of American History,* LV (1968), 54–72, and "Presidential Leadership in Foreign Affairs: William McKinley and the Turpie-Foraker Amendment," *American Historical Review,* LXXII (1967), 1321–35; and Lester B. Shippee, "Germany and the Spanish-American War," *ibid.,* XXX (1925), 754–77.

Among the published documentary material three collections are indispensable: *Correspondence Relating to the War with Spain . . .* (2 vols., Washington, 1902); *Spanish Diplomatic Correspondence and Documents, 1896–1900 . . .* (trans., Washington, 1905); and *Senate Reports,* 55 Cong., 2 Sess., No. 885 (Serial 3624). Regarding the *Maine* see *Senate Documents,* 55 Cong., 2 Sess., No. 207 (Serial 3610); *ibid.,* No. 230 (Serial 3610); *ibid.,* No. 231 (Serial 3610); and *House Documents,* 63 Cong., 2 Sess., No. 480 (Serial 6754). Valuable source material is also in *ibid.,* 55 Cong., 2 Sess., No. 405 (Serial 3692); *Senate Reports,* 54 Cong., 2 Sess., No. 1160 (Serial 3474); and *Senate Documents,* 54 Cong., 2 Sess., No. 104 (Serial 3470).

### Territorial Expansion in the 1890s

Regarding the moves toward expansion made by Blaine at the beginning of the decade see Alice F. Tyler, *The Foreign Policy of James G. Blaine* (Minneapolis, 1927); Albert T. Volwiler (ed.), *The Correspondence between Benjamin Harrison and James G. Blaine, 1882–1893* (Philadelphia, 1940); Volwiler, "Harrison, Blaine, and American Foreign Policy, 1889–1893," *Proceedings of the American Philosophical Society,* LXXIX (1938), 637–48; and Harry T. Peck, "A Spirited Foreign Policy," *Bookman,* XXI (1905), 369–79. Regarding Blaine's aspirations for a naval base in Haiti see Ludwell L. Montague, *Haiti and the United States, 1714–1938* (Durham, N.C., 1940); Rayford W. Logan, *The Diplomatic Relations of the United States with Haiti, 1776–1891* (Chapel Hill, 1941); Frederick Douglass (the American minister to Haiti at the time), "Haiti and the United States: Inside History of the Negotiations for the Môle St. Nicolas," *North American Review,* CLIII (1891), 337–45, 450–59; and *Senate Executive Documents,* 50 Cong., 2 Sess., No. 69 (Serial 2611).

For the battle of Manila Bay and wartime events concerning the Philippines see the comprehensive history by William C. Forbes, *The Philippine Islands* (2 vols., Boston, 1928); and, for the general setting, John A. S. Grenville, "Diplomacy and War Plans in the United States, 1890–1917," *Transactions of the Royal Historical Society*, XI (1961), 1–12. Dealing specifically with policy toward the Philippines is Leon Wolff, *Little Brown Brother: How the United States Purchased and Pacified the Philippine Islands at the Century's Turn* (New York, 1961). Several books deal with broader subjects but have perceptive sections about the Philippines: Alfred L. P. Dennis, *Adventures in American Diplomacy, 1896–1906* (New York, 1928); Julius W. Pratt, *Expansionists of 1898: The Acquisition of Hawaii and the Spanish Islands* (Baltimore, 1936); Ernest R. May, *Imperial Democracy: The Emergence of America as a Great Power* (New York, 1961); John A. S. Grenville and George B. Young, *Politics, Strategy, and American Diplomacy: Studies in Foreign Policy, 1873–1917* (New Haven, 1966); and Philip S. Foner, *The Spanish-Cuban-American War and the Birth of American Imperialism, 1895–1902* (2 vols., New York, 1972). Regarding McKinley's role see two good biographies: Margaret Leech, *In the Days of McKinley* (New York, 1959); and H. Wayne Morgan, *William McKinley and His America* (Syracuse, 1963). For occasional sidelights on important participants see: Gardner W. Allen, *Papers of John Davis Long, 1897–1904* (Boston, 1939); Russell A. Alger, *The Spanish-American War* (New York, 1901); and George Dewey, *Autobiography...* (New York, 1913). Able studies of the Navy Department's aspirations regarding the Philippines are: William R. Braisted, *The United States Navy in the Pacific, 1897–1909* (Austin, 1958), and "The Philippine Naval Base Problem, 1898–1909," *Mississippi Valley Historical Review*, XLI (1954), 21–40; and Seward W. Livermore, "American Naval Base Policy in the Far East, 1850–1914," *Pacific Historical Review*, XIII (1944), 113–35. Directly related to Dewey and Manila Bay are: Ronald Spector, "Who Planned the Attack on Manila Bay?" *Mid-America*, LIII (1971), 94–104; Edwin Wildman (American vice-consul at Hong Kong in 1898), "What Dewey Feared in Manila Bay, as Revealed by His Letters," *Forum*, LIX (1918), 513–35; Thomas A. Bailey, "Dewey and the Germans at Manila Bay," *American Historical Review*, XLV (1939), 59–81; and Admiral von Diederichs (who commanded the German squadron at Manila Bay in 1898), "A Statement of Events in Manila Bay, May–October, 1898," *Journal of the Royal United Service Institution*, LIX (1914), 421–46. Some useful material is in *Senate Documents*, 55 Cong., 3 Sess., No. 62 (Serial 3732), Pt. 1.

A valuable book about the peace treaty is H. Wayne Morgan (ed.), *Making Peace with Spain: The Diary of Whitelaw Reid, September–December, 1898* (Austin, 1965). An article that apparently influenced McKinley is John Foreman, "Spain and the Philippine Islands," *Contemporary Review*, LXXIV (1898), 20–33. Paolo E. Coletta has written two illuminating articles: "Bryan,

McKinley, and the Treaty of Paris," *Pacific Historical Review,* XXVI (1957), 131–46; and "McKinley, the Peace Negotiations, and the Acquisition of the Philippines," *ibid.,* XXX (1961), 341–50.

On the international situation as it affected the decision to annex the islands see James K. Eyre, Jr., "Japan and the American Annexation of the Philippines," *Pacific Historical Review,* XI (1942), 55–71, and "Russia and the American Acquisition of the Philippines," *Mississippi Valley Historical Review,* XXVIII (1942), 539–62. Documents relating to the treaty are in *Senate Documents,* 55 Cong., 3 Sess., No. 62 (Serial 3732), Pts. 1, 2, and 3. See also *ibid.,* 56 Cong., 2 Sess., No. 148 (Serial 4039).

Contemporary periodical articles give insight into the great debate centering on the annexation of the Philippines. The many articles include: John R. Procter, "Isolation or Imperialism?" *Forum,* XXVI (1898), 14–26; Charles Denby, "Shall We Keep the Philippines?" *ibid.,* pp. 279–81; Carl Schurz, "Thoughts on American Imperialism," *Century Illustrated Monthly Magazine,* XXXIV (1898), 781–88; Whitelaw Reid, "The Territory with Which We Are Threatened," *ibid.,* pp. 788–94; George W. Melville, "Our Future on the Pacific—What We Have There to Hold and Win," *North American Review,* CLXVI (1898), 281–96; Andrew Carnegie, "Distant Possessions—The Parting of the Ways," *ibid.,* CLXVII (1898), 239–48; and George H. Knoles (ed.), "Grover Cleveland on Imperialism" (a Cleveland letter dated Nov. 9, 1898), *Mississippi Valley Historical Review,* XXXVII (1950), 303–4. Richard E. Welch, Jr., *Imperialists vs. Anti-Imperialists: The Debate over Expansion in the 1890's* (Itasca, Ill., 1972), is a helpful little book with contemporary material.

Books by or about some of the leading debaters are illuminating: George F. Hoar, *Autobiography of Seventy Years* (2 vols., New York, 1906); Richard E. Welch, Jr., *George Frisbie Hoar and the Half-Breed Republicans* (Cambridge, Mass., 1971); John A. Garraty, *Henry Cabot Lodge: A Biography* (New York, 1965); Howard K. Beale, *Theodore Roosevelt and the Rise of America to World Power* (Baltimore, 1956); and David H. Burton, *Theodore Roosevelt: Confident Imperialist* (Philadelphia, 1969). See also the perceptive study by Robert L. Beisner, *Twelve against Empire: The Anti-Imperialists, 1898–1900* (New York, 1968); and Richard E. Welch, Jr.'s thoughtful essay, "Motives and Policy Objectives of Anti-Imperialists, 1898," *Mid-America,* LI (1969), 119–29.

A classic article on the Anti-Imperialist League is Fred H. Harrington, "The Anti-Imperialist Movement in the United States, 1898–1900," *Mississippi Valley Historical Review,* XXII (1935), 211–30. A good, longer, and more recent study is Maria C. Lanzar, "The Anti-Imperialist League" (a number of articles in *Philippine Social Science Review,* 1930–1933). See also Erving Winslow, "The Anti-Imperialist League," *Independent,* LI (1899), 1347–50.

The Philippines were not, of course, the only areas into which the United

States expanded at the end of the century. For Hawaii and Samoa see above, "Hawaii and Samoa." Regarding Guam see Earl S. Pomeroy's interesting study, mainly, however, concerned with the twentieth century, *Pacific Outpost: American Strategy in Guam and Micronesia* (Stanford, 1951); and Leslie W. Walker, "Guam's Seizure by the United States in 1898," *Pacific Historical Review*, XIV (1945), 1–12. Edward Van Dyke Robinson, "The Caroline Islands and the Terms of Peace," *Independent*, L (1898), 1046–48; and Pearle E. Quinn, "The Diplomatic Struggle for the Carolines, 1898," *Pacific Historical Review*, XIV (1945), 290–302, have material about the Caroline Islands.

In recent years many scholars have written about the outburst of territorial expansion. Ernest R. May's thoughtful *American Imperialism: A Speculative Essay* (New York, 1968), deals mainly with the 1890s and considers such matters as "The Structure of Public Opinion" and "New Turns in Thought." Longer-range studies are Albert K. Weinberg, *Manifest Destiny: A Study of Nationalist Expansionism in American History* (Baltimore, 1935); Frederick Merk, *Manifest Destiny and Mission in American History: A Reinterpretation* (New York, 1963); and Richard Van Alstyne, *The Rising American Empire* (New York, 1960). Van Alstyne sees the annexation of the Philippines as in line with American tradition, an interpretation contrasting with that of Samuel F. Bemis, *A Diplomatic History of the United States* (New York, 1955), ch. 26. There are several excellent studies dealing with shorter periods. Walter LaFeber, *The New Empire: An Interpretation of American Expansion, 1860–1898* (Ithaca, 1963), and William A. Williams, *The Roots of the Modern American Empire: A Study of the Growth and Shaping of Social Consciousness in a Marketplace Society* (New York, 1969), stress economic factors. On the other hand, each of the following three studies has a broader, more variegated approach: Pratt, *Expansionists of 1898;* May, *Imperial Democracy;* and David F. Healy, *US Expansionism: The Imperialist Urge in the 1890s* (Madison, 1970). Robert G. Neale, *Great Britain and United States Expansion: 1898–1900* (East Lansing, 1966), is an able monograph about a smaller topic. Two helpful little books are Alexander E. Campbell (ed.), *Expansion and Imperialism* (New York, 1970); and Thomas G. Paterson (ed.), *American Imperialism and Anti-Imperialism* (New York, 1973). The latter has an excellent bibliography. A thoughtful critique of the expanding-market explanation of American foreign policy is Marilyn B. Young, "American Expansion, 1870–1900: The Far East," in Barton J. Bernstein (ed.), *Towards a New Past: Dissenting Essays in American History* (New York, 1968), pp. 176–201.

As regards those persons opposed to imperialism in the late 1890s see E. Berkeley Tompkins, *Anti-Imperialism in the United States: The Great Debate, 1890–1920* (Philadelphia, 1970). Beisner, *Twelve against Empire,* is excellent on the anti-imperialists in the last two years of the century. For the important year 1898 see Welch, "Motives and Objectives" (cited above). Healy, *US Expansionism,* has a helpful section on anti-imperialism. The anti-imperialists themselves have been subjected to much examination. Fred H. Harrington, "Literary Aspects of American Anti-Imperialism, 1898–1902," *New England Quarterly,* X (1937), 650–67, discusses them as intellectuals. John W. Rollins, "The Anti-Imperialists and Twentieth Century American Foreign Policy," *Studies on the Left,* III (1962), 9–24, views them as really imperialists, because they favored commercial expansion abroad. Christopher Lasch, "The Anti-Imperialists, the Philippines, and the Inequality of Man," *Journal of Southern History,* XXIV (1958), 319–31, argues that they were racists. Paterson, *American Imperialism,* is especially valuable for bibliography.

For background on the Open Door notes of 1899 see A. Whitney Griswold, *The Far Eastern Policy of the United States* (New York, 1938), a classic study now somewhat outmoded, in places, by new interpretations and material. Paul A. Varg, *Missionaries, Chinese, and Diplomats: The American Protestant Missionary Movement in China, 1890–1952* (Princeton, 1958), and *The Making of a Myth: The United States and China, 1897–1912* (East Lansing, 1968), are both excellent books that put the notes in perspective. See also the penetrating book by Akira Iriye, *Across the Pacific: An Inner History of American–East Asian Relations* (New York, 1967). Two interesting articles are also useful for perspective: Thomas J. McCormick, "Insular Imperialism and the Open Door: The China Market and the Spanish-American War," *Pacific Historical Review,* XXXII (1963), 155–69; and Paul A. Varg, "The Myth of the China Market, 1890–1914," *American Historical Review,* LXXIII (1968), 742–58. Charles S. Campbell, *Special Business Interests and the Open Door Policy* (New Haven, 1951), considers business influence on the McKinley administration. An interesting study about economic factors is Thomas J. McCormick, *China Market: America's Quest for Informal Empire* (Chicago, 1967). Somewhat broader in approach, but still stressing economics, is Marilyn B. Young's perceptive study, *The Rhetoric of Empire: American China Policy, 1895–1901* (Cambridge, Mass., 1968). Books dealing with larger topics, but having useful sections on the September notes, are: Dennis, *Adventures in American Diplomacy;* Charles S. Campbell, *Anglo-American Understanding, 1898–1903* (Baltimore, 1957); and Healy, *US Expansionism.* Regarding the two principal American authors of the notes see William R. Thayer, *The Life and Letters of John Hay* (2 vols., Boston, 1915); Tyler Dennett's fine biography, *John Hay: From Poetry to Politics* (New York, 1933); Paul A. Varg, *Open Door Diplomat: The Life of W. W. Rockhill* (Urbana, Ill., 1952), and "William Woodville Rockhill and the Open Door Notes," *Journal of Modern History,* XXIV (1952), 375–80. For a stimulating but perhaps overdrawn interpretation that sees the Open Door policy as a key to general United States foreign policy in the twentieth century see William A. Williams, *The Tragedy of American Diplomacy* (Cleveland, 1959). An early article of interest, partly because written by an influential person who advocated a strong policy, is James H. Wilson, "America's Interests in China," *North American Review,* CLXVI (1898), 129–41. A little material is in *House Documents,* 55 Cong., 2 Sess., No. 536 (Serial 3692).

## The Anglo-American Rapprochement and Related Developments

Three books (written by Canadian, British, and American authors) deal specifically with Anglo-American relations around the turn of the nineteenth century, and all of them should be consulted: Lionel M. Gelber, *The Rise of Anglo-American Friendship: A Study in World Politics, 1898–1906* (London, 1938); Alexander E. Campbell, *Great Britain and the United States, 1895–1903* (Glasgow, 1960); and Charles S. Campbell, *Anglo-American Understanding, 1898–1903* (Baltimore, 1957). See also C. S. Campbell, *From Revolution to Rapprochement: The United States and Great Britain, 1783–1900* (New York, 1974), and "Anglo-American Relations, 1897–1901," in Paolo E. Coletta (ed.), *Threshold to American Internationalism: Essays on the Foreign Policies of William McKinley* (New York, 1970).

Bertha A. Reuter, *Anglo-American Relations during the Spanish-American War* (New York, 1924), is the only book exclusively devoted to the subject indicated by the title. In his *Great Britain and United States Expansion: 1898–1900* (East Lansing, 1966), Robert G. Neale has added many significant points of detail. Two perceptive articles by Geoffrey Seed analyze aspects of Britain's reaction to American imperialism: "British Reactions to American Imperialism Reflected in Journals of Opinion, 1898–1900," *Political Science Quarterly,* LXXIII (1958), 254–72; and "British Views of American Policy in the Philippines Reflected in Journals of Opinion, 1898–1907," *Journal of American Studies,* II (1968), 49–64. Dealing mainly with other topics, but shedding some light on the Anglo-American rapprochement, are: Alfred L. P. Dennis, *Adventures in American Diplomacy, 1896–1906* (New York, 1928); and John A. S. Grenville's fine study, *Lord Salisbury and Foreign Policy: The Close of the Nineteenth Century* (London, 1964).

Each of the books noted above, by Gelber, A. E. Campbell, and C. S. Campbell, examines all or most of the topics considered in the following paragraphs; and for many of the topics, as they affected Anglo-American relations, they are the best sources of information. But in addition certain other books and articles should be consulted.

Contributing to the rumors about an Anglo-American alliance was an article by Colonial Secretary Joseph Chamberlain: "Recent Developments of Policy in the United States and Their Relation to an Anglo-American

Alliance," *Scribner's Magazine*, XXIV (1898), 674–82. An article by former Secretary of State Richard Olney, speaking in warm terms of Great Britain, may also have fed the speculation about an alliance: "International Isolation of the United States," *Atlantic Monthly*, LXXXI (1898), 577–88. Other contemporary articles, some of them by prominent men, projecting an alliance or, at least, close relations were: James Bryce, "The Essential Unity of Britain and American," *Atlantic Monthly*, LXXXII (1898), 22–29; A. V. Dicey, "England and America," *ibid.*, pp. 441–45; Carl Schurz, "The Anglo-American Friendship," *ibid.*, pp. 433–40; Charles Waldstein, "The English-Speaking Brotherhood," *North American Review*, CLXVII (1898), 223–38; Richard Temple, "An Anglo-American *Versus* a European Combination," *ibid.*, pp. 306–17; and Charles W. Dilke, "The Future Relations of Great Britain and the United States," *Forum*, XXVI (1899), 521–28. See also a lecture by Charles A. Gardiner, *The Proposed Anglo-American Alliance . . .* (New York, 1898).

On the Joint High Commission of 1898–1899 see C. S. Campbell, *Anglo-American-Understanding*, ch. 4; A Canadian Liberal, "The Anglo-American Joint High Commission," *North American Review*, CLXVII (1898), 165–75; and John W. Foster (a member of the American delegation), *Diplomatic Memoirs* (2 vols., Boston, 1909).

Mary W. Williams, *Anglo-American Isthmian Diplomacy, 1815–1915* (Washington, 1916), and W. Stull Holt, *Treaties Defeated by the Senate: A Study of the Struggle between President and Senate over the Conduct of Foreign Relations* (Baltimore, 1933), are informative on the negotiations of the Hay-Pauncefote treaty.

Regarding Alaska see Norman Penlington, *The Alaska Boundary: A Critical Reappraisal* (Toronto, 1972); and C. S. Campbell, *Anglo-American Understanding*, chs. 6, 14, 15.

Calvin DeA. Davis, *The United States and the First Hague Peace Conference* (Ithaca, 1962), handles the topic adequately. Documentary material is in James B. Scott (ed.), *The Proceedings of the Hague Peace Conferences . . .* (5 vols., New York, 1920–21); and *The Hague Conventions and Declarations of 1899 and 1907 . . .* (New York, 1915).

John H. Ferguson, *American Diplomacy and the Boer War* (Philadelphia, 1939), is the only book on the subject. Two short articles by the pro-British Alfred T. Mahan are significant: "The Transvaal and the Philippines," *Independent*, LII (1900), 289–91; and "The Boer Republics and the Monroe Doctrine," *ibid.*, pp. 1101–3. Everett P. Wheeler, "The Uprising of a Great People," *ibid.*, pp. 114–16, and Montagu White (a Boer official), "The Uprising of a Great People," *ibid.*, pp. 373–76, illustrate the sharply different opinions prevalent in the United States. On a touchy subject see W. L. Penfield, "British Purchases of War Supplies in the United States," *North American Review*, CLXXIV (1902), 687–701.

No book deals exclusively with the general subject of Anglo-American economic, cultural, ideological, and personal relations as they affected the rapprochement. In addition to the books cited in the first paragraph of this section, see Harry C. Allen, *Great Britain and the United States: A History of Anglo-American Relations (1783–1952)* (New York, 1955); Bradford Perkins, *The Great Rapprochement: England and the United States, 1895–1914* (New York, 1968); Henry Pelling, *America and the British Left, from Bright to Bevan* (London, 1956); Clifton K. Yearley, Jr., *Britons in American Labor: A History of the Influence of the United Kingdom Immigrants on American Labor, 1820–1914* (Baltimore, 1957); and David H. Burton, "Theodore Roosevelt and His English Correspondents: The Intellectual Roots of the Anglo-American Alliance," *Mid-America*, LIII (1971), 12–34, and *Theodore Roosevelt and His English Correspondents: A Special Relationship of Friends* (Philadelphia, 1973).

Anglo-Saxonism was rampant in the United States and Great Britain in the 1890s. Recent scholarly works touching upon Anglo-Saxonism in the nineteenth century are: Christine Bolt, *Victorian Attitudes to Race* (London, 1971); Thomas F. Gossett, *Race: The History of an Idea in America* (Dallas, 1963); and Edward N. Saveth, "Race and Nationalism in American Historiography: The Late Nineteenth Century," *Political Science Quarterly*, LIV (1939), 421–41. Contemporary books of some influence were: Josiah Strong, *Our Country: Its Possible Future and Its Present Crisis* (New York, 1885); James K. Hosmer, *A Short History of Anglo-Saxon Freedom . . .* (New York, 1890); and Edmond Demolins, *Anglo-American Superiority: To What It Is Due* (London, 1898); see also an earlier study that attracted much attention: Joseph A. Gobineau (like Demolins, a Frenchman), *Moral and Intellectual Diversity of Races* (Philadelphia, 1856). John R. Dos Passos, *The Anglo-Saxon Century and the Unification of the English-Speaking People* (New York, 1903), although published too late to be read in the late 1890s, was written by a contemporary and expressed current ideas. The many contemporary articles about Anglo-Saxonism include: George B. Adams, "The United States and the Anglo-Saxon Future," *Atlantic Monthly*, LXXVIII (1896), 35–44, and "A Century of Anglo-Saxon Expansion," *ibid.*, LXXIX (1897), 528–38; Walter Besant, "The Future of the Anglo-Saxon Race," *North American Review*, CLXIII (1896), 129–43; David Mills (the Canadian Minister of Justice), "Which Shall Dominate—Saxon or Slav?" *ibid.*, CLXVI (1898), 729–39; and B. O. Flower, "The Proposed Federation of the Anglo-Saxon Nations," *Arena*, XX (1898), 223–38.

# Index

382 INDEX

# The Transformation of American Foreign Relations 1865–1900

by

## CHARLES S. CAMPBELL

In 1865 the United States had just emerged from the Civil War, of necessity an isolationist period in foreign relations and one marked by special hostility toward the British, who, though avowedly neutral, had scarcely concealed their Southern sympathies. By 1900 the country's foreign affairs were characterized by friendship—still rather guarded—for the British and by an overseas expansionist policy firmly established with the acquisition of the Philippines in 1899.

In this book, the only comprehensive study of United States foreign relations during the latter decades of the nineteenth century, Mr. Campbell explains vividly and authoritatively how and why these transformations occurred, giving the details of the great debate on overseas expansion and of the intricate diplomacy, including international arbitration, that led to the settlement of the disputes with the British. Throughout he emphasizes the relationships between elements in United States domestic history (politics, ideology, economics) and developments in foreign relations.

*This book, complete in itself, is one of a number to appear under the general title* The New American Nation Series. *For a description of the project, see the back of the jacket.*

*16 pages of halftones; 11 cartoons; maps*

*Jacket illustration: Signing the Armistice with Spain, August 12, 1898 (reproduced by permission of The Huntington Library, San Marino, California)*